Engaging Characters

Murray Smith

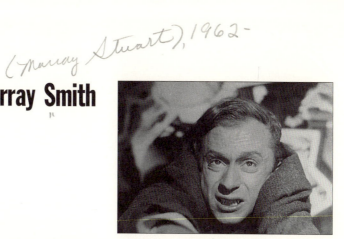

Engaging Characters

Fiction, Emotion, and
the Cinema

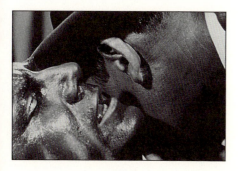

Clarendon Press · Oxford

1995

Oxford University Press, Walton Street, Oxford OX2 6DP

Oxford   New York
Athens   Auckland   Bangkok   Bombay
Calcutta   Cape Town   Dar es Salaam   Delhi
Florence   Hong Kong   Istanbul   Karachi
Kuala Lumpur   Madras   Madrid   Melbourne
Mexico City   Nairobi   Paris   Singapore
Taipei   Tokyo   Toronto
and associated companies in
Berlin   Ibadan

Oxford is a trade mark of Oxford University Press

Published in the United States
by Oxford University Press Inc., New York

British Library Cataloguing in Publication Data
Data available

Library of Congress Cataloging in Publication Data
Data available
ISBN 0–19–818240–6
ISBN 0–19–818347–X (Pbk)

1 3 5 7 9 10 8 6 4 2

Typeset by Graphicraft Typesetters Ltd., Hong Kong
Printed in Great Britain on acid-free paper by
Biddles Ltd, Guildford and King's Lynn

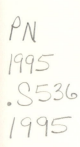

For my parents

Acknowledgements

Over the course of writing this book I have benefited from the help and goodwill of many people. First, I must thank all those who were a part of my life at the University of Wisconsin–Madison, where this work took its initial form. In particular, thanks go to Don Crafton, Sarah Cunningham, Darrell Davis, Susan Feagin, Kevin Heffernan, Charlie Keil, Katie Lynes, Pete Lutze, Rick Maxwell, J. J. Murphy, Deb Navins, Carl Plantinga, Ron Radano, Kristin Thompson, and Greg Taylor; and especially to David Bordwell, who has been a constant source of intellectual inspiration. Elsewhere, Richard Allen, Noël Carroll, Dirk Eitzen, Thomas Elsaesser, Tom Gunning, Lynne Kirby, Ed Tan, John O. Thompson, and Malcolm Turvey have provided ideas and encouragement; while the three Press readers of the manuscript, Christopher Butler, Richard Maltby, and the Unnamed have, I am sure, saved me from many embarrassments. Elizabeth Cowie, Michael Grant, Alan Millen, and Steve Neale have proven to be gracious and supportive colleagues (and friends). Thanks are due also to Jeffrey Peacock, for his unique insights and perspective, and for help with Russian. In addition to many years of friendship, Kath Dymoke provided me with expert advice on contracts, much to the chagrin of my publisher. Notwithstanding, my editors, Andrew Lockett and Vicki Reeve, have been a pleasure to work with; and I must thank Lynn Childress and Elizabeth Stratford for their rigorous copy-editing. A graduate scholarship from the University of Wisconsin–Madison helped me to complete an earlier version of this study, while grants from the British Academy and the Colyer-Fergusson Charitable Trust have enabled me to illustrate this book with frame enlargements. I must also thank Maureen Humphries for lightening the administrative load associated with this task; Jim Styles and Spencer Scott for processing, printing, and photographic advice; and Anna Miller for bibliographic sleuthing. Earlier and abridged versions of Chapters 3 and 6 have appeared, respectively, as 'Altered States: Character and Emotional Response in the Cinema', *Cinema Journal*, 33: 4 (Summer 1994), and 'Cognition, Emotion and Cinematic Narrative', *Post Script*, 13: 1 (Fall 1993). I have also borrowed the odd paragraph or sentence from the following articles: 'Film Noir, the Female Gothic and *Deception*', *Wide*

Angle, 10: 1 (1988); 'The Influence of Socialist Realism on Soviet Montage: *The End of St. Petersburg, Fragment of an Empire* and *Arsenal*', *Journal of Ukrainian Studies*, 19: 1 (Summer 1994); 'Film Spectatorship and the Institution of Fiction', *Journal of Aesthetics and Art Criticism*, 53: 2 (Spring 1995); and 'The Logic and Legacy of Brechtianism', in David Bordwell and Noël Carroll (eds.), *Post-Theory: Reconstructing Film Studies* (Madison: University of Wisconsin Press, 1995). I thank the editors and publishers of each of these volumes for permission to reprint the respective sections.

On a personal level, Guy Reynolds, Caroline Anton-Smith, Ito Peng, André Sorensen, my brother, sister, and above all my parents, have all helped me through a sometimes bumpy re-entry into British culture, during which I put this work into its final form. Miri Song has helped me immeasurably with every phase of the project, from conception to writing to editing. Thanks go to her in particular for that clever transposition which turned an ugly neologism into a neat phrase—and for everything else which cannot be expressed so concisely.

M.S.

Lewisham
September 1994

Contents

Figures and Frame Enlargements

Figures

Frame Enlargements

Acknowledgements: *The Man Who Knew Too Much*, © Paramount Pictures. *Saboteur*, ©
Universal City Studios, Inc. Courtesy of MCA Publishing Rights, a Division of MCA Inc. *The
Suspended Vocation*, Institut National de l'Audiovisuel, Bry-sur-Marne. *New Book*, Semafor
Film Studio, Łódź. *North by Northwest*, © 1959 Turner Entertainment Co., All Rights Re-
served. *L'Argent*, Robert and Mylène Bresson.

Introduction

The crowd is a being that remembers and imagines, a group that evokes other groups much like itself—audiences, processions, parades, mobs in the street, armies. They imagine that it is they who are experiencing all these adventures, all these catastrophes, all these celebrations. And while their bodies slumber and their muscles relax and slacken in the depths of their seats, they pursue burglars across the rooftops, cheer the passing of the king from the East, or march into a wide plain with bayonets or bugles.

Jules Romains[1]

FERDINAND [*in French*]. I've always wanted to know what exactly the cinema is.
GIRL [*in English*]. He says he wants to know exactly what is movies.
SAMUEL FULLER [*in English*]. Well, a film is like a battleground.
GIRL [*in French*]. The film is like a battleground.
FULLER. Yes . . . Love.
GIRL. Love.
FULLER. Hate.
GIRL. Hate.
FULLER. Action.
GIRL. Action.
FULLER. Violence.
GIRL. Violence.
FULLER. Death.
GIRL. And Death.
FULLER. In one word . . . Emotion.   *Pierrot le fou* (Jean-Luc Godard, 1965)

With characteristic bluntness, Sam Fuller gets to the heart of the matter—or, at least, the heart of a matter. Our propensity to respond emotionally to fictional characters is a key aspect of our experience and enjoyment of narrative films. Most frequently, we talk of this type of experience in terms of 'identification'— 'I could really identify with *x*,' we might say; or, alternatively, 'the film left me cold—I mean, I couldn't identify with *any* of the characters.' The word itself is ultimately less important than the model of experience to which it points. While the language of 'identification' is the most common idiom in which we speak of such powerful emotional responses, there is, in the vernacular, a range of other terms which refers to the same model of experience ('empathy', and 'absorption', for example). Our everyday conception would seem to have a long and complex genealogy, deriving from the Aristotelian concept of catharsis, notions of sympathy and empathy stemming from the eighteenth century, and the specifically psychoanalytic concept of 'identification'. The stance taken towards identification has varied dramatically over the history of cinema, from the awed fascination of Jules Romains, to the contempt and suspicion expressed by those in the Brechtian tradition, such as Noël Burch, who describes identification as a form of 'bondage'.[2]

The responses, and in particular the emotional responses, of spectators to fictional characters in film are, then, my concern in this study. I propose some answers to the following questions. What is the nature (the logic, the rationality) of our responses to fictional characters? In what sense, if any, do we take characters in films to be real persons? Is such a (mis)perception a prerequisite for having an emotional response to a fictional character? If filmic characters aren't real people, what are they? What exactly do we mean when we say that we 'identify' with a particular character? What are the various senses of this term, and can they be developed into a systematic explanation of emotional response to fictional characters in cinema? These questions may lead to other, even more complex ones. What, for example, is the significance of our emotional responses to characters with respect to the social and ideological import of narratives? What are the social and psychological functions of cinematic 'identification'?

The everyday concept of identification, it might be urged, is an explanation of why and how spectators respond to fictional characters. What, then, does the everyday notion of identification tell us about the phenomenon under scrutiny? The scenario it presents looks something like the following. We watch a film, and find ourselves becoming attached to a particular character or characters on the basis of values or qualities roughly congruent with those we possess, or those that we wish to possess, and experience vicariously the emotional experiences of the character: we identify with the character. Romains's depiction of the cinematic audience, quoted at the beginning of this introduction, draws on this model. Leo Handel cites some responses to his survey undertaken in the 1940s which conform to this kind of explanation: 'These actresses I mentioned are great. They make me feel every emotion of their parts. I feel as if it were myself on the screen experiencing what they do.'[3] Even politicians appeal to the concept. 'Sitting in darkened cinemas,' writes Roy Hattersley, 'I forgot about my crew-cut and corduroy trousers and identified with the elegant figure [Rex Harrison] in silver grey suiting.'[4] We may refer to this as the 'folk model' or 'folk theory' of spectatorial response to character.[5] By this I mean that it is a widely used and understood mode of describing and explaining a common experience, but one which lacks comprehensiveness, coherence, and systematicity. The model rests upon two basic concepts: 'character' and 'the spectator', and a cluster of implications about the relationship between these two entities. The model implies a singular and unyielding relationship between the spectator and a character; it conflates perceiving and constructing a character with affectively responding to a character; and it produces a crude, dualistic model of response, in which we either identify, or we don't. There is also often the sense—as in the quotation from Handel—that the vicarious experience of the spectator involves a loss of normal consciousness, a more or less 'willing suspension of disbelief', to use Coleridge's celebrated phrase. These assumptions are somewhat inchoate; for the purposes of everyday discussion, they need be nothing more. Thus I do not deny that the folk model offers some sort of description and explanation, but rather I suggest that it does not offer a very good one.

Of course, I am not the first to formulate a model of spectatorial response to character which attempts to go beyond the folk theory. Bertolt Brecht argued that the way in which we respond emotionally to characters in fictions lies at the heart of the tendentious and ideological effects they may have. In doing so, he marked out a set of interrelated phenomena—rationality, emotion, narrative, and narrational form—which lie at the heart of this study. For Brecht, traditional (or what he referred to as 'Aristotelian' or simply 'dramatic') theatrical form and realist staging techniques effect an 'illusion of reality' in which spectators experience the fictional world as real, through a powerful empathy with the protagonist. The emotional potency of such empathy prevents critical reasoning, that is, the possibility of seeing undesirable outcomes as contingent and socially determined, not inescapable, natural necessities.[6] Brecht's work thus intersects with two long-standing topoi of Western thought, namely the *paradox of fiction* (the idea that in responding to fictions we behave at once as if we know, and as if we do not know, that we are perceiving a mere fiction), and the *reason–emotion antinomy* (the idea that emotion and reason are at odds with one another), both of which are considered and rejected in Chapter 2.

Brecht is also exemplary of a widespread suspicion of the traditional, novelistic conception of character—of characters as 'rounded' figures mimicking the culturally stressed complexity and uniqueness of real persons—a suspicion echoed and amplified by (among others) the practitioners of the *nouveau roman* and structuralist literary theory. Commenting on the displacement of this conception of character in twentieth-century fiction, Nathalie Sarraute describes the typical character of a nineteenth-century novel, emblematized by Balzac's Eugenie Grandiet, as

richly endowed with every asset, the recipient of every attention; he lacked for nothing, from the silver buckles on his breeches to the veined wart on the end of his nose. Since then he has lost everything: his ancestors, his carefully built house, filled from cellar to garret with a variety of objects, down to the tiniest gew-gaw; his sources of income and his estates; his clothes, his body, his face. Particularly, however, has he lost that most precious of all possessions, his personality—which belonged to him alone—and frequently, even his name.[7]

The confluence of Brechtianism with the modernist literary tradition Sarraute refers to has led to a theoretical orthodoxy for which treating characters in any way as if they were real, especially by responding emotionally to them, is regarded as at best naïve and at worst pernicious.[8] Throughout this study I identify this orthodoxy with 'the structuralist tradition'— by which I mean to denote a strand of thought which can be traced from the Russian Formalists (especially Shklovsky) through French structuralism (Lévi-Strauss, Barthes, Todorov) and into post-structuralism (Barthes, Cixous). The strand I am interested in is precisely that concerned with character, and this should not be mistaken for the larger fabric of any of these theoretical movements, each of which interweaves many other concerns and arguments. Indeed, the breadth and diversity of 'structuralism' is testified to by the fact that many of the ideas of Czech structuralism, most especially its effort to reveal the social and historical embeddedness of formal structures and our responses to them, are akin to my own.[9] While I am critical of this orthodoxy, I have striven to preserve what seem to me the important insights of structuralism. My stance towards the structuralist tradition I hope escapes obsessive criticism as much as slavish imitation—the twin towers, it is said, of intellectual servitude.

At the broadest level, my thesis in this study is that characters are central to the rhetorical and aesthetic effects of narrative texts. Character structures are perhaps the major way by which narrative texts solicit our assent for particular values, practices, and ideologies. As these opening remarks suggest, this argument has the distinction of being at once widely held and deeply unfashionable; pervasive in practice but spurned in theory. I have divided this study into two parts which on the whole match the two ambitions of the work, though these goals are inevitably intertwined throughout: to advance a polemical argument concerning the social functions of character 'identification', and the relationship of these to notions of 'aesthetic' experience (Part I), and to map out a descriptive poetics of character (Part II), on the assumption that the latter lends detail and precision to the former. One of the major problems with discussions of character, emotional response, and 'identification' is the imprecision and plasticity of terminology. Both 'identification' and the equally pervasive 'point of view' tend to designate a variety of quite distinct processes. Criticism often runs together seeing with a character, having access to a character's actions and thoughts, and sympathizing with a character, as we will see shortly in a brief analysis of criticism of Jonathan Kaplan's *The Accused* (1988). While some theorists have attempted to make important discriminations, the tendency is simply to extend one of the governing metaphors. Kristin Thompson, for example, writes of 'ideological point of view', as well as 'spatial', 'temporal', and 'causal point of view'.[10] We will never prise these distinctive phenomena apart so long as we are seduced by the attractions of elaborating a single metaphor. Thus I propose replacing blanket terms such as 'identification' and 'point of view' with a system which posits several distinct *levels of engagement* with fictional characters, which together comprise what I call the *structure of sympathy*.

Within the discipline of film studies, any study addressing these questions over the last twenty-five years would almost inevitably be grounded in psychoanalysis. Since the framework of my analysis is drawn from analytic philosophy and cognitive anthropology rather than psychoanalysis, some comment is necessary here. It is worth noting the oddity of this situation: in most fields of enquiry, it would be an appeal to psychoanalysis, rather than a decision not to appeal to it, that would require a defence. Noël Carroll has dubbed 'psychoanalytic imperialism' the presumption that psychoanalysis is a necessary or uniformly desirable approach, irrespective of even its own principle that it should be applied only where conventionally rational approaches fail to explain a given phenomenon.[11] Psychoanalytically inclined critics have paid scant attention to the myriad ways in which psychoanalysis can and has been challenged as a whole—on grounds of methodology, of evidence, and of coherence. But this is not the place for a serious or extensive discussion of these 'transcendental' issues. My more modest goal here is to outline the ways in which the use of psychoanalysis has often led to descriptive inaccuracies and explanatory simplifications in the discussion of both the form and rhetoric of films, and the way in which spectators engage with such form. Psychoanalytic criticism is not alone in suffering from these deficiencies, but it is perhaps more noticeable in the light of the purported sophistication of its model of 'identification'. Indeed, the very elaborateness of the psychoanalytic theory of mind has obscured its bluntness as an instrument of narrative analysis. Moreover, important as these descriptive failings are in and of themselves, they also perpetuate a particular view of mainstream filmmaking which at once overestimates the power of films made in this formal mode to simply 'subject' spectators, and underestimates the potential of such films to engage spectators in a thought-provoking manner.

The Accused provides a useful reference point for this discussion for several reasons. Based on a true story, the film concerns the gang rape of Sarah Tobias (Jodie Foster). Beginning in the immediate aftermath of the rape, the film traces the experiences of Tobias as she faces the prejudices of the American legal system. The first phase of the narrative concerns the compromises made by Tobias's lawyer Katheryn Murphy (Kelly McGillis) in order to ensure that the rapists are put away: the reduction of charges from rape to 'reckless endangerment'. The second phase traces Tobias's angry reaction to this redefinition of the rape which effectively violates her a second time, and Murphy's attempt to reverse the compromise (and redeem herself) by bringing charges of 'criminal solicitation' against the men who goaded and cheered the rapists on. Murphy wins the case, but only on the basis of the testimony of Kenneth Joyce (Bernie Coulson), who witnesses the gang rape in its entirety before reporting the incident to the police. The film thus explicitly tackles questions of sexuality and power, and the ways in which the ideology of patriarchy is operative in American society—questions on which psychoanalysis might be thought to be on its 'own' territory. The film was commercially successful and generally well received within the mainstream press, but much of the academic criticism of the film has been hostile. Such criticism is emblematic of the way in which an amalgam of critical assumptions concerning 'identification', fusing psychoanalysis with both Brechtian and structuralist ideas, has become dispersed and institutionalized.[12]

The first thing we might note about this criticism is the way it employs a heavily deterministic rhetoric: one critic, for example, writes that *The Accused* 'railroads' the spectator into a certain kind of response.[13] Such language has the effect of both simplifying the form of the text, and entirely negating the spectator as an active participant in the production of meaning. These problems in the conception of the spectator as 'subject' are examined in Chapter 2. The second tendency which stands out is the representation of our responses to characters in terms of a singular 'identification', along with the assumption that this can only be disrupted by an equally wholesale 'alienation' or 'distanciation'— a duplication, in this respect, of the everyday, 'folk' model of identification. Discussing Joyce's testimony concerning the rape, rendered through flashback, one critic argues that the 'crosscutting allows the audience to identify with Joyce . . . the jury can only see through Kenneth Joyce's eyes—the flashback is *his* flashback'.[14] Another talks of the 'spectator's perspective' being 'incorporated into that, and only that, of Kenneth Joyce'; a little later this is restated in that admixture of psychoanalytic and Brechtian terms characteristic of contemporary theory: 'Such suturing and identification allows for, in Martin Esslin's words, the drawing of "each individual member of the audience into the action by causing (them) to identify (themselves) with the hero to the point of complete self-oblivion".'[15]

And yet, if we look closely at the film, it seems that anything but a singular 'identification' is produced. A fundamental problem here is that two distinct processes—in my terms, levels of 'engagement'—are confused. The first of these, what I will call *alignment*, concerns the way a film gives us access to the actions, thoughts, and feelings of characters. The second, *allegiance*, concerns the way a film attempts to marshal our sympathies for or against the various characters in the world of the fiction. Now clearly these phenomena interact, but they are not reducible to a singular 'identification'—and especially not if that is understood as 'self-oblivion'. As we will see in later chapters, it is quite possible for a film to 'align' us with an unsympathetic character, a situation which is occluded by an undifferentiated concept of 'identification'.

The structure of alignment throughout the film is more complex than the comments quoted above suggest. At different points in the film, the action follows Tobias, Joyce, Murphy, the investigating lieutenant, Tobias's friend Sally (another waitress at the bar), even the barman. The result is that the film gives us access to the thoughts and feelings of a range of characters, interleaving the attitudinal perspectives and interests of all the participants. This structure is mirrored in the representation of the rape itself. As Mallorie Cook indicates in her essay on the film, the rape is 'narrated' by Joyce, in the sense that we witness the rape as a flashback when he is on the witness stand. While the visual representation of the rape is intitiated as a flashback by Joyce's testimony, and while the scene certainly stresses Joyce's experience by cutting to shots of him both in the bar and on the witness stand (what I will call *keying* in Chapter 5), the representation of the rape is much more multi-layered than the notion of a total 'identification' with Joyce implies. The narration of the film shuttles our optical perspective through virtually all of those present: Joyce, Tobias, the rapists, Sally, those goading and cheering. We see shots of all of these characters, showing us how they relate to the event (ranging from intense pleasure and excitement to horror), and shots representing their optical viewpoints. The tuning of the sequence to Joyce's emotional 'key' does not amount to the negation of all other perspectives on the action.

Similarly, the film is more complex in terms of allegiance than the psychoanalytically informed accounts suggest. For the latter, the figure of Cliff 'Scorpion' Albrecht (Leo Rossi) is central. 'Scorpion' is one of the three men tried for inciting the rape. During the rape, he acts as a grotesque master of ceremonies, clapping and cheering and directing other men to engage in the rape itself. Earlier in the film, after Murphy has compromised on the original charge and the three rapists have been imprisoned for 'reckless endangerment', 'Scorpion' encounters Tobias in a record store and taunts her cruelly. 'Scorpion' is thus set up as a figure of almost metaphysical evil. Alongside 'Scorpion', Joyce looks suitably angelic, and it is this Manichaean opposition which produces the comforting 'identification' with Joyce, the 'good man' who is revolted by rape and ultimately acts in spite of masculine peer pressure. As Cook writes, '*The Accused* enhances the effect of identification through setting totally despicable characters in opposition to the film's point of identification'.[16]

What this description leaves out is the range of other men implicated in the rape, who are depicted as neither monstrous nor angelic but rather as, well, regular guys. One of the rapists is a 'good-looking' college boy; one of them is taunted by 'Scorpion' for sexual inadequacy. The other onlookers, though not characterized in detail, are depicted as unremarkable, blue-collar men. Moreover, the middle-class men in the film—the lawyers—are generally represented as cynical and unsympathetic. And the treatment of the rape as a spectacle of pleasurable violence by the blue-collar men in the bar is echoed by Murphy's male colleagues' attendance at an ice hockey game (the violence of which unsettles Murphy). In so far as 'Scorpion' is different in degree but not in kind from the other male characters, he is not depicted as an 'aberration'.[17] The film posits a continuity of masculinity across the different men which implicates the ordinary men in the act of rape, rather than exempting them from it.

None of this is meant to suggest that The Accused is a great triumph for radical feminism. A careful description of the formal complexity of the film does not inexorably lead to a sentimental aggrandizement of it. The film can be criticized for selecting an unrepresentative case—in so far as a charge is brought, and the outcome is conviction—and for omitting entirely any consideration of the difficulties faced by rape victims after a conviction has been obtained.[18] It is hardly a surprise that the film compromises its feminism; the more pertinent task is to examine how it represents what it represents within the formal and institutional constraints of Hollywood. Nor is this meant to imply that we should not consider the relationship between the form of films and ideology. We could hardly avoid doing so in the case of The Accused. Rather, it is to suggest that there are problems with the methodology and critical vocabulary of certain widespread approaches, psychoanalysis among them, and that the latter does not have an exclusive patent on questions of desire, gender, and ideology.

Two assumptions in particular of most psychoanalytic criticism with respect to the relationship between form and ideology mark it off from the perspective of this study. The first is the idea that the appeal of cinema as a whole is to be explained primarily in visual terms, an assumption at the heart of criticism deriving from the work of Jean-Louis Baudry and Christian Metz in the late 1960s and early 1970s. For Metz and Baudry, the fundamental pull of the cinema lies in its restaging of the Lacanian 'mirror stage', an effect dependent on the very technology or 'apparatus' of cinematic representation rather than a particular use of it. One could hardly deny that the visual basis of cinema is an important fact, though it is evidently more important to some forms of filmmaking than others, and there are many other visually-based media; but admitting this does not commit one to an explanation of the fascination of cinema in terms of Lacanian psychoanalysis. In any case, the view assumed by this study is that the appeal of cinema is heterogeneous and cannot be reduced to a single principle: films are visual spectacles, but they are also aural experiences, and they engage us in a variety of imaginative and epistemological forms, of which fictions and documentaries are the most common. In part as a reaction against the stress on the sensory, and especially visual, peculiarities of film in recent (indeed most) film theory, this study emphasizes the imaginative functions that fiction films share with fictional representations in other media.

Within this framework, ideological beliefs and values—those which can be explained by the social interests and power of groups within a society—are understood as emerging from the concrete uses of devices and structures in particular contexts, by particular agents, and directed towards specific ends. It is with respect to this issue that the second major difference between this study and the most dominant psychoanalytic approaches of recent years becomes clear. For many psychoanalytic theorists, the cinematic apparatus as such—or, indeed, narrative form as such—is (always-already) ideological (whether that ideology is conceived as bourgeois or patriarchal). In the words of Jacqueline Rose, a certain ideology is 'latent' in the system of 'cinematic specularity' itself—a formulation which clearly echoes the earlier arguments of Baudry and Metz.[19] The cinematic apparatus is not a technology that only becomes ideological when it is used for certain goals, representing particular subject-matter in specific ways. I do not wish to dispute that the cinema, as a technology, emerged from a bourgeois and patriarchal society—but I do argue that the potential uses and effects of a technology may outstrip its origins, and that this is certainly the case with the ideological effects of cinema. Finally, I am not suggesting that psychoanalysis is irrelevant to the study of cinema, so much as questioning its status as a 'metapsychology' of cinema. One cannot dispute the significance of psychoanalysis as a cultural belief system—as a doctrine which wields considerable social force—and later chapters discuss films in relation to psychoanalysis in this sense.

So much for a broad overview of the premises and goals of this study, and its relationship to other theoretical approaches. At a more detailed level, the study breaks down in the following way. Chapter 1 argues that the concept of 'character' is a basic element of narrative itself and cannot be reduced to some more fundamental element. In the second chapter, I examine the concept of 'the spectator', the other key term in any analysis of 'identification'. In particular, I try to resolve some of the difficulties of the concepts of 'consciousness' and 'the unconscious' as they are applied to cinematic spectators, by appealing to a 'cognitive-anthropological' model of mind very different from the psychoanalytic one drawn on by post-structuralist theorists like Baudry, Metz, and Althusser. My method here is to provide a detailed explication of this alternative model, the purpose of which is to demonstrate the potential scope of the theory. I argue that it may be useful in dealing with a wide range of questions, from questions peculiar to specifically filmic perception, to broad questions about the relations between narrative representations and ideology. Aside from my comments here and questions raised here and there throughout the study, I do not engage in a critique of other models, as exhaustive critical overviews are already available.[20] At this juncture, an appraisal of the virtues of the cognitive anthropological model seems more valuable than further carping about the deficiences of other models. I let the analyses in Part II of a very diverse group of films stand as evidence of the fertility, versatility, and subtlety of the model of 'character engagement'.

Chapters 1 and 2, then, engage in a debate with structuralism and post-structuralism concerning our assumptions regarding the elements of a theory of character and 'identification'. They thus serve to clear the ground for Chapter 3, in which I present an alternative model of 'identification'. This is the pivotal chapter in the study, in which the interrelations among the various concepts discussed separately in other chapters are explicated. Readers unfamiliar with or uninterested in the questions raised by structuralism and post-structuralism may find the first two chapters irrelevant or unnecessary; for these readers, Chapters 3 through to the Conclusion stand, I hope, as a more-or-less coherent, self-contained whole.

In Chapters 4, 5, and 6, I examine each of the principal levels of engagement in greater detail: alignment, allegiance, and *recognition*, the more basic level at which spectators grasp and construct characters. In each case, I provide an overview of the assumptions and attitudes within film theory, criticism, and even filmmaking, which have pertinence to the level of engagement under scrutiny. In this sense, my project is metacritical: an effort to make explicit tacit critical assumptions and practices, especially where these conflict with avowed theoretical positions, in order to clarify and, where necessary, critique them. Following these metacritical overviews, I present detailed analyses of individual films. The films have been chosen in order to demonstrate the distinctiveness of the various levels of engagement; often, non-classical films serve this purpose best. Nevertheless, in each case I have striven to establish the classical norms of the level of engagement in question, the non-classical examples further illuminating and being illuminated by the classical norms.

In the Conclusion, I attempt to provide a partial answer to the most general and the most difficult of the questions posed at the beginning of this chapter: what are the social and ideological functions of character engagement ('identification')? In this way, my study seeks to relate 'character' to the question of spectatorship. Hence, my goal is not simply to produce a typology or poetics of character, but rather a psychology and sociology of spectatorial responses to character, understood as elements of narrative film structure. I suggest that 'identification' may function in a variety of ways with respect to ideology, having the potential both to reinforce and to question norms. 'Identification' does not, therefore, always accommodate the spectator to prevailing ideological norms, as the Brechtian model suggests. Implicit in this argument is a defence of the potential of traditional characterization and emotional response, and the classical film or 'movie' which depends on them; of the ability of such movies to engage spectators in sophisticated, imaginative ways. Movies are enormously diverse in terms of both their ideological character and aesthetic interest, a fact which is hardly recognized by those schemes which conflate the description of broad formal patterns ('classical mode') with ideological or aesthetic assessments, as in the work of Baudry. Just as the ideology of a particular film may transcend or subvert the prevailing ideology of the period in which the general form of the film, or indeed the technology itself, was developed, so its aesthetic value cannot be divined simply by placing it in such a broad category, itself assigned a place in a contingent aesthetic hierarchy (the presumption being that 'art' films are by definition superior to Hollywood movies). Most art of any kind is mediocre, but we are as likely to find aesthetically intriguing work in movies as in more esoteric and exclusive forms.

Lastly, a word or two concerning my presuppositions with respect to the concept of 'classical cinema', and indeed the very notion of 'cinema' itself. The historiographic view that underpins my use of the notion of 'classicism' is derived from David Bordwell, Janet Staiger, and Kristin Thompson's *The Classical Hollywood Cinema*.[21] The fundamental tenet of this study is that 'Hollywood', as both an ideology and a set of institutions, stabilized a cluster of formal practices which have proven enormously enduring and influential on mainstream narrative filmmaking world-wide. So formidable and pervasive has the 'classical mode' become that most alternative cinematic aesthetics—Soviet montage, the American avant-garde, and so forth—have defined themselves against this 'classical' background. The classical mode, however, should not be thought of as a pigeon-hole, a rigid category with necessary and sufficient conditions.[22] Categories like 'classical fiction film', 'art movie', and 'documentary' are rather defined by prototypes or 'central' examples, with diffuse boundary zones shading into one another, enabling a degree of flexibility on the spectator's part in the way that particular films are apprehended. Just as a robin is a 'better' (more central) example of the category 'bird' than is an emu because an emu cannot fly, so *Casablanca* (Michael Curtiz, 1942) is a more typical instance of a classical film than *The Lady from Shanghai* (Orson Welles, 1948), because the latter lacks some but not all of the features that would mark it clearly as a classical Hollywood film (ultimate clarity with respect to character motivation, for example). (As a result, Welles's film might be construed as a different type of film: an art film or an auteur film, for example.) The notion of a classical mode is designed, then, to capture a psychological reality in the way films are categorized and so understood; the critical act of situating a given film in relation to the classical mode is the beginning, not the end, of analysis.

A related assumption concerns the delimitation of this study, on the whole, to fiction *films*—that is, fictions made in the first instance for the cinema. In the eyes of some theorists, marking cinematic fiction off from other cultural forms has become an intolerably artificial gesture in the light of the convergence of the film, television, and video industries. They would point out that our experience of fiction films blurs with our experience of, for example, televisual fiction and fan discourse in various media; and that many viewers see most of the films that they see on television and video rather than in the cinema. All of this is true. Such experience also overlaps with our experience of literary fiction, oral storytelling, documentary film, and television—all cultural forms that I touch on at various points. While there is no impermeable barrier between cinematic fiction and these other forms of cultural life, however, it is nevertheless distinct. Watching a film in a cinema is not exactly like watching TV or reading a novel for technological, institutional, and 'spectatorial' reasons: cinemas are public spaces eliciting expectations, norms of behaviour, and types of experience different from those prompted by the domestic locus of TV viewing. Whatever one thinks about the debate surrounding the censorship and distribution of so-called 'video nasties', the fact that many groups within our society believe that these various media should be regulated differently is evidence that audio-visual texts do not simply exist in a diffuse cultural ether, but in distinct, material forms. Any form of cultural analysis must slice into the cultural flux, and any such incision is necessarily 'artificial' in that it involves selection and emphasis, but the angle of the slice in this case is motivated by these materially and psychologically real factors.

1. Jules Romains, 'The Crowd at the Cinematograph' (1911), trans. Richard Abel, in Richard Abel (ed.), *French Film Theory and Criticism: 1907–39*, i (Princeton, NJ: Princeton University Press, 1988), 53.
2. Noël Burch, *Theory of Film Practice*, trans. Helen R. Lane (Princeton, NJ: Princeton University Press, 1981), 135.
3. Leo Handel, *Hollywood Looks at its Audience: A Report of Film Audience Research* (Urbana: University of Illinois Press, 1950), 147. Cf. another one of Handel's respondent's remarks: 'A good emotional actress makes you feel as if you were living her part yourself' (p. 149).
4. Roy Hattersley, 'Endpiece: What Would the Rake Make of our Progress', *Guardian*, 18 Nov. 1991, 24.
5. See George Lakoff, *Women, Fire, and Dangerous Things: What Categories Reveal about the Mind* (Chicago: University of Chicago Press, 1987), 118.
6. See the various essays collected in *Brecht on Theatre: The Development of an Aesthetic*, trans. and ed. John Willett (London: Methuen, 1964), e.g. 'A Dialogue about Acting', 'Indirect Impact of the Epic Theatre', 'A Short Organum for the Theatre', and 'From the *Mother Courage* Model'. Brecht comments directly on Balzac, as an example of traditional, novelistic characterization, in 'Remarks on an Essay', Fredric Jameson (ed.), *Aesthetics and Politics* (London: Verso, 1980), 78–9.
7. Nathalie Sarraute, *Tropisms and the Age of Suspicion*, trans. Maria Jolas (London: John Calder, 1963), 84.
8. W. J. Harvey comments on a parallel hostility in certain Cambridge and 'New' critics in *Character and the Novel* (Ithaca, NY: Cornell University Press, 1965), Appendix II: The Attack on Character.
9. F. W. Galan, *Historic Structures: The Prague School Project, 1928–1946* (Austin: University of Texas Press, 1985); J. G. Merquior, *From Prague to Paris: A Critique of Structuralist and Post-Structuralist Thought* (London: Verso, 1986), 27.
10. Kristin Thompson, *Breaking the Glass Armor: Neoformalist Film Analysis* (Princeton, NJ: Princeton University Press, 1988), 169.
11. Noël Carroll, *Mystifying Movies: Fads and Fallacies in Contemporary Film Theory* (New York: Columbia University Press, 1988), 52.

12. I consider *The Accused* and its critical reception at greater length in 'The Logic and Legacy of Brechtianism', in David Bordwell and Noël Carroll (eds.), *Post-Theory: Reconstructing Film Studies* (Madison: University of Wisconsin Press, 1995).

13. Patrice Fleck, 'The Silencing of Women in the Hollywood "Feminist" Film: *The Accused*', *Post Script*, 9: 3 (Summer 1990), 54.

14. Ibid. 54–5.

15. Mallorie Cook, 'Criticism or Complicity? The Question of the Treatment of Rape and the Rape Victim in Jonathan Kaplan's *The Accused*', *CineAction* 24/25 (1991), 84–5.

16. Ibid. 85; cf. Fleck, 'Silencing of Women', 53–4.

17. Fleck, 'Silencing of Women', 54.

18. See Carol Clover, *Men, Women, and Chainsaws: Gender in the Modern Horror Film* (London: BFI, 1992), 146–7.

19. Jacqueline Rose, 'Paranoia and the Film System', *Screen*, 17: 4 (Winter 1976–7), 89; Jean-Louis Baudry, 'Ideological Effects of the Basic Cinematographic Apparatus' (1970), trans. Alan Williams, *Film Quarterly*, 28: 2 (Winter 1974–5), 39–47; Christian Metz, *Psychoanalysis and Cinema: The Imaginary Signifier*, trans. Celia Britton, Annwyl Williams, Ben Brewster, and Alfred Guzzetti (London: Macmillan, 1982).

20. Carroll, *Mystifying Movies*; Richard Allen, *Projecting Illusion* (Cambridge: Cambridge University Press, 1995); David Bordwell, *Narration in the Fiction Film* (Madison: University of Wisconsin Press, 1985), ch. 2; Andrew Britton, 'The Ideology of *Screen*', *Movie*, 26 (Winter 1978–9), 2–28; Terry Lovell, *Pictures of Reality: Aesthetics, Politics and Pleasure* (London: BFI, 1983); and George M. Wilson, *Narration in Light: Studies in Cinematic Point of View* (Baltimore: Johns Hopkins University Press, 1986), ch. 10.

21. *The Classical Hollywood Cinema: Film Style and Mode of Production to 1960* (New York: Columbia University Press, 1985).

22. Andrew Britton, 'The Ideology of the Pigeonhole: Wisconsin Formalism and "The Classical Style"', *CineAction!* 15 (Winter 1988–9), 47–63.

Part One

He used a set of elegant gestures to accent the comedy of his bent, hopeless figure and wore a special costume, dressing like a banker, a cheap, unconvincing, imitation banker. The costume consisted of a greasy derby with an unusually high crown, a wing collar and a polka-dot four-in-hand, a shiny double-breasted jacket and grey-striped trousers. His outfit fooled no one, but then he didn't intend it to fool anyone. His slyness was of a different sort.

Nathaniel West, *The Day of the Locust*

The Saliency of Character

MRS VALE. Where did these flowers come from?
CHARLOTTE VALE. New York.
MRS VALE. Who sent them?
CHARLOTTE VALE. I can't remember the name of the florist, but I'm sure it's on the box.
MRS VALE. You know very well what I mean. What man sent them?

Now, Voyager (Irving Rapper, 1942)

The term 'character', in its most basic sense, typically denotes a fictional analogue of a human agent. Although this concept of character is everywhere assumed in everyday discourse about narratives, it has taken a beating at the hands of both writers and narrative theorists in the twentieth century. Modernist novelists from D. H. Lawrence to Alain Robbe-Grillet, literary critics such as L. C. Knights and Q. D. Leavis and, most proximately for the purposes of this study, structuralist narrative theorists, have all argued that 'character' is of marginal relevance to narrative—if not simply 'dead'. Against the grain of these sentiments, I want to argue in this chapter for the necessity of the concepts of agency and character in our apprehension of fiction films (and indeed, narratives in general). Our imaginative engagement with fictional narratives requires, I will argue, a basic notion or human agency or 'personhood', which is a fundamental element of both our ordinary social interactions and of our imaginative activities.

In so arguing for the fundamental role of character in our engagement with fiction, I contradict one of the 'axioms' of contemporary theory, as expressed by Edward Branigan in the following way: 'Character is a construction of the text, not *a priori* and autonomous. It is not a "first fact" for literary criticism through which the remainder of the text is interpreted, made intelligible.'[1] Briefly, while I agree with Branigan's premises (that characters are constructs, that they are not autonomous), I argue that his conclusion (that they are not privileged aspects of narratives in terms of their 'intelligibility') does not necessarily follow from them. Character structures are not privileged aspects of narrative films from every point of view (if we wish to understand editing rhythms, for example, we might wish to start by timing shot lengths); but if we wish to understand 'identification', and how narrative films are 'made intelligible', then I contend that character is central. My house is undoubtedly a construction, and it is not autonomous in that it relies on the city water system, electrical system, and gravity. Nevertheless, it has a certain saliency in my life, if we wish to have an understanding of how I experience my life in the space of the city.

Thus, I will not argue for a return to the pre-structuralist conception of character, of the type that sees realist characterization as the only legitimate goal of narrative fiction, a view in which characters should transcend the work in which they are produced and take on an independent, albeit merely imaginative, existence. Rather, I wish to argue that our 'entry into' narrative structures is mediated by character. A distinction can usefully be made here between a free-standing ('autonomous') structure, and an out-standing element of a structure. Characters form salient nodes of narrative structures, but they do not stand outside them. The idea I am advancing is one usually lost in the void between the humanist and the structuralist conceptions of character; but it is precisely the inadequacy of both positions that calls for a more complex view of the issue. Consider again our experience of social existence. Even if we acknowledge the massive determining power of material and ideological structures, our immediate experience of the social world is through agency—agents filling the roles assigned to them by these structures. It is, in fact, quite rare for us to be confronted by a literally faceless bureaucracy: computers notwithstanding, we still deal with human agents like policemen, bank clerks, and university deans. Though they may offer us nothing more than a blank stare, it is still an expression fixed on a human face.

One of the earliest articulations of the contemporary devaluation of character—preceding Propp's analysis of the Russian folktale by some three years—occurs in Boris Tomashevsky's 'Thematics', published in 1925: 'The story, as a system of motifs, may dispense entirely with [the protagonist] and his characteristics.'[2] Tomashevsky's introduction to the same essay, however, insists on the importance of thematic interest and emotional arousal in the construction and experience of narrative forms; and these, he makes clear, are organized around characters.[3] Tomashevsky develops his argument by showing how a particular anecdote is constructed so as to produce a pun on the verb 'to know'. The *raison d'être* of the anecdote is the pun; the other aspects of the short narrative—namely, characters— leading up to it are incidental. But Tomashevsky immediately qualifies his argument, stating that 'in its concrete form, the

dialogue always fixes upon some kind of protagonist . . . some character is necessary to hold the anecdote together'.[4] In general, however, structuralism and
post-structuralism have extracted and taken up Tomashevsky's initial statement ('The story may dispense'), while ignoring the qualifications.

There are two particularly problematic aspects of structuralist theories of
character that I want to emphasize. The first is the implication that spectators
build characters in an entirely inductive fashion, on the basis of the particular
'differential network' of the text in question.[5] Consider the following statement
made by A. J. Greimas:

A character in a novel, supposing that it is introduced by the attribution of a name
conferred on it, is progressively created by consecutive figurative notations extending
throughout the length of the text, and it does not exist as a complete figure until the
last page, *thanks to the cumulative memorizing of the reader.* (emphasis added)[6]

On this view, the text is a closed structure in which, in the words of Marc
Vernet, 'a character does not define herself *per se* . . . because she articulates
herself in networks formed by the attributes of other characters'.[7] We will see
later in this chapter how this contrasts with a more dynamic model of the
construction of character, in which the viewer uses cultural models and stereotypes to 'fill out' the information provided by the text; much more than
memory is at stake here. Far from being a hermetically closed system, the text
relies upon assumptions and expectations brought to it by the spectator. For
example, we assume—until cued otherwise—that a character will have one
body, individuated by a particular set of physical features, just as a person does.
Moreover, we could never grasp such a set of features in a purely differential
manner. I could tell you that my nose—to take but a single feature—is not
aquiline, not Roman, not birdlike, not bulbous, not . . . an infinite number of
things, none of which would enable you to grasp the specificity of it. Persons,
and by extension characters, are not defined solely in a differential manner. If
we characterize John as 'very English', the trait certainly does rely on a set of
contrasts with other proposed 'national identities'—John is reserved, not expressive—but all this tells us is that John instantiates a certain social type, not
how he instantiates it.

It might appear that this argument is successful only with respect to cinematic characters, in which the physical uniqueness of a real person (a performer)
represents in an iconic and indexical fashion the physical uniqueness of a fictive
person (the character). That is, the cinematic image not only resembles the
performer, but was formed by light bouncing off the performer and registering
on the photographic emulsion, impressing a physical trace or 'index' of the performer on it. No such transfer occurs in literary narrative, in which characters
can surely only be created through the contrasts internal to the particular language in which the narrative is written. But this assumes a wholly implausible

view of language itself, based (once again) on the idea that meaning is generated solely through the differences among terms contained within a closed system. Such contrasts would be quite meaningless if words did not also acquire meaning ostensively, that is, through reference: the meaning of 'bulbous' is grasped by a consensus within a language community that the word indicates a certain physical quality, which can be perceived and pointed to in many objects, not simply through its contrasts with other terms ('aquiline', 'birdlike', and so forth).[8]

The second aspect of structuralist theories of character that I wish to emphasize is a tendency towards abstraction, that is, towards transforming the traits embodied by particular characters into general states or thematic motifs. Roland Barthes, for example, writes: '[W]hen a single sequence involves two characters . . . it comprises two perspectives, two names (what is *Fraud* for the one is *Gullibility* for the other)'.[9] Similarly, David Bordwell describes the protagonist of Robert Bresson's *Pickpocket* (1959) 'as the point of intersection of two lines of material, becoming the splice between domesticity and petty crime'.[10] While most structuralists follow Aristotle in maintaining a notion of agency, albeit subordinated to plot structure, the nature of this agency remains inchoate. The differences between human agency and non-human agency are played down— perhaps as a consequence of this tendency towards abstraction. Greimas's concept of *actant*, for example, can be instantiated by human agents, inanimate objects (like magic rings or pencils), or abstract concepts (like destiny).[11] Of course, I do not wish to argue that human agents are the only agents of causality in narratives, but I do want to argue that human agency has a centrality to our comprehension of narratives, and not just in a quantitative sense (i.e. in most narratives, most actions are performed by human agents). I will go on to argue that our understanding of non-human agents (animals, inanimate objects, abstract concepts, social forces, natural forces, deities) is modelled on our understanding of humans to a large degree. Arguing that human agency is central to our comprehension of narrative in this sense is, of course, quite different from simply equating all types of agents by divesting narrative of any special place for the human; or, in the language of post-structuralism, by 'decentring man'.

The Person Schema and Primary Theory

James Phelan has pointed out that any 'talk about characters as plausible and possible persons presupposes that we know what a person is. But the nature of the human subject is of course a highly contested issue among contemporary thinkers.'[12] While this would be regarded as a truism by most contemporary theorists of film and literature, only a fraction of the voluminous literature on personal identity to which Phelan alludes has been drawn upon.[13] Certain overlooked theories of 'personhood', I want to suggest, may provide the most cogent basis for a theory of character.

Specifying the particular conceptions of 'the person' held within cultures (or indeed, across cultures or by sub-cultures within a larger culture) will be important in dealing with specific modes of film and their likely audiences. As analogues of human agents, characters depend not only on a general conception of human agency but also on conceptions of social roles specific to cultures. A limited, 'narrow' sense of personhood, on the basis of which such cultural variations are produced, nevertheless seems inescapable in any discussion of narrative, and hence, following Tomashevsky, of character. In 'A Category of the Human Mind: The Notion of Person; the Notion of Self', Marcel Mauss presents a history of the concept of personhood in Western culture, arguing that this narrow, universal category of the self was successively developed, from the notion of *personnage*, in which the individual is defined principally by her role within a social system, to the notion of *moi*, identified as the modern conception of interiorized, monadic selfhood. Mauss traces this development through the ascription of legal rights and moral qualities to the person, through its metaphysical enshrinement, to the psychological reification of the concept.[14] A similar proposal is made by Clifford Geertz, who argues that particular cultural conceptions of personhood answer to general 'existential problems', and that even within societies which stress the significance of the person as a role-player within a larger system, expressions of the person as an individual self are present.[15] The narrow, fundamental category of the human agent (on which culturally specific developments are based) may be taken to include:

1. a discrete human body, individuated and continuous through time and space;
2. perceptual activity, including self-awareness;
3. intentional states, such as beliefs and desires;
4. emotions;
5. the ability to use and understand a natural language;
6. the capacity for self-impelled actions and self-interpretation;
7. the potential for traits, or persisting attributes.

A human agent must have the features and capacities listed above, or something like them, in order to fulfil a social role. To be a subject—to perform a socially prescribed function—one must first be an agent in at least this limited sense. By extension, so must characters, as the imagined, fictive counterparts of human agents. I shall refer to this basic set of capacities as the 'person schema'.[16] A schema is a 'mental set' or conceptual framework which enables us to interpret experience, form expectations, and guide our attention (Chapter 2 discusses schema theory in detail). In constructing characters, we begin with this basic schema and revise it on the basis of the particular data in a particular text. This information is itself likely to elicit culturally specific imagery concerning particular social roles, stereotypes, and so forth. But the framework provided by the person schema undergirds the process as a whole.

Precisely what defines this basic notion of 'personhood' is contestable. At this point, though, I will attempt only to defend the notion of the person schema as a conceptual assumption. Steven Lukes suggests that to assume a fundamental category of personhood

is to say that a certain structure of thinking about persons arises out of completely general features of social existence . . . and is in this sense unavoidable to minimally rational beings in all cultures, though they may be differently expressed and understood, and with greater or less clarity or depth, and may even be explicitly denied within certain theoretical traditions or in certain segments of people's lives.[17]

The 'person schema' is thus part of a certain common core or 'bridgehead' of assumptions shared by all cultures, along with, for example, those beliefs represented by our everyday notion of causality. Without this set of assumptions, no intelligible interaction of any sort would be possible between radically different cultures. Now this 'bridgehead' may be 'floating'—what an anthropologist initially takes to be common ground may well have to be revised. But some common ground must still exist if the two cultures in question are both to be recognized as, simply, human societies.[18] As Roy D'Andrade has queried: if cultures are completely 'incommensurate', and the anthropologist can never hope to learn an alien cultural model, as the relativist argues, 'one would wonder how the children [of these cultures] could learn the model'.[19] Granting the existence of such cross-cultural convergences does not depend on seeing them as 'natural' or 'biologically determined', but rather on recognizing that there are certain regularities in human physiology and in the physical environment which all human societies face, which have given rise to common conventions and practices. Of course, no society is defined exclusively by such 'contingent universals', but it seems equally unlikely that they are entirely absent from any society.[20]

Lukes's argument is derived from the work of the anthropologist Robin Horton, which in turn attempts to ground empirically the central ideas of P. F. Strawson. Horton argues that common to all cultures are 'two distinct yet intimately complementary levels of thought and discourse',[21] which he terms 'primary theory' and 'secondary theory'. The former contains those ideas operative in the immediate physical interaction of the everyday world, and varies little from culture to culture; while secondary theory consists of the 'hidden' entities (such as spirits or, in modern Western societies, atoms) which provide explanation for those aspects of the world beyond the grasp of primary theory, and varies immensely from culture to culture. Primary theory 'provides the cross-cultural voyager with his intellectual bridgehead'. It conceives of the world as filled with 'middle-sized . . . enduring, solid objects . . . interdefined, in terms of a "push–pull" conception of causality, in which spatial and temporal contiguity are seen as crucial to the transmission of change'. Most importantly, from our perspective, 'primary theory makes two major distinctions amongst its objects: first, that between human beings and other objects; and second, among human beings, that between self and others'.[22] The important implication is that human agency has a distinctness and a saliency in everyday life cross-culturally; and that, by analogy, characters have a salience in our comprehension of narrative which is not merely the product of the individualism of modern Western culture.

As an illustration of the distinction between primary and secondary theory, consider the analysis of the beliefs among the Nuer that 'twins are one person' and that 'twins are birds', presented by E. E. Evans-Pritchard.[23] At first blush, these statements seem to fly in the face of the distinction Horton proposes, since they conflict with our everyday assumptions that human twins are distinct persons, and that they are simply humans, and not also birds. Indeed, it was precisely such apparently radical—incommensurable—differences between cultures that led Lévy-Bruhl to explain pre-industrial, tribal societies by attributing 'pre-rational' mentalities to their members. But Evans-Pritchard argues that this mistakes the place and function of such statements, which are operative in the domain of religious ritual, not the everyday world. Of the first claim, that 'twins are one person', Evans-Pritchard writes:

Their [i.e. the twins'] single social personality is something over and above their physical duality, a duality which is evident to the senses and is indicated by the plural form used when speaking of twins and by their treatment in all respects in ordinary social life as two quite distinct individuals.[24]

And of the second claim:

[The Nuer] are not saying that a twin has a beak, feathers and so forth. Nor in their everyday relations with twins do Nuer speak of them as birds or act towards them as though they were birds. They treat them as what they are, men and women.[25]

Twins take on an extra, symbolic quality as part of a symbolic system which attempts to explain larger questions and phenomena than are encountered in day to day, pragmatic living. The ascription of birdlike qualities to twins, and the purported unity of twins, then, are elements of the secondary theory of the Nuer, which do not inhibit their recognition, in the world of primary theory, as discrete human agents (any more than our scientific understanding of humans as chemical systems stops us from using an everyday conception of them as human agents).[26] In a similar fashion, Geertz's study of Balinese notions of personhood suggests that even within a culture which, unlike ours, emphasizes the shared traits and responsibilities of members of various kinship structures, a basic notion of individual, personal agency persists and finds some cultural expression.[27]

If a central aspect of Horton's primary theory is the distinction between human and non-human, a further feature of it lies in the use of the human as a model for understanding non-human forces and entities—a phenomenon recognized in the concepts of 'animism' and 'personification'.[28] The analogy between human and non-human may be more or less complete: we may treat things like the weather, animals, and computers, as 'intentional systems', that is, as entities with beliefs and desires, intentions and hunches, and so forth, even though they lack other features of the person schema.[29] In addition to the perceptual salience discussed above, then, human agency also has an explanatory salience in narrative comprehension. More precisely, we may say that human agency functions as an heuristic in explaining non-human agency, in that we often make sense of non-human agency using the person schema. Animal heroes, for example, have bodies, intentional states, emotions, the capacity for self-impelled action, and physiological and dispositional traits. They cannot communicate verbally but they manage through other means. Enough of the person schema holds for the sake of an imaginative project in which an animal features as a major agent.[30] The perceptual and explanatory salience of the human agent within primary theory helps to explain why the notion of character—once again, understood as the fictional analogue of the human agent—is so central to the folk model of 'identification', and suggests that it should play a fundamental role in any more sophisticated theory of our responses to fictional narratives.

Durkheim suggested that the individual has 'a double existence . . . the one purely individual and rooted in our organisms, the other social and nothing but an extension of society'.[31] The value of Durkheim's observation, and the importance of recognizing a cross-cultural notion of personhood, is that we acknowledge a material basis for the (re)production of 'egocentric' conceptions of the human agent characteristic of modern Western societies, which theories of 'subjectivity' have attacked. To recognize such a basis is not necessarily to reify the modern, bourgeois concept of 'individualism', or to turn it into a metaphysical category. Rather, it is to acknowledge that our cultural notions are constructed out of some material; bodily and mental individuality is a constant which cultures may or may not emphasize. To argue that such cultural notions are somehow constituted *sui generis* is to deny oneself the possibility of a complete explanation of 'personhood' and fictional character, and it is to miss an important element in the explanation of the tenacity of the ideology of 'individualism'.

Human Embodiment

. . . these men are no longer the anonymous tokens for a defeated tribe, they are individual people—laughable, to be sure, in their helpless confusion, but our very laughter presupposes an imaginative effort to see the scene enacted in front of us, to think not only of the 'what' but also of the 'how'.[32]

The person schema includes the idea that a person typically has, or is, a discrete human body.[33] Human individuality, as a set of physiological and neurological facts, is a contingent universal: there is nothing logically binding about the discreteness of human bodies, but, for the moment at least, this is the way humans are constructed. Perhaps one day neurology will enable us not only to separate the hemispheres of the brains of individuals (as it already can), but to link up the hemispheres of different bodies: my right hemisphere with your left hemisphere. Perhaps each body would be under the partial control of the two brains, each still physically housed in distinct bodies. (Devotees of Joseph Mascelli's *The Atomic Brain* (1964) or Carl Reiner's *All of Me* (1984) will recognize the plot type.) But these are not physical possibilities, let alone prototypical features, of human agents as we understand them now. The point of the speculation is to establish some of the basic physical constraints within which human societies work.

The physiological fact of bodily human discreteness presents another problem for the structuralist view of character. Consider the following, wholly unremarkable, statement: 'Cagney's closeness (on screen) to his mother is important because it "exonerate[s] the nastier actions of the Cagney character".'[34] A structuralist theory of character would have difficulty in articulating a basic claim such as this one; are we to say, following Barthes, that Intimacy exonerates Cruelty? That is, we can ascribe certain abstract thematic qualities to a character in a static fashion, but as soon as we attempt to render their narrative function, we find ourselves forced into the use of much more traditional idioms. In Raoul Walsh's *White Heat* (1949), Cagney plays a typically psychopathic gang leader, Cody Jarrett. The conflicting elements of Jarrett's character can be seen in the contrast between, on the one hand, the moment when he viciously kicks his 'moll' Verna (Virginia Mayo) from a chair and, on the other hand, Jarrett's pathetic collapse into his mother's lap. These are fictional actions performed by fictional agents, but they do not drift around in some Platonic world of Ideal Forms. Even if we accept the practice of turning every kind of agent and action into an abstraction, and thereby risk making an allegory of every narrative, we may ask what brings the two abstract qualities together into a structural relationship, such that one can be said to affect the other? What, that is, if not the embodiment of the character—the fact that, under normal circumstances, *a person, and by extension a character, occupies a single body*? However we might wish to qualify notions of the unity and continuity of consciousness of persons and characters, the assumption of a discrete, continuous body is what makes possible the kind of ordinary assessment made about the role of Cagney's image noted above. As Richard Dyer writes, 'the disunity created by attaching opposing qualities to [the images of certain stars is] nonetheless rendered a unity simply by virtue of the fact that each was only one person' (where the 'one body : one person' assumption is implicit).[35] Philosophers are fond of defamiliarizing this assumption with bizarre cases of multiple personality and brain division of the type noted above; but these cases can only be as troubling as they are because the assumption they challenge is so firm and taken for granted.

Dyer develops a view of characterization that emphasizes the analysis of hidden, social contradictions within the images of stars, whilst acknowledging the place and function of individual bodily discreteness and 'unity'. His use of 'unity', however, conflates 'unity' with 'continuity'. Critics such as Dyer could not talk about 'disunified' characters unless against a background of at least bodily continuity; for without such continuity, we would have separate rather than split subjects. The continuity of personhood does not only make possible the kind of reconciliation of conflicting qualities that Dyer writes of; more fundamentally, it enables us to talk of conflicted persons, split subjects, and 'disunified characters' in the first place.

Some narrative artists have tried to undermine the prototypical equation of the individual character (and thus person) with a single, discrete body. The playwright Caryl Churchill (in *Light Shining in Buckinghamshire* (1976)), and filmmakers as diverse as Maya Deren (*At Land* (1944) and *Ritual in Transfigured Time* (1946)), Oshima Nagisa (*The Story of a Man Who Left His Will on Film* (1970)), Raul Ruiz (*The Suspended Vocation* (1977)), Yvonne Rainer (*Kristina Talking Pictures* (1976) and *The Man Who Envied Women* (1985)), and Luis Buñuel (*That Obscure Object of Desire* (1977)), have all constructed narratives in which two or more actors play single characters. Without homogenizing these diverse works, they can be seen to share a strategy of characterization which attempts to cut away the physical ground of bodily continuity and discreteness in order to reveal both the common and conflicting interests in a society more clearly. Churchill herself has written of *Light Shining in Buckinghamshire*:

The characters are not played by the same actors each time they appear. . . . This seems to reflect better the reality of large events like war and revolution where many people share the same kind of experience. . . . When different actors play the parts what comes over is a large event involving many people, whose characters resonate in a way they wouldn't if they were more clearly defined.[36]

Similarly, in the Buñuel film, 'desirability' is a quality of the social category Woman, not a trait of any individual woman; while Oshima's *The Story of a Man Who Left His Will on Film* constructs characters who are logically contradictory, as a metaphor for certain ideological contradictions (and perhaps the very notion of ideological contradiction itself), again as a way of undercutting the 'unifying' power of the discrete body of the person and the typical character.[37]

The powerful estrangement effected by these strategies can only be accounted for, however, by the fact that they overturn not simply established narrative convention, but extremely basic assumptions about persons in the real world—the cluster of properties I have termed the person schema.[38] Buñuel and Oshima conflate individuality—the set of physiological constants discussed above—with individualism, a cultural development in which the individual human becomes the overriding legal and moral unit. It is a strategic conflation, with an artistic and epistemological end in view: shocking us into a realization of the fact that in spite of our bodily and neurological discreteness, we share roles and interests with other human agents. But as theorists, we have to disentangle this conflation in order to understand why it is so estranging, in the sense that a profound interruption on the level of basic narrative comprehension may lead to a new awareness of certain social facts. The inductive nature of the structuralist model (see above, p. 19) cripples its ability to account for the difficulty of comprehension and the thematic implication in these cases. If characters are formed solely on the basis of a 'network of differential elements'[39] internal to the particular text, with no mimetic constraints or assumptions, why should there be any difficulty in constructing a character with two sets of physical features?

To avoid misunderstanding, I should emphasize that my argument here is neither metaphysical nor ahistorical. The 'multiple performer–single character' strategy is only disorientating if we assume that the human figures in the cinematic or theatrical representation are characters, that is, fictional analogues of persons. They can, of course, represent other entities. We can imagine a kind of filmmaking in which many performers represent a single entity without this causing any confusion. Allegories may use human figures to represent abstract qualities in this way. Abstract qualities are not tied to the discrete human body in the way that characters, as analogues of human agents, are. In such texts, the human figure performs a very different function from that which it performs in the realist narrative film, and so the formal dynamics and conventions of comprehension are changed. Only when the human figure is used to represent a person does the multiple performer strategy 'roughen form' so notably.[40]

The representation of characters, then, depends upon conventions, such as the convention that a character will be represented by a single performer. (Of course, given that the 'one performer : one character' convention has been almost universally upheld throughout the history of cinema, it is, for us, second nature: but it is *second* nature, a convention.) The convention is not, however, arbitrary: it is motivated by both the function it performs and the material conditions of its making. If the goal is the presentation of concrete persons, then the 'one performer : one character' convention suits the task well, since it fits with our assumption that concrete individuals are possessed of one body, and only one body. But other conventions can perform this function, and certain conditions will lead to the adoption of a different convention even where the same representational goal prevails. Small theatre companies, for example, often use a 'single performer : multiple character' convention, in which each performer undertakes a number of roles, for pragmatic and economic reasons. Thus, the choice we have in conceptualizing the nature of realist representation is not simply between arbitrary cultural convention and universal nature, as John Frow (among others) has argued.[41] Rather, we need to consider the goals of representation, the conditions in which the act of representation is undertaken, and the ways in which these two factors constrain and motivate the particular convention chosen. The arbitrariness of the relationship between signifier and signified, so cardinal to structuralism, cannot be taken to be a quality of every form and medium of representation, nor to be operative at every level of representation. The notion that we have to make a choice in theorizing character between nature (characters are persons) and convention (characters are textual effects) is spurious; characters are not persons, but analogues of persons, and representational conventions underpin the analogy.

There is a great deal more to be said about performative conventions, in both theatre and film, concerning the ratio of performer(s) to character(s). Alongside the 'one performer : one character' convention, there are clearly traditions in which it is quite conventional for a single performer to play many characters—one-man shows and stand-up comedians, for example. Spalding Gray is a (high-brow) contemporary exponent of this tradition. It may be that this type of virtuoso multiple performance is rooted in oral storytelling, in which the narrator may adopt the voices of many characters. This would explain why this convention seems so familiar, and so much less unnerving than the alternative in which a single character is represented by more than one performer. It is perhaps in virtue of this troubling quality that the writers and filmmakers discussed above have used this convention to challenge the social norm of individualism. Tom Gunning has also suggested that these performer : character 'ratios' may carry different implications in different media and genres. A black performer in a white role might be accepted by a theatre audience where it would not be by a film audience, for example.[42] Examples of this kind introduce another level of complexity into the discussion, since they raise issues not only of comprehension but of propriety: white performers in black roles, or children in women's roles, are conventions we still understand but which are no longer generally acceptable. Context again is vital in an understanding of convention.

My argument here is both analogous with and historically related to arguments made by Ian Watt with regard to the 'formal realism' of the novel, and by E. H. Gombrich with regard to the differences of form and function in, on the one hand, Greek and, on the other hand, pre-Greek and medieval visual art. Watt argues that the novel broke with the conventions of previous prose fiction (allegory, romance, fabliau) as a result of a shift in focus from 'universals' to 'particulars': 'particular people in particular circumstances' rather than 'general human types'.[43] Conventions of naming, for example, shifted so as to place the emphasis on the particularity of narrative agents—full proper names, rather than symbolic tags or epithets focusing our attention on a quality: Pamela Andrews rather than Mr Badman or Talkative. The new convention of designating a character with a complete and plausible proper name performed the function of creating individuated, person-like agents more effectively than did the overtly emblematic name or 'charactonym'.[44]

Similarly, Gombrich argues that the systematic development of illusory techniques of visual representation was prompted by a shift from a concern with representing universals (dominant in pre-Greek and medieval art) to the rendering of particulars, including particular persons and particular stories (in Greek and post-Renaissance European art): with the 'how' as well as the 'what'.[45] With respect to this function, perspective (like the proper name in narrative representation) does have a real advantage over other systems of visual representation. If the aim is to suggest to the viewer a particular event viewed from a specific vantage point, perspective is superior to other systems of visual representation. That the function came into being is a contingent fact of Western history; once the function is in place, certain conventions serve it more or less adequately. Similarly with the 'one performer : one character' convention: in the context of the goals of realist narrative—which, like the Greek art Gombrich discusses, are those of particularity—the convention really is more effective. It is more faithful to reality than would be a convention in which one performer played several characters, or several performers played a single character. Buñuel and Churchill know this: the departure from the convention is undertaken in the knowledge that the convention is widely assumed. These texts do not attempt simply to re-create the conventions of medieval allegory, but rather set up a field of tension between the very different functions of the individual human figure in realist fiction, on the one hand, and allegory, on the other. Form, in these instances, 'roughens' our perception of function.

The Proper Name and the Body

Roland Barthes has argued that the proper name performs the function I have ascribed to the body in film, that of gathering the traits of a character together, making them legible as the traits of *a* character: 'Sarrasine is the sum, the point of convergence, of: turbulence, artistic gift, independence, excess' and so forth.[46] But Barthes goes further, proposing that in literature the 'Proper Name' necessarily attaches a psychological depth and complexity to an agent, 'something like *individuality*, in that, qualitative and ineffable, it may escape the vulgar bookkeeping of compositional characters'.[47]

Now it is true that the body in film and the proper name in literary fiction provide more than a mere 'point of convergence' for the traits of a character; they also elicit the person schema. We 'gestalt' or organize the particular qualities conveyed to us about a character around and upon those more basic capacities of the human agent (although this initial construal is always subject to revision). It is this movement that turns the structuralist's 'bundle of relations'[48] into a character. But, *contra* Barthes, there is nothing 'ineffable' or 'illusory' about this; the proper name and/or the body perform these functions for all characters, for the Man with a movie camera as much as for Dorothea Brooke, Ethan Edwards, or Hank Quinlan. Dziga Vertov's *The Man with a Movie Camera* (1928) is the epitome of 'anti-psychological' cinema, but we still assume that the Man—and the other human figures represented in the film—possess the capacities and features described by the person schema. And it is in this sense that the schema is not simply the product of bourgeois society. The person schema functions as an enabling framework, part of the material out of which particular types of characterization can be constructed. As we have already seen in Watt's argument, the proper name tends to highlight the particularity of characters, but this need not be construed as a form of mysticism (the ascription of a 'soul' to a character). And in any case, proper names do not only individuate agents; they also perform a typifying function, since proper names bear connotations of, among other things, nationality, gender, region, and class.

Barthes's comments indirectly raise the issue of the degree of similarity between characters in cinematic and linguistic narrative respectively, and thus of the degree of overlap between filmic and literary theories of character. I am not arguing for two theories of characterization, one for written fiction and one for film and other iconic media. Indeed, we need some explanation of characters in written fiction for a theory of character in film, because not all cinematic characters are realized through the visual and auditory representation of their bodies. Most fiction films include peripheral, and sometimes major, characters who are alluded to in the dialogue but who are never visually rendered: Sean Regan in Howard Hawks's *The Big Sleep* (1946), for example, is represented only by references to him in dialogue, while the authoress of the eponymous letter in Joseph Mankiewicz's *A Letter to Three Wives* (1949) is rendered only through a voice-over. And there are those films, like Hollis Frampton's *Poetic Justice* (1972), which disdain iconic footage altogether and tell their stories entirely through titles.

Clearly there are differences in both the ways we standardly apprehend characters in film and written fiction, and in the different potentials the two media have for disrupting this process in various ways, because of the dominance in one of linguistic signs and of iconic signs in the other.[49] But the person schema is just as fundamental to the comprehension of character on the basis of linguistic cues as it is to iconically rendered character. A novel might designate a character using a proper name and pronouns; it might describe or imply nothing about the face, body, or voice of the character; but we will assume that the character possesses these attributes, at least until something in the text states or implies otherwise. Characters are not disembodied clusters of traits until their physiognomies are described; they simply have unspecified physiognomies. The person schema, as an instrument of the imagination, takes us beyond what is stated or implied by the story just as surely in literary narrative as it does in the movies.

To summarize, then, I am arguing that character, as the fictional analogue of the human agent, is a salient element of narrative structure which should not be thought of as merely one more culturally contingent structural effect or 'illusion', the 'textual character-effect'.[50] Characters are constructs, as the structuralist argues, but they are constructs formed on the basis of a perceptual and explanatory schema (the person schema) which makes them salient and endows them with certain basic capacities. Particular characters drawing on culturally specific schemata are built upon this foundation. And as with all schemata, the person schema is subject to revision: we may apply the person schema to a brain-damaged individual, and be forced to revise it on discovering that the individual lacks certain capacities presupposed by the schema. The primary-theoretical notion of the person schema will not be sufficient for our discussion of character engagement, but it is a necessary condition to establish the saliency of character. Character construction is a process of modelling, in which the spectator 'projects' a schema (initially, the person schema) and revises it on the basis of the particular text; we do not inductively construct characters every time we watch a film via the simple accumulation of differential features (as both Greimas and Vernet imply). Character construction is thus a dynamic process in which the person schema and cultural models allow us to leap ahead of what we are given and form expectations. If this is correct, there are some dramatic consequences for our assumptions about the relationship between actions and agents. Rather than agents coming into being as the result of actions, as the structuralists, and indeed Aristotle, argue, actions themselves may stand out because they are performed by fictional human agents, who are salient because of the person schema.

Character and Mimesis

An interesting metatheoretical question arises out of the foregoing discussion. I have argued that the structuralist theory of character makes a number of counter-intuitive claims which it seems impossible to maintain in practice, and which are challenged by other research, such as the anthropological material concerning primary theory. What prompted the construction of a theory that is so difficult to sustain? Answering this question will serve to highlight still more emphatically the differences between the structuralist model and the theory that I am advancing.

To talk of a character, in the view of many contemporary theorists, is inevitably to invite an exploration of a being with an unfathomable psychological depth, the very complexity and partial opacity of the character being the mark of her plausibility. The plausibility of a character—its perceived mimetic adequacy—is only a result of its conforming to a particular, bourgeois ideology of autonomous individuality, not to some absolute or incorrigible reality. These attitudes are the legacy of the anti-mimetic thrust of much twentieth-century criticism, beginning with the Russian Formalists, and supplemented by a certain strand of Marxist theory. For Viktor Shklovsky, characters are not fictional human agents but 'threads' which hold narratives together.[51] Shklovsky's importance as a precursor to French structuralism becomes clear if we juxtapose another of his remarks with a statement made by Tzvetan Todorov:

A painting is something constructed according to laws proper to it, and not some imitative thing.[52]

[O]ne can speak of the *vraisemblance* of a work in so far as it attempts to make us believe that it conforms to reality and not to its own laws. In other words, the *vraisemblable* is the mask which conceals the text's own laws and which we are supposed to take for a relation with reality.[53]

The quotation from Shklovsky points to a general problem in Formalist and structuralist discussions of realism: a conflation of the natural and the mimetic. The first terms from each of two pairs of logical opposites—'natural–conventional', and 'mimetic–abstract (non-mimetic)'—are conflated, with the result that mimesis is associated exclusively with a view of art as a copying of reality ordained by natural processes, rather than the creation of representations through conventions agreed upon by human communities. Barthes's concept of 'naturalization'—the idea that bourgeois representations present themselves as natural objects rather than cultural artefacts—is in effect the structuralist reconceptualization of mimesis. Viewed as 'naturalization', mimesis is intrinsically insidious, and understanding texts through character is the most basic form of naturalization. A similar view is implicit in Shklovsky's comment: a painting (and he is discussing a representational piece) is 'constructed', and therefore, according to his logic, not 'imitative'. There is, however, no reason why we cannot view Shklovsky's representational painting as both conventional and imitative. Indeed, praising something for its 'realism' depends implicitly on recognizing that it is not of the same order as the thing imitated, that an effort of construction was necessary to produce the effect. In other words, that it is conventional.

I concur with Kristin Thompson when she argues—drawing on the Russian Formalists—that 'realism' is an effect, and that as a consequence we should analyse the conventions of the artwork rather than assess it for any transcendant referential adequacy. My point is that this 'reality-effect' is, *contra* Shklovsky, generated by a mimetic act, even if the object of the imitation is a moving target—that is, that notions of the real are, in certain ways, historically defined. Thompson herself provides several examples. The aleatory narrative of Vittorio de Sica's *Bicycle Thieves* (1948) 'seems to recreate the rhythm of real events',[54] she argues. In other words, the aleatory narrative convention captured an aspect of reality, as it was understood by a certain community at a certain moment, more adequately than did the Hollywood narrative convention. In claiming that art sometimes strives to imitate an aspect of a historically contingent reality, we do not necessarily lose sight of its conventionality.

The anti-mimetic arguments of the structuralist tradition are deployed against a naïve view of mimesis, in which narratives and other forms of representation are thought to re-present 'transparently' a set of events which have occurred or which might occur, often dubbed 'reflectionism'. The structuralist riposte to this view is that there is nothing to reflect; narrative representations do not reflect reality but bestow meaning and order on what would otherwise be 'mere sequence without beginning or end'.[55] As both Paul Ricoeur and David Carr have argued, however, what this critique overlooks is that what narratives represent—human social life—already has an implicit narrative structure: the structure of human action.[56] Like narrative, human agency is intrinsically temporal, moving between past experiences, present states, and anticipations and intentions directed towards the future. Like narratives, human agents select through attention certain experiences and exclude others, in the course of planning and remembering. Thus, in selecting and ordering events, narrative representations amplify a process already at work in social action and interaction. Narrative extends the habit of 'configuration' central to the thought and action of the agent. In Carr's words, the ' "configuration" effected by narrative is not grafted onto something figureless, faceless, but upon a life in which narrative structure is "prefigured" '.[57] None of this is to deny that narratives effect a (re-) shaping (refiguration) of what they represent, nor that that reshaping may be a distortion. Rather, it is to deny that narrative representation as such distorts reality, and to suggest that the manner in which narrative structure echoes and grows out of the temporal and intentional dimensions of human agency provides further evidence for the centrality of character in our apprehension of narrative.

Many post-structuralists also regard the Formalist position on character as inadequate. John Frow, for example, argues that 'any account of character must inevitably rely upon a systematic preconception of the structure of the self'.[58] He goes on to present a psychoanalytic framework, which he regards as 'the basis of all historically specific regimes of identification',[59] to replace both the old humanist theory and the 'structuralist reduction'. His move is similar to my own, in the sense that he realizes the need to posit some theory of the person, although of course the notion of the person schema is quite different from the psychoanalytic account that he presents. What is interesting here is that neither Frow nor I have escaped the mimetic approach to character, nor the need to assume some basic human material as the background to historical and cultural difference. Indeed, I want to argue here that, in so far as we maintain a notion of character at all, as the fictional analogue of the human agent, it is impossible to escape a certain kind of mimetic assumption. Put another way, a mimetic assumption is embedded in the very concept of character. I do not mean that we are compelled to see narratives from a simple reflectionist perspective in order to talk about characters. But even as we drop the requirement for a global referential adequacy—a sense in which the art-work reflects the 'totality' of reality—in comprehending narratives we are still initially obliged to adopt certain mimetic assumptions in order to get the game going. I believe that those assumptions about human agency given above are the most basic and inescapable. But whether or not the reader is persuaded by that argument, I wish to show that other attempts, such as Frow's, are every bit as mimetic as my own and the old humanist whipping boy. We are all acknowledging something in the text we call 'character', and believe it can be explained by recourse to a particular psychology. In other words, to admit a notion of character at all is to acknowledge an element of narrative texts which is analogous to the human agent, and *it is thus in the positing of a notion of character that a mimetic relationship is assumed to obtain between fictional narratives and the world*. From this point on, the argument can only be about what psychology, or theory of the human agent, we model character on; and to what degree and in what ways this model is or is not historically and culturally variable.

A post-structuralist might suggest that she escapes any notion of mimesis by arguing that 'real persons', like characters, are nothing more than texts. In stating that 'real persons' are texts, the post-structuralist foregrounds the idea that persons are constructs, subjects of social structures, rather than unique, individual essences. But if this is true of 'real persons', it must certainly also be true of fictional characters. This, however, brings us back to the basic idea that characters are analogues of persons. The mimetic relationship holds, except now we have texts imitating texts rather than rounded characters imitating complex persons. My point in laying this out is to suggest that where such a position is taken, it repeats the very error derided in humanist criticism. Mimesis does not disappear in the shift to conceiving the human agent as social subject rather than individual essence. The way out of this impasse I have tried to suggest in the first section of this chapter: acknowledge that character is a mimetic construct; make the distinction between the universal and culturally-specific levels of character; and attempt to suggest where the line is to be drawn between those two levels, admitting that the line is a provisional one, subject to revision in the light of further anthropological study and conceptual scrutiny. I am not, therefore, arguing for an incorrigible conceptual foundation, so much as arguing that all theoretical discourse contains within it foundational assumptions, and that it is better to argue about which are the most plausible assumptions for us, than to pretend that we can escape them altogether.

Most contemporary discussions of character—meaning those which have followed and taken account of the structuralist critique—mark out the debate on character as between those who see characters as real people and those who see them as elements of texts; in the words of Rimmon-Kenan, 'People or words?'[60] For Boris Uspensky, the habit of discussing 'characters as real people', one practised by the 'naïve reader' and 'traditional criticism' alike, amounts to a kind of violation of the 'frame' between art and life, equivalent to 'the murder by a medieval audience of an actor who played Judas . . . and the famous attempt of a New Orleans audience upon the life of an actor who played Othello'![61] This, however, radically misconstrues what people (naïve or sophisticated, critics or not) do when they discuss characters in the same way that they discuss real people. The antithesis between 'people' and 'words' is a false one. To my knowledge, no humanist critic has ever argued that characters are real. Rather, they argue that characters can be successfully lifelike in so far as they give the impression of 'roundness', of a depth and complexity of motivation which is adumbrated but never exhausted by the fiction in which they appear.[62] In other words, they see them as analogues of persons, on the model of the modern, bourgeois concept of the self (Mauss's *moi*). The humanist may well deny that her conception is culturally embedded, but she does not argue that these characters are not textually produced. Frow likewise sees characters as analogues of human agents, but the model for the person is Freud instead of Descartes. The challenge would be to devise a concept of character which is not an analogue of the person; then we might have a truly non-mimetic theory of character. But to do so would so strongly violate our most basic assumptions about what the notion of character is, and what critical function it performs, that it would not be recognizable as a concept of character.

1. Edward Branigan, *Point of View in the Cinema: A Theory of Narration and Subjectivity in Classical Film* (New York: Mouton, 1984), 12.
2. Boris Tomashevsky, 'Thematics' (1925), in Lee T. Lemon and Marion J. Reis (trans. and eds.), *Russian Formalist Criticism: Four Essays* (Lincoln: University of Nebraska Press, 1965), 90. Vladímir Propp's *Morphology of the Folktale*, 2nd edn., trans. Laurence Scott and Louis A. Wagner

(Austin: University of Texas Press, 1968), is often cited as a key text in the displacement of character in the study of narrative.

3. Ibid. 65–6, 90.

4. Ibid. 91. Kermode has a similar account of the development of character out of a series of actions, in the context of his discussion of the Gospels and *midrash*. See Frank Kermode, *The Genesis of Secrecy: On the Interpretation of Narrative* (Cambridge, Mass: Harvard University Press, 1979), ch. 4.

5. Jonathan Culler, *Structuralist Poetics: Structuralism, Linguistics and the Study of Literature* (London: Routledge and Kegan Paul, 1975), 235–7, criticizes Todorov's remarks on character in a similar fashion. In general, Culler recognizes many of the problems of the structuralist account of character, but he does not pursue the implications of his criticisms, which would entail the very different account of character argued for here.

6. A. J. Greimas, 'Actants, Actors and Figures', in *On Meaning: Selected Writings in Semiotic Theory*, trans. and ed. Paul J. Perron and Frank H. Collins (Minneapolis: University of Minnesota Press, 1987), 119.

7. 'Ainsi un personnage ne se définit jamais *per se* . . . parce qu'ils s'articule aux réseaux formés par les éléments des autres personnages' (Marc Vernet, 'Le Personnage de film', *Iris*, 7 (Oct. 1986), 85).

8. See Christopher Butler, *Interpretation, Deconstruction, and Ideology: An Introduction to Some Current Issues in Literary Theory* (Oxford: Clarendon Press, 1984), 47–59; and Noël Carroll, 'Belsey on Language and Realism', *Philosophy and Literature*, 11: 1 (Apr. 1987), 124–35.

9. Roland Barthes, 'Introduction to the Structural Analysis of Narratives' (1966), in *A Barthes Reader*, ed. Susan Sontag (New York: Hill and Wang, 1982), 277.

10. David Bordwell, *Narration in the Fiction Film* (Madison: University of Wisconsin Press, 1985), 290. See also Victor Erlich's remarks on this subject, in *Russian Formalism: History—Doctrine*, 3rd edn. (New Haven, Conn.: Yale University Press, 1981), 195–6.

11. A. J. Greimas, 'Elements of a Narrative Grammar', in *On Meaning*, trans. and ed. Perron and Collins, 71. See also Shlomith Rimmon-Kenan, *Narrative Fiction: Contemporary Poetics* (London: Methuen, 1983), 34.

12. James Phelan, *Reading People, Reading Plots* (Chicago: University of Chicago Press, 1989), 11.

13. Alongside the implications of psychoanalysis, we should note the analytic writings (particularly those spawned by P. F. Strawson's *Individuals: An Essay in Descriptive Metaphysics* (London: Methuen, 1959), and the more recent work of Derek Parfit in *Reasons and Persons* (Oxford: Clarendon Press, 1984)), and those emerging from sociology (Simmel, Mauss) and anthropology. Of these various bodies of work, film and literary theory have engaged in earnest only with the psychoanalytic tradition.

14. Mauss's essay is contained in Michael Carrithers, Steven Collins, and Steven Lukes (eds.), *The Category of the Person: Anthropology, History, Philosophy* (Cambridge: Cambridge University Press, 1985).

15. Clifford Geertz, 'Person, Time and Conduct in Bali', in *The Interpretation of Cultures* (New York: Basic Books, 1973), 360–411.

16. The 'person schema' presented here does not coincide in detail with Mauss's category of the person. The idea of a 'person schema' was prompted by David Bordwell, *Making Meaning: Inference and Rhetoric in the Interpretation of Cinema* (Cambridge, Mass.: Harvard University Press, 1989), 152, although I have revised the version of the schema he posits. I should also indicate that I am using the term 'person' interchangeably with 'human agent', and therefore do not intend that the word 'person' carry the moral implications it often does in philosophical discourse. Of course, 'human' is often substituted for 'person' in moral discourse, as in the notion of 'human rights'. But again, it is not part of my project here to argue that the perceptual category under discussion entails or implies any moral status. See Anthony Kenny, 'Are You a Person?', *New York Times Book Review*, 27 Aug. 1989, 21.

17. Steven Lukes, 'Conclusion', in Carrithers, Collins, and Lukes (eds.), *Category of the Person*, 288;

cf. Geertz, *Interpretation of Cultures*, 363; and Richard A. Shweder and Edmund J. Bourne, 'Does the Concept of the Person Vary Cross-Culturally?', in Richard A. Shweder and Robert A. LeVine (eds.), *Culture Theory: Essays on Mind, Self, and Emotion* (Cambridge: Cambridge University Press, 1984), 188.

George Lakoff, *Women, Fire, and Dangerous Things: What Categories Reveal about the Mind* (Chicago: University of Chicago Press, 1987), 37, also raises the possibility of positing certain human capacities which may be, in his words, 'underutilized' within a given culture. One virtue of this kind of model is that it enables us to recognize extremes of cultural diversity as utilizing certain basic human material, without moralizing as to its being 'natural' or 'unnatural'.

18. Lukes, 'Conclusion', in Carrithers, Collins, and Lukes (eds.), *Category of the Person*, 297–8.

19. Roy D'Andrade, 'A Folk Model of the Mind', in Dorothy Holland and Naomi Quinn (eds.), *Cultural Models in Language and Thought* (Cambridge: Cambridge University Press, 1987), 145.

20. On the notion of contingent universals, see Thomas MacCarthy, 'Ironist Theory as a Vocation', *Critical Inquiry*, 16: 3 (Spring 1990), 644–55.

21. Robin Horton, 'Tradition and Modernity Revisited', in Martin Hollis and Steven Lukes (eds.), *Rationality and Relativism* (Oxford: Basil Blackwell, 1982), 228.

22. Ibid. 228. The features of primary theory, Horton argues, are indispensable instruments for the 'kind of social co-ordination that is distinctive of the human species' ('Material Object Language and Theoretical Language: Towards a Strawsonian Sociology of Thought', in S. C. Brown (ed.), *Philosophical Disputes in the Social Sciences* (Brighton: Harvester Press, 1979), 199), amongst which the use of co-operative manual technology is prominent (Horton, 'Tradition', in Hollis and Lukes (eds.), *Rationality and Relativism*, 233).

23. E. E. Evans-Pritchard, *Nuer Religion* (Oxford: Clarendon Press, 1956).

24. Ibid. 128.

25. Ibid. 131.

26. Birds, whose young usually hatch in groups, are considered by the Nuer to be 'children of God'. Thus it is through the material analogy of multiple birth that twins come to be ascribed the special spiritual qualities of birds. Ibid. 130.

27. Geertz, *Interpretation of Cultures*, 406.

28. George Lakoff and Mark Johnson, *Metaphors We Live By* (Chicago: University of Chicago Press, 1980), 33–4, 132–3; Kathleen V. Wilkes, *Real People: Personal Identity without Thought Experiments* (Oxford: Clarendon Press, 1988), 97–9.

29. Ibid. 97–8.

30. This is not to imply that all 'animal' films need to present their protagonists as modified human agents; Robert Bresson's *Au Hasard Balthasar* (1966) is one obvious counter-example. My point is simply that many—probably most—narratives in which animals figure as prominent agents treat these animals in this way.

31. Emile Durkheim, quoted by Lukes, 'Conclusion', in Carrithers, Collins, and Lukes (eds.), *Category of the Person*, 286.

32. E. H. Gombrich, *Art and Illusion: A Study in the Psychology of Pictorial Representation* (Princeton, NJ: Princeton University Press, 1969), 136.

33. Cf. Jonathan Glover, *I: The Philosophy and Psychology of Personal Identity* (London: Allen Lane, 1988), 76: 'one body corresponds to one person' (under normal circumstances). Some philosophers argue that bodily identity is neither a sufficient nor a necessary condition of personal identity. Bernard Williams, however, argues persuasively for the difficulty of excluding bodily identity as a necessary (though not sufficient) condition of personal identity: 'when we are asked to distinguish a man's personality from his body, we do not really know what to distinguish from what' (*Problems of the Self: Philosophical Papers 1956–72* (Cambridge: Cambridge University Press, 1973), 12). In any case, the imagined cases used to undermine bodily identity or continuity as a condition of personal identity—brain switches, for example—do not affect our prototype of the human agent or person; and it is with this prototype that we

are concerned. See also Georges Rey, 'Survival', in Amélie Oksenberg Rorty (ed.), *The Identities of Persons* (Berkeley: University of California Press, 1976), 57–9; and Wilkes, *Real People*, 109, 120.

34. Richard Dyer, *Stars* (London: BFI, 1979), 57.

35. Ibid. 30.

36. Caryl Churchill, *Churchill Plays: One* (London: Methuen, 1985), 184–5.

37. Branigan, *Point of View*, 143–67.

38. An illuminating contrast can be drawn here with those soap operas in which a character's role is taken over by a new performer. In such cases, the change is clearly signalled to the spectator, and so the mimetic assumption is, at least temporarily, suspended. The difficulty and shock of the Buñuel example derives from the fact that the shift in performer is both sudden (we are not warned) and unmotivated: the strategy lacks even the generic motivation that explains and codifies the soap opera example. Thanks to Craig Fischer for bringing the example to my attention.

39. 'un faisceau d'éléments *différentiels*' (Vernet, 'Le Personnage de film', 85). This phrase is derived from Claude Lévi-Strauss's essay 'La structure et la forme', in which the author also uses the phrase 'paquets d'éléments différentiels'. See Claude Lévi-Strauss, *Anthropologie structurale II* (Paris: Plon, 1973), 161–2, 170.

40. The notion of 'roughened' or 'impeded form' is derived from Viktor Shklovsky, 'The Resurrection of the Word', in S. Bann and J. E. Bowlt (eds.), *Russian Formalism* (New York: Barnes and Noble, 1973), 47; and 'Art as Device', *Theory of Prose*, trans. Benjamin Sher (Elmwood Park, Ill.: Dalkey Archive Press, 1990), 13.

41. John Frow, 'Spectacle Binding: On Character', *Poetics Today*, 7: 2 (1986), 228.

42. In conversation, Madison, Wisconsin, May 1991.

43. Ian Watt, *The Rise of the Novel* (Berkeley: University of California Press, 1957), 15.

44. Thomas L. Van Laan, *The Idiom of Drama* (Ithaca, NY: Cornell University Press, 1970), 76; quoted by Dyer, *Stars*, 122.

45. Gombrich, *Art and Illusion*, 116–45.

46. Roland Barthes, *S/Z*, trans. Richard Miller (New York: Hill and Wang, 1974), 191.

47. Ibid. 191.

48. The phrase 'un faisceau de relations' is used by Philippe Hamon, 'Pour un statut semiologique du personnage', in Roland Barthes *et al.* (eds.), *Poétique du récit* (Paris: Seuil, 1977), 125.

49. On this question with respect to literary narrative, see Uri Margolin, 'Introducing and Sustaining Characters in Literary Narrative: A Set of Conditions', *Style*, 21: 1 (Spring 1987), 107–24; for some general comments on the different potentials of cinematic and literary fictions with regard to character subjectivity, see the analysis of Karel Reisz's *The French Lieutenant's Woman*, in Seymour Chatman, *Coming to Terms: The Rhetoric of Narrative in Fiction and Film* (Ithaca, NY: Cornell University Press, 1990).

50. Hamon, 'Pour un statut', in Barthes *et al.* (eds.), *Poétique du récit*, 120: 'l'effet-personnage du texte'.

51. Shklovsky, 'The Structure of Fiction', *Theory of Prose*, 66; cited by Kristin Thompson, *Breaking the Glass Armor: Neoformalist Film Analysis* (Princeton, NJ: Princeton University Press, 1988), 41.

52. Quoted by Thompson, ibid. 197, from Victor Chklovski, *La Marche du cheval*, trans. Michel Pétris (Paris: Éditions Champ Libre, 1973), 87–8.

53. Tzvetan Todorov, 'Introduction: Le Vraisemblable', *Communications*, 11 (1968), 3; quoted and trans. Culler, *Structuralist Poetics*, 139. A slightly different version of this essay appears in translation in Todorov, *The Poetics of Prose*, trans. Richard Howard (Ithaca, NY: Cornell University Press, 1977).

54. Thompson, *Breaking the Glass Armor*, 207.

55. Hayden White, 'The Value of Narrativity in the Representation of Reality', in W. J. T. Mitchell (ed.), *On Narrative* (Chicago: University of Chicago Press, 1981), 23; cf. Christian

Metz, 'Some Points in the Semiotics of Cinema', in *Film Language*, trans. Michael Taylor (New York: Oxford University Press, 1974): the cinema can 'be considered as a *language* . . . to the extent that [its] elements are not traced on the perceptual configurations of reality itself (which does not tell stories)' (p. 105).

56. Paul Ricoeur, *Time and Narrative*, i, trans. Kathleen McLaughlin and David Pellauer (Chicago: University of Chicago Press, 1984), 54–64; David Carr, 'Discussion: Ricoeur on Narrative', in David Wood (ed.), *On Paul Ricoeur: Narrative and Interpretation* (London: Routledge, 1991), 162–6.

57. Carr, 'Discussion', 169; Carr is here paraphrasing Ricoeur, *Time and Narrative*, i, 54, 64.

58. Frow, 'Spectacle Binding', 248.

59. Ibid. 243.

60. Rimmon-Kenan, *Narrative Fiction*, 31.

61. Boris Uspensky, *A Poetics of Composition: The Structure of the Artistic Text and Typology of a Compositional Form*, trans. Valentina Zavarin and Susan Wittig (Berkeley: University of California Press, 1973), 138–9, and note 16.

62. W. J. Harvey, for example, argues that 'it is part of any character's mimetic adequacy that he should resist the encroaching lucidity of the reader' (*Character and the Novel* (Ithaca, NY: Cornell University Press, 1965), 71).

The Imaginative Spectator

High structuralism was never more strident
than in its annunciation of the end of man.
Foucault struck the characteristically prophetic
note when he declared in 1966: 'Man is in the
process of perishing as the being of language
continues to shine ever more brightly upon
our horizon.' But who is the 'we' to perceive
or possess such a horizon? In the hollow of
the pronoun lies the aporia of the programme.

Perry Anderson[1]

'An action', writes Jon Elster, 'is the outcome of a choice within constraints.'[2] The choice embodies an element of freedom on the part of the agent; the constraint an element of necessity. This is not, of course, a very remarkable definition of what an action is, other than for its clarity. But it is a description which is deeply alien to the philosophy which underlies the dominant strain of contemporary film theory. Within that theory, the very notion of agency has been supplanted by that of subjectivity, where that term implies not merely the mental dimension of existence, but subjection as the nature of that existence.[3] This negation of agency in the social realm is the direct counterpart to the structuralist reduction of character in narrative discussed in the last chapter. Contemporary cultural theory has obsessively theorized the element of constraint in action, while marginalizing, and in some cases explicitly negating, the element of freedom. (The one major exception to this generalization is reception theory, which I comment on in the final section of this chapter.) This is a liability for any theory which wants to explain—and even advance the cause of—social and individual change. Placing an extraordinary emphasis on the determination of an agent's actions by the various social, and particularly linguistic, structures within which she exists, the following statement (on *The Accused*) is characteristic of contemporary theory and criticism: '[T]he film's formal structure . . . serves to construct and hold the spectator as moral subject, allowing for no active production of meaning on the part of the spectator.'[4] (The fact that the film has—self–evidently—'allowed for' the critic's own critical 'production of meaning' escapes her attention.)

When it comes to the cinema and spectatorship, the sort of activity we are talking about is psychological—acts of mental assent and dissent—but the issues are the same. Are spectators simply 'positioned', or do they respond to texts in a more flexible way? If we grant that there is an element of freedom in our responses, exactly how does it work, and what is its relationship to the undoubted presence of the element of constraint? In what sense(s) is the spectator 'conscious'—or, conversely, how and in what ways (if any) does the apprehension of fiction films involve a 'loss of consciousness' on the spectator's part? Sketching an answer to these questions will be the burden of this chapter, but it will be helpful to look briefly at the ways in which contemporary theory has nullified the activity—the measure of freedom—of the spectator. My approach here will be conceptual rather than historical, since my priority here is to outline my own position, rather than exhaustively critique other positions (a task that has already been undertaken by several authors).[5] In the remainder of the chapter I argue for an alternative conception of the spectator, in which the spectator's relationship to both particular texts, and to ideology in general, is mediated by her imaginative capacities. Spectators, I will argue, are neither deceived with respect to the status of representations, nor entirely caught within the cultural assumptions of those representations. Moreover, against a tradition extending back to Plato, I will argue that emotional responses to fiction should be regarded as neither symptom nor cause of the purported 'positioning' of the spectator by the text. Far from being merely impulsive, unconscious, or bodily responses antithetical to rationality, emotions—whether elicited by real events or fictions—form part of an integrated cycle of perception, cognition, and action.

Subjection, Perception, and Cognition

It doesn't make sense to deceive . . . [t]hat's like saying someone's being phoney at a costume party.[6]

The most basic way in which the spectator has been conceived as 'subjected' is with respect to her perception of the cinematic image. More often an assumption than an argument—shared by theorists as diverse as Jean-Louis Baudry, Noël Burch, Jurij Lotman, Christian Metz, Jean Mitry, Laura Mulvey, and Constance Penley—Hollywood films have long been treated as a particularly potent form of 'dramatic illusion'. The spectator is tricked into holding false beliefs about the status of the object she is perceiving, mistaking representation for referent, as in a *trompe-l'œil* painting. For Uspensky, as I have already noted, even to talk of characters as analogues of real persons is to fall prey to such an illusion. The notion of illusion is compelling because it explains the apparent paradox of fiction, that we sometimes respond to fictions as if they were real, while we know that they are not. The paradox—most vividly realized in our emotional responses to fictions—is thus resolved with the suggestion that, at least for the duration of our engagement with the representation, we are deceived, mistaking the representation for reality. The particular potency of cinematic illusion is said to derive from the combination of qualities specific to film as a medium (the conjoining of photographic 'indexicality' with move-ment, for example), together with the adaptation of 'realist' or 'illusory' narrational forms originally developed in other media (painting, theatre, liter-ary fiction), which are said to mask the factitious nature of representation.

In the most influential formulation, Christian Metz has argued that the spec-tator's attitude towards the filmic image is one of 'disavowal': the spectator knows that what she is watching is only a representation, but believes that it is real.[7] Metz is careful to distance himself from any straightforward notion of deception, preferring the term 'impression' to 'illusion'. But Metz is equally clear that the spectator's experience must be conceptualized in terms of *belief* in the reality of what is in fact only a representation. Metz argues that the spectator of the 'traditional fiction film' at certain moments drifts into a de-ceived, dreamlike state, in which the represented world is experienced as a reality.[8] The 'credulous spectator' (who believes in the reality of the repres-ented action) at this moment dominates and displaces the 'incredulous spec-tator' (who knows that the action is merely represented). The appeal of disavowal is twofold. First, it echoes the older and more widespread notion of the 'suspension of disbelief', in so far as the latter implies a structure of knowl-edge (voluntarily) embedded within (self-)deception. Secondly, it coheres with a more general appeal to psychoanalysis as a theoretical context for cinema. Metz spends little time considering explanatory alternatives to the complex and paradoxical notion of disavowal; the need for such a concept is treated as self-evident. Rather than interrogating the apparent paradox of spectatorship, Metz embraces the paradox because of its congruency with psychoanalysis, for which disavowal is both a defining moment in the development of the individual subject, and a pervasive 'structure of belief'.[9]

Metz's argument, is, however, fundamentally implausible. The spectator must be aware of the representational status of a representation at all times in order to respond appropriately to it. Whenever a fiction film departs from represent-ing an action in real time, there can be no doubt that we are attending as much to the textuality of the fiction as to what it represents. Consider the following sequence from George Miller's *The Road Warrior* (aka *Mad Max II*, 1982), the climax of the final chase. Max has sent the Feral Kid out onto the hood of the truck to retrieve a cartridge. This action is cross-cut with the leader of the rival gang (the Humungus) racing ahead and turning his vehicle in the direction of the truck. As the Feral Kid reaches for the cartridge, Wez, the rival second-in-command, suddenly rears up from the front of the truck. Wez and Max struggle over the Feral Kid. The narration then cuts to the Humungus's car accelerating headlong towards the truck. The close proximity of the two vehicles and the great velocity of each suggest that they will collide in a split-second. The collision is delayed by some eight seconds, though, as the narration cuts between the faces of Max, the Feral Kid, a POV shot of the Humungus's vehicle, Wez's face, and a POV shot of Max's truck. Then the crash occurs.

The sequence involves a quite conventional (if virtuoso) expansion of the implied 'real' time of the event in the diegesis. In order to understand this feature of the sequence, we must attend to the fact that we are watching a representation, that a narrational agency (conceived as either author, narrator, or simply narration) represents the action for us and manipulates the temporal dimension of it. This sense of a narration guiding our attention is a part of our experience of all types of representational texts—including 'classic realist' ones, with their purported 'transparency' of style, designed to maximize the 'illusory' effect.[10] If we did not posit some such narrational agent, we would interpret the sequence as representing a crash in a world with alternative physical laws, in which less ground is covered by bodies moving at given speeds than in the real world. We realize that the norms of physical behaviour which have governed the fictional world throughout the film still hold. This might seem an exceptional case, but from how many fiction films is this kind of manipulation of temporal duration absent? The same goes for spatial manipulations, which are even more obviously omnipresent, since we rarely, if ever, look into the space of the represented world as if it were continuous with the space we inhabit in the theatre. As spectators we must be aware that we are watching a narrated fiction in order to make the kinds of adjustments in perception necessary in a sequence such as that from The Road Warrior. Even the most basic comprehension of a fiction film requires that we never cease to attend to the fact that it is a representation built on conventions.

The Road Warrior draws attention to another way in which realist texts require recognition as texts, and do not simply 'absorb' the spectator into the diegesis. Even though the story world as a whole is governed by the same physical laws as the real world, certain characters within the film obey different physical laws. The Gyro Captain is invested with a magical ability to escape physical harm, whether in the case of falling from the sky in his gyroplane, or wandering in the desert for days without food or water. Major characters are likewise superhumanly resilient. They are, however, set against a background of minor characters who are much closer to the actual world in their (in)ability to withstand physical blows. This kind of variation in the physical laws which govern different types of characters—major, comic, and minor—is, I would suggest, not atypical of realist films.

The kind of intense mental absorption in fiction that the notion of 'illusion' attempts to account for is better explained without the notion of a mistaken belief in the reality of what is represented. Fiction films, I will argue in this chapter, offer us a set of perceptions and sensations which form the basis of an imagined, fictional world. The strategies of the 'traditional fiction film' do not so much efface the work of representation, as direct our attention towards what is represented, rather than towards the means of or the context of representation, in the way that, for example, Vertov's *The Man with a Movie Camera* (1928) does. The channelling of our attention towards, on the one hand, the action represented or, on the other hand, the material of representation, however, is a separate matter from our belief in the literal reality of the representation. As the discussion of *The Road Warrior* seeks to demonstrate, even where our concentration is keenly focused on the represented action, it is inconceivable that we could both understand the fiction and cease to believe that it is a fictional representation.

The 'illusion of reality', however, is not construed by all theorists in such a literal sense. For some, we are not subject to a deception in having false beliefs about the status of the representation, but rather false beliefs about the world represented by the representation. 'Illusory' representations may not lure us into a perceptual trap in which we mistake them for actual events, but they 'subject' us in so far as we understand them as mere transcriptions of reality: '[T]he film does not conceal its operations but it offers them as a transposition of a pre-existent reality.'[11] Just as we can always tell a carbon copy from an original, but assume that all the information from the original has printed through with no significant transformation, we are not deceived with respect to the status of the representation, so much as naïve with respect to how it represents what it represents. Post-structuralist theorists have argued that much of what we take to be 'reality' is a matter of social convention, which we have come to accept as familiar, plausible, and perhaps natural, by force of habit. What is at stake here is not so much the spectator's consciousness of representations *qua* representations (actual events vs. represented events) then, but their consciousness of what leads them to find certain representations plausible, others less so (plausible representations vs. implausible representations). Indeed, the literal interpretation of 'illusion' might be thought of as a straw man, were it not for the fact that the confusion between 'the actual' and 'the plausible' is often encouraged. Brecht, for example, regarded the 'Aristotelian' theatre as mystifying at once the nature of theatrical representation and the nature of what was represented. The 'illusion' of an actual event was integral to the 'illusion' that certain features of human existence are immutable. In this way, an argument for deception at the level of perception is conjoined with an argument for subjection at the level of cognition, with the result that the two issues are often conflated.[12]

A host of critical terms are, for the purposes of my argument, cognate with 'plausibility': verisimilitude, naturalization, the notion of 'realism' as a 'doxa' or set of opinions.[13] All of them imply that our assessments of the plausibility of texts depend on the degree to which the particular text conforms to a set of beliefs about reality, rather than an objective world standing outside of all beliefs and values. What we take to be a free judgement of the plausibility of a work is thus determined in advance by the very beliefs and values that the practices and representations of our society instil in us. Later in this chapter I will suggest a way in which the insight behind these notions can be reconceived and preserved, but it is first important to see the difficulties that arise in the case of one variant, the Althusserian notion of 'interpellation'.

We find in Althusser's writing an important model for the deterministic rhetoric of contemporary film criticism. Althusser's early essay 'The "Piccolo Teatro": Bertolazzi and Brecht' (1962) develops what is essentially an early version of the theory of ideological interpellation. In this essay, Althusser claims that before a spectator identifies psychologically with any individual character, her very attendance in the theatre is an occasion for a cultural and ideological 'recognition'—a term meant to imply a spontaneous, unreflective mode of existence, a lack of self-knowledge. It is implied that this recognition is unconscious:

what, concretely, is this uncriticized ideology if not simply the 'familiar,' 'well-known,' transparent myths in which a society or an age can recognise itself (but not know itself), the mirror it looks into for self-recognition, precisely the mirror it must break if it is to know itself?[14]

(In Althusser's later work in which the term 'interpellation' is coined, the mirror metaphor is linked with the Lacanian notion of the 'mirror stage', thus locating ideological subjection in the most basic awareness of self.)[15] As spectators, we are 'already ourselves in the play itself, from the beginning . . . the play itself *is* the spectator's consciousness—for the essential reason that the spectator has no other consciousness than the content which unites him to the play in advance.'[16] Thus, texts which appeal to the 'transparent myths' of a society will be perceived as 'realistic', because they are found to be plausible and familiar; texts which challenge them will be rejected as 'unrealistic'.

The concept of central interest here is that of 'consciousness'. As the title of the essay indicates, Althusser is attempting to reconceptualize Brecht's theory of 'alienation' in structural terms. If we can reduce Brecht's dramaturgy to a single ambition, it is surely to produce a 'true' (fuller, more complete) consciousness in the spectator. However, one of the very premises of structuralism, in its reaction against phenomenology, is the denial that subjects (spectators) can ever have a consciousness of the structures which determine their existence.[17] I will argue against this later in the chapter, but what is important here is the difficulty Althusser has in marrying the Brechtian ambition (which he wishes to maintain) with this tenet of structuralism. On the one hand, the concept of 'recognition' is highly deterministic, suggesting that the spectator is entirely caught in a hermetically sealed bubble of ideology: '[W]e are first united by an institution—the performance, but more deeply, by the same myths, the same themes, that govern us without our consent, by the same spontaneously lived ideology.'[18] On the other hand, some of Althusser's descriptions suggest that spectators can achieve some form of true consciousness (consciousness of the real conditions of class society), which is 'visible to the spectator in the mode of a perception which is not given, but has to be discerned, conquered and drawn from the shadow which initially envelops it, and yet produced it'.[19]

The struggle in this essay between the possibility of consciousness and the incarceration of the spectator in an eternally benighted 'in-structuredness' is resolved, in favour of the latter, with the introduction of Lacanian concepts in later essays. Althusser's final suggestion is that the essay he has just written in fact represents the play itself continuing its work through him; in the familiar structuralist dictum, language speaks us, we do not speak language:

I look back, and I am suddenly and irresistibly assailed by *the* question: are not these few pages, in their maladroit and groping way, simply that unfamiliar play *El Nost Milan*, performed on a June evening, pursuing in me its incomplete meaning, searching in me, despite myself, now that all the actors and sets have been cleared away, for the *advent* of its silent discourse?[20]

This is an attempt to deflect the objection that the subject 'Althusser' has a true consciousness of the working of a play and its relations to ideology and the real conditions of existence, and has made this consciousness available to the reader. And yet Althusser cannot evade the active construction: 'I look back . . .' The essay presents the bizarre spectacle of a theorist actively and consciously theorizing that he cannot theorize his own activity and consciousness. Althusser cannot escape ascribing agency and consciousness (of some sort) to at least one figure: himself. Althusser is haunted by pronouns, emblems of the ghost of agency in the purportedly impersonal structuralist machine.

Cognition and Imagination

In addition to the descriptive failings of contemporary theory sketched in the introduction, then, it is riven by contradictions in so far as it assumes—indeed, cannot escape—the very concepts and phenomena it seeks to indict. In the case of Althusser's theory of interpellation, consciousness and agency stubbornly reappear; in the case of structuralist narrative theory, the importance of character, and the intrinsically mimetic nature of character, continually resurface. In clarifying the nature of the parallels between persons and characters, Robin Horton's argument for a cross-cultural distinction between human and non-human was important. The second fundamental distinction Horton notes within 'primary theory'—between self and others—relates directly to our primary concern here: understanding and 'identification' between and among different persons, and between real persons (spectators) and imagined, fictive persons (characters). Imagination will be a key concept in examining the relationship between self and others—a term which, like identification, is extremely elastic in meaning and will therefore require precise definition. Unlike identification, however, imagination has largely been ignored by contemporary cultural theory.

I introduce the concept of imagination as a way of countering the determinism at the heart of concepts like subjection and 'interpellation'. In doing so, I am cognizant of both the looseness of the term, and its association with a debilitatingly impressionistic and a- (or even anti-) theoretical critical stance. I tackle both by proposing a specific and detailed definition, which situates imagination within the framework of cognitive psychology. I will not argue that imagination constitutes a kind of utopia of mental freedom. The topography of imagination as I will develop it is not that of untrammelled, virgin territory; it is criss-crossed by culturally established routes. Cognitive anthropologists have developed a range of concepts which enable us to explain both 'subjectivity' (the structuring of individual consciousness and imagination by cultural and ideological forces) and agency (the way in which individuals use these structures in order to act within them and on them). Thus, far from losing sight of the constraints on thought and agency that structuralism stresses, the cognitive account of the imagination incorporates them.

One of the central concepts in cognitive theory is the 'schema'. A schema (plural, schemas or schemata)[21] is a pattern which allows the mind to organize and process the mass of sensory data it constantly receives. Such patterns allow us to predict and postulate outcomes on the basis of partial information: schemata allow us 'to go beyond the ideas overtly expressed by providing the elaboration, explanation, and interconnections that we call *understanding*'.[22] Moreover, such mental activity is also characterized by the productivity traditionally associated with the concept of imagination, as George Lakoff acknowledges in his extensive use of the term in his study of schemata and categorization.[23] A given schema will provide an outline of events or features, with 'slots' for the major agents, events, props, or possible outcomes. On the basis of such schemata, we decide how to act, and we form expectations concerning the results of our actions and those of others. If someone extends their hand and suspends it at waist height in front of me, I make sense of this gesture as a civil invitation to enter into the social ritual of 'shaking hands', probably a preface to conversation with this person. To do this, I activate a number of schemata involving patterns of social etiquette, schemata which I have learned as part of my socialization into Western culture.

This is an extremely simple example; cognitive psychologists have also studied the processing of narrative discourse and the recall of stories.[24] E. H. Gombrich explains both artistic production and perception using schema theory: an artistic style, he writes, 'like a culture or a climate of opinion, sets up a horizon of expectation, a mental set [= schema], which registers deviations and modifications with exaggerated sensitivity'.[25] Partly on the basis of schema theory, cognitive anthropologists have developed the notion of 'cultural models': prototypical scenarios which generate 'simplified worlds' of types and events.[26] These models enable us to identify agents and events rapidly from a few salient details: we do not need to draw an inductive picture, from the ground up, of every new agent (real or fictional) that we encounter. In a later chapter, I discuss how we swiftly identify the likely traits and overall personality of Ben McKenna (James Stewart) on the basis of a very few features revealed in the opening moments of The Man Who Knew Too Much. In this case, our rapid categorization of the character is accurate, but a film (or any work of narrative fiction) may just as legitimately invite us to make the wrong inference(s): such is the strategy of many mystery films, like Robert Siodmak's The Spiral Staircase (1946), in which our suspicions do not easily flow towards the guilty party because he appears to embody only virtuous qualities.[27]

The central point of schema theory is that in comprehending social events and signs, we are constantly activating and situating them within schemata. As Gombrich states, '[A]ll culture and all communication depend on the interplay between expectation and observation, the waves of fulfillment, disappointment, right guesses, and wrong moves that make up our daily life.'[28] In order for the physical gesture (the hand suspended in mid-air) to become a sign (of civility), a certain amount of mental activity has to occur, which semiotics has tended to ignore. Schema theory, then, can be used in a theory of the mental representation of social practices, beliefs, and values, and to elucidate the relationship between imagination and ideology.[29]

Cognitive theory proposes neither a 'transcendental' nor a 'voluntarist' subject, fully 'self-present' and autonomous, entirely in control of her desires and aware of her motivations. Schema theory regards human behaviour as basically goal-directed, but the parameters within which these goals are set are not necessarily, and certainly not wholly, available to agents, as these parameters are automatized. 'Automatized' or 'overlearned' mental processes are 'beneath consciousness' in the sense that they are usually performed quickly and unreflectively, but they are 'conscious' in that they are accessible to reflection (in contrast to 'non-conscious' and 'unconscious' processes).[30] The cluster of assumptions that constitutes the person schema is automatized in this sense: we take it for granted that a character has just one body, but we can be brought to reflect on this contingent fact of human physiology, as both filmmakers and philosophers have proven (see Chapter 1). In addition, both general cultural and specifically ideological beliefs and values—those that arise and function in relation to a society's power structures—can be conceptualized in the cognitive model as automatized, and therefore apparently natural, habits of mind. Automatized schemata constitute the ground on which everyday, conscious behaviour is based. Cognitive anthropologists have used various phrases to capture the nature of such knowledge: 'presupposed worlds' and 'taken-for-granted worlds', for example. Dorothy Holland and Debra Skinner have commented on the difficulty many subjects have in making such knowledge explicit, a problem explained in part by Edwin Hutchins's characterization of its 'referential transparency'. Such knowledge is 'often transparent to those who use it. Once learned, it becomes what one *sees with*, but seldom what one *sees*.'[31]

Schema theory is informed by a realist, constructivist epistemology in which sense-data from the external world are organized by mental structures; it is neither an empiricism which sees the mind as a *tabula rasa* passively accepting the imprint of an immanently meaningful world, nor an idealism which regards the mind as entirely unconstrained in its construction of 'reality'. As Gombrich writes, our 'need to organize and interpret does not mean that we are helplessly caught in our interpretation. We can experiment and through trial and error learn something about such impressions. An alternative interpretation may drive out the accepted one and reveal a glimpse of the reality behind it.'[32] Agency is conceived as occurring within a cycle of action and perception: the human agent 'perceives as the basis of action; each action affords new data for perception'.[33] Emotion too is a part of this cycle, as we will see later in this chapter. Perceptions and actions may give rise to particular emotions, but these emotions, in turn, function as 'patterns of salience' and thereby influence future perceptions and actions. We need not posit a wholly unified being in order to retain a notion of rational agency, so much as a 'loose integration' of schemata such that an agent is capable of purposeful action.

If we underline the fact that many schemata are culturally specific, it should be clear that schema theory offers an alternative model for conceptualizing the 'spontaneous' activity characterized by Althusser as 'ideology'. The important difference from the Althusserian account, as we shall see, lies in the detail and complexity with which schema theory enables us to approach ideology, a model of mental activity which accounts for both conformity to the 'spontaneous' and developments away from it (in other words, changes in what is conceived as 'the familiar', and the possibility of an awareness that what is familiar may shift). In the broader terms set out at the opening of this chapter, schema theory enables a model of ideology that accounts for both freedom and constraint. If film viewing is modelled on the lines of an action/perception cycle, we can no longer conceive of films and spectators as bound in a mutual strait-jacket of ideological confirmation and reinforcement.

Cultural schemata are learned and sustained within a given cultural environment. For this reason they become automatized: drawn upon as if by reflex, though they are learned rather than innate. We do not 'think about' the ritual of the handshake as we participate in it because it is so familiar and automatized. Similarly, tacit beliefs—those which are evident from behaviour rather than expressed (cognized, reasoned out) by agents—may be regarded as automatized schemata. When such schemata interlock, they may function as ideologies, which 'succeed to the extent that they exclude conflicting schemas from consideration, making their reality untenable'.[34] 'Tenability' here is akin to both Althusserian 'familiarity' and the structuralist concept of naturalization, in that it is a quality that arises from conformity among a set of ideological beliefs about the world, rather than conformity between such beliefs and a reality outside of all ideologies. But conceiving of ideology as a network of automatized beliefs allows for both the constraining power of ideology, and the possibility of moving within and even beyond these constraints (which does not, of course, entail that in doing so we can exist outside of any and all constraints).

The ritual of the handshake becomes automatized and 'transparent', continually reinforced by the cultural context in which it is a norm. But in a different culture with a very different ritual of introduction, we would be 'conscious of' the handshake schema: in essence, the action would become 'defamiliarized' or 'alienated'. Schema theory is thus a fruitful context for reconsidering Shklovsky's concept of *ostranenie* and its Brechtian elaboration, *Verfremdung*.[35] It also challenges 'the unconscious' and repression as the dominant concepts by which we model ideology. Automatization provides a better explanation of what most theorists are driving at when they talk of ideology as 'unconscious'. Automatized practices and beliefs are indeed 'beneath consciousness', but they are not repressed. On the contrary, they are assumed: the vehicle rather than the object of thought. Conceived as automatized, 'unconscious' practices and beliefs are capable of being brought to consciousness; in the right context, we may be brought to reflect upon them. Aside from the dislocating experience of immersion in an alien culture, we should also include self-reflective activity, and in particular the socially sanctioned spaces for such activity—certain kinds of education, and the aesthetic domain—as such contexts.

An objection to the picture of 'active consciousness' being developed here is that there is a crucial gap between activity, conceived as the activation of learned schemata, and truly critical activity, in which such schemata are critically reflected upon.[36] To discuss them in the same breath is to confuse apples and oranges. If the claim is that humans do not typically have self-consciousness of any kind, it seems counterintuitive, and incoherent when claimed by someone reflecting on the nature of consciousness. The notion of 'referential transparency' points to the difficulty of a reflective awareness of our most fundamental cultural models, not its impossibility. With an understanding of 'unconscious' beliefs as tacit and automatized rather than repressed, it could be argued that high-level culturally specific schemata are the most susceptible to critical reflection. There are, *pace* Rube Goldberg, only so many ways to grasp a rock or fashion a wheel; but there are many ways in which we can organize a society (who will fashion the wheels?).

A handshake is usually held for two or three seconds, but occasionally one or both of the agents involved may grasp the other's hand for longer, for an entire sentence or more. The latter is not our first expectation, but it is an option held within the schema, accommodated through our experience with many thousands of handshakes, and so we are not thrown into crisis by the change. This is recognized in schema theory in the concepts of 'default values' and 'hierarchies'. Each 'slot' of a schema has a number of hierarchically ordered alternatives, the default value constituting the prototypical case. As with schemata in general, default values and hierarchies may embody ideological conceptions. There is one example with which we are all familiar: the default value of the generic pronoun *he* is male. That is, there is evidence that both men and women instantiate the supposedly generic form of 'he' with a male representative, and that women must take an additional step of altering the instantiation if they are not to exclude themselves from the 'address' of the pronoun. This is a powerful example of the way a cultural model may embody the viewpoint of a dominant group within society, hence 'muting' other groups and thus functioning ideologically.[37] In fact, the default hierarchies of a great many schemata are ordered according to patriarchal prejudice. Consider the following puzzle:

A father and his son are driving along a motorway. An accident occurs. The father is killed instantly, while his son is severely injured. In the operating theatre, the old surgeon looks at the young man and exclaims, 'My God, it's my son!' How can this be?

The difficulty caused here lies in the instantiation of the word 'surgeon'. The default value for the gender of 'surgeon' is male, due to both the historical reality of, and representations of, hospital life in which labour is divided between male doctors and female nurses. This creates a paradox: how can the father have been killed in the car and yet be operating on his son? The solution is, of course, that the boy's mother is the surgeon. (John Ford's *7 Women* (1966) exploits precisely this default value. A group of women missionaries await a new doctor, identified in advance only as 'Dr Cartwright'. Expecting a man, the women—and perhaps the audience—are shocked when the doctor arrives, a young woman played by Anne Bancroft.) The solution may be temporarily blocked because we automatically fill the gender 'slot' in the surgeon schema with a male representative. But the riddle is usually quickly solved, because a female surgeon is neither logically impossible nor empirically so rare (in real hospitals or in representations). The possibility is ranked, however, lower on the default hierarchy (although not so low in 1994 as it probably was in 1966, when Ford made 7 Women). In the words of George Lakoff, default hierarchies can 'accommodate stripeless tigers and white gold',[38] even though such odd-ities will not be the default value. Moreover, as the 'surgeon schema' suggests, default hierarchies may change historically as social practices shift. Schemata, then, have a certain degree of flexibility built into them; they should not be thought of as rigid sequences which either explain experience fully or fail completely.

In phenomenological and affective terms, the testing of belief-schemata against new experience may result in continued conformity to an ideology, question-ing the authorities who espouse the ideology, conceptual conflict, or the more or less drastic revision of beliefs. A variety of factors affect this hesitation among assimilation (fitting new experience into pre-existing schemata), accommodation (revising schemata to accommodate unfamiliar aspects of new experience), and wholesale rejection of social schemata. These range from, in Marx's words, the 'dull compulsion' of immediate material needs (food, shelter, warmth), to the degree of support one finds in the social environment for schemata which oppose those of the dominant ideology, to the very difficulty of developing schemata which genuinely do break with the existing ideology in which the agent has been socialized. Mary Crawford and Roger Chaffin develop this last point with reference to 'muted group' theory. Distinguishing between 'background' and 'experience', they argue that radical differences in background (one's history of experience) may be obscured by viewpoint (the perspective one adopts on a situation). The schemata which comprise our cultural models of gender may be biased to represent male experience; and in this sense women may have no choice in adopting a 'masculine' viewpoint on even their own experience: 'Because the male viewpoint is diffuse and pervasive, neither men nor women can readily step in and out of it as they attempt to apprehend their experi-ences.'[39] Arguing that such ideological breaks are possible, however, does not depend upon positing a voluntarist subject, nor does it assume that all social phenomena are explicable in terms of the goals of individual agents—some agents are supra-individual, and some events are unforeseen and unintended consequences of actions. But it does depend upon a view of human cognition as imaginative precisely in the sense that, no matter how far our beliefs and values are initially shaped by the social structures in which we are immersed, we are capable of expanding and adapting our existing conceptual frameworks through new experience, including our experience of fictional representations.

Representation and Mimesis

Traditionally, the relationship between fictional representations and the world has been described by the concept of mimesis: the imitation of human action by the body or voice, or in the media of stone, paint, the written word, the photographic or cinematic image. The concept of mimesis—along with those of agency, consciousness, and imagination—however, has been virtually excised from the vocabulary of contemporary theory. Where it is maintained at all, it is, as we have seen, in the transmogrified form of verisimilitude or naturalization, where it is cast as a form of deception. Mimesis—the 'reality-effect' —is regarded as an illusion fostered by conformity to accepted representational codes. 'Reality' itself is a tissue of representations. For post-structuralism, reality is either swept up entirely into textuality (as in Derrida's oft-cited slogan, 'there is nothing outside the text'), or else it is reduced to a purely physical world, outside of human action and meaning.[40] If this were literally true, however—if there was nothing outside the text—we would not be able to discriminate real actions from representations, and clearly we routinely do this. The lesson to be learned from the fact that social reality is already invested with symbolic meaning (and is in this sense 'textual') is not that the idea of mimesis collapses, but that it requires more careful definition. The idea of mimesis— whether it goes by that name or any other—is not easily snuffed out, as we have already seen in the case of the concept of character.

Mimesis need not be associated exclusively with theories which claim that art does or ought to *reproduce* reality (however that may be defined: physically, socially, phenomenologically, psychologically, spiritually). The perception of representations can be deemed a mimetic process in the sense that in the act of comprehension the spectator or reader must appeal not only to knowledge of textual and artistic conventions (genre conventions, editing conventions, and so forth) but also to knowledge of the real world, in whatever way that is defined for particular audiences. I do not assume that the external world, that which is imitated or referred to, is simply 'out there', with literary and filmic representations pointing to them in a purely secondary or parasitic fashion. Rather, I argue that in comprehending such representations we must employ, at least initially, the same schemata through which we understand reality. Christopher Butler explicates this modified mimetic theory succinctly:

Most theorists of world–text relationships have concerned themselves with matters of correspondence: what one can say or cannot say about the actual relationship of text to world: to say, for example, that we can refer to Russia or Paris but not to fictional characters because they do not 'exist'. But I am arguing for a relationship which is consistent with the shifting, culturally relative, and often metaphorical frameworks through which we 'see' the world in the first place.[41]

Seeing characters as persons is a central aspect of such a mimetic act, bringing both the person schema and culturally specific role-schemata (like the surgeon schema) into play. A mimetic theory of this sort assumes that when we engage with a fiction by watching a film or reading a book, we do so on the basis of knowledge developed in a much broader sphere than the merely fictional. Our earlier experiences with fiction are an important part of this general 'encyclopaedia' of knowledge; the institution of fiction is a part of our social reality. But it is just that, a part of our more general experience; to equate fictional experience with real experience is to render the concept of 'fiction' vacuous. Butler describes this 'encyclopaedia' and its relation to mimesis in the following passage:

At its largest, this set of propositions comprises our most general beliefs about the world, which we bring to the beginning of the text, and which may have to be discarded for the purposes of the text (if for example we are reading fantasy literature). In reading, our contextual conception of the world and the text's own projection inevitably confront one another. We must see the text, at least initially, as mimetic, since our knowledge of the meaning of its expressions is so largely drawn from experience.[42]

The mimetic reading strategy is nothing more than a mimetic hypothesis: an approach we take at the outset and subject to modification. The mimetic hypothesis is made in the context of and tempered by the knowledge that we are processing an artefact, a narrated representation, as the sequence from *The Road Warrior* demonstrated. Far from there being a necessary tension or mutual exclusivity between textuality and mimesis, the two factors dynamize and complement each other. To respond to fictional works we have to begin with our experience of the world. But fictional texts ask us to revise the assumptions, beliefs, and values that we bring to them in a myriad of ways: fictional worlds can propose alternative physical laws, histories, moral codes, and social rituals. As Paul Ricoeur has written, one of the functions of fiction is 'to suspend our attention to the real, to place us in a state of non-engagement with regard to perception or action . . . [i]n this state of non-engagement we try new ideas, new values, new ways of being-in-the-world'.[43] Traffic between world and text, then, runs in both directions: we need our experience of the world to 'get into' the text, but the text itself may transform the way we understand and experience the world.

Fiction and Emotion

Emotional responses to fiction occupy a special place in debates concerning the mimetic nature of fictional narrative, probably because they reveal the power of fiction most viscerally. For the Brechtian tradition, emotional responses to

fiction of an 'empathic' kind lock us into the perspective of individual characters, blocking a more interrogatory relationship with characters and the narrative as a whole. Rather than transforming our understanding of the world,
emotive ('Aristotelian') narratives divert our critical attention away from the
world, by providing a safe, protected sphere in which we can experience sorrow, anger, outrage—and congratulate ourselves on our sensitivity—without
having to act on these emotions. Rather than developing and intensifying
our understanding of the world, emotional responses to fiction only serve to
siphon off energies which might otherwise have transformed the world. In
short, empathic emotions are an instrument of subjection.

This view of the nature and effects of emotional response, I want to argue,
is reductive and ill-conceived. There is, however, a puzzle prior to the questions raised by Brecht concerning the consequences of emotional response to
fiction. For certain authors, the key question concerns the grounds upon which
we respond emotionally to fictions in the first place: how is it that we can be
moved at all by what we know to be non-existent? The question of emotional
response returns us, in other words, to the purported 'paradox' of fictional
response discussed at the beginning of this chapter: the idea that in engaging
with fictions we behave as if we both believe and do not believe in the reality
of the fictional events. Approaching this issue from the perspective of specifically emotional responses, however, provides no further arguments or
evidence for the existence of the supposed 'paradox' than did considering our
responses more broadly.

Colin Radford approaches this question by first considering emotions in
relation to real events. Radford argues that our emotional responses to actual
events depend upon our believing that the given event has actually occurred.
If I find a friend slumped over a bar, in the process of consuming a bottle of
whisky, and my friend explains that his sister has just died in a road accident,
I will experience sorrow and grief in sympathy with my friend. If, however, my
friend then breaks out into a smile, nudges me in the ribs and says 'fooled you!'
I will no longer feel any form of pity for my friend. The object of the emotion—the belief that my friend's sister has died—has disappeared (a new emotion might appear with a different object: anger at having been so deceived).[44]
For an aesthetic parallel, we might think of a film like *David Holzman's Diary*
(1967, directed by Jim McBride), which presents itself as a documentary, by the
observance of certain stylistic codes, only to undercut this at the end by the
revelation that the film was scripted and performed by actors.

With similar examples as the basis of his discussion, Radford then goes on
to question how we can ever be moved by fictional entities and events which
we never believe to be actual, for example the character Anna Karenina. Anna
Karenina is the mental equivalent of the sister now known not to be dead. If
the latter fails to move us, why should the former? An 'inconsistency' arises,

then, because belief in the reality of agents and events appears to be a criterion of emotional response in the case of our everyday affairs, but not in the case of our experience of fiction. The problem, as Radford sees it, 'is that people *can* be moved by fictional suffering given their brute behaviour in other contexts where belief in the reality of the suffering described or witnessed is necessary for the response'.[45] Proffering several possible solutions to this paradox, he concludes that none are satisfactory and declares that emotional responses to fiction are not merely inconsistent with our emotional responses to actual events, but absurd, 'unintelligible', and 'unmanly'.[46]

A further feature of Radford's argument, then, is an implicit privileging of emotional responses to real events over emotional responses to fictional events. That we respond emotionally to real events is, to use Radford's phrase, a 'brute fact' of human existence; that we can also respond emotionally to fictional events is merely 'inconsistent' with this 'brute fact'. Radford never explains why emotional responses to fictional events should not also have the status of 'brute fact'. No argument is offered as to why the inconsistency between the two responses results in one being accepted, the other being deplored. By working initially from the scenario involving emotional responses to actual events, Radford has constructed the argument in such a way as to block alternative explanations of emotional responses to fiction. Radford begins by describing the nature of and criteria for emotional responses to real events, including the crucial criterion that we believe that the event has or is occurring. In doing so, he implicitly establishes this criterion as a norm for all emotional responses (whether to fictions or real events). In such a light, emotional responses to fiction cannot but seem irrational and incoherent. But why should we accept this as a condition of all emotional response, when our experience of fictions tells us otherwise?

Radford anticipates the objection that he has created a problem by failing to recognize two senses of the phrase 'being moved', one applying to real situations, one to fictional situations.[47] However, he claims that the fact of similarity between emotional response to real events and that to fictional events means that we cannot ignore the crucial difference, that is, that belief does not seem to be necessary in the case of fiction. But this merely repeats the structure of the essay as a whole, by regarding emotional response to fiction as secondary and parasitic, and therefore not truly separable or distinct from emotional response to actual events. It might appear that emotional responses to real events have a utility that emotional responses to fiction do not have: fear of real dangerous animals, for example, helps us to live longer, while fear of fictional Green Slime does not. As we will see, however, emotions constitute a crucial 'motivational supplement' in the conduct and explanation of human action, and emotions are learned through both actual experience and through fictional and other representations.

Radford's conundrum, concerning the sudden deflation of our emotional responses in his core scenario, can be explained without creating a hierarchy between acceptable emotional responses (to real events) and 'unintelligible' ones (to fictional events). We need to recognize that there are two forms of emotional response, one to actual events, and one to fictional events, which share many features but which are not structurally identical. They differ precisely with respect to the nature of the object of the emotion. In a response to an actual situation, we must believe that the object (the event to which we react) must exist or have existed. In a response to a fictional text, we merely imaginatively propose to ourselves that the object exists: we do not require any existential commitment.[48] In responding to what is clearly a fictional event, we do not assess the object for its referential validity.

We can conceive of these two types of response as two categories defined by prototypes rather than necessary and sufficient conditions. The prototype of a category functions as a norm against which other members are judged: an apple is a 'more central' example of the category 'fruit' than is a tomato; an unmarried, male civil servant is a 'better' example of the category 'bachelor' than Tarzan or the Pope, even though all three are 'unmarried adult males'. Many categories defined by prototypes also exhibit fuzzy, overlapping boundaries rather than rigid limits.[49] (Prototype categorization is thus closely linked with default values and hierarchies: in our society, a woman can be a surgeon, but the prototypical surgeon is male.) In the case at hand, 'fictional representation', on the one hand, and 'historical' or 'documentary representation', on the other, may be viewed as two overlapping categories, each characterized by this 'centrality gradience' and fuzziness at the peripheries of the category. Most representations are obvious and clear examples of either fiction or documentary, but some, like *David Holzman's Diary*, Orson Welles's *F for Fake* (1973), and Wim Wenders's *Lightning Over Water* (1981), are not so easily categorized and may invite us to draw on both the fictional and the non-fictional norm; hence, the notion of overlap between the two categories. Such representations, which commingle the representation of real events with fictional ones, are sometimes discomforting because we are invited to respond to them according to two very different, and in some ways conflicting structures of emotion.

Conceiving of emotions in this fashion allows us to explain Radford's conundrum. The purportedly true stories which are revealed as false effect a sudden shift in the prototype we appeal to, which results in the collapse of the initial emotional response. The rules have been changed; the drunken, deceiving friend asks us to switch suddenly from one mental structure to another, from believing in an actual event to entertaining the idea in the imagination. In addition, this model can help us explain the complex and various responses we may have to 'mixed' representations, that is, texts like the quasi- and ersatz-documentaries noted above; or films like Radu Gabrea's *A Man Like Eva* (1983) and Richard

Brooks's *In Cold Blood* (1967), which do not purport to be historical transcriptions, but nevertheless draw on well-known historical events as material for the fiction ('based on a true story'); or Dušan Makavejev's *Innocence Unprotected* (1968) and Haskell Wexler's *Medium Cool* (1969), which, in different ways, interweave fictional and documentary representations, both 'referring' to the same story world. Wexler's film achieves this by shooting performers representing fictional characters in the actual space of Chicago during the 1968 Democratic convention and subsequent riots, Makavejev's by weaving together documentary and newsreel material from the Second World War with footage from a fiction film made during the same period. Viewing a film as a fiction, we will be untroubled by the degree of accuracy of the text with respect to the historical material: for the purposes of our emotional responses, the actual existence of the events portrayed is not at issue. Christopher Butler has suggested that this argument might be pushed further to acknowledge that the process of learning to identify particular emotions with particular situations is facilitated as much through our experience of fictions as through our experience of reality. '[H]aving an emotion', Butler writes, 'is not something that is intrinsically tied to real life objects at all. . . . We need to be able to learn to operate on the boundary between the real and the fictional in deciding, eg., what the moral *consequences* of having those emotions might be. But not, I think, in learning/acquiring them.' This underlines the fact that emotional responses to real events cannot be seen as more significant and legitimate than emotional responses to fictions.[50]

If, however, we do not view a film as a pure fiction and activate (as the text may invite us to) the pertinent historical background, then we may be discomfited by the text's inconsistent adherence to what we accept as 'the facts'. Imagine a 'docudrama' about the fall of the Czechoslovakian Communist Party in 1989. The film begins by following events as they are generally accepted to have occurred. But then we are told that Václav Havel was endowed with supernatural powers by virtue of a visitation from benign aliens. His influence spreads so that a utopian era descends upon Europe by 1991. Events leading up to this, initiated by Havel, include the downfall of Margaret Thatcher. In other words, in the manner of 'magic realism', the film mixes accepted facts of history with obvious flights of fancy. The film never abandons reference to certain actual events, and thus does not invite us to abandon entirely the mode of response appropriate to actual events for the response appropriate to fictional events. As in Radford's problem case, there is a disjunction between the two structures, but in this case the disjunction is sustained and used as an artistic strategy. The point here is not to make a moral judgement about playing with the boundaries of fiction and the actual, but to explain one factor in the unsettling nature of such 'mixed' representations. We are invited to draw upon the two structures of emotion simultaneously, not to reject one for the other as in the case of the 'trick' story so important to Radford.

Reason and Emotion

The work of art is apprehended through the feelings as well as through the senses. Emotional numbness disables here as definitely if not as completely as blindness or deafness.[51]

The barely disguised discomfort with emotion, and more especially with emotional responses to fiction, in Radford's essay, has deep roots in the Western tradition. The paradigmatic expression of this distrust of emotion in twentieth-century aesthetics is surely to be found in the work of Brecht, for whom empathic emotional responses deaden our rational capacities. The attitude of both Brecht and Radford fits into a tradition of thought that goes as far back as the Stoics and Plato, one that has been dominant in Western thought,[52] though in Brecht's case this aversion may have been justifiably heightened by the centrality of spectacular, emotive aesthetics in Nazi culture (most obviously embodied by Wagner). Similarly, the association of emotion with (dangerous) femininity, present in Radford's essay, extends back through the Enlightenment to Platonic philosophy: in the *Phaedo*, Socrates chides Apollodorus 'for his womanish tears'.[53] This 'domineering dichotomy between the cognitive and the emotive',[54] and the concomitant association of emotion with irrationality, is among the 'Enlightenment' attitudes which post-structuralism has sought to discredit.[55]

But post-structuralism has not acknowledged the massive revision of notions of 'rationality' undertaken in the last thirty years by cognitive theorists and some philosophers. For these authors, 'rationality' is no longer conceived as a set of timeless, abstract procedures divorced from the particularities of culture and the perceptual and nervous systems of the human body. Abstract, 'transcendental' rationality has been complicated, and to some degree undermined, by a range of theorists. On the one hand, cognitive theorists have examined techniques and patterns of human reasoning which, while not traditionally 'rational' (i.e. describable in the abstract language of mathematical logic) are pervasive and effective.[56] From another angle, emotion has enjoyed a resurgence in respectability among philosophers of mind, who have argued that emotion is a part of human systems of reason. In general, human cognition—the features and patterns of practical human thinking, including emotion—has supplanted the consideration of abstract rules of logic. It should be noted, though, that what has been established are the many inadequacies of the reason–emotion antinomy, in which emotion is consigned to the status of a mere impediment to reason and action. We have yet to see a complete theory of the interrelations between cognition (inference-making, memory, hypothesizing, and so forth) and affect.

An initial defence of the 'rationality of emotion' may be made on the grounds that emotions are only distinguishable on the basis of certain identificatory beliefs. Emotions are neither merely bodily sensations (as in the Cartesian argument) nor psychic 'energy' (as in the Freudian model): they are composed

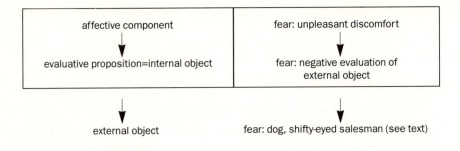

Figure 2.1   Objects of emotion

of affect and cognition. Anger, for example, rests upon the agent's belief that someone (or something) has injured her interests; fear rests upon the belief that something threatens the agent's interests. The rationality of the emotion can therefore be assessed along with that of the belief: if the belief is unjustified, and the evidence is before the agent holding the belief, then both the belief and the emotion are irrational.

This 'cognitivist' or 'judgementalist' account of emotion is the type that Radford assumes in mounting his attack upon emotional responses to fiction.[57] Since spectators do not seem to believe that fictions are real, they should not, rationally, experience any emotional responses to fiction. So the abundant and often intense emotional reactions spectators often have to fiction are 'incoherent'. Obviously, then, a strictly 'judgementalist' account of emotions, in which their justification or rationality is reduced to the assessment of the rationality of their identificatory beliefs, is not compatible with the model I am developing.

'Cognition', however, is not synonymous with 'belief'. Patricia Greenspan revises the strict judgementalist account by splitting the object of the emotion (the someone or something about which the belief is held, or intentionally directed at) into an internal and external object. The latter is a real object (the dog that we fear, the student we are angry at) while the internal object is the *evaluative proposition* in which we mentally assess and take a stance towards that object: 'the dog is dangerous', 'the student has embarrassed me'. The identificatory belief is thus replaced by an identificatory evaluation. The structure of an emotion may thus be represented as in Fig. 2.1. By separating out these two layers, Greenspan is able to demonstrate, via a number of case-studies, that such evaluative propositions need not and often do not involve the kind of assent we associate with belief. Rather, we may 'hold them in mind', without believing them. Furthermore, Greenspan argues, such evaluative propositions may be 'appropriate' (the parallel to 'rational' with respect to beliefs) where the equivalent belief would not be. Thus, the assessment of the appropriateness (roughly, 'rationality') of an emotional response does not reduce to the assessment of the rationality of a belief, as it does for the pure 'judgementalist'. For example, in dealing with a salesman, something about his behaviour makes me suspicious of him (suspicion is here understood as a weak form of fear). Though I am unable to identify reflectively what it is about his behaviour that produces this discomfort, it is something about his behaviour that initiates the distrust—say, his subtle refusal to make eye contact. It is not a paranoid projection on my part; I simply have difficulty pinning down exactly what I am reacting to. In such a case, Greenspan argues, it would be irrational to believe 'the salesman is untrustworthy', but holding this as an evaluative proposition in mind, and consequently experiencing the emotion of suspicion, may be appropriate. 'Appropriateness', then, is a measure of the 'backward-looking' rationality of the emotion: to what degree is it warranted by the situation (even where a belief parallel to the identificatory evaluation would not be)?

Greenspan adds another criterion of rationality by which an emotion may be judged, that of 'adaptiveness'. An emotion is adaptive if it serves some goal of the agent; it is an instrumental or 'forward-looking' criterion. If a principal aim of mine is not to be stiffed by the car salesman, because I have the limited funds of a graduate student, then the emotion of suspicion (which does not amount to a belief in the salesman's untrustworthiness) is, in principle, ad-aptive, since it keeps me alert to his actions and statements.[58] Ronald de Sousa, in work formulated at roughly the same time as Greenspan's, puts forward two very similar notions of rationality (which may be applied to emotions, among other phenomena): 'cognitive rationality' and 'strategic rationality' (parallel to Greenspan's criteria of appropriateness and adaptiveness).

There is a further point of overlap between de Sousa and Greenspan worth pursuing here. Both discuss the tendency of emotions to resist revision or elimination in the light of further evidence which undermines the evaluative proposition, or what de Sousa labels the 'inertia' of emotions. An old and trusted friend shows up who happens to have dealt with the salesman on several occasions, and swears that he's honest—and yet, I'm still suspicious. De Sousa suggests that this inertia occurs because of the bodily component of emotions: physiological arousal does not simply disappear when the evaluation or belief which produced it does. This is surely one of the features of emotion which figures prominently in traditional critiques of emotion. Emotion over-whelms us, 'distorting' or obscuring our vision, leading us to ignore the evid-ence before our eyes. Greenspan, however, suggests how even this inertia, at first blush nothing more than a Cartesian 'animal spirit', may play a crucial role in reasonable deliberation and action:

Suspicion registers information of a sort that, in many cases, has to be absorbed quickly, on the basis of a few perceptual cues, as a check on any tendency towards overhasty trust. *It would not have quite the same force for action, moreover, if it were readily modified in light of further evidence.* Something like this seems to be generally true of emotions:

Their affective components serve to add force to 'snap' evaluations, where the evidence at hand, even if not decisive, is significant enough to warrant holding them in mind (emphasis added).[59]

The quotation succinctly suggests the way in which emotions, for Greenspan, are systematically integrated with perception, cognition, and action, rather than standing in opposition to them. Our perception becomes attuned to certain aspects of a situation because we are 'holding in mind' a 'propositional feeling' (Greenspan's most concise definition of an emotion). Both Greenspan and de Sousa view emotion as a necessary 'motivational supplement' to logic. In other words, emotions function partly as focusing and guidance systems. In the suspicion case developed above, suspicion (the affect combined with the evaluative proposition) directs my attention to what the salesman is saying, how he is trying to sell me the car, what he is omitting from his spiel. Excitement at the prospect of owning that '58 Chevrolet, by contrast, may lead me to ogle the well-preserved tailfins, rather than paying attention to the warnings the (honest!) salesman is giving me about the clutch. I ask different questions, and different factors are dominant in my reasoning. The two emotions lead to different

patterns of salience among objects of attention, lines of inquiry and inferential strategies. . . . Logic leaves gaps. So long as we presuppose some basic or preexisting desires, the directive power of 'motivation' belongs to what controls attention, salience, and inference strategies preferred.[60]

The model of emotion developed by Greenspan and de Sousa has pertinence to the model of character engagement that I lay out in Chapter 3, and explain in detail over Chapters 4, 5, and 6. Specifically, it relates to the notion of allegiance, a term chosen precisely to evoke the combination of cognitive evaluation and affective arousal described by Greenspan. Allegiance denotes that level of engagement at which spectators respond sympathetically or antipathetically towards a character or group of characters. It rests upon an evaluation of the character as representing a desirable (or at least, preferable) set of traits, when compared with other characters within the fiction. This basic evaluation is combined with a tendency to arousal in response to the character. That is, the level of intensity of the arousal may vary, and the type of emotion experienced will shift depending on the situation in which the character is placed, but both these factors are determined by an underlying evaluation of the character's moral status within the moral system of the text. Thus, when a character to whom I am morally sympathetic is placed in a dangerous situation, I may experience unease or fear for the character. When the sympathetic figure is tortured by a villainous character, I am outraged and frustrated. But as the villain receives his come-uppance at the hands of the character, I experience relief, satisfaction, even joy. All of these particular emotions (with their distinct identificatory evaluations) depend on the underlying sympathetic allegiance.

I have characterized the spectator as an imaginative agent—an agent who knowingly fulfils certain institutional roles; whose mental life is constrained by particular beliefs and values, but whose imaginative capacities allow for change in what is assumed—automatized—and what is questioned; an agent for whom emotional response is part of a larger cycle of action, perception, and cognition, rather than an impediment to any of these. In certain respects, the stress on the 'element of freedom'—on agency itself—evokes the emphasis in reception and 'reader-response' theory on the role of the reader or spectator in the constitution of meaning. Indeed, one might see the development of film theory over the last ten years in terms of two strands of 'reception' theory, both reacting against the concept of the 'subjected' spectator associated with the semiotic and psychoanalytic theory of the 1970s and early 1980s. The first strand represents an effort to describe the mental activity and creativity of the spectator, in the context of cognitive theory; while the second is concerned with the study of empirical, socially situated spectators, focusing on how specific audiences have 'appropriated' particular texts.[61] While my own work clearly falls into the first of the groups, it intersects with and complements the second in important ways.

The model of the spectator developed here stresses the active, creative work of the spectator in the course of interpreting the material and structures of the text, and in this respect resembles the depiction of the reader in the work of Wolfgang Iser, and other phenomenological reader-response theorists.[62] However, the context of the imaginative activity of the perceiver is more social than Iser allows. In this respect, the theory I have expounded is more closely allied with those theorists who concern themselves with the text as an object of appropriation, in the sense that a perceiver's apprehension of a text will be informed by their socially formed desires, values, and interests. However, I do not see these imaginative appropriations of texts as mere acts of self-projection in which the 'text' can be construed in any way, according to the interests and desires of a particular 'interpretive community', to use the phrase coined by Stanley Fish.[63] This is so for three reasons. First, while in theory any narrative could be appropriated by any social group to serve its distinctive desires and interests, different texts will suit different needs to different degrees. In other words, while texts can sustain extremely varied interpretations, at a certain level texts are determinate and will thus resist certain uses and facilitate others. As Dirk Eitzen has put it, 'We don't need a theory of the resisting spectator. What we need is a theory of the initiating spectator and the resisting text.'[64] If you want to reaffirm your faith in the potential for human goodness and divine justice, Frank Capra's *It's a Wonderful Life* (1946) will prove more amenable to this desire than Fritz Lang's *M* (1931) or R. W. Fassbinder's *The Bitter Tears of Petra Von Kant* (1973). The second difficulty with the idea of the wholesale 'appropriation' of texts by perceivers is that while the depiction of the perceiver empowered by the assumptions of her 'interpretive community' would appear to be the obverse of the perceiver subjected by the text, both exclude the possibility that a text might transform (temporarily or permenantly) a spectator's beliefs and values by articulating new possibilities. Part of the interest of fictional representations, and thus of our motivation in engaging with them, is to be confronted with the unfamiliar. Total predictability is not thought to be a good recipe for a fiction film by either the most extreme experimentalist or a Hollywood producer; and yet if the apprehension of fiction amounted to no more than socially determined self-projection, it would have precisely this tedious result. My third objection to the Fishian position follows on from the second: if it is argued that spectators or readers construe texts entirely according to the dictates of their ideology and class position, and that nothing in a text can cause a spectator to question or suspend a belief, then the spectator is still subjected, but now to the larger 'text' of a particular ideology or interpretive community. Far from being the obverse of subjection, 'self-'projection is simply a variant of it.

While it would be absurd to deny that spectators bring particular beliefs, desires, and interests to the text, they are not the only or indeed the first ones to do so. Filmmakers themselves do. Filmmakers—like all artists—make films in the knowledge of the beliefs, values, and interests of society, whether their goal is to affirm, to challenge, or simply to defamiliarize them. Using this knowledge, they use stereotypes and other aesthetic devices in order to create particular effects: John Ford knew that the first thought of a contemporary spectator on hearing the word 'Dr' uttered would probably be of a male character, and he used this social knowledge in designing *7 Women* for a specific effect. Put another way, 'filmmaker' and 'spectator' are not particular individuals, but roles taken on by individuals; and the filmmaker is the first spectator of her work. What a critic does, then, in boldly declaring that 'the spectator responds in such and such a way', or more defensively, 'the text asks the spectator to feel such and such', is not to assume an all-powerful text and a prostrate spectator, but a spectator who responds to the text with a knowledge of all the relevant conventions that the text draws upon for the particular effect in question. Neither does this assume that this is all that a spectator may do— simply that the text is designed to elicit this response from an appropriately knowledgeable spectator.

In the following chapters, then, I will be making claims about 'the spectator's' responses to various films. Like other film critics, most of my claims about how the spectator responds are based on (informed) assumptions and guesses about what it is to be 'appropriately knowledgeable', rather than on actual responses. I do not claim to be describing a more empirically verified or verifiable spectator than other narrative theorists, but I do believe that it is a theoretical depiction compatible with empirically described spectators, in so far as the model facilitates, instead of conflicting with, a historical approach. For some narrative theorists, a kind of division of labour has opened up between 'narrative theory' and 'reception theory', in which questions of response—especially evaluative and emotional response—are hived off to 'reception theory'.[65] This is, however, a misleading division. Any criticism focusing on the reception of texts in concrete contexts requires a precise model of the ways in which texts create the rhetorical and moral structures to which spectators respond (whether that response, in a given situation, amounts to assent or resistance to these structures).

While this work is, then, clearly a contribution to the 'cognitive' strand of film theory, it is one that complements historically focused work on specific, socially situated audiences. Schema theory allows us to fill in more or less historical and cultural detail in considering specific audiences in relation to specific films or film cycles. We can begin with a very abstract spectator, with the minimal capacities for comprehending a narrative. In understanding more delimited audiences and their reactions, we will need to know more about the cultural models that they both employ in understanding, and learn from (among other things), films. And in analysing how such models are learned and undergo change, we must also consider how such models are represented, cognized, and affectively charged in the minds of individual agents, with an understanding of emotion as an integral aspect of human perception and cognition, not something opposed to them. Maintaining the pervasive antinomies of the psychological and the social, of reason and emotion, and of subjection and unconstrained freedom, will ensure that the spectator remains a dim figure at the back of the academic auditorium.

1. Perry Anderson, *In the Tracks of Historical Materialism* (London: Verso, 1983), 52.
2. Jon Elster, *Sour Grapes: Studies in the Subversion of Rationality* (Cambridge: Cambridge University Press, 1983), p. vii.
3. Mary Ann Doane could not be more explicit: 'The subject is not synonymous with the "self," still less is it compatible with any notion of agency . . . the subject is more accurately understood as "subject to" rather than "subject of"' (*The Desire to Desire: The Woman's Film of the 1940s* (Bloomington: Indiana University Press, 1987), 9–11).
4. Mallorie Cook, 'Criticism or Complicity? The Question of the Treatment of Rape and the Rape Victim in Jonathan Kaplan's *The Accused*', *CineAction* 24/25 (1991), 80.
5. See the references in the Introduction, note 20.
6. Jaron Lanier, Virtual Reality engineer, quoted in Teresa Carpenter, 'Slouching Toward Cyberspace', *Village Voice*, 12 Mar. 1991, 36.
7. Christian Metz, *Psychoanalysis and Cinema: The Imaginary Signifier*, trans. Celia Britton, Annwyl Williams, Ben Brewster, and Alfred Guzzetti (London: Macmillan, 1982), 69–74.
8. See Metz's remarks on 'perceptual transference', ibid. 101–8.

9. Ibid. 70.

10. In these terms, *The Road Warrior* is a 'realist' film. The futuristic setting of the film no more excludes it from the category than do the quasi-mythical domains of Westerns. For a recent and careful (re-)definition of the 'transparency' of classical style, see George M. Wilson, *Narration in Light* (Baltimore: Johns Hopkins University Press, 1986), 50–61.

11. Pierre Sorlin, *European Cinemas, European Societies 1939–90* (London: Routledge, 1991), 139.

12. Brecht's position in this debate is discussed at greater length in my 'Character Engagement: Fiction, Emotion and the Cinema', Ph.D. thesis (University of Wisconsin–Madison, 1991).

13. See e.g. Roland Barthes, *Mythologies*, trans. Annette Lavers (New York: Noonday Press, 1990); *S/Z*, trans. Richard Miller (New York: Hill and Wang, 1974), 206; *Roland Barthes by Roland Barthes*, trans. Richard Howard (London: Macmillan Press, 1977); and Tzvetan Todorov, 'Introduction to Verisimilitude', *The Poetics of Prose*, trans. Richard Howard (Ithaca, NY: Cornell University Press, 1977).

14. Louis Althusser, *For Marx*, trans. Ben Brewster (London: Allen Lane, 1969), 144.

15. According to Lacan, the 'mirror stage' is that moment in the development of the child when, in seeing herself in a mirror, she 'misrecognizes' herself as a separate, unified being. See Louis Althusser, 'Ideology and Ideological State Apparatuses (Notes towards an Investigation)' and 'Freud and Lacan', in *Lenin and Philosophy and Other Essays*, trans. Ben Brewster (London: New Left Books, 1971), 121–202.

16. Althusser, *For Marx*, 150.

17. Or at least, an important strain of structuralism, which would include Althusser. See J. G. Merquior, *From Prague to Paris: A Critique of Structuralist and Post-Structuralist Thought* (London: Verso, 1986), 1–6; and Claude Lévi-Strauss, *The Savage Mind*, trans. unknown (Chicago: University of Chicago Press, 1966), 252.

18. Althusser, *For Marx*, 150.

19. Ibid. 146; cf. 142. Ideology is still described in this essay as a 'false consciousness', although in later essays Althusser breaks away from the realism implicit in the wording—i.e. that there could be a 'true consciousness'.

20. Ibid. 151.

21. There is some disagreement about the plural form of schema, with the virtues of articulatory ease (schemas) pitted against those of grammatical correctness (schemata). I have opted for the latter; some authors referred to, however, use 'schemas'—Arbib and Hesse, most contributors to the Holland and Quinn volume.

22. Mary Crawford and Roger Chaffin, 'The Reader's Construction of Meaning: Cognitive Research on Gender and Comprehension', in Elizabeth A. Flynn and Patrocinio Schweickart (eds.), *Gender and Reading: Essays on Readers, Texts, and Contexts* (Baltimore: Johns Hopkins University Press, 1986), 11.

23. George Lakoff, *Women, Fire, and Dangerous Things: What Categories Reveal about the Mind* (Chicago: University of Chicago Press, 1987).

24. Schema theory as used here originated with Frederic Bartlett, *Remembering: A Study in Experimental and Social Psychology* (Cambridge: Cambridge University Press, 1932). Comparable concepts in cognitive theory are 'scripts' and 'frames'. These concepts are reviewed in Deborah Tannen, 'What's in a Frame? Surface Evidence for Underlying Expectations', in Roy O. Freedle (ed.), *New Directions in Discourse Processing* (Norwood, NJ: Ablex, 1979). Mark Johnson, *The Body in the Mind: The Bodily Basis of Meaning, Imagination, and Reason* (Chicago: University of Chicago Press, 1987), provides an overview and considers the relationship between schemata, imagination, and bodily experience. Crawford and Chaffin, 'The Reader's Construction of Meaning', provide a good summary of the fundamental tenets of schema theory, and an extensive bibliography. For specifically aesthetic uses, see the works by E. H. Gombrich, David Bordwell, Edward Branigan, James Peterson, and Kristin Thompson cited in the bibliography.

25. E. H. Gombrich, *Art and Illusion: A Study in the Psychology of Pictorial Representation* (Princeton, NJ: Princeton University Press, 1969), 60.

26. Dorothy Holland and Naomi Quinn (eds.), *Cultural Models in Language and Thought* (Cambridge: Cambridge University Press, 1987).

27. For any experienced mystery movie spectator, however, the situation is more complex. They have the additional textual schema which tells them that it is rarely the most obvious suspect, and often the least likely candidate, who is in fact the perpetrator of the crime.

28. Gombrich, *Art and Illusion*, 60.

29. I should stress that I am not claiming that schema theory provides a comprehensive account of human consciousness, but rather provides a model of a particular feature of human cognition. In other words, I share the scepticism of philosophers like John Searle who argue that 'self-consciousness' is a rabbit that will never be pulled out of a schematic hat, no matter how complex the schemata become. The role of schema theory in my argument is to emphasize features of human cognition, bearing on narrative and ideology, of which contemporary theory takes no account, not to provide an exhaustive account of human consciousness.

30. Non-conscious processes are those 'reflex' perceptual and conceptual activities over which we maintain no control and of which we are unaware. When we see movement in a narrative film, as a result of the 'phi phenomenon', we cannot decide to watch the individual frames instead, and neither can we reflectively observe ourselves performing the transformation of single still frames into a continuous, moving image. Unconscious processes are those purportedly repressed activities of which we have no conscious awareness but which may affect our conscious behaviour.

31. Dorothy Holland and Debra Skinner, 'Prestige and Intimacy: The Cultural Models behind Americans' Talk about Gender Types', in Holland and Quinn (eds.), *Cultural Models*, 79; Edwin Hutchins, *Culture and Inference: A Trobriand Case Study* (Cambridge, Mass.: Harvard University Press, 1980), 12.

32. Gombrich, *Art and Illusion*, 363.

33. Michael Arbib and Mary Hesse, *The Construction of Reality* (Cambridge: Cambridge University Press, 1986), 52.

34. Ibid. 131; see also Naomi Quinn and Dorothy Holland, 'Culture and Cognition', in Holland and Quinn (eds.), *Cultural Models*, 11.

35. The conceptual and biographical links between *ostranenie* and *Verfremdung* are discussed by John Willett in *Brecht on Theatre: The Development of an Aesthetic* (London: Methuen, 1964), 99. They are also discussed in a series of articles in *Screen*: Ben Brewster, 'Introduction to "Documents from *Novy Lef*"', *Screen*, 12: 4 (Winter 1971–2), 59–66; Stanley Mitchell, 'From Shklovsky to Brecht: Some Preliminary Remarks Towards a History of the Politicisation of Russian Formalism', *Screen*, 15: 2 (Summer 1974), 74–81; and Ben Brewster, 'From Shklovsky to Brecht: A Reply', *Screen*, 15: 2 (Summer 1974), 82–102.

36. Mike Budd and Clay Steinman, 'Television, Cultural Studies, and the "Blind Spot" Debate in Critical Communications Research', in Gary Burns and Robert J. Thompson (eds.), *Television Studies: Textual Analysis* (New York: Praeger, 1989), 14–15.

37. See Crawford and Chaffin, 'The Reader's Construction of Meaning', 16.

38. Lakoff, *Women, Fire, and Dangerous Things*, 116.

39. Crawford and Chaffin, 'The Reader's Construction of Meaning', 25. This parallels the arguments of Mulvey and Doane concerning female spectators, in which the latter ultimately can only adopt a position prescribed by patriarchy. The theory advanced here, however, would take the psychoanalytic theory as its object, seeing it as an elaboration of the patriarchal culture it seeks to explain.

40. Cf. the quotations from Hayden White and Christian Metz in Chapter 1, note 55.

41. Christopher Butler, *Interpretation, Deconstruction, and Ideology: An Introduction to Some Current Issues in Literary Theory* (Oxford: Clarendon Press, 1984), 53.

42. Ibid. 7. See also David Novitz, *Knowledge, Fiction and Imagination* (Philadelphia: Temple University Press, 1987), 122.

43. Paul Ricoeur, 'The Function of Fiction in Shaping Reality', trans. David Pellauer, in Mario J.

Valdés (ed.), *A Ricoeur Reader: Reflection and Imagination* (London: Harvester-Wheatsheaf, 1991), 128. Ricoeur's use of the term 'engagement' here is very different from my own. See also Paul Ricoeur, *Time and Narrative*, i, trans. Kathleen McLaughlin and David Pellauer (Chicago: University of Chicago Press, 1984), ch. 3.

44. This is a version of the scenario presented in Colin Radford and Michael Weston, 'How can We be Moved by the Fate of Anna Karenina?' *Proceedings of the Aristotelian Society*, Supplementary Volume 49 (1975), 68. Radford and Weston contribute independent essays under this common title.

45. Ibid. 72.

46. Ibid. 69, 70. Though related, the paradox that troubles Radford is not identical to the paradox embraced by Metz under the rubric of 'disavowal'. For Metz, the spectator of a fiction film at once knows that it is a representation of fictional events and believes that the events really occur. For Radford, readers or spectators suffer from no such equivocation as they engage with a fiction; they know it is fictional. The paradox enters in the need for belief as a condition of emotional response in the context of ordinary experience, and the absence of this condition in the context of fiction.

47. Radford, 'How can We be Moved', 72 and 75–6.

48. Eva Schaper, 'Fiction and the Suspension of Disbelief', *British Journal of Aesthetics*, 18 (1978), 31–44; Peter Lamarque, 'How Can We Fear and Pity Fictions?', *British Journal of Aesthetics*, 21: 4 (Autumn 1981), 291–304; and Noël Carroll, *The Philosophy of Horror; or, Paradoxes of the Heart* (New York: Routledge, 1990), 79–87.

49. Lakoff, *Women, Fire, and Dangerous Things*, part i.

50. Cf. Ronald de Sousa, *The Rationality of Emotion* (Cambridge, Mass.: MIT Press, 1988), 181–4. Butler's remarks were made in a publisher's review of this study. Dirk Eitzen has argued that not only 'mixed mode' narratives, but fully-fledged documentaries—like *The Civil War*—are often viewed as fictions, in the sense that viewers are not concerned with the referential validity of particular events and persons represented, so much as their dramatic force. Many spectators 'regard *The Civil War* primarily as drama and . . . either accept or ignore both its propositional claims and the ways in which it selects and emphasizes material' ('The Reception of *The Civil War* and the Popular Conception of History', unpublished manuscript, 1992, 15).

51. Nelson Goodman, *Languages of Art: An Approach to a Theory of Symbols* (Indianapolis: Hackett, 1976), 248.

52. See Patricia Greenspan, *Emotions and Reasons* (New York: Routledge, 1988), 177; Martha Nussbaum, *The Fragility of Goodness: Luck and Ethics in Greek Tragedy and Philosophy* (Cambridge: Cambridge University Press, 1986), 382–91; John McCrone, *The Myth of Irrationality: The Science of the Mind from Plato to Star Trek* (London: Macmillan, 1993).

53. Nussbaum, *Fragility of Goodness*, 131; see also her comments on Locke, 16.

54. Goodman, *Languages of Art*, 247–8.

55. Cf. the conference on 'emotion and reason' at the Center for Twentieth Century Studies, University of Wisconsin–Milwaukee, Apr. 1990.

56. Lakoff, *Women, Fire, and Dangerous Things*; Philip Johnson-Laird, *Mental Models: Towards a Cognitive Science of Language, Inference, and Consciousness* (Cambridge: Cambridge University Press, 1983); Stephen Kosslyn, *Image and Mind* (Cambridge, Mass.: Harvard University Press, 1980); Daniel Kahneman, Paul Slovic, and Amos Tversky (eds.), *Judgment under Uncertainty: Heuristics and Biases* (Cambridge, Mass.: Harvard University Press, 1982); Richard Nisbett and Lee Ross, *Human Inference: Strategies and Shortcomings of Social Judgment* (Englewood Cliffs, NJ: Prentice-Hall, 1980).

57. This view of emotions is generally traced back to Aristotle, and has many modern exponents, from psychologists like Schacter and Singer and George Mandler, to philosophers, such as O. H. Green, Errol Bedford, and Robert Solomon. Though I will go on to qualify this position, it is a crucial starting-point from which to distinguish emotions, which have a cognitive component, from 'objectless affect', denoted in these schemes by terms such as 'mood'.

58. I add the clause 'in principle' to indicate that, along with Greenspan, I am aware that an adaptive emotion may become maladaptive: my suspicion can turn into a kind of paranoia, and I find myself unable to trust any salesman enough to purchase a car. But as Greenspan points out, this is hardly a sufficient argument to demonstrate the general irrationality of emotions. My practice of eating is, in principle, a necessary and, in so far as it generally sustains my well-being, perfectly rational practice. But, just as with the adaptive emotion, a practice which is useful in principle may become harmful to my basic interests (in the case of eating, staying alive): I eat so much of the wrong kind of food that I harm myself. See Greenspan, *Emotions and Reasons*, 94 and 187 n. 7.

59. Ibid. 93–4.

60. De Sousa, *Rationality of Emotion*, 196–7.

61. The most substantial work of this type in film studies to date is Janet Staiger's *Interpreting Films: Studies in the Historical Reception of American Cinema* (Princeton, NJ: Princeton University Press, 1992).

62. Wolfgang Iser, *The Implied Reader: Patterns in Communication in Prose Fiction from Bunyan to Beckett* (Baltimore: Johns Hopkins University Press, 1974).

63. Stanley Fish, *Is There a Text in this Class?* (Cambridge, Mass.: Harvard University Press, 1980).

64. Dirk Eitzen, 'Negotiated Readings of *The Civil War*: A Cognitive Perspective', paper delivered at the 1992 Society for Cinema Studies Conference, University of Pittsburgh, 11; cf. Paul B. Armstrong, *Conflicting Readings: Variety and Validity in Interpretation* (Chapel Hill: University of North Carolina Press, 1990), 119. To those critics who believe that we should stop assuming even a minimally determinate text, and simply analyse the responses of empirical spectators to texts, we must put the question: why should we treat these responses as any more determinate than the film itself? Are not these responses likely to be construed in entirely different ways by critics with different interests? Analysing empirical responses to films displaces but does not solve the problems at stake here.

65. See e.g. Seymour Chatman, *Story and Discourse: Narrative Structure in Fiction and Film* (Ithaca, NY: Cornell University Press, 1978), 125–6; and Philippe Hamon, 'Pour un statut semiologique du personnage', in Roland Barthes *et al.* (eds.), *Poétique du récit* (Paris: Seuil, 1977), 151–2.

Part Two

Every literary work of any power—whether or not
its author composed it with his audience in mind—is
in fact an elaborate system of controls over the reader's
involvement and detachment along *various* lines
of interest.

Wayne C. Booth, *The Rhetoric of Fiction*

Engaging Characters

The last two chapters have examined in detail the two essential concepts underlying the everyday model of identification: the spectator and character. Having a better grasp of these two concepts, we are now in a position to refine this model, and to address the key question posed in the introduction: what are the various senses of the term 'identification', and how can they be developed into a systematic explanation of emotional response to fictional characters? I argue that we need to break the notion down into a number of more precisely defined concepts: recognition, alignment, and allegiance. These concepts are, however, systematically related, together constituting what I term the *structure of sympathy*. I then argue that the three basic levels of engagement must be supplemented by concepts accounting for 'empathic' phenomena—affective mimicry and emotional simulation—if a comprehensive theory of 'identification' is to be constructed. Finally, I discuss the relationship between the structure of sympathy and these empathic processes. (Figure 3.1, at the end of this chapter, lays out in a spatial fashion the various concepts and their interrelations.)

Throughout the chapter, I place the various levels of engagement in the context of theories of narrative and narration: in Chapter 1 I argued that characters are salient elements of narrative structure, but we should never lose sight of the fact that characters are, nevertheless, parts of larger structures.

Imagination and Narration

Whatever else it is, engaging with fiction is a species of imaginative activity, not in the traditional and derogatory sense of 'the flight of fancy', but rather in two more complex senses. First, in comprehending, interpreting, and otherwise appreciating fictional narratives, we make inferences, formulate hypotheses, categorize representations, and utilize many other cognitive skills and strategies which go well beyond a mere registration or mirroring of the narrative material.[1] Secondly, fictions prompt and enrich our 'quasi-experience', that is, our efforts to grasp, through mental hypotheses, situations, persons, and values which are alien to us.[2] Our imaginative activity in the context of fiction is, however, both guided and constrained by the fiction's narration: the storytelling force that, in any given narrative film, presents causally linked events occurring in space across time.

The Russian Formalists devised two basic concepts for the analysis of narrative: *story* (fabula) and *plot* (syuzhet). While the plot refers to the narrative material as it is presented to the viewer or reader (in terms of order, duration, and frequency), the story refers to the reordering and 'filling-in' of this material according to a causal logic. The narration, then, is the force which guides the viewer in the reorganization of the plot into the story, or the construction of the story on the basis of the plot.[3] Moreover, a narration may be usefully described in terms of three principal qualities: knowledgeability, communicativeness, and self-consciousness.[4] The knowledgeability of a narration pertains to the 'range' and 'depth' of story information to which it claims access. A narration may have great range, moving freely among different groups of characters and across time. On the other hand, it may restrict itself spatially and temporally to the actions of a single character. Furthermore, a narration can provide access not only to the 'objective' world of the story, but also to the purely subjective experiences of characters, through dream imagery, for example. Such variations pertain to the depth of the narration.

Once the narration has established a certain range and depth of knowledge, it may communicate narrative information to the viewer to a greater or lesser degree. The narrations of detective movies tend to be uncommunicative or 'suppressive', forcing the spectator to speculate about basic narrative events. By contrast, melodramatic narration tends to be highly communicative, revealing character traits and states so that we may watch for the development of these states in the light of new events. The communicativeness of a narration can only be ascertained by assessing the degree to which it provides the viewer information to which it has shown itself to have access, through an established pattern of knowledgeability. The self-consciousness of the narration arises partly out of the interplay of its knowledgeability and its communicativeness. A narration which establishes itself as having access to the actions of a character, and then overtly denies us access to an important action performed by that character, foregrounds itself, and so becomes 'self-conscious'. A narration may establish itself as self-conscious in other ways: by using particularly unusual or virtuosic techniques, it can reveal an 'awareness' that it is addressing an audience. The knowledgeability of a narration will be of particular importance in analysing the relations which may obtain between characters and spectators, as I will discuss in more detail later in this chapter and in Chapter 5.

I want to propose that fictional narrations elicit three levels of imaginative engagement with characters, distinct types of responses normally conflated under the term 'identification'. Together, these levels of engagement comprise the 'structure of sympathy'. In this system, spectators construct characters (a process I refer to as *recognition*). Spectators are also provided with visual and aural information more or less congruent with that available to characters, and so are placed in a certain structure of *alignment* with characters. In addition, specatators evaluate characters on the basis of the values they embody, and hence form more-or-less sympathetic or more-or-less antipathetic *allegiances* with them. Thus, the larger question I began with can be broken down into the following questions: how does a narration generate the characters on which it depends? What is the nature of the 'filtering' which seems to occur when a particular character becomes the conduit for narrative information? And how does our 'attraction to' (or 'repulsion from') a character affect our experience of the text?

As the ultimate 'organizer' of the text, the narration is the force which generates recognition, alignment, and allegiance, the basic components of the structure of sympathy. From this perspective, recognition, alignment, and allegiance are intermediary abstractions—neither as concrete as the particular devices which materially comprise the film, nor as abstract as the 'reference' narration, which describes the overarching, apersonal agency of control in the text.[5] The narration uses the various cinematic techniques in order to produce these subsystems; and different techniques become prominent with both each of the three intermediary structures, and with different types of film. Recognition, for example, is usually dependent on a legible and consistent representation of the human face and body, a fact which becomes clear in those films which refuse to follow this practice. These intermediary abstractions gain their critical *raison d'être* via their ability to explain those aspects of textual functioning which pertain to our responses to fictional characters.

The narration may stymie the three processes which are the focus of my attention. If the attributes of a character are continually in flux, or if we see only one part of a character, then recognition will be retarded and perhaps prevented. An extremely suppressive narration may block our access to character subjectivity. The narration may assign traits to a character which are quite contradictory in terms of their moral 'valence', thus problematizing allegiance. The narration may be concerned with the agency of natural forces and institutions. In each of these cases, however, the three processes are still pertinent; the narration disrupts the typical or classical functioning of the process in question, but does not eliminate it. More radically, a narration may direct our attention to peripheral, 'forceless' objects, as in the lingering shots of rooms and doorways in the films of Straub and Huillet, or the so-called 'pillow' shots in the films of Ozu. Such cases border on the domain of non-narrative form, where the construct of character becomes irrelevant.

Responding to fictional characters is, to repeat, a kind of imaginative activity. Every fictional text requires a minimal inferential activity, which may be thought of as the basis of imagination. The fiction itself provides material for and shapes the 'quasi-experience' that it is the business of the imagination, in our sense of the term, to generate. Our experience of fiction is unlike imagination in other contexts (such as day-dreaming) in that it is enabled and constrained by texts which determine, at the very least, some features of our imagining. Of course, every imaginative act is 'constrained' in the sense that it depends on the resources provided for the subject by her experiences within a particular culture; but our experience of fiction is peculiar, in the context of imagination in general, in the degree to which, and the ways in which, it is guided. Having outlined the concept of narration, the force which guides and constrains the spectator, let us consider further 'the beholder's share'—the imaginative activity of the viewer.

In *The Thread of Life*, Richard Wollheim makes a 'fundamental distinction, corresponding to a big divide between two modes of imagination': 'central' imagining and 'acentral' imagining.[6] A rough guide to the distinction can be found in linguistic clues. While central imagining is often expressed in the form 'I imagine . . .', acentral imagining is expressed in the form 'I imagine that . . .' If we say, 'I imagine jumping from the top of the building', we imply that we represent this event to ourselves, as it were, from the 'inside': I imagine, for example, the view I would have as I fall, the nauseating sensation I experience as my body picks up speed, and so forth.[7] Or again, in imagining being revolted by the smell of rotten eggs, I recall the characteristic sulphurous stench. Central imagining is not, however, limited to such physical and spatio-temporal conjectures: it may also involve simulations of the internal states and values of the person or character functioning as the vehicle of the central imagining.[8] By contrast, in imagining *that* I am revolted by the smell, I need generate no such olfactory 'image';[9] in 'imagining *that* I jump from the building', I do not represent the event to myself with any of 'indexical' marks of the imagined action—for example, transporting myself imaginatively into the appropriate position. I do not place myself 'in' the scenario, so much as entertain an idea, but not from the perspective (in any sense of the term) of any character within the scenario.[10]

In so far as our experience of fiction is comprised of acts of imagination prompted by fictional texts, we may use Wollheim's distinction in order to pinpoint a crucial dividing line among models of 'identification' (defined broadly as attempts to deal with the question of how spectators relate to fictional characters). Everyday talk about identification tends to depend upon a singular and monolithic conception, in which we are said to experience vicariously the thoughts and feelings of the protagonist: in Wollheim's terms, unalloyed central imagining.[11] While no theory of cinematic identification is so simplistic, the stress on experiencing the narrative through an identification with (a) particular character(s) is carried over into many more elaborate theories. Robin Wood's early work, for example, argues that Hitchcock plays with our sympathies, asking us to imagine centrally the experiences of various characters. Wood's defence of Hitchcock is based upon a valorization of both the power and function of this aesthetic. Hitchcock's films draw us 'in' so completely that we 'become' the protagonist—'[t]he characters of *Psycho* are *one* character, and that character, thanks to the identifications the film evokes, is us'[12]—and this identification has a 'therapeutic' effect.

The stance of semiotic and psychoanalytic film theorists towards the central–acentral division is somewhat more complex. Part of the difficulty in placing psychoanalytic theory in these terms is the degree of mismatch—if not incommensurability—between the two approaches. Christian Metz, for example, makes identification with characters 'secondary' to the 'primary' experience of identification with the camera, which is ultimately a form of identification with the self. This seems to bring forward acentral imagining, in so far as identification with characters is subordinated, but since 'secondary identification' is conceived of as an extension of identification with the self, central imagining is ultimately what is at stake.

In much of the work on identification following Metz, the emphasis remains on central imagining. For example, Laura Mulvey's influential work suggests that classical cinema produces a consistently masculine subject position for the spectator, and this occurs largely through identification with the male protagonist.[13] Taking up Metz's notion of identification across a range of characters or 'subject positions'—hardly more than a note in *The Imaginary Signifier*[14]—other psychoanalytic theorists have advanced the idea of 'multiple identification'. Rather than conceiving of the spectator as identifying with a single character or subject position, the spectator's locus of identification shifts across various characters, each representing a distinctive role in a given fantasy. Elizabeth Cowie, for example, draws on Freud's essay 'A Child is Being Beaten' in order to suggest that in Max Ophuls's *The Reckless Moment* (1949) the spectator shifts through identifications with 'the diverse positions [of] father, mother, child, lover, wife, husband, each of which are never finally contained by any one character'.[15] Most recently, Carol Clover has argued that, in the contemporary horror film, 'We are both Red Riding Hood *and* the Wolf; the force of the experience, in horror, comes from "knowing" both sides of the story.'[16] Of course, in all these approaches, characters as such are purportedly epiphenomenal—figures of an illusory stability, effects of the underlying structures of fantasy. Although these models allow for far more subjective fluidity than does Mulvey's, and some of them explicitly allow for acentral positions, the focus nevertheless remains overwhelmingly on central processes. The fundamental experience for the spectator is the perception of narrative action through identification with subject positions instantiated by characters, even if this involves shifts from character to character over the course of the film as a whole.

Reacting to this stress on central imagining in contemporary psychoanalytic theory, Noël Carroll has argued unequivocally that spectators never really adopt the viewpoint (in a general, rather than a purely optical, sense) of characters. Although Carroll does not couch his argument in Wollheim's terminology, it amounts to the idea that fiction furnishes us only with opportunities for acentral imagining. Carroll suggests that the very term 'identification' is misleading because it implies that spectators centrally imagine the fictional events of a narrative as if they were the protagonist. In Carroll's words, 'identification' implies a kind of 'fusion' of or 'mind-meld' between spectator and character. Carroll argues that the concept of *assimilation*[17] more accurately describes the structure of interaction between spectators and fictional characters. When the spectator Charles sees a fictional character faced by the Green Slime—to use the dramatis personae of Carroll's analysis[18]—he does not experience an emotion identical to that of the character. Rather than experiencing *fear of the Slime*, Charles experiences *anxiety for the character as she faces the Slime*. Charles imagines that the character faces the Slime, rather than imagining facing the Slime himself (i.e. Charles does not adopt the character's position as a vehicle for an act of central imagining). Charles never loses sight of the oblique or acentral relation that he, as a spectator, maintains towards events and characters in the fictional world:

In order to understand a situation internally, it is not necessary to identify with the protagonist. We need only *have a sense of* why the protagonist's response is appropriate or intelligible to the situation. With respect to horror, we do this readily when monsters appear since, insofar as we share the same culture as the protagonist, we can easily *catch-on to* why the character finds the monster unnatural. However, once we've assimilated the situation from the character's point of view, we respond not simply to the monster, as the character does, but to a situation in which someone, who is horrified, is under attack (emphasis added).[19]

By its very nature, Carroll seems to argue, engaging with fiction prompts acentral imagining (unlike, say, fantasies, dreams, or hallucinations, all centrally imaginative phenomena).

One clarification is important, however, regarding Carroll's use of the phrase 'point of view' in this passage. Carroll is not suggesting that we first centrally imagine the event, and then acentrally imagine it. Understanding the situation from the character's 'point of view', in Carroll's sense, entails only an understanding of the interests and judgements of the character. This is clear when Carroll writes that assimilation requires that spectators have 'a sense of the character's internal understanding of the situation', but that spectators 'need not replicate the mental state of the protagonist, but only know reliably how she assesses it' (emphasis added).[20] Thus, in Ridley Scott's *Alien* (1979), we understand the situation from the 'point of view' of Sigourney Weaver in so far as we understand that the fear that she experiences arises because she judges that the alien is revolting and dangerous, and because she sees it as being in her interest to preserve her life. We do not need to experience the occurrent emotion of fear in order to understand the situation 'internally'. The phrase 'point of view', in other words, has a very different meaning for Wollheim and Carroll respectively, and I do not take it to mean anything akin to 'central imagining' for Carroll.[21]

Carroll does not deny that spectators may share certain emotional states with characters: 'we tend to be reviled by the monster in the same way that the character is.'[22] Spectators may share both the evaluation and arousal characteristic of an emotion with a character. Indeed, Carroll challenges Kendall Walton's view that such states are merely 'quasi-emotions'. The issue at stake here is the mechanism by which this 'parallel' emotion is generated. For Carroll, the mechanism is acentral: there is no sense that we come to share a character's emotion through some sort of central imagining. Rather, we comprehend, evaluate, and respond to the character's situation and interests: I take this to be the meaning of the rather vague verbs ('have a sense of', 'catch-on to') I have emphasized in the long quotation above. Sharing basic cultural concerns and symbolic systems with a character, we are likely to assess and react to horrific monsters in the same way as the character. But, precisely because we share these assumptions, we do not arrive at the 'parallel emotion' through centrally imagining ourselves as the character in the situation. Rather, we comprehend the character and the situation, and react emotionally (if we react at all) to the thought of *the character in that situation* (as opposed to the thought of *being the character in that situation*).

It is important not to confuse two issues here, which relate to a strong and a weak version of the fallacious conception of identification. First, there is the

question of whether a spectator mistakes a representation for an actual referent, as discussed in Chapter 2. Secondly, we can ask whether the spectator, in
engaging with fiction, imagines the events centrally (a claim usually indicated
by a term like 'empathy' or 'identification') or acentrally (as in Carroll's 'assimilation'). Often the 'illusion' theory of fiction is yoked with a notion of identification. This issues in the 'stronger' of the two versions: not only do we mistake
the representation for its referents, but we mistake ourselves for (or 'lose ourselves in') the protagonist (version 1). But it is quite possible to conceive of a
spectator centrally imagining while never mistaking representation for referent
—just as it is possible for us to imagine what another person must feel like in
their situation, without for a moment confusing ourselves with that other person.
This is the 'weaker' version of the identification thesis (version 2). There is also
a third, related concept, although it is not commonly referred to by the term
'identification.' We might be said to imagine *ourselves in the situation* (as distinct
from imagining *being the character in the situation*)—Ripley might climb into the
exoskeleton in order to combat the mother alien in *Aliens* (James Cameron,
1986), but I, Murray Smith, would be paralysed by fear (version 3). Whether
in the strong or the weak version, identification depends on the idea that the
spectator's traits and mental states are modelled on those of the character, not
that the character functions as a vacant 'holding bay' into which the spectator
projects her own attributes. This is what distinguishes (1) and (2) from (3), and
is an implication of the notion of 'identification' worth retaining, even if we
reject the concept as a whole. We will return to this point later in my argument, where I discuss the desire to experience new and unfamiliar situations
and values as an underlying motivation for engaging with fictions.

Carroll's discussion does not distinguish between the strong and weak versions of the the notion of identification, but it is clear that the concept of
assimilation is intended to supplant both. As such, we may regard Carroll's
argument as one answer to the question posed at the beginning of the chapter.
In general, I share Carroll's scepticism towards models of spectatorial response
to character which place central imagining at centre stage. The problem with
all three of the variants of 'identification' is that they found our experience of
fictions on the idea of central imagining. Whether we are said to mistake
ourselves for the central character (1), imagine the events of the narrative from
the (physical and mental) perspective of the character (2), or imagine ourselves
in the exact situation of the character (3), our experience of fiction is conceived
as one in which we apprehend the fictional world 'through' a particular character.
What varies is the role and strength of the word 'through' in each version.

Carroll's argument, along with those discussed in Chapter 2, licenses us to
reject (1) outright. (2) and (3), however, do not suffer from the same kind of
intrinsic, conceptual flaws. Both of them describe types of imagining which
fictions might prompt. My objection to these versions of 'identification' is more

empirical in nature. What fictions generally offer us are imagined scenarios which we are invited to experience from a variety of perspectives. As we shall see in Chapter 5, very few films provide us with continuous and exclusive access to a particular character, a precondition of sustained, prompted central imagining. (We are, of course, free to centrally imagine being a character 'unprompted'—when the fiction guides our attention elsewhere—but if we do so we are not engaging with the fiction in the sense I have in mind.) As a result, we are likely to imagine what a fiction film depicts acentrally, as well as from the central perspectives of certain characters and even, perhaps, the central perspective of ourselves were we in that situation. Important aspects of the institution of fiction include assessing the claims of rival perspectives based on different experiences of the same situation (Little Red Riding Hood vs. the Wolf), and assessing the differences between our own responses to a situation, and those of particular fictional characters. Unlike Carroll, therefore, I will argue that central imagining plays a very important role in our experience of fiction, although the central imagining is unlikely to be restricted to that based upon a single character, and whatever central imagining the narrative elicits is embedded within an overall structure of acentral imagining.

While the structure of sympathy is an acentral structure, then, it contains and draws upon central imagining. Central imagining, or what psychologists call *empathy*, can in turn be broken down into a series of more narrowly defined mechanisms: emotional simulation, motor and affective mimicry, and autonomic reactions like the startle response. These phenomena function as 'comprehension mechanisms' which feed into the structure of sympathy, working with other cognitive processes (perception, inference, schematic processing) in the construction of characters and narrative situations, but may also function as a subsystem *at odds with* the structure of sympathy. One of the key mechanisms for arriving at the kind of acentral assessments Carroll posits may be a form of imaginative 'simulation' of the mental states of characters. While such simulation may not be necessary, it is not uncommon. A comprehensive theory of spectatorial response to character must incorporate these phenomena in addition to the more familiar cognitive, acentral processes that Carroll believes exhaustively describe the nature of our responses to character. We must address, therefore, both acentral imaginative processes and these central or empathic phenomena, in formulating a theory of character engagement.

The Structure of Sympathy

We now need to outline the three levels of engagement which comprise the structure of sympathy (recognition, alignment, and allegiance), and the interrelations among them. These levels and their interactions are then examined in more detail through an analysis of Hitchcock's *The Man Who Knew Too Much* (1956). Before I define the components of the structure of sympathy, however, a word of clarification on their status. Each concept, in one sense, describes a level of narrative structure which relates to character. I have endeavoured, though, to frame the definitions in such a way as to emphasize the co-operative activity of the spectator which works with these narrative systems. In a fuller sense, then, the concepts of recognition, alignment, and allegiance denote not just inert textual systems, but responses, neither solely in the text nor solely in the spectator. This caveat is in part designed to distinguish my model of spectatorial engagement from 'hypodermic' models, in which the spectator is conceptualized as the passive subject of the structuring power of the text. The narratological work presented here is an attempt to understand the ways in which texts produce or deny the conditions conducive for various levels of engagement, rather than the ways they enforce them. In the succeeding chapters, this general claim will be examined in more detail with respect to each of the components of the structure of sympathy.

Recognition

Recognition describes the spectator's construction of character: the perception of a set of textual elements, in film typically cohering around the image of a body, as an individuated and continuous human agent. Recognition does not deny the possibility of development and change, since it is based on the concept of continuity, not unity or identity. Recognition requires the referential notion of the mimetic hypothesis, as defined in Chapter 2: it is not simply a function of a self-enclosed text (in whatever medium). While understanding that characters are artifices, and are literally no more than collections of inert, textually described traits, we assume that these traits correspond to analogical ones we find in persons in the real world, until this is explicitly contradicted by a description in the text, forcing us to revise a particular mimetic hypothesis. Characters, and fictional worlds in general, rely upon this process in order to be mentally represented at all. The mimetic hypothesis underpins more complex engagements built upon recognition; for example, we would not find ourselves attracted to (and so could not become allied with) an inert bundle of traits. We perceive and conceive of characters as integral, discrete textual constructs. Just as persons in the real world may be complex or entertain conflicting beliefs, so may characters; but as with persons, such internal contradictions are perceived against the ground of (at least) bodily discreteness and continuity.

Recognition has received less attention than any other level of engagement in studies concerned with character and/or identification, probably because it is regarded as 'obvious'. Certainly, in most films, it is rapid and phenomenologically 'automatic'. The importance of the level becomes apparent in those films which undercut or retard recognition. Films as different as Alexander Dovzhenko's *Arsenal* (1929), Christopher Maclaine's *The End* (1953), Raul Ruiz's *The Suspended Vocation* (1977), and Luis Buñuel's *That Obscure Object of Desire* (1977) all problematize the process of recognition, but to ends rather more diverse than can be captured by a single, gross function such as 'distanciation' or the 'laying bare of the device'. Even the post-structuralist might welcome an explanation of recognition. If characters are really such fragmentary bundles of relations, then some significant mental activity must give rise to our experience of them as continuous wholes.

Alignment

The term *alignment* describes the process by which spectators are placed in relation to characters in terms of access to their actions, and to what they know and feel. The concept is akin to the literary notion of 'focalization', Gérard Genette's term for the way in which narratives may feed story information to the reader through the 'lens' of a particular character, though 'identification' is more commonly appealed to: 'The final scene confines itself to what Marlowe, inside a parlor with a killer, could perceive; the film never depicts action outside the house unless he sees it. To a great extent, our "identification" with a film's protagonist is created by exactly this systematic restriction of information.'[23] I propose two interlocking functions, *spatio-temporal attachment* and *subjective access*, cognate with the concepts of narrational range and depth discussed earlier in this chapter, as the most precise means for analysing alignment.[24] Attachment concerns the way in which the narration restricts itself to the actions of a single character, or moves more freely among the spatio-temporal paths of two or more characters. Subjective access pertains to the degree of access we have to the subjectivity of characters, a function which may vary from character to character within a narrative. (Genette uses the metaphor of 'screening' to describe this aspect of narration. An 'even screening' is produced by a narration which gives us equal access to the internal states of all characters.)[25] Together these two functions control the apportioning of knowledge among characters and the spectator; the systematic regulation of narrative knowledge results in a *structure of alignment*.

Perceptual alignment—optical POV and its aural equivalent—is regarded as simply one resource of the narration in controlling alignment. The absence of a level of engagement founded upon optical POV will seem perverse to some readers. I shall try to show that POV is not, as is assumed by most models of 'identification', privileged in providing us with uniformly greater access to characters' states than other devices. Such an assumption both overstates the importance of POV to 'identification', and at the same time occludes the wide variety of other functions that POV may perform—for example, concealing the identity of the looker, a function it often performs in the horror film (consider John Carpenter's *Halloween* (1978), for example, in which POV shots rendering Michael Myer's vision proliferate). As I will argue in Chapter 5, POV neither entails, nor is essential to, recognition, alignment, or allegiance. All three levels of structure can operate without POV, and with the self-evident exception of perceptual alignment, the use of POV does not necessarily result in our recognizing a character, being aligned with a character, or being allied with a character.

Allegiance

Allegiance pertains to the moral evaluation of characters by the spectator. Here we are perhaps closest to what is meant by 'identification' in everyday usage, where we talk of 'identifying with' both persons and characters on the basis of a wide range of factors, such as attitudes related to class, nation, age, ethnicity, and gender ('I could really identify with Virgil Tibbs, having experienced that kind of racial hostility myself'). Allegiance depends upon the spectator having what she takes to be reliable access to the character's state of mind, on understanding the context of the character's actions, and having morally evaluated the character on the basis of this knowledge. Evaluation, in this sense, has both cognitive and affective dimensions; for example, being angry or outraged at an action involves categorizing it as undesirable or harmful to someone or something, and being affected—affectively aroused—by this categorization. On the basis of such evaluations, spectators construct moral structures, in which characters are organized and ranked in a system of preference. Many factors contribute to the process of moral orientation (the narrational counterpart to moral structure), and hence to allegiance: character action, iconography, and music are particularly salient. (I use the word 'moral' rather than 'ideological' to describe this level of engagement for two reasons. First, with respect to characters, ideological judgements are typically expressed as moral evaluations; and secondly, assessing the overall ideology of a text may involve factors other than those pertaining to its characterological structure.)[26]

For many psychoanalytic film theorists, POV is inseparable from allegiance. Laura Mulvey treats the POV shot as central to the masculine address of classical cinema, articulating scopophilia more clearly than any other device. Rather than being conceived as a tool for a variety of human needs and purposes, looking is inextricably bound up with the development of sexual difference and the inequities of power under patriarchy. POV, as the pre-eminent cinematic device for the representation of looking, is thus intrinsically value-laden: indeed, Mulvey talks of the spectator of Hitchcock's *Vertigo* (1958) as being caught in the 'moral ambiguity' of looking.[27] My model can accommodate such an association between POV and allegiance, but only by construing Mulvey's argument as a historical and cultural claim which addresses the way in which certain devices (like POV shots) have been used in the service of certain ideological purposes—the use of the POV shot as an extension of patriarchal, scopophilic behaviour, for example. In Chapters 5 and 6, I examine certain films in a historical context using psychoanalysis in this way (although psychoanalytic ideas concerning 'the gaze' in particular are not central in these analyses). Treating POV in this fashion allows us to recognize the massive variety of other functions performed by POV: the representation of a character's longing for drinking water, for example, in Hitchcock's *Lifeboat* (1944). If the various psychoanalytic accounts of cinema are to represent themselves as more general theories, then they must show how scopophilia and voyeurism illuminate such instances of POV.

Neither recognition nor alignment nor allegiance entails that the spectator replicate the traits, or experience the thoughts or emotions of a character. Recognition and alignment require only that the spectator understand that these traits and mental states make up the character. With allegiance we go beyond understanding, by evaluating and responding emotionally to the traits and emotions of the character, in the context of the narrative situation. Again, though, we respond emotionally without replicating the emotions of the character. For example, in watching a character perform certain actions, and in seeing the character adopt a certain kind of posture and facial expression, we may infer that the character is in a certain kind of mental state, or possesses certain traits—say, anger as the state, or brutality as the trait. These inferences contribute both to our recognition of the character, and to the pattern of alignment, since we are dealing here partly with a question of subjective access; but such inferences in no way mandate that the spectator be moved to think or feel (let alone behave) in the same way. If we do go on to be moved, by engaging with the character on the level of allegiance, our responses are at a tangent to those of the character: they are acentral, sympathetic rather than empathic. In order to respond emotionally in this way, the perceiver must first understand the narrative situation, including the interests, traits, and states of the characters. I do not mean to imply that the spectator's understanding and evaluation of the traits of a character must be either complete or immutable in order for allegiance to occur, but merely that at a given moment in the narrative the spectator must believe that she has some basis for evaluation, in the form of beliefs about what traits comprise the character in question. We will see how this contrasts with empathic emotional responses which do not require such an understanding.

It is in view of these conditions that recognition, alignment, and allegiance comprise a structure of sympathy, where that term is distinguished from empathy precisely in virtue of its acentrality. In understanding 'why the protagonist's response is appropriate or intelligible to the situation',[28] it is only necessary that we have what we take to be, at that moment in the course of the narrative, reliable information about the traits and states of the character, and about the situation in which the character is placed. In sympathizing with the protagonist I do not simulate or mimic her occurrent mental state. Rather, I understand the protagonist and her context, make a more-or-less sympathetic or antipathetic judgement of the character, and respond emotionally in a manner appropriate to both the evaluation and the context of the action.

The Man Who Knew Too Much (Hitchcock, 1956)

Much of the the critical and theoretical comment on the work of Hitchcock has centred on the notion of identification. In particular, critics have observed that his work sometimes elicits a paradoxical identification with villainous, unsympathetic characters. Robin Wood, for example, writes of Hitchcock 'playing identification techniques *against* the natural gravitation of our sympathetic concern';[29] while Raymond Durgnat writes of the '"fishtail" of contradictory identifications and condemnations as we discover the several layers of Norman Bates'.[30] For these reasons, Hitchcock's films provide a particularly good test case for the theory of character engagement. *The Man Who Knew Too Much* will serve to illustrate the concepts of recognition, allegiance, and alignment. Later in the chapter, I consider it alongside Hitchcock's *Saboteur* (1942) and begin to sketch an explanation, filled out in more detail in Chapter 6, of our sympathy for the devil in these films.

The Man Who Knew Too Much may be divided into two, broad movements. Jo and Ben McKenna (Doris Day and James Stewart), an American couple, are vacationing in Morocco with their son Hank (Christopher Olsen). In the course of their travels, they befriend a Frenchman, Louis Bernard (Daniel Gélin), and a retired English couple, the Draytons (Brenda de Banzie and Bernard Miles). Bernard is murdered, but he attempts to pass information regarding a plot to assassinate a French minister on to Ben McKenna with his last words. The Draytons, it emerges, are in some way connected with the murder of Louis Bernard; they kidnap Hank in order to silence Ben McKenna. The Draytons hold Hank in captivity in England; the McKennas pursue them largely without the aid of the police. Hank is located in a London Embassy and is recovered via a ruse in which Jo McKenna, a professional singer, entertains guests at the Embassy with a (loud and lengthy) rendition of 'Que Sera, Sera'. Recognizing the song, Hank whistles it, enabling his father to locate him.

In the first movement, which extends up to the beginning of the McKennas' hunt for Hank in Britain, we recognize the major characters (a process that I examine in relation to the film in more detail in the next chapter) and we are aligned exclusively (with a few brief exceptions) with the McKennas. At the same time, this first movement establishes a moral structure which ensures that our allegiance is with the McKennas. In the second movement, the structure of alignment develops so as to disperse our attention over several characters, rather than exclusively attaching us to the McKennas. Moreover, while the McKennas remain the moral centre of the film, the moral structure of the film fragments in the second movement. Let us consider these developments in more detail.

The first movement of the film both attaches us to the McKennas and provides the spectator with access to their subjectivities. That is, the narration follows the spatio-temporal path of the McKennas, only occasionally breaking away to reveal action occurring in a different location; and the McKennas are subjectively transparent, revealing their inner states through actions, expressions, and language. By contrast, when the narration does break momentarily from the McKennas—just prior to the stabbing of Louis Bernard, for example—the characters we witness are largely opaque: we see their actions, but have no access to their subjectivities. (Indeed, the film persistently elicits curiosity by introducing secondary characters—Louis Bernard, the Draytons, the assassin, Ambrose Chappell Jnr.—in this obtuse fashion.) It is this combination of transparency and opacity, couched in a pattern of spatio-temporal attachment which emphasizes the McKennas, which creates the sense that narrative information is being 'filtered' through the McKennas. (Except in the case of POV shots and diegetic voice-overs, film cannot filter narrative information through a character in the direct fashion of a literary narrative, written in the voice of a homodiegetic narrator. And even in the case of the POV shot, the generalization does not hold up, as we will see in Chapter 5.)

Up until the murder of Louis Bernard, the McKennas have functioned as an 'alignment unit': that is, the narration has followed them as a couple, much of our access to their thoughts deriving from dialogue between them. The murder results in the splitting of this unit, aligning us more closely with Ben McKenna during the murder and in its immediate aftermath. The murder scene is one of the few occasions within this first movement when the narration attaches us to action other than that involving the McKennas; and yet it ultimately functions to underscore our alignment with Ben McKenna. Since these are, on the face of it, contrary effects, a more detailed examination of the sequence is warranted.

The action takes place in a market-place, where the McKennas are spending a leisurely morning with the Draytons. The narration first aligns us with the McKennas. The Draytons are looking after Hank, and this second group occasionally crosses the path of the McKennas. The narration then breaks with this restriction, in order to follow a scuffle and chase which erupts in the market: Louis Bernard is being pursued (frame 1). Bernard is stabbed (frame 2), staggers towards the group formed by the McKennas and the Draytons, and falls on Ben McKenna. Through a sequence of tighter and tighter shots, and the dimunition of background noise, the narration attaches us to Ben McKenna's actions and experience ever more exclusively (frames 3–10). The apex of this movement occurs in the shot represented by frames 9 and 10, in which the camera tracks in towards the characters as Bernard whispers into Ben's ear. Though the shot is not subjective in any obvious sense, it mimics for the spectator the way Ben has been drawn down by Bernard. Over these shots, Bernard communicates some fragmented information regarding the assassination plot; the spectator's alignment with Ben is cemented here, since only the spectator and Ben are party to these revelations. The more omniscient narration during the chase which precedes Bernard's death in fact functions to highlight this exclusive alignment of the spectator with Ben. In this sense, if we take the sequence as whole, the brief 'decentring' of the McKennas only serves to place the subsequent narrational isolation of Ben McKenna in relief.

Following this incident, Ben is interviewed by the police, and then receives a threatening phone call in which he is informed that Hank has been kidnapped. Back at the hotel, he tells Jo about the phone call, and his realization that the Draytons must have been the agents of the kidnapping, thus reforming

Frames 1–4 The Man Who Knew Too Much: the murder of Louis Bernard

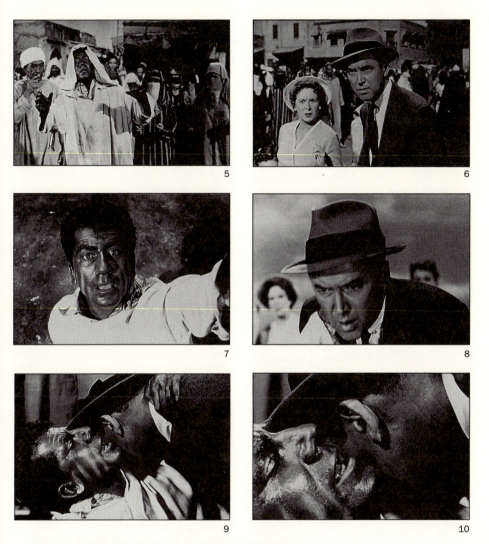

Frames 5–10 The Man Who Knew Too Much: the murder of Louis Bernard

the earlier 'alignment unit'. This is crucial in reifying a moral structure in the film: from the beginning the McKennas have been presented as a sympathetic couple, but no definitively antipathetic character emerges until this moment. The narration sets up a 'Manichaean' moral structure: a simple opposition of groups representing opposed values. The narration has provided us with our villains—for the moment, at least. The pattern of exclusive attachment to the McKennas is important here, since we later discover that Mrs Drayton is a most half-hearted and guilt-ridden kidnapper. But the Hitchcockian narration does not choose to reveal this to the spectator at this point, thus inviting the Manichaean response. In this way, the alignment structure affects the pattern of moral orientation. Distinguishing alignment from allegiance does not at all deny that the two systems interact. That is why they are defined as operating within a larger system: the structure of sympathy.

The first movement of the film climaxes with the argument between the McKennas in their hotel room in Marrakesh, and their telephone call with Hank, which follows their arrival at Heathrow airport in London. As with the stabbing scene, these scenes function to concentrate our attention more keenly on the characters with whom we are aligned, in this case, both the McKennas. Aside from a brief argument with Buchanan, a British police official, the McKennas are isolated in these scenes. The narration thus dovetails alignment and allegiance: we have been aligned with the McKennas from the beginning of the film, a pattern underlined by their isolation in these scenes; and during the same portion of the film the moral structure clarifies into a dualistic opposition, thus intensifying our sympathy for the McKennas. The text is so organized that at precisely the point where our allegiance is most strongly elicited, any 'interference' from action involving other characters is excluded. The first movement of the film, then, leads to this convergence of alignment and allegiance, the optimal conditions for an intense and unqualified sympathetic engagement with the McKennas.

The second movement of the film disperses and fragments this convergence, all the time maintaining our sympathetic engagement with the McKennas. Within the structure of alignment, this dispersal occurs as the narration becomes increasingly omniscient; in our terms, the narration attaches us to multiple characters and, again in contrast to the first movement of the film, gives us access to the subjectivities of characters other than the McKennas. The once exclusive pattern of attachment splinters in two ways. Ben and Jo search for Hank separately, effecting a sustained (rather than temporary, as in the first movement of the film) division of the sympathetic characters. Secondly, and more importantly, the narration now periodically aligns us with the Draytons, beginning with the sequence in which the assassin is instructed by Mr Drayton. Up to this point in the film, the narration has only momentarily strayed from aligning us with either Ben or Ben and Jo together.

This increasing omniscience does not only manifest itself in the attachment to a greater number of characters than in the first movement of the film. This shift is mirrored by a change in the 'texture' of the narration—that is, the quality of the narration on a shot-by-shot, 'micro-' level, as opposed to its global qualities established across entire segments—which self-consciously interrupts the flow of character action and reaction by foregrounding elements of the diegesis of which the characters are unaware. The most striking case involves the stuffed animals which intrude upon our attention when Ben visits the taxidermists in search of Hank, commenting ironically on the misperception—shared by Ben and, by virtue of the structure of alignment, the spectator—of the Chappells as a gang of menacing criminals. We will examine this scene, and the idea of the texture of narration, in more detail in Chapter 5.

Parallel with these shifts in the structure of alignment, the narration also complicates the moral structure of the film. In aligning the spectator with the Draytons in the scene in which the assassin receives his instructions, the narration posits a new moral opposition among the kidnappers, between Mrs Drayton, on the one hand, kind and protective towards Hank, and Mr Drayton, the assassin and Hank's guard on the other. The opposition mirrors the larger one that crystallizes at the end of the first movement, between the McKennas and the Draytons. The film thus effects a series of reversals with respect to Mrs Drayton, switching from antipathy to sympathy twice (we will look at the other, earlier instance in the next chapter). The split between the Draytons performs an even more complex function in the way that it parallels and overshadows a more subtle division that opens up between Ben and Jo McKenna.[31] After the kidnapping, the domineering, controlling traits of Ben McKenna take on a much more troubling and unsympathetic aspect. Up to this point, the difficulties caused in the marriage by Ben's 'benign' patriarchal dominance have been revealed in dialogue—most obviously, in references to Jo's unwillingly abandoned singing career—but largely anaesthetized by the ludic tone of the family scenes. After the kidnapping, however, Ben's control over Jo is cast in a more sinister light, particularly in the scene in which he cajoles her into taking tranquillizers (frame 11). A major thematic concern of the second movement of the film is the (relative) re-empowerment of Jo McKenna within the marriage—she is proven to be at least as capable and insightful in the 'masculine' business of the hunt for the kidnappers—and the consequent renewal of the marriage. However, in moral terms, this division is very minor compared with that between the McKennas and the Draytons, and the new split between

Frames 11–12 The Man Who Knew Too Much: Ben McKenna restrains his wife; Mrs Drayton's fearful expression

11   12

Mr and Mrs Drayton. The latter both plays out in more extreme form, and yet diminishes by comparison, the conflict between the McKennas. None of these intricacies undermine our sympathy for the McKennas as a couple, and it is in this sense that they remain the moral centre of the film. The narration manages to introduce moral complexity with respect to the protagonists, without undermining the strong 'melodramatic' opposition set up in the first movement.

Some of the consequences of these complications in the patterns of alignment and allegiance are manifested in the climactic scene in the Embassy. Mr Drayton leaves the basement of the Embassy to fetch Hank from the room upstairs in which he is being held by Mrs Drayton. He is planning to strangle Hank. In the next shot, Ben heads up the stairs of the Embassy from the ground floor, following the sound of his son whistling 'Que Sera'. The narration then cuts to Mrs Drayton in the room with Hank. She is desperately trying to save Hank. Someone starts to pound on the door. Do we guess that it is Ben—or Mr Drayton? Our hesitation is integral to the effect of suspense, but what I am interested in here are the factors which bear on our hypotheses. The moral opposition between Mr and Mrs Drayton is important because, generically, we expect a confrontation between a sympathetic and an antipathetic character.[32] On these grounds, then, it is likely to be Mr Drayton rather than Ben. (In addition, what I will call 'affective mimicry' supports the hypothesis that Mr Drayton is breaking the door down. Fear (that it is her husband at the door) is clearly the emotion communicated by Mrs Drayton's facial and vocal expressions (frame 12); affective mimicry describes the phenomenon whereby we not only recognize but mimic an emotion expressed by another.) Against this, however, inference based on narrative context should lead us to the opposite conclusion: Ben surely has less ground to cover, since he begins from the ground floor rather than the basement. It is my experience that for most spectators, the combined effects of allegiance and mimicry override the purely cognitive assessment of narrative space. Thus, the information provided by the mechanism of central imagining in this case coheres with the structure of sympathy.

The second movement of the film thus complicates the pattern of moral orientation, without displacing the McKennas as the moral centre of the film, and replaces an exclusive alignment with the McKennas with a structure of alignment in which we are alternately aligned with the McKennas and the kidnappers. These shifts occur for the sake of generating suspense. The first movement, however, is important to the creation of this suspense in a different way. The exclusive alignment with the McKennas, combined with the Manichaean moral structure, create the optimal conditions for an intense, sympathetic engagement with them; and this emotional bond carries through the second movement of the film, in spite of the self-conscious, mocking interventions of the narration, ensuring that when the narration does disperse our attention by developing an alternating alignment pattern, we still care enough about the characters to want a good outcome for them. To borrow a phrase from the detective fiction writer P. D. James, suspense depends on both devices and desires.

Two further points regarding the structure of sympathy in general emerge from this analysis of *The Man Who Knew Too Much*. First, in contrast to the folk model of identification, engagement within the structure of sympathy is conceived as a plural phenomenon. According to the commonplace conception of character identification, as described in the introduction, we watch a film, and find ourselves becoming attached to a particular character on the basis of qualities roughly congruent with those we possess or wish to possess, and experience vicariously the emotional states of this character: we identify with the character. It should now be clear that this scenario conflates many different kinds of response to character, some purely cognitive, some both cognitive and affective, and implies that this articulation of the various kinds of response is the only significant one. Our examination of *The Man Who Knew Too Much* illustrates the way in which spectators may recognize, align, and ally themselves with characters in complex patterns which may preclude or transcend a single, strong engagement with a single character. One of the advantages of positing a number of different levels of engagement is that we can see how our relationship with a central character is inflected by adjacent engagements at the same or different levels, which may compete or co-operate with a dominant engagement. Broadly speaking, plural engagement can work in two ways. We may respond differently to the same character at different points in the film, as, strikingly, in the case of Mrs Drayton; and we may engage simultaneously with different characters in different ways within a given sequence in the film. Plural identification—the ramification of character engagement through the variables of level of engagement, number of characters, and time—lies at the heart of the complexity of experience that narrative fiction can offer us.

In spite of this, the great bulk of theoretical speculation on the question of 'identification' has been concerned with sympathetic reactions to characters reflecting the values already held (consciously or unconsciously) by the spectator—which should hardly surprise us, since this is the relationship built-in to the word 'identification'. And this is another good reason to drop the term in favour of another, more neutral term, like engagement. For engaging with characters may result in—if I can risk a hideous neologism—'alterification' at least as much as 'identification'; narratives (including popular ones) are not only about reconfirming and restaging the familiar, the same old story. The interest and fascination of narratives may equally well derive from the representation of the unfamiliar, the spectator's 'quasi-experience' of the new. *The Man Who Knew Too Much* draws on stereotypes and generic narrative patterns, and yet, unquestionably, it engages our interest by eliciting sympathetic (and antipathetic) responses towards characters undergoing experiences of traumatic loss, violation, and self-questioning that few of us will have direct experience of, and none in the precise configuration put forward by the narrative. Fiction enables, in Stephen Greenblatt's words, a kind of 'imaginative mobility' which has been almost entirely obscured by the stress on 'subjection'—ideological determination—in contemporary theory.[33] I must stress that I am not appealing to a notion of imagination or aesthetic experience that takes us beyond or outside the social, but rather one that fosters new perspectives on the social—that facilitates imaginative mobility within social 'space'.

One fairly obvious motivation for engaging with fictions is the desire to be (or at least, imagine being) in some way more powerful than one actually is—politically, socially, intellectually, or physically. Centrally imagining being the character may perform this function. The role of centrally imagining *oneself* in the fictional situation lies in providing the necessary contrast with such centrally imagined empowerment: in this situation, I could not or would not (be able to) react as this character does. Cast as 'escapism', such experience is usually either trivialized or demonized: harmless distraction from one's everyday worries and limitations, or an illusory respite from oppressed existence which in reality only serves to perpetuate it. While I would not want to deny that engaging with fictions might be trivial or deleterious in particular cases, it would seem facile and reductive to subsume all fictional experience under these rubrics. The play of centrally imagining being the character and being oneself in the character's situation, within the acentral structure of sympathy, has the potential to expand our experiential repertoire in a non-trivial and non-pernicious fashion. Even the simplest fiction which offers us a brute fantasy of physical empowerment must, by definition, involve a complementary awareness of our actual lack of power—an experience which does not necessarily foster satisfaction with our present lot. I will take up these issues again in Chapter 6 and in the Conclusion.

As a result of the typicality of plural engagement, states such as 'identification' and 'empathy' as traditionally defined, in which we are completely absorbed or 'possessed' by a particular character, are rare (if we grant that such states, strictly defined, are possible at all). Identification or empathy even by the weaker definition (version 2) would entail, at the very least, that we have recognized a character, have complete access to her knowledge and other mental states, and are sympathetic with the character. It would further require that this engagement is only reinforced by our engagements with other characters: that we are aligned exclusively with this character, and that a firm antipathy is elicited towards all characters whose interests and actions are detrimental to the interests of our 'identification figure'. No complicating sympathy for characters representing other values or goals is possible. We have seen how even in *The Man Who Knew Too Much*, the director so lauded for his skill in eliciting 'identification' varies the patterning of alignment and allegiance far more than this scenario would suggest. Such conditions exist, I submit, only in a very few agitational ('propaganda') films and melodramas.

The second feature of the structure of sympathy that emerges from the analysis of *The Man Knew Too Much* is that the three basic levels of engagement which comprise it may interact in various ways. Traditional aesthetic concepts, such as 'empathy' (in the Brechtian sense) and catharsis, might be explained with more precision in terms of such complex patterns of engagement. But it is important here to recognize that the three basic levels, though they always interact in actual films, are distinct phenomena which should not be conflated. William Lustig's *Maniac* (1982), for example, develops an alignment pattern in which the narration attaches us to a subjectively transparent protagonist whose actions (a series of horrible rapes, murders, and scalpings) are morally repugnant, denying most viewers the necessary conditions for a sympathetic allegiance with the character.[34] Similarly, Steven Spielberg's *Schindler's List* (1994) aligns us in certain sequences with Amos Goeth (Ralph Fiennes) (for example, as he shoots at the Jewish boy who has failed to remove every blemish in Goeth's bathtub); and Hitchcock's *Spellbound* (1945) provides a yet briefer example, in which we are at one point perceptually aligned, through a POV shot, with Dr Murchison (Leo G. Carroll), the film's chief villain. In all these cases we are, as it were, made to 'identify' informationally with a character from whom we are—simultaneously—emotionally alienated. The distinction between alignment and allegiance attempts to capture this split. None of this is to deny, however, that structures of alignment affect structures of allegiance, as we saw with respect to our changing evaluations of Mrs Drayton, and will see again in subsequent chapters (see in particular the analysis of *Le Doulos* is Chapter 6).

Empathy

By the imagination we place ourselves in his situation, we conceive ourselves enduring all the same torments, we enter as it were into his body, and become in some measure the same person with him, and thence form some idea of his sensations, and even feel something which, though weaker in degree, is not altogether unlike them.[35]

Popular culture is rife with allusions to empathy. Deckard hunts replicants in Ridley Scott's *Blade Runner* (1982) using an empathy test which allows him to discriminate humans from androids, while drugs known as 'empathogens' are used to 'enhance' television viewing in *Wild Palms* (Oliver Stone, 1993). The cartoon baby Leviathan is made to ingest a medicine that goes by the name of 'Empatheen', to improve his sense of fellow-feeling for the other characters in the strip.[36] But like 'identification', empathy is only loosely defined in everyday discourse. Empathy is generally thought of as the adoption in a person of the mental states and emotions of some other person. In contemporary social

psychology, much debate hinges on whether empathy is to be defined principally as the cognitive ability to 'perspective-take', that is, to imagine being in
the situation of the perceived or target subject; or whether empathy is more
appropriately defined as the replication of the emotions of the other. For these
reasons I have chosen to set the debate up in this chapter using terminology
(i.e. central and acentral imagining) less burdened with conflicting historical
associations, and the inevitable variation in sense which accompanies the spread
of a word into the vernacular.

As a scientific concept, empathy is still alive because in spite of the confusions and disagreements regarding the precise definition of the term, there is
a consensus that a certain range of phenomena are usefully gathered under it.
These phenomena all pertain to reactions we have to the states of others which
are distinct from sympathy in that they do not require the perceiver to share
any values, beliefs, or goals with the perceived. Centrally imagining a scenario
from the attitudinal perspective of a person other than oneself is distinct from
acentral imagining, or sympathy, by virtue of the subject's 'emptying out' of
her own qualities in order to simulate the states of the target subject: it is not
a question of sharing but of imaginative substitution. Acentral imagining and
sympathy, and central imagining and empathy are then, respectively, cognate
terms. And just as the structure of sympathy breaks down into more particular
processes, so the notion of central imagining or empathy breaks down into
further mechanisms, distinguished according to the role of volition within them.
While *emotional simulation* is voluntary, *motor* and *affective mimicry* and *autonomic reactions* are involuntary. We will see that the nature of at least one of
these mechanisms has important ramifications for the relationship between
sympathy and empathy, not least in our aesthetic experience.

Emotional Simulation

In a scene in Joseph Lewis's *The Big Combo* (1955), a gang leader pushes a
hearing aid into the ear of a policeman investigating him and alternates shout-
ing and playing frenetic jazz music into the microphone of the earpiece. The
cop winces with pain. The gang leader has borrowed the hearing aid from his
subordinate McClure, played by Brian Donlevy, who looks on as his boss tor-
tures the prisoner. McClure winces as well—which is remarkable, since, without his hearing aid, he can hear virtually nothing (as we discover in a later
scene, when McClure's assassination is represented from his aural perspective
—that is, silently). So why does McClure flinch? He is engaging in emotional
simulation.

The concept of emotional simulation as discussed by Robert Gordon is perhaps the most obviously related to central imagining of all the concepts I
consider here.[37] Indeed, Wollheim also uses the term 'simulation' to describe

central imagining, although he does not draw on the recent psychological work that forms the basis of Gordon's argument. Gordon begins, however, not with imagination, but with practical reasoning. In its simplest form, practical reasoning involves hypothesizing how I will act in some situation. Gordon shows how such 'hypotheticopractical' reasoning,[38] which involves speculation about and 'simulations' of one's own feelings in future situations, extends to simulations of the intentional states of other persons, as a means of predicting their behaviour. Such predictions are most obviously seen in games. Playing chess, I do not try merely to predict what I would do in my opponent's situation, but what she would do in that situation (cf. the discussion of varieties of central imagining above, pp. 79–80). To this end, I might 'simulate a lower level of play, trade one set of idiosyncracies for another, and above all pretend ignorance of my own intentions'. We do not lose ourselves in the other, but imagine possessing certain predicates of the other.

Gordon goes on to suggest that these simulated predicates might include not only beliefs[39] and desires but also emotions. Observing the behaviour of a person in a certain situation about which we have limited knowledge—as is often the case with a character in a fiction—we imaginatively project ourselves into their situation, and hypothesize as to the emotion(s) they are experiencing. For example, when we encounter the black American soldier in the second episode of Roberto Rossellini's *Paisà* (1946), we do not know why he is chattering incoherently. Is he drunk? Shellshocked? Deranged? Emotional simulation may be the method we employ to fathom his behaviour.

At the opening of *Deception* (1946, directed by Irving Rapper), a female character, played by Bette Davis, arrives at a cello recital being performed by a male character, played by Paul Henreid. (Neither of the characters is named at this point.) An expression which seems to suggest both anticipation and anxiety appears on her face as she watches the recital. The lush romanticism of the piece underscores the strength of the emotion being experienced by her, without specifying the emotion any more clearly. Perhaps she has arrived late to the performance of a loved one, and is experiencing relief and joy that she has not missed what is clearly to be regarded as an impassioned performance. Perhaps this is the expression of an admiring but jealous rival musician. Perhaps the Davis character is a music critic, arriving late to the performance of a musician known and not highly regarded by her, and surprised by the quality of this performance. (Of course, such hypothesizing will work within the constraints of the two stars' personae, but these still leave the situation and emotions underdetermined.) As we hypothesize, we may 'try on' these emotions (along with the other intentional states)—imagining a general anxiety to attend the concert (the state which seems clearest), and then extending our minds toward the states suggested above. We simulate what seems most evident, in order to build a fuller picture, and hence to predict the behaviour of the agent.

The delayed exposition of *Deception* makes the process of simulation-and-hypothesis-formation particularly evident. Arguably, emotional simulation takes on a larger role as a mechanism of discovery the more underdetermined the narrative representation. On this account, while every narrative leaves some room for this kind of simulation, art films would invite the process much more than classical films (since the classical film produces much greater redundancy, and progressively narrows the range of plausible hypotheses regarding a character's future actions).[40]

Gordon appeals to a computer metaphor in order to capture the nature of this 'hypotheticoemotional reasoning':

our emotion-producing system may be run off-line, disengaged from its natural input and output systems. Hypothesis testing [is] again central to the methodology, whether such testing is carried out consciously or not. One ['tries on'] various emotions, seeking the best fit to the observed situation (with the appropriate spatiotemporal shifts, along with other 'indexical' shifts) and the observed behavior, engaging in further pretending where necessary.[41]

Such emotional simulation constitutes a form of 'affective trial and error'[42] through which we build up a picture of the states of others (or, in a fictional context, characters). If this is correct, then one of the very mechanisms through which we form beliefs about the traits and occurrent states of characters—the kind of information on which the structure of sympathy depends—is, in fact, a form of empathy. For in simulating an emotion or any other intentional state, we are not merely recognizing or understanding it, but centrally imagining it.

Affective Mimicry

Facial and gestural expression plays an important role in the visual media of art, film, and the theater. . . . When humans deal with humans, animals with animals, or when a cat and his owner try to get along with each other, they constantly read their partner's external behavior and control their own. This seems a remarkable achievement once we realize that the eyes of the person or of the cat see nothing but a relief of muscles and bones covered with skin and subjected to various displacements, contractions and expansions. What can such purely physical patterns have in common with states of mind, which offer no perceivable shape? What makes us see pleasure in a smiling face?[43]

I flip the TV on after an exhausting day and I am confronted by the image of a middle-aged man crying. Characteristically, the man's face is framed in close-up, so that his expression is absolutely legible. Without any knowledge of the character, or what is at stake in the larger framework of the narrative, before I know it, a lump forms at the back of my throat. The term *mimicry* has been applied to this kind of reaction, which relies not on a voluntary act of imagining and simulation—as in the case of emotional simulation—but upon an almost 'perceptual' registering and reflexive simulation of the emotion of another person via facial and bodily cues.

The notion of mimicry has its modern scientific roots in the work of Theodor Lipps, although similar ideas can be found much earlier, in the writings of, for example, Leonardo da Vinci and Adam Smith.[44] *Einfühlung*, for Lipps, described a kind of involuntary neuromuscular response to physical forms. He refers to the phenomenon at one point as 'kinaesthetic mimicry'. Looking at a Doric column supporting a stone arch provokes an imitative muscular reaction in us, based on our knowledge of the kind of forces bearing on the column. These in turn are registered in the observer's consciousness as 'activity' or 'inner motions'. Such reactions extend to our observation of human postures and expressions:

We do not know how or why it happens that a glimpse of a laughing face, or a change in that contour of the face, especially the eyes and mouth, which we associate with the phrase 'laughing face' should stimulate the viewer to feel gay and free and happy; and to do this in such a way that an inner attitude is assumed, or that there is a surrender to this inner activity or to the action of the whole inner being. But it is a fact.[45]

Arnheim's comments, at the head of this section, seem to have been inspired in part by Lipps; and while the concept of *Einfühlung* was a central element of the cluster of aesthetic assumptions that Brecht sought to overthrow, Eisenstein embraced the very similar notion of 'expressive movement' in his contemporaneous Marxist aesthetic.[46]

The modern descendant of Lipps's concept also spans the range from purely muscular to affective responses. In *motor mimicry*, we mimic the muscular actions of the subject we are observing. Watching a basketball player set and then throw, our bodies may—especially if we are watching closely and have a keen interest in the outcome—tense up, in imitation of the muscular control being exercised by the player. Smith captured this well: 'The mob, when they are gazing at a dancer on the slack rope, naturally writhe and twist and balance their own bodies, as they see him do, and as they feel that they themselves must do if in his situation.'[47] Something similar seems to occur when we prepare ourselves for performing some physical task requiring great skill or strength. Preparing myself for the high jump, I subliminally rehearse the muscular actions which I will fully realize in a few moments. Motor mimicry is a weak or partial simulation of a physical motion.

Beyond establishing the presence of such muscular activity (through electromyography), one of the advances made by recent work on such 'mimicry' has been the connection of purely muscular mimicry with *affective* mimicry. The connection is made by Lipps, but, as Arnheim queries, how can purely physical patterns evoke subjective states? There are two stages to the answer.

First, Paul Ekman and his associates have done much to substantiate the claim that certain 'basic' affects (happiness; sadness; surprise/fear; disgust; anger) are associated cross-culturally with certain expressions.[48] Consequently, when we mimic patterns of facial muscles, we are able to recognize at least these basic affective states.[49]

Mimicry, however, performs no earth-shattering role in enabling us to recognize these affects through facial expression. If we accept that certain expressions are cross-culturally understood as expressions of particular affective states, we do not need to mimic them to recognize them as such, any more than we need to 'mimic' the waving of branches to know that the wind is blowing, or 'mimic' a person waving semaphore flags in order to understand their meaning. The second necessary element in explaining affective mimicry derives from the notion of 'feedback'. A vestige of the account of emotions posited by William James and C. G. Lange,[50] the facial feedback thesis holds that in adopting a facial expression apposite to a particular emotion, our subjective experience of the emotion is intensified.[51] In other words, if we mimic a facial expression apposite to a basic affect, we do not merely see and categorize a certain expression and hence affect, we experience it, albeit in weaker form (just as the examples of motor mimicry assumed only a partial replication).[52]

Unlike emotional simulation, the action of mimicry is not performed voluntarily, or with specific reasons on specific occasions. Rather, it functions almost as a 'sixth sense', a physiological mechanism by which we constantly probe the meaning of our environment. Indeed, on some occasions, the involuntary nature of the process leads to a certain incongruency: Ekman has spoken of the 'qualifier smile', in which a subject smiles in mimicry of someone who is criticizing her—while smiling.[53] Clearly, there is nothing for the subject to be happy about, but the involuntary mimicry takes over, at least initially. Mimicry of facial muscles is usually invisible (hence the value of electromyography in the detection of such movements), though the examples already provided suggest that acts of motor mimicry are often quite visible. The founding scenario most often invoked by psychologists expounding the concept is the smile of a baby in response to the smile of the mother. Furthermore, there seems to be a number of situations in which adult humans show an 'unarticulated' awareness of the effects of affective mimicry. For example, we often appreciate people with 'infectious grins'; and most of us recognize the strategy of overcoming depression by placing ourselves in social situations, where we know that we are likely to be 'forced' to smile by the environment, that is, a gregarious gathering of smiling faces.[54]

The relevance of such affective mimicry to our responses to characters may not be clear, as most films present us with many cues, aside from facial expressions and bodily motions, through which we make sense of the narrative situation, including the intentional states of characters—dialogue, for example.

There is no reason to believe that mimicry is suspended altogether in such cases—consider the case of Mrs Drayton's fear of Mr Drayton, for example—but its role is certainly more apparent in two, more unusual types of representation. First, there are those visual representations in which we are denied all cues aside from those provided by facial expression and bodily posture. Consider, for example, paintings like Edvard Munch's *The Scream* or some of the photographs of Cindy Sherman, which present the viewer with legible facial expressions without a fully specified narrative context. Turning to film, we might consider avant-garde and art films which suppress information which would unambiguously explain a character's expression (Werner Schroeter and Kenneth Anger come to mind). Secondly, the role of mimicry is revealed in a different way by those films which minimize facial and bodily expressivity. Bresson's *L'Argent* (1983) is one such film, and we will examine it at length in Chapter 5. The film not only uses an inexpressive performance style, but also employs an editing strategy in which shots of objects and isolated limbs are placed at dramatic points where we would expect facial expressions in close framing. This technique, I suggest, excises the constant, low-level mimicry which accompanies our viewing of classical films like a 'sixth sense'. This absence is one major factor which accounts for the emotionally austere quality of Bresson's films. To reiterate, such cases only clarify the role of mimicry by, in the first case, forcing the spectator to rely on it to an unusual degree, and in the second, removing it as a factor altogether. Mimicry is certainly not limited to these relatively unusual cases.

Gordon makes a passing remark on the relationship between mimicry and simulation which raises a problem for the cognitive theory of emotions discussed in Chapter 2. He suggests that mimicry pre-empts much of the work of both emotional simulation and ordinary cognitive inference, 'leaving only the specific content of the emotion to be determined by testing'.[55] How can we be said to 'replicate' an emotion, though, if we have not yet determined its structure and object? Mimicking an expression tells us nothing of the evaluative proposition of the person or character, nor of the object towards which it is directed. And according to the cognitive view, emotions are differentiated from one another according to the 'judgement' or 'evaluation' in question—'that snake may cause me harm', in the case of fear, 'my mother has died' in the case of sorrow. Gordon implies, however, that we can recognize a broad emotion-type through mimicry, and fill in the details (i.e. the specific evaluative proposition) of the situation as we learn more. It is for this reason that I have used the qualifier 'affective' rather than 'emotional', in order to make it clear that mimicry pertains only to those basic affects which are distinguishable physiologically, and via feedback, subjectively. In these cases—but in these alone—I do not need to understand the specific evaluations of a person or character in order to grasp the basic affect-type being experienced by that figure, because it is discernable through the feedback chain of expression, physiology, and subjectivity—that is, through affective mimicry.[56]

There remains one kind of empathic process to discuss: autonomic reactions, such as the startle response in which we jump at a sharp, loud noise or a violent, unexpected movement within the frame. Like motor and affective mimicry, autonomic reactions are involuntary. If we jump at the sudden appearance of the nurse in Rob Reiner's *Misery* (1990)—standing over the crippled hero in his bed, in the middle of the night—it is a reflex reaction. (If the shock is created by a sound, the sound must be diegetic if the reactions of spectator and character are to be causally identical, although a startling non-diegetic sound—say, a sudden blast of music—produces a parallel, and pragmatically identical, reaction.) Along with simulation and mimicry, such autonomic reactions bind spectator and character together in a qualitatively different manner to that which we find in the structure of sympathy. We experience an identical shock to the character, and in this sense the response is central or empathic. In this case, however, the response does not arise from an engagement with the character, as it does with both simulation and mimicry, but directly from the represented visual or aural environment in which the character moves. Both the character and the spectator react to the unexpected noise or movement, rather than the spectator responding 'through' the response of the character. This does not preclude a spectator both responding to a noise or movement autonomically and mimicking or simulating a character's emotions in an actual viewing. The point here is to distinguish the different kinds of response which may, phenomenologically, overlay and succeed one another. Let us turn to such interactions.

Character Engagement

We are now in a position to discuss the relations among the structure of sympathy, simulation, mimicry, and autonomic responses, and thus to come to grips with the model of character engagement as a whole. There are two key differences between the structure of sympathy (acentral imagining) on the one hand, and those reactions examined under the aegis of empathy (central imagining) on the other. First, the sympathetic phenomena require comprehension of the narrative situation and characters, unlike the empathic phenomena. Secondly, in the case of sympathetic responses, we cognitively recognize an emotion and then respond with a different but appropriate emotion based on our evaluation of the character, while in the case of the empathic responses, we simulate or experience the same affect or emotion experienced by the character.

Typically, however, both emotional simulation and affective mimicry function *within the structure of sympahy*. They are among the mechanisms through which we gain an understanding of the fictional world and the characters who inhabit it. They are subordinate to the overarching structure of sympathy in that initial simulations and mimickings of the emotional states of characters are constantly filled out, modified, sometimes overturned by our cognitive construction of the narrative (that is, by what we come to know through our ordinary perceptual, conceptual, and inferential processing). In *Deception*, for example, our initial simulations of the mental states of the heroine give way to the subsequent narrative knowledge we gain through the action: she is the lover of the musician, not a rival. In this sense, if we wish to characterize the overall structure and nature of our responses to fictional characters, we must argue that such responses are *acentral*. The structure of sympathy usually acts centripetally, 'pulling in' the insights of simulation and mimicry and affording them no privilege over more cognitive assessments. The typical functioning of empathy—of simulation and mimicry—is thus twofold: first, to act as a searchlight or probe in our construction of the narrative situation; and secondly, to generate in the viewer, in somewhat attenuated form, the predominant emotions of the characters in the story world. They function to 'attune' the spectator to the emotional tenor of the narrative. It is the absence of this rough affective matching that creates the emotionally oblique quality of the films of Bresson.

At this juncture, however, we must focus on one of the differences between simulation and mimicry, in order to grasp a possible functional difference. Recall that an important feature of mimicry which marks it off from both the structure of sympathy and emotional simulation is that it is involuntary.[57] This enables it to break away from the structure of sympathy on occasion; or, to put it differently, mimicry may produce responses which prove difficult for the structure of sympathy to assimilate (cf. the incongruity of the 'qualifier smile', discussed above). Hitchcock's *Saboteur* provides an instructive contrast to *The Man Who Knew Too Much* in this respect. In *The Man Who Knew Too Much*, we saw that our affective mimicking of Mrs Drayton's fear might override our cognitive assessment of the situation. In this case, the affective mimicry works in concert with the structure of sympathy and the generic character of the film. In *Saboteur*, the viewer is, similarly, encouraged to construct a moral structure in which she is strongly allied with the hero Barry Kane, against the gang of saboteurs. While in certain respects the film resists the Manichaean moral structure often used by war dramas, the saboteur himself, Fry (Norman Lloyd), is a truly repugnant character. He is defined almost wholly by his function as a saboteur, which obviously elicits a negative evaluation in the context of the film; the only significant development of Fry's character occurs in the final scene, in which he responds in an unctuous manner to the interest shown in him by Kane's girlfriend (frame 13). This 'interest' is actually a ruse designed to delay Fry at the top of the Statue of Liberty, while police rush to the scene. The ruse succeeds, and Fry is pursued on to the torch of the statue by Kane. Defying Kane with an arrogant smile, Fry loses his footing; Kane reaches out and grabs him. As Fry dangles—literally by the threads of his jacket, which gradually tear—we see his terrified expression, framed in medium close-up (frames 14 and 15). Our experience of Fry's predicament is prolonged by a series of shots alternating medium close-ups of his face with long shots of the statue and close-ups of the fraying jacket. Finally, Fry falls to his death (frame 16); Kane climbs back to safety and embraces his girlfriend. This 'triumphant' ending, however, is strangely qualified. While the structure of sympathy leads us to find satisfaction in the pursuit and sufferings of the saboteur—a kind of poetic justice—the mimicry provoked by the close-ups of him conflicts with those responses. The impact of affective mimicry runs against the grain of the sense of triumph and resolution invited by the structure of sympathy. Mimicry denies us the uncomplicated satisfaction that the hitherto wholly unsympathetic portrayal of Fry would otherwise offer us, in the form of his comeuppance. Hitchcock is reported to have subsequently regretted this effect,[58] and

Frames 13–16 Saboteur: Fry falls from the Statue of Liberty

13

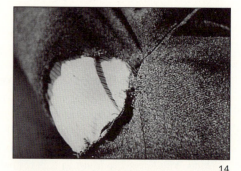
14

15

16

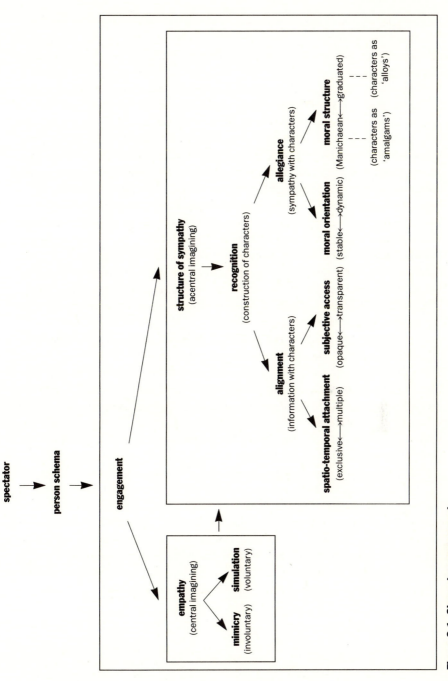

Figure 3.1 Character engagement

it is striking that in *Lifeboat* (1944)—his next-but-one film, and another narrative dwelling on wartime loyalties and ethics—the murder of the duplicitous U-boat captain is handled so that he is entirely hidden from us, thus prohibiting mimicry.

One might object that affective mimicry is still operating with the structure of sympathy in this case. Mimicking the terror of the saboteur, we have a palpable sense of his vulnerability which the film has denied us previously, and as a result we evaluate him differently. The moral structure is changed, our sympathetic engagement complicated, and it is this shift that accounts for our divided reaction. The choice between these different explanations of our response seems to depend upon whether we see the example as different in degree or in kind from the typical functioning of affective mimicry, as a probe and an affective 'interface'. But in choosing the second, more modest explanation, we are still acknowledging that affective mimicry has an extraordinary power to disrupt and force a reorganization of the moral structure at a given moment in a film. In some cases, then, affective mimicry overwhelms other forms of response which comprise the structure of sympathy. Certain filmmakers, like Hitchcock, have recognized this and incorporated such effects into their stylistic rhetoric.

The distinctions made in the model of character engagement enable us to describe and explain our variegated responses to character in a more subtle and discriminating way than the uniform concept of identification allows. The various aspects of the model are mapped out in Figure 3.1, which I urge the reader to use as a guide and reference point over the next three chapters. These chapters deal with each of the three levels of engagement which comprise the structure of sympathy in more detail. In each case, I provide an overview of the role of particular cinematic techniques in fulfilling the functions required by the level of engagement in question, from both a logical and a historical point of view. These broad commentaries are followed by analyses of particular films which are intended both to underline the distinctness of each level of engagement and to show how they may affect each other. This is quite different, of course, from collapsing the various concepts which comprise the model of character engagement back into a single, homogeneous phenomenon—just as there is a difference between mistaking the wood for the trees and acknowledging that there is both a wood and several varieties of tree.

---

1. Two works which advance a view of imagination as central to human rationality and productivity are George Lakoff, *Women, Fire, and Dangerous Things: What Categories Reveal about the Mind* (Chicago: University of Chicago Press, 1987); and, from a more purely philosophical perspective, David Novitz, *Knowledge, Fiction and Imagination* (Philadelphia: Temple University Press, 1987).

2. The notion of 'quasi-observation' is posited by Jean-Paul Sartre in *The Psychology of the Imagination*, trans. unknown (London: Methuen, 1972); and developed by Paul Taylor, who writes of 'quasi-experience' in 'Imagination and Information', *Philosophy and Phenomenological Research*, 42 (1981), 211–14.

3. Boris Tomashevsky, 'Thematics', in Lee T. Lemon and Marion J. Reis (trans. and eds.), *Russian Formalist Criticism: Four Essays* (Lincoln: University of Nebraska Press, 1965), 66–9, 75–7.

4. David Bordwell, *Narration in the Fiction Film* (Madison: University of Wisconsin Press, 1985), 57–61.

5. Edward Branigan, *Point of View in the Cinema: A Theory of Narration and Subjectivity in the Classical Film* (New York: Mouton, 1984), 40.

6. Richard Wollheim, *The Thread of Life* (Cambridge, Mass.: Harvard University Press, 1984), 74.

7. The linguistic distinction is made in Richard Wollheim, *On Art and the Mind* (Cambridge, Mass.: Harvard University Press, 1974), 59, not in *The Thread of Life*. The distinction should not be confused with the one made in the latter work, in which similar linguistic cues are used to suggest a broader distinction between iconic and non-iconic mental states.

   Wollheim makes a further subdivision within central imagining, between central (where the position occupied is that of a central figure in the imagined scenario) and 'peripheral' imagining (where the position occupied is that of a minor figure within the imagined scenario). For example, in imagining a wedding, we could centrally imagine it from the position of the bride (central) or from the position of a member of the congregation (peripheral). The major divide lies between these two forms of imagining and acentral imagining.

8. Wollheim, *On Art and the Mind*, 75.

9. I add this second example in order to make it clear that central imagining is not a synonym for mental visualizing, though the latter can be an example of central imagining. This is a problem because of the visual 'bias' embedded in the 'imagination' word group, and because many authors, Wollheim included, choose to discuss these broader concepts with examples which involve visualization.

10. The distinction is not dissimilar to that between sympathy and empathy, as those terms are often defined. I regard acentral imagining as cognate with sympathy, and central imagining with empathy. However, because of the great variety of senses attaching to 'empathy' and 'sympathy' in the vernacular, I shall refrain from using them until I have clarified my position with less encumbered terminology.

11. See the Introduction, p. 2 and n. 3.

12. Robin Wood, *Hitchcock's Films Revisited* (New York: Columbia University Press, 1989), 147.

13. Laura Mulvey, 'Visual Pleasure and Narrative Cinema', *Screen*, 16: 3 (Autumn 1975), 12.

14. Christian Metz, *Psychoanalysis and Cinema: The Imaginary Signifier*, trans. Celia Britton, Annwyl Williams, Ben Brewster, and Alfred Guzzetti (London: Macmillan, 1982), 55–6.

15. Elizabeth Cowie, 'Fantasia', *m/f* 9 (1984), 101. For a similar argument, see Janet Bergstrom, 'Enunciation and Sexual Difference', *Camera Obscura*, 3/4 (Summer 1979), 57–8. Linda Williams also stresses divided and multiple 'identifications' in ' "Something Else Beside a Mother": *Stella Dallas* and the Maternal Melodrama', *Cinema Journal*, 24: 1 (1984), 2–27.

16. Carol Clover, *Men, Women, and Chainsaws: Gender in the Modern Horror Film* (London: BFI, 1992), 12.

17. The reader should not confuse this with the notion of assimilation discussed in Chapter 4, which refers to the revision and adaptation of schemata.

18. Carroll derives these characters from a scenario initially used by Kendall Walton in 'Fearing Fictions', *Journal of Philosophy*, 75: 1 (Jan. 1978), 5–27, which has since become a touchstone in the debate on emotional response to fiction.

19. Noël Carroll, *The Philosophy of Horror; or, Paradoxes of the Heart* (New York: Routledge, 1990), 95–6.

20. Ibid. 95.

21. The only occasion when Carroll develops an example which clearly would count as an instance of central imagining occurs in Carroll, *The Philosophy of Horror*, 80. But here, the

context is ordinary action (walking near a cliff edge and imagining falling over it). Whenever Carroll discusses fiction, the paradigm becomes acentral imagining.

22. Noël Carroll, *Mystifying Movies: Fads and Fallacies in Contemporary Film Theory* (New York: Columbia University Press, 1988), 247.

23. Bordwell, *Narration in the Fiction Film*, 65.

24. The notion of spatial attachment is derived from Boris Uspensky, *A Poetics of Composition: The Structure of the Artistic Text and Typology of a Compositional Form*, trans. Valentina Zavarin and Susan Wittig (Berkeley: University of California Press, 1973), 58.

25. Gérard Genette, *Narrative Discourse: An Essay in Method*, trans. Jane E. Lewin (Ithaca, NY: Cornell University Press, 1980), 162.

26. The term 'allegiance', and the idea of moral structure, are posited by Carroll in 'Toward a Theory of Film Suspense', *Persistence of Vision*, 1 (Summer 1984), 65–89.

27. Mulvey, 'Visual Pleasure', 16.

28. Carroll, *The Philosophy of Horror*, 95.

29. Wood, *Hitchcock's Films Revisited*, 223.

30. Raymond Durgnat, *The Strange Case of Alfred Hitchcock; or, the Plain Man's Hitchcock* (London: Faber, 1974), 37. See also Carroll, 'Toward a Theory of Film Suspense'.

31. On the parallels between the McKennas and the Draytons, see Dave Kehr, 'Hitch's Riddle', *Film Comment*, 20: 5 (May–June 1984), 15.

32. Carroll, 'Toward a Theory of Film Suspense', 71–3.

33. See Stephen J. Greenblatt, 'Culture', in Frank Lentricchia and Thomas McLaughlin (eds.), *Critical Terms for Literary Study* (Chicago: University of Chicago Press, 1990), 232.

34. This, of course, assumes that the spectator believes that it is wrong to rape, murder, and scalp. But I see no problem in assuming that most spectators do believe this. One does not need to posit that horror movie viewers have a secret urge to murder, scalp, or rape in order to explain how such viewers enjoy these films. But that is not a problem germane to this study.

35. Adam Smith, *Theory of Moral Sentiments* (1759) (Clarendon Press: Oxford, 1976), 6.

36. Peter Blegvad, 'Leviathan', *Independent On Sunday*, 10 April 1994, 51.

37. See Robert M. Gordon, *The Structure of Emotions: Investigations in Cognitive Psychology* (Cambridge: Cambridge University Press, 1987), 149–55.

38. Ibid. 140.

39. For Gordon, we simulate not beliefs, but knowledge; simulating a set of mental propositions other than the ones we regard as knowledge is, for him, the foundation of the concept of belief. But this aspect of Gordon's argument does not affect my own.

40. Noël Carroll, in conversation, Madison, Wisconsin, December 1990.

41. Gordon, *Structure of Emotions*, 152–3.

42. Susan Feagin, 'Getting Into It', unpublished manuscript, 1990, 21.

43. Rudolf Arnheim, *Art and Visual Perception: A Psychology of the Creative Eye* (The New Version) (Berkeley: University of California Press, 1974), 445–6.

44. On da Vinci, see E. H. Gombrich, 'The Edge of Delusion', review of David Freedberg, *The Power of Images*, *New York Review of Books*, 15 Feb. 1990, 6–9.

45. Theodor Lipps, 'Empathy and Aesthetic Pleasure' (1905), in Karl Aschenbrenner and Arnold Isenberg (eds.), *Aesthetic Theories: Studies in the Philosophy of Art* (Englewood Cliffs, NJ: Prentice-Hall, 1965), 409.

46. The notion of 'expressive movement' was advanced by Eisenstein and Tretyakov as a type of 'attraction': 'It is precisely expressive movement, built on an organically correct foundation, that is solely capable of evoking the emotion in the spectator, who in turn reflectively repeats in weakened form the entire system of actor's movements: as a result of the produced movements, the spectator's incipient muscular tensions are released in the desired emotion' (Sergei Eisenstein and Sergei Tretyakov, 'Expressive Movement', trans. Alma H. Law, *Millennium Film Journal*, 3 (Winter/Spring 1979), 36–7).

47. Smith, *Theory of Moral Sentiments*, 10.

48. Paul Ekman (ed.), *Emotion in the Human Face*, 2nd edn. (Cambridge: Cambridge University Press, 1982), 149.

49. Note that the claim here is that such mimicry occurs only with respect to these basic affects (physiologically distinct affective states) and not with what we defined as emotions (those affective states which can only be defined in relation to a cognitive judgement) in Chapter 2. For this reason, I write of affective rather than emotional mimicry.

50. Roughly speaking, the view of emotion developed by James and Lange holds that the subjective experience of an emotion is really a by-product of the physical reactions (like running away, in the case of fear) which accompany them. This contrasts with the folk model of emotion, which conforms quite closely with the generally accepted philosophical understanding of the relation between the subjective experience of an emotion and an accompanying action, which holds that the action is caused by the feeling of the emotion, not vice versa. For a clear overview and critique, see Gordon, *Structure of Emotions*, esp. 89.

51. This is also connected with the idea that the basic emotions are physiologically distinguished, also supported by Ekman. See Paul Ekman, Robert W. Levenson, and Wallace Friesen, 'Autonomic Nervous System Distinguishes among Emotions', *Science*, 221 (Sept. 1983), 1208–10; and R. B. Zajonc, 'Emotion and Facial Efference: A Theory Reclaimed', *Science*, 228 (Apr. 1985), 15–21.

52. Cf. Feagin, 'Getting Into It', 8.

53. Paul Ekman, 'About Face: Information Signalled by Facial Expression', Hilldale Lecture Series, University of Wisconsin–Madison, Sept. 1990.

54. Ibid.

55. Gordon, *Structure of Emotions*, 153.

56. Ekman's recent work on emotion (Ekman, Levenson, and Friesen, 'Autonomic Nervous System') suggests that the autonomic nervous system does distinguish among emotions. But Ekman does not contend that his findings completely overturn the intuitions of cognitive views of emotion. Rather, he argues that they need to be modified and combined with his results, perhaps in the way that Gordon suggests.

57. Douglas Chismar, 'Empathy and Sympathy: The Important Difference', *Journal of Value Inquiry*, 22 (1988), 260, 265 n. 14.

58. Durgnat, *Strange Case of Alfred Hitchcock*, 181.

The Threshold of Legibility: Recognition

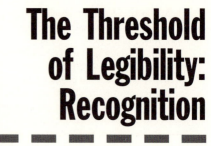

Faces and names, I wish they were the same
Faces and names only cause trouble for me
Faces and names
If we all looked the same and we all had the
    same name
I wouldn't be jealous of you or you jealous of
    me

> Lou Reed and John Cale, *Songs for Drella*

In Chapter 1, we examined the notion of the 'person schema', which, it was argued, must underlie any response to a narrative agent as a person-like, human figure. In this chapter, we will consider the manner in which this schema, in different ways and to different degrees, is instantiated and elaborated by different kinds of narrative filmmaking. The person schema, in other words, represents a conceptual structure central to human cognition in general; while recognition represents the first and most basic of a series of specifically narrative phenomena which arise from this more general structure, and which I attempt to describe in this work. I take as a norm the spectator's apprehension of an agent as *individuated* and *continuous* (or *re-identified*) and reserve the term recognition to refer to this norm. While individuation poses the question, 'What are the criteria for the numerical distinctness of persons who have the same general description?', re-identification asks: 'What are the criteria for reidentifying the same individual in different contexts, under different descriptions, or at different times?'[1] Re-identification is dependent on individuation: we cannot re-identify a character unless we have individuated her. Taken together with individuation, the re-identification of the character constitutes her recognition. A little later in the chapter I analyse the opening of Hitchcock's *The Man Who*

Knew Too Much in order to delineate how a character comes to be recognized, to be perceived as individuated and continuous. But recognition, in this sense, in fact depends upon some prior operations. Prototypically, these operations interlock, undergirding recognition; but they can be separated, and by prising them apart we reveal some stages of 'proto-recognition' which are themselves significant.

The first of these operations is already familiar to us from the work of Robin Horton, discussed in Chapter 1. Fundamental to human perception and cognition is an ability to distinguish humans from other objects and agents. This may seem painfully obvious, but it is worth restating if only to draw our attention to the way in which this very basic distinction can be aesthetically exploited. There is a startling moment in Fritz Lang's *Kriemhild's Revenge* (Part Two of *The Nibelungen*, 1924) in which our ability to discriminate human from non-human is temporarily undermined. In extreme long-shot, we see what appears to be a plain strewn with boulders and other rock formations. Suddenly, the rock formations split apart, and we realize that we are actually watching a crowd of villagers being pursued by warriors on horseback. In a similar fashion, horror films exploit the distinction between human and non-human by blurring it: at what point, in the course of David Cronenberg's *The Fly* (1986), does Seth Brundle cease to be human and become insect? The premisses of such narratives puncture our normal confidence in making such discriminations; that is one reason that they are horrific.

The warriors in *Kriemhild's Revenge* become discriminable as human agents once they move, but they remain indistinguishable from each other: we can assign each of them some basic traits (Teutonic, belligerent, masculine) placing them in a certain class of persons, but nothing allows us to discriminate one from another within this class. Such figures are hardly the peculiar possession of mythological epics, however. Indeed, they are commonplace in classical films. In this context, one critic has polemically labelled such unindividuated characters 'stick figures':

Once again [in Oliver Stone's *Born on the Fourth of July* (1989)] we are being called upon to sit through yet more post-war propaganda which works assiduously, ad nauseam, to celebrate the angst of the invader while the Vietnamese flit across the screen as stick figures of no consequence.[2]

We understand what John Pilger means by the phrase. A stick figure has a body, a face, can speak a natural language, and so forth; but it does not possess—for the spectator—a particular, recognizable body, face, or idiolect, which would serve to distinguish it from other human agents.

It is also possible to represent a human figure that does not even possess the kind of typifying trait borne by the warriors in *Kriemhild's Revenge*, or the Vietnamese extras in *Born on the Fourth of July*; a human agent endowed only with the 'abstract' features of the person schema. In written fiction, an agent may be designated using a marker free of all denotative and connotative clues with which we might classify the agent (sex, nationality, ethnicity)—something like a Robbe-Grilletan 'X'. In an iconic medium like film, however, it is very difficult to imagine such a colourless designation, one which would not provide some information about what classes of human the agent belongs to, no matter how rudimentary: androgynous/feminine/masculine; African/Asian/Caucasian/etc.; and so forth. Can a human body be filmically represented in such a way that it does not instantiate any typifying traits? Perhaps the closest we can come to such a case involves the use of focus, filters, or processing to blur the features of the figure to the point that they become unknowable. Consider, for example, the out-of-focus images of an approaching figure in Harmonica's flashbacks in Sergio Leone's *Once Upon a Time in the West* (1968). Over the course of the film, these images become more legible, until finally we discern the features of first, a man, and ultimately, Harmonica's enemy, Frank. But in what ways can we reliably classify this figure when we first see it? What does it tell us? Very little—nothing—beyond the fact that it is a human. Of course, all sorts of generic and narrative expectations allow us to reduce the infinity of possibilities; in all probability, it is a gunfighter, a whore, or a settler. But the point here is to suggest just how little a filmic image can give us in isolation: thus, I am not concerned with what the image implies or suggests in the context of narrative and genre, but with what the spectator can glean about the figure represented from such an image in and of itself. There are cases in film, then, in which an unambiguously human figure is represented which lacks not only individuating, but even any clear typifying traits.

There is a widely held assumption in contemporary theory, of Brechtian provenance, that the individuation of an agent suppresses the kind of typifying trait discussed above in relation to the stick figures in *Kriemhild's Revenge* and *Born on the Fourth of July*. From our perspective, this seems to be a rather odd claim. For if we can individuate an agent, we must be able to place the agent within some class: if an agent's body and face are legible enough to individuate the agent, we will surely be able to discern something about the age, or the sex, or the race of the figure. In order to be understood, the Brechtian argument must be placed in the context of certain cultural assumptions which equate individuality with autonomy, in the sense of a freedom from any form of social determination (the context, that is, of the *moi* culture analysed by among others Marcel Mauss (see Chapter 1)). (The Barthesian argument that proper names bestow a mysterious, soul-like individuality upon a character only makes sense in the same context; for most proper names not only designate an individual but typify that individual. John and Justin are likely to hail from very different socio-economic backgrounds.) What our examination of the stages leading up to 'recognition' reveals is that this antagonistic relationship between individuality and typicality is historically contingent, not necessary. Georg Lukács's counter-claim—that it is possible to yoke together the individual and the social in the representation of a character, and that the personal aspects of a character do not necessarily mask or displace the social dimensions—thus gains credibility.[3] Still, the cultural and historical association of individuality with autonomy, and hence with an exclusive, suppressive relationship to the social, encouraged certain filmmakers to develop strategies whereby the individuation of characters could be held in check. Dovzhenko's *Arsenal* is such a case, and we will return to this film at the end of the chapter.

Unity, Continuity, and the Body

In Chapter 1, I argued that embodiment was a central component of the person schema. We would expect, then, the perceptible, exterior traits of perform-ers—the body, the face, the voice—to play a central role in the individuation and re-identification of characters.[4] A point of clarification may be necessary here. I am treating, perhaps unconventionally, not only psychological disposi-tions but also bodily attributes as character traits. I do this for two reasons. First, although we usually assume that bodily attributes are relatively fixed, they are, like psychological dispositions, subject to change, and not merely through the process of ageing: plastic surgery or injury may, for example, intervene. Secondly—and more importantly—bodily attributes can and often do imply psychological traits: shifty eyes, an honest face.[5] (Physiognomy, of course, attempted to transform this loose and impressionistic cultural phenom-enon into a science.) Pondering a magic trick in which a peasant and an em-peror are made to switch personalities, Bernard Williams wonders what the criteria of success would be: 'The voice presumably ought to count as a bodily function; yet how would the peasant's gruff blasphemies be uttered in the emperor's cultivated tones, or the emperor's witticisms in the peasant's growl?'[6] In other words, in considering questions of identity, it is difficult to disentangle the bodily from the psychological. The traits and occurrent states of characters are available to spectators principally through performative factors: the body, the face, the voice, and the actions performed through these physical attributes. We will return to these matters in the next chapter.

Re-identification establishes the continuity, not the unity, of the character, at least not in the sense in which the term 'unity' is most frequently used in contemporary theory, to refer to an unchanging, identical core—a soul, an ego—underlying physical and dispositional changes.[7] That is, re-identification allows us to say that a certain figure is continuous with a figure apprehended at an earlier or later point in the narrative, by virtue of certain bonds of sim-ilarity and causality,[8] whether these be psychological or physical. It does not allow us to say that a character is 'unified', in the sense of being harmonious, homogenous, consistent; comprised of traits and mental states among which there is no actual or potential conflict or contradiction. The paradigm from which this sense of 'unified' derives is psychoanalysis; the human subject is said to be 'split' or 'disunified' as a result of the disjunction between the primary and secondary processes. That a human subject—or a character—can be disunified in this sense depends, however, on the continuity established by re-identification. Dora is 'split' or 'disunified' because two sets of conflicting traits and desires are instantiated by a single, bodily continuous agent. If the conflicting sets were not instantiated by *a* subject, the problem of disunity would not arise; there would simply be two subjects, rather than an internally riven, split subject.[9] A character must be continuous before we can talk not only of unity and disunity, but of 'roundness', 'flatness', and any other attributes which derive from the way in which the traits of a given character are interrelated.

The concept of continuity is open to challenge, of course. What happens to a person's identity when the two halves of their brain are separated? What happens when Madonna's brain is transplanted into Divine's body? But I am not trying to establish a watertight philosophical case, a set of irrefutable laws, for the metaphysical identity of persons. Rather, I am seeking to lay out the perceptual and cognitive norms by which we apprehend persons, and hence, in certain ways, characters. Indeed, it is only against such norms that the kinds of conundrum represented by commissurotomy (brain dissection) and brain switching hold their fascination. Such cases produce interesting cases at the periphery of our category of personhood, and bring to our attention the facets of our automatized, everyday prototype schema, but they do not change it.

Recognition in film, then, is normally dependent upon exterior, perceptible traits—the body, the face, and the voice. As we saw in Chapter 1, this assumption highlights the contrast between my theory of character and those derived from structuralist literary theory which assume that proper names are the pre-eminent textual elements ensuring character continuity: 'As soon as a Name exists (even a pronoun) to flow toward and fasten onto, the semes become predicates, inductors of truth, and the Name becomes a subject.'[10] While there is no denying that this is a norm in literary narrative, it is a norm that can be flouted, as it is by William Faulkner in *The Sound and the Fury* (1929), where two proper names designate four characters, thus forcing the reader to establish individuation and continuity by other means. In the fiction film, language (in the form of titles, dialogue and voice-over) can and often does play a role in character recognition, but I ascribe primacy to the iconic representation of the body, voice, and face as together they form the bedrock of recognition in most films,[11] as their real presence does in life. In the words of Jonathan Glover, 'To see someone is to see a body.'[12] We usually encounter persons first 'through' their bodies and are assured of re-identification when we are familiar with the body of the person.

Two questions arise here. First, how does the account that I have proposed deal with characters whose continuity does not depend on the continuity of a single performer's body—as in *Once Upon a Time in the West* in the case of Harmonica, or in any film which traces the growth of a character from childhood to adolescence by using two or more performers to represent the character at different stages of their existence? Unlike the brain–body switches, such cases can hardly be characterized as perplexing but peripheral; these are common and conventional. The answer here is that we accept the convention precisely on the grounds that each performer represents a temporally distinct part of the character's life. (Using multiple performers to represent a single character within the same temporal span is an entirely different matter, and one to which I turn below.) Moreover, we expect there to be some degree of similarity between the performers; and if little similarity obtains, we expect some causal explanation of the disjunction—plastic surgery, for example—or else we criticize the film as shoddy or implausible. (We need only add that shoddiness and implausibility may be the desired effects.) Once again, we see that continuity depends on similarity and causal dependence, not identity or unity.

The second question pertains to characters rendered solely by linguistic devices—names, pronouns, descriptions—whether in film, in the form of dialogue, voice-over and titles, or written on the page in literary narrative, or spoken by an oral storyteller. Again, such characters form a populous and quite unremarkable group in our experience of cinematic fiction, and they are the very stuff of verbal narrative. What role do bodily features play in guaranteeing the continuity of these characters? None, directly; naturally we rely on the names, pronouns, and descriptions interlocking and interreferring, if we are to construct *a* character, that is, to perceive textually dispersed devices as referring to an agent rather than several discrete agents. But to return to a point made in Chapter 1, the person schema, once evoked in relation to an agent—in the case which interests us here, by a name, pronoun, or description—brings with it the body, which becomes an imagined or inferred locus of continuity. As Amélie Rorty notes, 'Bodily continuity stands behind the assurance of personal pronouns.'[13] Persons are often referred to by several names—first, family, nickname—but their referential convergence is underwritten by a continuous body.

While it has been observed that the body individuates characters,[14] little attention has been paid to its role in providing continuity, perhaps because this undermines the structuralist argument, examined in Chapter 1, that 'individuality' (in reality) and 'character' (in representations) are no more than effects of language:

What gives the illusion that the sum [of semes] is supplemented by a precious remainder (something like *individuality*, in that, qualitative and ineffable, it may escape the vulgar bookkeeping of compositional characters) is the Proper Name, the difference completed by what is *proper* to it.[15]

My argument is not that language cannot perform the same functions (designation and prediction) in cinema as it does in literature with respect to character. Rather, it is that in film, typically we are confronted initially by an iconic rendering of the character, and in this sense recognition depends directly on the physical features of the character; and that in written fiction, and in the case of those cinematic characters generated initially or entirely by linguistic devices, those devices serve to evoke the person schema, of which a central component is the idea that a person is embodied. If the body of a character is neither seen nor described, it is still assumed.

Recognition in cinematic fiction is, then, a process in which iconic renderings of the physical features of the body, face, and voice typically play an important role, though language may contribute and interact with them. The Vietnamese extras in *Born on the Fourth of July* are not recognizable, in my sense of the term, because we can neither individuate nor re-identify them. They are discriminable individuals, in so far as we know that they are discrete agents, persistent through time. But the stick figures are not individuated in the sense that we cannot know, in any given perception of one of them, if it is a stick figure we have seen before, or simply another member of the same class. Precisely because stick figures are not individuated, they cannot be re-identified.

Elaborating Character

Beyond recognizing characters, we may discriminate degrees of complexity, fixity, stereotypicality, plausibility, artificiality, attachment, and subjective transparency among them, as we will see in subsequent analyses. E. M. Forster's distinction between 'round' and 'flat' characters represents an attempt to capture such dimensions, but collapses them into a simple opposition. Characters may be unidimensional, defined by a single trait; or they may be a composite of many traits, and hence more complex. A character may shift over the course of the narrative in terms of the number of traits which are attributed to her, or the interrelation among traits assigned to the character may change; thus characters are more or less fixed. The trait, or cluster of traits, ascribed to a given character may conform with or depart from a stereotypical person-type available within the culture as a whole, or within a tradition of fiction, to a greater or lesser degree. This will affect the degree to which we find a character plausible: in some cases and for some audiences, the mark of plausibility will be a high degree of conformity with a stereotype; in other cases and for other audiences, just the opposite will be true—the plausible character is the character that 'goes beyond' or breaks with familiar types. (Plausibility is thus not reducible to stereotypicality.) The constructed or artificial nature of characters may be stressed to different degrees, relative to their mimetic qualities; the artificiality of the major characters in *Pierrot le fou* is foregrounded to a far greater degree than it is in the case of Popeye Doyle in *The French Connection*. A film may attach us to a character to varying degrees; the narration may directly represent the actions of that character continuously, intermittently, or not at all (that is, a character may be represented only in the recountings of other characters). And a character's traits and subjective states may be more or less transparent to us. (We will return to questions of attachment and subjective access in the next chapter.) These various dimensions overlap and interlock in particular cases, but in principle none is reducible to any other one.[16]

Though I have made several basic distinctions between character types, between recognized characters and various types of unindividuated figure, and among recognized characters with respect to their complexity, fixity, stereotypicality, plausibility, artificiality, centrality, and transparency, I wish to distance myself from some character typologies which bear a superficial resemblance to my model, such as Forster's division between 'round' and 'flat' characters.[17] I believe my model could easily accommodate such distinctions. A flat character would be one that never challenges the stereotype schema it invokes on its first appearance. A round character would be one where the initial schema is subject to considerable revision. In the case of the flat character, however, there is always the potential for such a challenge to the stereotype schema as long as the text continues; and the representation of the round character relies on the same storehouse of person-types, the same process of character construction, as the flat character. Categorizing characters as 'round' or 'flat' hypostasizes a dynamic process which must be undertaken in the construction of all characters. Consequently, I do not want to expend any energy on formulating such typologies, be they dualistic or more refined; with seven variables (and there are, doubtless, others) in place of Forster's two types, we would be here a long time. There is, however, a more important reason for my suspicion of character typologies, arising from a fundamental difference in method and intent between Forster and myself. My model attempts to represent and explain the phenomenology of character construction, and the distinctions I have proposed do not represent fixed types, but rather the parameters through which character construction must take place. Construction of both 'flat' and 'round' characters, along with other types we might capture with the more refined analysis outlined above, takes place on the basis of the same contrasts: human/non-human, individuated/undifferentiated, and continuous/discontinuous.

To recap: the principal materials for the narration, in eliciting character recognition, are bodily images (face, clothing, deportment, actions performed by the character), vocal cues, and language (proper names, 'titular' names which designate social roles like 'father', pronouns, descriptions) conveyed though title, dialogue, or voice-over narration, with bodily imagery assuming a historical and pragmatic though not logical primacy. In classical Hollywood films, bodily designation and predication typically mesh unproblematically with linguistic reference and description.[18] I take this to be the prototypical recognition scenario, a process so automatic in most films that it is completely taken for granted. Once I have considered this prototypical case, in which the process occurs unhindered, I will examine several films which use various strategies to undermine recognition, to different ends. These various alternative strategies will reveal some of the ways in which this general description of recognition has, perhaps inevitably, privileged certain classical norms. If such a slant is present, the emphasis in the following analyses on alternative formal strategies should redress the balance.

The Classical Prototype: The Man Who Knew Too Much (1956)

To exemplify the prototypical recognition scenario, I want to take a closer look at the opening of *The Man Who Knew Too Much*, thus developing the analysis of the film initiated in Chapter 3. Openings have a special function in our experience of narrative, because we base our viewing strategies and expectations on the information we receive at the beginning of a text, a phenomenon known as the 'primacy effect'.[19] The film begins as follows:

1.   Long shot [LS] of orchestra. Various titles are superimposed over the image of the orchestra, beginning with those of the film's two stars, James Stewart and Doris Day, followed by the title of the film. As the last credits for supporting players and crew are superimposed, the camera begins to track in towards the orchestra, gradually centring the cymbalist. As the piece played by the orchestra progresses to its climax, the cymbalist lifts his cymbals in readiness, and moves towards the front and centre of the composition. He crashes the cymbals, then holds them against his chest, facing outward, the lower part of his face being obscured by them. The final title fades up: 'A single crash of cymbals and how it rocked the lives of an American family.'

2.   Medium shot [MS]: Day on the left of the frame, Stewart on the right, with a young boy in between them. The characters are seated on the back seat of a bus. The camera tracks back along the aisle of the bus, revealing the presence of other passengers, mostly Arab.

3.   Medium close-up [MCU], exterior of the bus. The camera tracks back along the side of the bus, revealing the words 'Casablanca–Marrakesh' painted on its side.

4.   MS, as 2, with the following dialogue:

THE BOY. Daddy, you sure I've never been to Africa before? It looks familiar.
DORIS DAY [*smiling across at Stewart*]. You saw the same scenery last summer driving to Las Vegas.
THE BOY. Oh sure. Where Daddy lost all that money at the crap—
JAMES STEWART [*mock consternation on his face, turning to a smile as Day laughs*]. Hank!
HANK. Hey look! A camel!

The first titles, superimposed over the shot of the orchestra, 'JAMES STEWART / DORIS DAY', immediately provide us with schemata which will enable us to individuate the major characters and provisionally assign traits to them: the schemata that structure our knowledge of the 'star personae' of Stewart and Day. In the case of Stewart, these traits are (something like) loyalty, impetuosity, and moral uprightness; in the case of Day, homeliness,[20] professional competence, strong-willed independence, moderated by familial devotion. Common to both personae is a commitment to traditional family values. I will refer to these initial schemata, subject to ongoing revision, as 'character models'—cultural models (see Chapter 2) of character types. These may be prompted by factors other than star personae, as we will see, but in the prototypical classical film, the star system provides an especially well-developed set of character models. As James Naremore suggests, the 'surge of recognition and pleasurable anticipation most viewers feel [in recognizing stars at the beginning of a film] constitutes the most elemental form of identification, and it has an obvious value for . . . filmmakers'.[21]

As the camera moves towards the cymbalist in shot 1, we may hypothesize that he is to become a significant character, as the gradual movement to a medium-shot and central framing individuates him. But such a hypothesis proves to be incorrect. The second shot begins by framing the two major stars in the picture, with a small boy sitting between them. Thus posed as a family, nothing in the image violates the expectations we might have formed on the basis of the star schemata invoked by the titles. The track back within the bus, and the next shot of the exterior of the bus, provide information about the world in which these characters are situated.[22] The diegesis of the narrative has to be constructed just as the characters do. The story world is much less familiar to us than they are, but the film has provided us with a familiar anchor in the form of the two stars.

In shot 4, the young boy addresses Stewart as 'Daddy', thus reinforcing the hypothesis we have made on the basis of the first shot (that the three characters constitute a family). Titular names perform an important function in establishing and clarifying the relationships obtaining between characters. A few moments later, Stewart addresses the boy as 'Hank', endowing him with a proper name. In the ensuing dialogue, more specific traits of the characters are limned.

Ben is revealed to be 'good-humoured', by his light-hearted reaction to Hank's cheeky reference to Las Vegas; but also 'careless' or 'impetuous' by virtue of the action that Hank refers to.

Impetuous? Surely not. But according to the neo-Aristotelian position advanced by Seymour Chatman, we must ascribe this or a very similar trait to Ben McKenna: 'One who commits murder or usury is (at least) murderous or usurious.'[23] This is true enough for those characters which are no more than types, entirely defined by the principle narrative function they perform; but for more complex characters, a process of sorting between persisting and occurrent, and between central and peripheral, attributes is required. Consider, for example, the case of Donnelly (James Mason) in *The Reckless Moment* (Max Ophuls, 1949), who can hardly be summed up by reference to his initial narrative function as a blackmailer, since he becomes the protector and object of desire of the woman he initially tries to blackmail.

On the basis of both textual and mimetic schemata that the individuation of the character has triggered, we will hypothesize as to which of the occurrent attributes of the character are likely to be enduring, ranging from the very likely (bodily features) to the very unlikely (say, traits implied by the behaviour of a character unwillingly injected with a narcotic). This determines which of the attributes of the character are to be taken as traits (persisting attributes). This, of course, is integral to the act of re-identification: we can only know which attributes are enduring when a character is re-identified on the basis of an attribute we have seen before. The very act of re-identification on the basis of an attribute turns it into a trait. This is the operation which constitutes the shift from simply individuating a character to apprehending the continuity of the character. Moreover, those attributes of the character which we determine to be persisting—to be traits—may be more or less central to the character. It is apparent early in the narrative of *The Reckless Moment* that, for a blackmailer, Donnelly has a bizarrely compassionate streak, but initially this trait is peripheral to the central trait of 'criminal' predicated upon him by his blackmailing actions. (Indeed, the peripheral or secondary position of the trait may result in our interpreting his apparently solicitous behaviour as indicative of a trait of 'perverseness' rather than 'kindness'.) As the narrative evolves, however, the position of these traits is reversed, such that Donnelly's tenderness becomes central rather than peripheral. Attributes which are initially treated as merely occurrent or peripheral may thus be reactivated or resituated later in the narrative. Understanding a character of any complexity involves a process of reshuffling along these lines.

As we have seen, on the basis of the very first attributes of the character made available to us, we will appeal to schemata of person-types, drawn from our store of cultural conceptions, which enable us to produce hypothetically fuller versions of the character than the text, taken as an object, actually puts before us. As Glover puts it, 'We ascribe beliefs to others in clusters, often going well beyond any evidence we could explicitly cite.'[24] It would be a mistake to follow Barthes in treating this 'filling out' of characters as the ascription of an 'ineffable' essence which guarantees the individuality of characters; the elaboration I am discussing is an activity that relies on schemata of roles and person-types. Any additional qualities ascribed in this process will, therefore, be social and interpersonal rather than idiosyncratic. These character models are then tested against further information we receive about the character. Such information may invite us to revise, and even reject, the initial schemata to which we appealed, in order to incorporate the new material. In such cases we 'accommodate' the new data. Accommodation is the process of adaptation whereby a schema develops by incorporating new experience: either the default hierarchy becomes more elaborated, or an entirely new schema is developed. Alternatively, we might categorize the new information concerning the character as merely occurrent, and thereby not allow it to affect the schemata to which we have appealed. It is even conceivable that we could fail to register certain information altogether, due to the implementation of a rigid schema in which we believe strongly (such as a stereotype). In these cases, 'assimilation' occurs, where the strength of our schematic preconceptions actually 'blinds us' to certain data. In assimilation, the existing schema overrides the recalcitrant experience by processing what it can of the sense-data and effectively 'ignoring' (not noticing) the rest. As Gombrich writes, if schemata 'have no provisions for certain kinds of information . . . it is just too bad for the information'.[25]

How, then, does this bear on the dialogue in shot 4 concerning Stewart's loss of money in Las Vegas? Do we regard Ben as 'impetuous' on the basis of this incident? Actions are an important source of the traits which we assign to characters;[26] and the loss of this money constitutes a narrative action (albeit a recounted one) performed by the narrative agent designated by Stewart's body and provisionally individuated on the basis of his star persona (both the icon and the traits associated with it) and the information conveyed by the narrative so far. Now, it is most unlikely that the spectator will construct a model of Stewart's character which includes the trait 'prone to careless gambling', or 'extremely self-centred'. Logically this is quite possible. We don't, though, because we have already constructed a character model of Stewart's character (still unnamed) on the basis of his star persona, the clothing that he and his family wears, the genial atmosphere which prevails among the three members of the family, and the very fact that they are presented as a family, stereotypically a happy institution (within traditional ideology).[27] The force of the primacy effect is evident here. Imagine the disruption our character model would suffer if Stewart, brow creased, took an angry swipe at Hank in reaction to the boy's joke. The character model based on all the preceding factors 'prejudices' us, as it were, against the new information; to be more precise, it inclines us towards categorizing Stewart's behaviour in Las Vegas as occurrent or peripheral ('un-characteristic') rather than persisting or central ('characteristic'). Furthermore, our categorization of the act as occurrent is confirmed and 'justified' by the information which follows soon after: Stewart is a doctor. Doctors, according to the default hierarchy of the schema, are often family men but rarely compulsive gamblers. The original schema is reinforced, the act of gambling seems to have no generalizable force. At most, the action results in the ascription of a peripheral trait: the character is not 'careless' but 'occasionally careless'. (To repeat, this does not mean that the narrative may not activate such peripheral traits later, and prompt us to turn them into more central, less qualified traits. To some degree, the narrative of *The Man Who Knew Too Much* does this, as we discover that Ben is selfish and domineering: he won't adapt his career to facilitate Jo's, though he easily could, and he uses his authority as both husband and doctor to force her to take drugs against her will. No social schema—and in dealing with person-types and roles we have moved well beyond the basic person schema—is so powerful that it is incapable of being revised or overthrown.)

In shots 4 to 19, the three characters first talk about the landscape they are passing through, allowing the spectator to construct a more detailed picture of the story world. Hank then wanders up the aisle of the coach and, as the bus lurches, accidently pulls off the veil of a woman in purdah. Shots 20 to 30 represent the aftermath, in which the family meet a new character, Louis Bernard:

20.	MS Stewart and the helpful stranger.	STEWART. Just what was the trouble? THE STRANGER. Your little boy accidentally pulled off his wife's veil, you know?
21.	MCU, Hank on Day's knee.	DAY [*to Hank*]. Hank! STEWART. Oh, I want to introduce my wife, Mrs McKenna. MRS MCKENNA. How do you do?
22.	As 20.	THE STRANGER. How do you do, Mme., my name is Louis Bernard.
23.	As 21.	MRS MCKENNA. We thank you very much M. Bernard.
24.	As 20.	MR MCKENNA. Our son, Hank. BERNARD. Hello Hank.
25.	As 21.	HANK. You talk Arab talk.
26.	As 20.	BERNARD. A few words.
27.	As 21.	MRS MCKENNA. Why was he so angry? It was just an accident.
28.	As 20.	BERNARD. But the Moslem religion allows for few accidents.

29. MS Hank/Mrs McKenna   MR MCKENNA. Yeah, I suppose so.
on the left of the frame,   BERNARD [*gesturing to the seat in front of Hank*].
sitting, Mr McKenna/   May I?
Louis Bernard standing   MR MCKENNA. Oh yeah, sit down, right in front
on the right.   of Jo there.
30. MCU Bernard on the   BERNARD. Oh, I thought his name was Hank.
left, Mr McKenna on   MR MCKENNA. No, that's my wife's name. You
the right, Hank and Mrs   see 'J', 'O', no 'E'.
McKenna in between.   BERNARD. How different.
   MR MCKENNA. Short for Josephine. I've called
     her that for so long nobody knows her by
     any other name, do they?
   JO. No.
   HANK. I do. Mummy.
   MR MCKENNA. Oh yeah. Forgot about that.

Over these shots, the characters we have already individuated on the basis of star personae, bodily, facial, and vocal features, behaviour and dialogue, now become named. Not only does the narration contrive an introduction so that the names of the characters can be clearly articulated, but also a momentary confusion ('I thought his name was Hank') so that (1) Hank's name can be reiterated for the third time, (2) 'Mrs McKenna's' first name can be articulated—indeed, quite literally spelt out, and (3) the relationship between the the McKennas and Hank can be underlined once again ('Mummy': they are a family). In merely prompting further clarification of character traits and interrelationships, the function of the temporary confusion of character designation is just the opposite of sustained confusions or inconsistencies, as we will see below. The opening shots, in other words, produce an emphatic cross-referencing and redundancy of visual and verbal cues, both of a designatory (names and bodies) and predicatory order (names,[28] bodies, behaviour, dialogue).

In the shots which follow, 31 to 44, we are able to fill out our model of the McKenna family still further, thanks to Louis Bernard's questions. Ben is a practising doctor from Indiana, who was stationed in Casablanca during the war. Having attended a medical conference in France, he has decided to visit Morocco once again. Again, imagine instead the following: Ben becomes uncomfortable when asked about the reason for his visit. He avoids answering the question. Perhaps he is here to smuggle drugs to the USA. As a doctor he would know a quality drug when he saw it. Perhaps we should reconsider the relevance of that night in Las Vegas. . . . My point is that a different set of responses to Louis's questions could prompt us to revise our character model, to reconceive the model so that an occurrent attribute becomes a trait, or a peripheral trait becomes more central. As it is, Ben's answers fit smoothly into the character model already posited.

Our comparative lack of knowledge of Louis is emphasized by his reticence in the face of Jo's questions, and her suspicious stare at him in shots 38 and 43. Hank's anecdote about the snails again deflects attention away from Louis and to the family. In the following scene, Jo expresses her distrust of Louis to Ben, and chides him for being so forthcoming about his own life. This, in turn, prompts her to run through an inventory of the things that Louis now knows about them, providing yet more reinforcement of the basic traits of these characters.

This next scene follows Ben and Jo as they ride through Marrakesh to their hotel. This ride is set against the background of a mass of 'stick figures': the unindividuated bodies of the Moroccans. As I suggested above, such figures constitute an important type of human figure in Hollywood films. In classical films, however, significant action (action which has causal consequence) is generally restricted to recognized characters. We will see how some Soviet films from the 1920s challenge this distribution of significant action and complicate the relationship between these two classes of human figures (recognized characters and unindividuated characters).

The distinction between individuation and reidentification allows us to describe other kinds of character that fall in between the poles of full recognition, on the one hand, and a total absence of individuation, on the other. Once again, I am not interested in producing an exhaustive typology here, because such typologies do not accurately represent the dynamics of character construction. Rather, I want to provide a couple of examples to show how the approach taken here can make precise discriminations without recourse to a typology. Consider Louis Bernard. We know very little about Louis. The little he offers about himself (born in Paris, a businessman) has to be held in suspicion because he is so secretive. Nevertheless, we are capable of re-identifying him on the basis of his bodily traits. In other words, while certain actions of a character may cause us to ascribe dispositional traits to the character in only the most tentative fashion, we are still confident of our ability to re-identify that character on the basis of her bodily traits. The designatory function of the body is more reliable in these circumstances than is its predicatory function. Similarly, the character model we construct of the Draytons—the middle-aged couple who kidnap Hank—undergoes at least three major shifts over the course of the film, each time forcing us to assign a whole new set of dispositional traits to them. Yet we are still able to re-identify them on the basis of their bodily traits. Indeed, an ability to do so is crucial to the shock of having ascribed a wholly inappropriate set of dispositional traits to them. Bodily re-identification, as I argued earlier, necessitates a degree of individuation. As we can now see, however, bodily individuation massively underdetermines overall characterization. The Draytons, re-identified via their continuous bodies, are equally plausible, given the appropriate narrative information, as a kindly old couple and a pair of merciless villains.

Retarding Recognition: The Suspended Vocation and That Obscure Object of Desire

The prototypical classical film, then, quickly makes the central characters sali-ent and legible, through framing, shot-scale, blocking, dialogue, and so forth. Most of the expectations formed at the beginning of the film with regard to these characters will be reinforced, rather than undermined. There is, of course, some latitude here: delayed and 'false' recognition, of the type exemplified by the Draytons, can be more pervasive and emphatic, as it is in certain mystery and detective films. But there are still other possibilities, beyond the purview of classical form. In *Play Time* (1967), Jacques Tati plays havoc with our (in)ability to discriminate M. Hulot from a number of lookalikes, foiling recognition for largely comic purposes; while Raul Ruiz's *The Suspended Vocation* (1977) pro-vides an extreme contrast to the fluid process of character recognition facil-itated by *The Man Who Knew Too Much*. Many of the difficulties of both *The Suspended Vocation* and Buñuel's *That Obscure Object of Desire* (1977) relate to their Surrealist pedigree (directly, in the case of Buñuel's film; indirectly, in the case of Ruiz's film, which is based upon a novel by Pierre Klossowski). To cite Surrealism as an influence or context, however, is hardly to provide an ex-planation of the difficulties of these films. In what follows, I attempt to provide an explanation for one of these difficulties, namely the play with conventions of character continuity.

Often interpreted as an allegory of political in-fighting, *The Suspended Voca-tion* is a film which defies easy synopsizing, for reasons which will emerge. A young man, Jérôme, enters the priesthood as a means of controlling what he sees as 'evil urges', exemplified by his indulgence in a ménage à trois between himself, a friend, and his wife. Once in the Church, however, he finds himself buffeted by many warring factions, each advocating their own dogmas. (Many of these dogmas abrogate our mimetic expectations of what is acceptable within the Catholic church; for example, 'marriage is a necessity in the priesthood'.) Jérôme becomes involved in an intrigue with Malagrida, an old acquaintance and avant-garde painter, who is in hiding in the same abbey that Jérôme has been placed in, and who is attempting to seduce a nun within the abbey. In the final scenes of the film, Jérôme is informed that the Church has been secular-ized (!), and he attends a Mass where other members of the clergy watch in rapture as Malagrida performs the Eucharist. Finally, Jérôme declares that he is leaving the Church, as it has failed him. (For a more detailed breakdown, see the segmentation in the Appendix.)

The complications of the story are compounded by a curious narrational device. The film opens with two, simultaneous prefaces, one in the form of a title, the other a voice-over narration. The audience is informed that this film is in fact composed of two previous films also known by the name 'The Sus-pended Vocation', one, in black and white, from 1942, the other, in colour, from 1962, neither film having been completed. The prefaces also inform us that certain actors appeared in both versions, but it is not specified which performers are common to the two films which are to be intercut. In addition, though the first paragraph is identical, there are inconsistencies between the voice-over and the written preface: for example, the written preface claims that 'the present film tries to rediscover the spirit of the earlier footage', apparently referring to the first film, while the voice-over claims that the present film attempts to combine 'the most positive elements of the first two films'. The voice-over also indicates that the two earlier films were used by opposing factions within the Church to support their opposing theses. The inconsistencies between the written and spoken prefaces suggest that the present film, rather than resolving the inter-clerical struggle, has become another battleground for the conflicting factions. (This is also suggested by some later narrative contradictions; for example, the contradiction between segments 7 and 8.) Story and narration mirror each other in this respect.

The disorienting effect of these inconsistencies is exacerbated by the fact that the inconsistencies are themselves inconsistent. If the two prefaces systematically contradicted each other, point by point, we would simply conclude that we can take neither of them at face value. The effect of a few inconsistencies thrown into two generally consistent discourses is to make the spectator question herself as much as the text: did I misperceive or misread that, or was there a discrepancy? Such a reaction is made yet more probable by the speed with which the two prefaces are presented to us, and the fact that they are presented simultaneously. There is a sense of perceptual overload, which makes us suspect that the apparent inconsistency may be in our heads rather than on the screen.

The prefaces do not leave us with firm expectations. We expect two types of footage, but we have no idea which characters will be played by the same performers in the two types of footage, and which will be played by different performers. Retrospectively, the first clue to the fact that the protagonist, Jérôme, is played by two different performers, comes in the transition between segments 2 and 3. As Jérôme (in colour, played by Pascal Bonitzer) descends the stairs, he stops his companion, with the admonition 'Regarde!' (frame 17). The next shot (in black and white) appears to be an eyeline match, of two priests descending what appears to be the next flight of steps down (frame 18). It appears to be an eyeline match because the two characters in the earlier shot are staring down the stairs and are seen from a low-angle, while in the following shot the two new priests are seen from a high-angle—as if from close to the viewpoint of the first two characters. The next shot shows the second two priests emerging from the house; we now reidentify one of them as a character we have seen earlier in the film (in the opening segment). This character repeats the admonition heard from the character in the colour footage, 'Regarde!', and accompanies it with the same gesture: raising his right hand to stop his companion (frame 19).

The identical word and gesture, together with the shift from colour to black and white footage, certainly provide clues that the two performers may represent the same character, but the apparent eyeline match and the delay in matching of gestures and speech suggest just the opposite. The delay in assigning a proper name to the performers in question increases the likelihood of our not fusing them. Jérôme (C = colour) is not addressed as such until segment 10; Jérôme (B/W = black and white, played by Didier Flamand) not until segment 18. It is not until the transition between segments 10 and 11, and that between 19 and 20, that a more unequivocal link is made between Jérôme (C) and Jérôme (B/W). In the first case, an interview continues over a transition from colour to black and white (frames 20, 21, 22). In the second, there is a (near) match on action as Jérôme is pushed by the Painter Brother. If we are to perceive the two performers as designating the same character, we need such unequivocal cues. Where there are conflicting cues, as in the transition from segment 2 to 3, we will probably not fuse the performers into a single character, as this so strongly violates our mimetic assumptions. Persons, and person-like characters, have continuous bodies. So powerful is the assumption that a person is to be identified with a continuous body, that it will override other cues to the continuity between the two performers: for example, that they share many dispositional traits.

In the last third of the film, in which Jérôme resides in an abbey, a number of performers, playing the same characters, appear in both types of footage (most importantly, La Montagne and Jérôme's Father Superior). Curiously, they appear to be more or less the same age in both types of footage, although the preface has informed us that the black and white footage was shot twenty years prior to the shooting of the colour footage. This has the effect of flattening the differences between the two types of footage, and 'reproblematizes' the fusing of the two performers as the single character Jérôme. Just as we are settling into the convention of the two performers, appearing in distinct types of footage, designating the same character, the narration destabilizes the convention by drawing the two types of footage together through the performers common to both types of footage. For example, Jérôme's Superior, played by the same actor (Raoul Guillet) in the same costume, appears in segments 33 and 35 in black and white, and segment 36 in colour. As in the example concerning the transition from segment 2 to 3, these sequences put before us simultaneous, diametrically opposed cues. We are asked to integrate the two performers under the proper name 'Jérôme', by the shift in footage-type, and by causal continuity—in one shot Jérôme (B/W) moves towards his Superior, seen in the background of the shot (frame 23); the following shot, in colour, tracks from Jérôme (C) to the Father Superior (frames 24, 25), and both figures are in roughly the same positions as in the first shot (frame 23). But the sight of the same actor (Guillet) addressing two performers (Bonitzer and Flamand) invites us to construct two characters. Anti-mimetic conventions can be learned and accepted, but Ruiz's strategy is to reinsert more mimetic assumptions into the film just at the point when the spectator is becoming accustomed to the anti-mimetic convention. The rug of the mimetic hypothesis is never pulled from under our feet; it is jerked in opposing directions. Like Buridan's ass, we are caught between the two equidistant and equally tempting carrots of mimetic assumptions and the anti-mimetic conventions established, but then undermined, by the film.

I have dealt thus far with the difficulties of recognizing the central character of the film. The surrounding context offers little comfort to the queasy viewer. The film regularly withholds from us not only the proper names of important characters, but even their titular names, making it difficult to determine their relationship to Jérôme. For example, the Spiritual Director, first seen in segment 1, is undesignated as such until segment 36, and Euthanasian Persienne, who appears in segment 29, remains unnamed and untitled until segment 36. (Contrast this with the redundancy of relational cues provided by titular names in *The Man Who Knew Too Much*.) A pervasive haziness obscures all events and characters. Are the 'zones' literal or metaphorical? How many factions are there within the Church? Who is Jérôme really allied to? What are Malagrida's motives? Who is the mysterious character who both does and does not manage

colour   17

Frames 17–19 The Suspended Vocation: deferred recognition

b/w   18

b/w   19

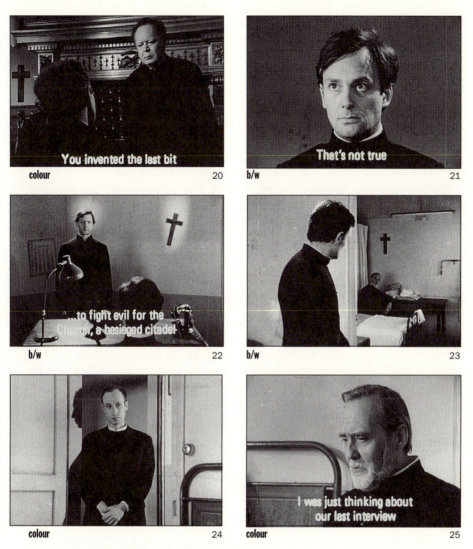

Frames 20–25 The Suspended Vocation: deferred recognition

to cross to 'the other zone' in the first third of the film? What happens to 'the rival' whom Jérôme claims to follow so closely in segment 4? The film generates a quagmire of indeterminacy, in contrast not only to the overdetermined clarity of classical films like *The Man Who Knew Too Much*, but also to the crystalline contradictions of Alain Resnais's *Last Year At Marienbad* (1961).

Nevertheless, *The Suspended Vocation* shares with Resnais's film that aggressive attitude towards character that has been a feature of a certain strand of modernist literary practice, in which 'the classical attributes of "character"—

proper name, physical and moral "nature"—have disappeared and along with them the signs that direct grammatical (pronominal) traffic'.[29] Ruiz's film does not eliminate these 'attributes', so much as scramble them, putting an interesting spin on D. H. Lawrence's metaphor of the 'allotrope' as a way of describing his attempt to break with classical characterization (an allotrope being a fixed substance which exhibits different physical properties in different conditions).[30] *The Suspended Vocation* literalizes the metaphor—Jérôme has a stable set of dispositions, but shifting physical properties—and in doing so, disrupts narrative comprehension far more than the dispositionally volatile, but nevertheless physically continuous, characters that Lawrence had in mind.

In conclusion, then, we can see that the film lacks the early and repeated meshing of proper names, titular names ('Daddy', Spiritual Director) and continuous bodies characteristic of the classical film. Both proper and titular names are withheld long after the characters have been introduced. In the absence of a secure linguistic reference point—the 'rigid designator' of a proper name—the designatory function of the body takes on an even greater burden in facilitating re-identification. But this, too, is denied. In classical films, there is a mutual reinforcement of the designatory and predicatory functions of the singular, continuous body (with the highly codified exception of duplicitous characters, like the Draytons). Ruiz's strategies shatter the coherence provided by such reinforcement, problematizing not only the recognition and construction of particular characters, but even our ability to discern how many characters exist in the story world (a process of disruption Ruiz's film shares with certain modernist novels like Faulkner's *The Sound and the Fury*). The play with character recognition in Hitchcock's film appears relatively tame. The abrupt switches in the dispositional traits assigned to villains like the Draytons in *The Man Who Knew Too Much* are made possible by the stability and continuity of the protagonists, both bodily and psychologically, and the constancy of the designatory function of the body in the case of the antagonists.

On the face of it, Luis Buñuel's *That Obscure Object of Desire* (1977) takes an even more radical step, by casting two performers in one of the central roles and providing no motivation whatsoever to explain the discontinuity: *The Suspended Vocation* at least provides the spectator with the preface. The disorientation produced by the sudden and unsignalled replacement of Carole Bouquet by Angela Molina as the character Conchita—purportedly the cause of a near-riot during a screening of the film in New York—is compounded by the flashback structure of the film. The opening scenes represent the virtual end of the story: Mathieu Fabert (Fernando Rey) leaves Sevilla having become frustrated with the continued resistance of Conchita to his desire for consummation between them. As he boards a train leaving for Madrid, Conchita, played by Bouquet, attempts to board the train. In response, Fabert douses her with a bucket of water. Soon after the train journey begins, Fabert responds to the chastising glances of his fellow passengers and reveals the background to this extraordinarily cruel act. The story is told through a series of flashbacks.

In the first flashback, we witness Fabert's first encounter with Conchita, again played by Carole Bouquet. As the first several appearances of Conchita are all performed by Bouquet, our mimetic assumption that Bouquet will continue to represent the character is reinforced. The continuity of character and performer, a strong tacit assumption at the outset, is made more emphatic by the flashback structure: we have seen Conchita close to the beginning of the fabula, and close to its end, and in both cases she is represented by the same actress. Consequently, when Angela Molina enters Fabert's bedroom as the maid Conchita, in the fifth segment of the film, the spectator is likely to be highly disoriented. We know that Fabert has asked Conchita to come to his room that evening, but when Molina enters, we are at least as likely to hypothesize that Fabert flirts with several maids, as to realize that Conchita is now being played by another performer—Fabert is, after all, the proverbial dirty old man.

The disorientation continues through the next few scenes, but eventually stabilizes. This is achieved by three formal strategies: the early and repeated use of the proper name 'Conchita', applied to both performers; the fact that the psychological traits of Conchita (memory, disposition towards Fabert) are constant; and the continuity of all the other characters around her, including her mother, her guitar-playing friend, and Fabert himself. There is none of the sustained instability characteristic of *The Suspended Vocation*. As in the latter, our mimetic assumption concerning the bodily continuity of persons is abrogated, but the anti-mimetic convention which replaces it is at least allowed to settle. There are many other inexplicable features of the world of the film: the sack that reappears (sometimes in the hands of minor characters, sometimes in the hands of Fabert) and the terrorist attacks. These are puzzling events, but they do not threaten basic narrative coherence to the degree that the 'double performer : single character' strategy does.

The double-performer strategy is, however, not just a technique designed to upset our comprehension temporarily; it also functions thematically. Offered no motivation at the levels of story, realism, or genre, the spectator reaches for what could be described as thematic motivation. The obscure object of desire is not this woman or that woman, Carole Bouquet or Angela Molina, but Woman Herself (the two actresses are very different physical types—one pale and lithe, the other dark and buxom—but they both conform to contemporary stereotypes of beauty). Mauss's terminology, discussed in Chapter 1, is useful in this context. The film asks the spectator of the *moi* culture, prone to perceiving persons first and foremost as monadic individuals, to think about sexual desire from the perspective of *personnage* culture, in which social role is emphasized over organic individuality. We are asked to see the roles under-lying our supposedly autonomous behaviour. This is reinforced by the many speeches made by Conchita where she explains to Fabert that she really cannot help her fickle behaviour: she is just doing what her socially defined role de-mands of her (for example, in the prostitution scene). *That Obscure Object of Desire* thus challenges the Western hypostasization of the organic self at both the level of comprehension and at the thematic level.

The foregoing analyses have assumed that films will utilize certain features of actual personhood, such as the individuation that the body and the face instantiate. Of course this represents a prejudice towards classical narrative style, in which the individuality of at least the major characters is established quickly and unambiguously, in large part, as we have seen, by the physical attributes of the body, the face, and the voice. The two alternatives analysed above rely on this individuation in order to confound it. In *The Suspended Vocation*, it is precisely because Pascal Bonitzer and Didier Flamand are each individuated by their bodies and faces, and look so different, that we have difficulty re-identifying Jérôme/Bonitzer as the same character as Jérôme/Flamand. There is, however, no injunction on filmmakers to make bodily in-dividuality legible, or to construct psychologically individuated characters. In-deed, there is no necessity for filmmakers to use iconic cinematographic images at all: some narrative films use nothing more than verbal language in the form of titles, such as Hollis Frampton's *Poetic Justice* (1972), in which characters are constructed much as they are in literature, through proper names, pronouns, descriptions, and the verbally described performance of narrative actions. Al-though the classical norms of live-action representation and bodily legibility are contingent in so far as they developed historically, they are still formidable norms, ones that films like *Poetic Justice* assume as a background in order to generate their novel effects.

Recognition and Distribution: Arsenal

I want to turn now to Soviet montage, a mode of filmmaking which gnaws away at the classical norms of character construction in a quite different way from *The Suspended Vocation* and *That Obscure Object of Desire* (though as we will see, the final aim has something in common with Buñuel's film). I will concen-trate here on Alexander Dovzhenko's *Arsenal* (1929), with some comments on related aspects of other Soviet montage films by V. I. Pudovkin and Friedrich Ermler. (Moreover, I will pick this thread up again in an analysis of Eisenstein's *Strike* in Chapter 6.) From the perspective of character recognition, there are two important aspects of *Arsenal*. The first concerns the relationship between narrative action, agency, and individuation; the second concerns the relation-ship between individuation, typage,[31] and the body.

Earlier I argued that in classical films significant action is restricted, on the whole, to individuated characters. Characters do not have to be major, in terms of the screen time they occupy, but if they perform an action which has causal consequences within one or more of the major lines of narrative development in the film, they will invariably be individuated. There is also a tacit 'distribution ratio' in classical films, in which, for the sake of narrative legibility and in accordance with the individualistic nature of causality in classical films, almost all significant narrative actions are performed by a restricted number of fully recognized agents, namely the major characters. The ratio of actions to agents in the classical film, then, is very high.

John Pilger's complaint about *Born on the Fourth of July* amounts to a call for a shift in which characters are individuated and given significant actions in classical films: a shift from Americans to Vietnamese. The Soviet filmmakers of the 1920s had something more fundamental in mind. Attention should be shifted to the proletariat, but such a shift involved not simply an inversion of narrative focus, but a radical change in the classical distribution ratio. Significant action is distributed across a far greater number of agents than in the classical film, and though individuated to a degree, it is the typicality of the agents that is foregrounded.

The narrative of *Arsenal* begins during World War I, and traces the history of the Ukraine in the aftermath of the War and into the Revolution. It uses many characters as vehicles for this historical narrative, centring on the struggle for the arsenal in Kiev in the last half of the film, as an emblem of the larger struggles against the counter-revolutionary forces in the Ukraine and throughout the Soviet Union. The film does feature a 'positive hero'[32] (frame 26)—an individuated, continuous character who reappears throughout the narrative—and yet this figure does not function as the pivot of the narrative structure in the way that the hero of a classical film does. The significance of the heroic individual is held in check by a number of strategies, structural and stylistic, which produce a 'mass hero'—a sense, that is, that the real protagonist of the film (and of the narrative of History, as described by Bolshevik doctrine) must be described in collective rather than individualistic terms.

The hero of the film, Timosh (Semyon Svashenko), does not appear in the first segment of the film, which lasts fifteen minutes. Within the film, Timosh's appearances are consistently framed and contextualized by an equal attention to other characters. For example, in segment 5, which depicts the ceremony celebrating Ukrainian independence, the narration concentrates on the action of the crowd before Timosh is even shown to be present. After a brief appearance, the narration cuts to the next segment. Here, Petlyura, the Ukrainian bourgeois leader, is imploring the soldiers to take up the nationalist cause. Again, it is some time before Timosh is shown to be present, and when he does appear, he makes his intervention, and the narration moves swiftly onto the

26

27

28

29

30

31

32

33

Frames 26–33 Arsenal: strategies of typification

34   35

Frames 34–35 Arsenal: strategies of typification

convention of Ukrainian landowners. A similar pattern is in evidence in all those sequences labelled (T) in the segmentation (see Appendix).

As in many of the Soviet experimental films from the 1920s, the responsibility for revolutionary action is distributed among many characters. Instead of highlighting Timosh by making him the initiator of all major revolutionary acts, many important actions are undertaken by peripheral characters. A munitions worker, who we see very briefly in segment 1, initiates the strike; and a member of the revolutionary committee, who speaks with Timosh in segment 4, commits the climactic murder of the bourgeois man in the final segment. These characters are individuated only in bodily terms, and each appears only twice in the course of the film; but they both perform actions as vital to the revolution as those undertaken by Timosh. Similarly, the climactic battle sequence of V. I. Pudovkin's *The End of St. Petersburg* (1927) (like *Arsenal*, a film commissioned to celebrate the tenth anniversary of the October Revolution) distributes significant actions among a host of 'minor' characters. The peasant protagonist plays the symbolic function of firing the signalling canon which begins the attack, but he is just one worker among many others we see in the build-up to the battle.

So far I have analysed the (re-)distribution of action among a greater number of characters than is the case in the classical paradigm. My second major point concerns the way in which such individuation as there is in *Arsenal* is held in check by various stylistic strategies. Stephen Heath has argued that, in film,

individuation is given in the very identification of agents as such. The interesting problem in film—a problem that has implications for political cinema—lies in its use of the *face*, the tendency—of which the close-up is the ultimate mode—to an 'inevitable' individuation round the *expression* of the character.[33]

Though I know of no piece of Soviet writing which poses the question as explicitly as this, such a wariness of the individualizing power of the face seems to inform Kuleshov's exhortations on the training of actors, and Eisenstein's acceptance of Lavater's theory of physiognomy for artistic purposes, a theory which he admits is nonsense as science.[34] Both were methods of controlling the potential 'psychologistic excess' of the individual face. (As with the Brechtian argument discussed earlier in the chapter, these ideas must be understood in the context of the cultural equation of individuality with autonomy.) Though Dovzhenko wrote nothing on the subject, *Arsenal* displays a remarkable range of compositional devices through which the uniqueness of the face is subordinated, if not erased entirely, such that the typical emerges with more force.

Some of these devices are quite straightforward: the use of long shots and extreme long shots, combined with lighting which either shrouds facial features in shadow or bleaches them through overexposure (frames 27, 28). (Similar techniques of 'defacement' are to be found in *The End of St. Petersburg*, dependent in the latter on framing rather than lighting or shot-scale.) An extension of this technique is silhouetting. At the beginning of the film, for example, a soldier and an officer are presented in direct confrontation in silhouette. The silhouette emphasizes their typifying, iconic traits: the round helmet and rifle of the infantryman contrasted with the cap and pistol of the officer (frame 29).

There are two further and related devices used by Dovzhenko. First, the film relates different characters through compositional and gestural similarity. The stance of the mother at the beginning of the film, for instance, is replicated by the nurse at the beginning of the scene in the makeshift hospital, two-thirds of the way through the film (frames 30, 31). The second device involves the casting of several performers each in several different roles (an inversion of the casting in the Ruiz and Buñuel movies, in which several performers play a single, central role). The nurse herself is played by the same actress who plays the Ukrainian mother in the sequence which marks the end of World War I. Ukrainian, French, and German veterans of the war return home to find their wives with illegitimate children, prompting them to ask the question (posed in the intertitles in each language): 'Who/Qui/Wer?' The same actress reappears as the Ukrainian mother near the end of the film, in a sequence parallel to the 'Who/Qui/Wer?' sequence, which cross-cuts a series of women asking questions ('Where is husband?', 'Where is son?') with symbolic vignettes of men and boys collapsing. (This technique resembles—in both form and effect—the casting strategy devised by Caryl Churchill for her play *Light Shining Over Buckinghamshire*; see Chapter 1.)

The 'Who/Qui/Wer?' sequence serves to introduce yet another related device: the national typing of each of the three couples is reinforced through iconography. The nationality of each of the soldiers is underlined by their different uniforms (frame 32), and, in the French vignette, a bust of Napoleon is visible in the background (frame 33). But at a level above the national typing, the figures are typified in class terms by the repetition of the same question in each language ('Who/Qui/Wer?'), and by the fact that all three mothers are posed and costumed so as to evoke traditional images of the Madonna with child. Perhaps the most striking example of this technique of class typification through *mise-en-scène* appears in segment 2, as the soldiers are retreating from the front. A Ukrainian soldier accuses a Russian soldier of being part of the Russian oppression the Ukrainians have suffered for three hundred years. Ironically, the two soldiers look almost identical in profile (it appears that the same actor played both soldiers) (frames 34, 35). As in the previous example, a near identity foregrounds the unity of characters, what makes them typical rather than individual: similarity in dress and identity in language in the first case, close resemblance of facial feature in the second. A similar technique is used by Friedrich Ermler in *Fragment of an Empire* (1929). In a scene representing the protagonist's traumatic memory of the Civil War, the same perfomer (Fyodor Nikitin) represents both the protagonist and a host of enemy soldiers. The sequence thus insists upon both individuality (by reminding us of the individual motivation of the flashback) and typicality (by suggesting that soldiers of opposing nations share class interests and identity).

In conclusion, then, we can see that *Arsenal* radically alters the classical pattern and ratio of distribution, in that action is spread across a great number of characters. In addition, style is used in such a way as to de-emphasize the individuality of these characters. From a completely different angle, we see once again that bodily individuation underdetermines psychological individuation, thus enabling both strategies of typification (as in the case of *Arsenal*) and strategies of misperception and reversal (as in the case of the Draytons in *The Man Who Knew Too Much*).

A rather different alteration of the classical distribution ratio may be found in such films as Oshima Nagisa's *Night and Fog in Japan* (1960), Miklós Janscó's *The Red and the White* (1967), Jean-Marie Straub and Danièle Huillet's *Not Reconciled* (1965), and R. W. Fassbinder's *The Third Generation* (1979). In such films, characters are individuated, and most significant actions are ascribed to these individuated characters, but the cast of individuated characters is so large, and the narrational patterns of the films so complex, that the spectator's ability to discern accurately which characters are which, and how they are interrelated, is attenuated, at least on a first viewing. In these films, the formal strategies of *Arsenal* are fused with those of *The Suspended Vocation*.

The final three case-studies in this chapter—*The Suspended Vocation, That Obscure Object of Desire*, and *Arsenal*—have all exploited and foregrounded the artificial nature of characters, that is, the fact that they need not be constrained by mimetic principles, to a greater degree than classical films like *The Man Who Knew Too Much*. Nevertheless, we should recall two points made earlier in this chapter. First, while the mimetic qualities of characters in classical films are stressed, spectators never lose sight of the fact that such characters are, like their modernist counterparts, artefacts. This is most obvious at those reflexive moments when a character talks about her character-type or the genre of the film, as Daisy Kenyon does in the film of the same name (see Chapter 5). But in a way, such examples divert our attention from a more fundamental point. The artificiality of character is constantly present in the representation of characters in the classical film: in the frontality of the positioning of characters, for example, the clarity of their dialogue or the seamless perfection of their skin. In other words, the artificiality of character is but one aspect of that more general awareness that we must have that we are watching a film (Chapter 2). The second point worth reiterating is that even anti-mimetic films like *The Suspended Vocation* rely upon, and indeed can taunt us with, mimetic assumptions: in this case, the assumption that a person has one discrete, continuous body. So we do not have a simple opposition between classical realism and modernist reflexivity, but a different articulation of and pattern of emphasis on the mimetic and artificial functions of character.

Ruiz pays a price, however, for the radically anti-mimetic strategies he employs, directed particularly against the process of character recognition. The profound disorientation at the level of character recognition threatens the very legibility of narrative. We may have emotions as we watch Ruiz's film—frustration, queasiness, amusement at the film's absurdities, and perhaps finally delight at having solved some of the intricate problems it poses for us—but these are not emotions directed at the characters as such. It is only when this most basic level of character engagement is secure that we are at all likely to respond emotionally to the mimetic functions of characters. Caught between mimetic and anti-mimetic conventions we are, again like Buridan's ass, starved—starved of those emotional nutrients that are the staple diet for spectators of classical films.

1. Amélie O. Rorty, 'Introduction', in Amélie Oksenberg Rorty (ed.), *The Identities of Persons* (Berkeley: University of California Press, 1976), 1–2.

2. John Pilger, 'Vietnam, Another Hollywood Fairy Story', *Manchester Weekly Guardian*, 11 Mar. 1990, 22.

3. Georg Lukács, *The Historical Novel*, trans. Hannah and Stanley Mitchell (Lincoln: University of Nebraska Press, 1983), 50. Genette, similarly, argues against the notion that individuality ('the idiosyncratic') and typicality ('the representative') are necessarily exclusive (Gérard Genette, *Narrative Discourse: An Essay in Method*, trans. Jane E. Lewin (Ithaca, NY: Cornell University Press, 1980), 184 n. 37).

4. See Bernard Williams, 'Personal Identity and Individuation', in *Problems of the Self: Philosophical Papers 1956–72* (Cambridge: Cambridge University Press, 1973), 12. The necessity for embodiment in re-identification may be grasped from the following thought experiment. How often do we say 'you seem familiar' in reference to the psychological qualities of a person we meet and seem to recognize? We might very well say to Peter, 'you remind me so much of Randy', on the basis of similar psychological traits, but we would only want to identify Peter with Randy if they also shared a number of physiological traits. As Kathleen Wilkes com-

ments: 'A mind achieves particularity, can be identified and reidentified, parasitically, only in terms of its realization and actualization' (*Real People: Personal Identity without Thought Experiments* (Oxford: Clarendon Press, 1988), 164).

5. Shlomith Rimmon-Kenan, *Narrative Fiction: Contemporary Poetics* (London: Methuen, 1983), 65; Amélie O. Rorty, 'A Literary Postscript: Characters, Persons, Selves, Individuals', in Rorty (ed.), *Identities of Persons*, 304.

6. Williams, *Problems of the Self*, 12.

7. e.g. John Frow, 'Spectacle Binding: On Character', *Poetics Today*, 7: 2 (1986), 228.

8. David Lewis, 'Survival and Identity', in Rorty (ed.), *Identities of Persons*, 17. In other words, any changes that occur between two successive states should be gradual rather than sudden, and there should be a causal relation between the first and second state. Where change is sudden, continuity may be saved by the causal connection; one aspect of the person in state (a) (say, the sudden memory of an infant trauma) may explain the rapid change resulting in state (b) (a typically non-violent man becomes a murderous maniac). In other words, particular models of personhood may function to 'unify' (provide continuity between) apparently radically dissimilar states. In this sense, in psychoanalysis the person is radically 'unified', since she contains a vast, repressed storehouse of memories which may always be appealed to in order to unify apparent discontinuity. On this point, see David Archard, *Consciousness and the Unconscious* (La Salle, Ill.: Open Court Publishing Co., 1984), 24.

9. The distinction between a criterion of 'continuity' and one of 'identity' or unity has existed since the seventeenth-century, Hume being associated with the former, Locke with the latter. The most influential contemporary argument in favour of the concept of continuity has been made by Derek Parfit, *Reasons and Persons* (Oxford: Clarendon Press, 1984); see also Rorty (ed.), *Identities of Persons*, a volume of essays, many of which comment on an earlier version of Parfit's argument.

10. Roland Barthes, *S/Z*, trans. Richard Miller (New York: Hill and Wang, 1974), 191.

11. In most classical films, the process of recognition depends more particularly on bodily and facial individuation. There are, though, many films which initiate recognition on the basis of the voice (Waldo Lydecker in Preminger's *Laura* (1944), for example); and some films sustain characters on vocal cues alone (as is the case with the characters in Chantal Akerman's *News from Home* (1976) and Patrick Keiller's *London* (1994)).

12. Jonathan Glover, *I: The Philosophy and Psychology of Personal Identity* (London: Allen Lane, 1988), 70.

13. Rorty, 'Introduction', in Rorty (ed.), *Identities of Persons*, 8.

14. Though it is not a merely metaphorical individuation, and need not be taken as masking the inscription of social traits, as both Stephen Heath and John Fiske argue, sustaining the Brechtian argument examined earlier in this chapter. See Heath, 'Film and System: Terms of Analysis', Part II, *Screen*, 16: 2 (Summer 1975), 104; and Fiske, '*Cagney and Lacey*: Reading Character Structurally and Politically', *Communication*, 9 (1987), 401.

15. Barthes, *S/Z*, 191. Cf. Jonathan Culler, *Structuralist Poetics: Structuralism, Linguistics and the Study of Literature* (London: Routledge and Kegan Paul, 1975), 235.

16. I have deliberately avoided terms like 'unity' and 'consistency', because it would be difficult to free them of the wide and imprecise meanings which attach to them. Nevertheless, in positing the seven variables, I am seeking to chart the same conceptual space that such terms as 'unity' and 'consistency' point towards.

17. E. M. Forster, *Aspects of the Novel* (London: Edward Arnold and Co., 1927).

18. I am using the terms 'designation' and 'reference', and 'description' and 'predication', respectively, as synonyms. From here on, when referring to these functions in film, I use the terms 'designation' and 'predication', because description and reference have more specifically linguistic associations (apparent especially in the term 'description').

19. David Bordwell, *Narration in the Fiction Film* (Madison: University of Wisconsin Press, 1985), 38.

20. I do not mean by this adjective 'unattractive', a sense which it carries in American English. Rather, I mean to capture the unthreatening, familiar, 'girl-next-door'-ish quality in Day's persona.

21. James Naremore, *Acting in the Cinema* (Berkeley: University of California Press, 1988), 213. On the foreshadowing of characters by the star personae of the performers who represent them, see David Bordwell, Janet Staiger, and Kristin Thompson, *The Classical Hollywood Cinema: Film Style and Mode of Production to 1960* (New York: Columbia University Press, 1985), 14–15. The effect is particularly clear in those films which delay our understanding of a character played by a star. The opening of *Possessed*, for example, withholds information which would explain Louise Howell's distracted state, but the schemata provided by the Crawford persona add up to a character model which allows us to infer and hypothesize about the history of the character.

22. The order of the exterior and interior shots here is slightly unusual: a more typical classical opening scene would begin with the exterior shot of the bus and then cut to the interior of the setting.

23. Seymour Chatman, *Story and Discourse: Narrative Structure in Fiction and Film* (Ithaca, NY: Cornell University Press, 1978), 109.

24. Glover, *I: Philosophy and Psychology of Personal Identity*, 115.

25. E. H. Gombrich, *Art and Illusion: A Study in the Psychology of Pictorial Representation* (Princeton, NJ: Princeton University Press, 1969), 73.

26. For a discussion of this pertaining to literature, see Uri Margolin, 'The Doer and the Deed: Action as a Basis for Characterization in Narrative', *Poetics Today*, 7: 2 (1986), 205–25. I examine the moral and emotional dimensions of narrative actions in Chapter 6.

27. I am not ignoring the way in which Hitchcock undermines these conventional assumptions about the family later in the movie. Rather, I am pointing to the way the same assumptions are used earlier in the film in order to contain the hints we are given concerning Ben McKenna's more selfish traits; to make, in other words, these traits peripheral rather than central at this point in the film.

28. Though I argued above that proper names can be 'hollow' in a way that bodies cannot be— as in the case of the name 'X'—proper names can, of course, provide us with information. The name 'Louis Bernard' implies that the character is French.

29. Genette, *Narrative Discourse*, 246. See also Nathalie Sarraute, 'The Age of Suspicion', in *Tropisms and the Age of Suspicion*, trans. Maria Jolas (London: John Calder, 1963).

30. D. H. Lawrence, *The Letters of D. H. Lawrence*, ed. Aldous Huxley (London: Heinemann, 1932), 197–8.

31. The notion of the type, important in the letters of Engels, the work of the Russian radical democrats of the nineteenth century, and Lukács, denotes a character whose emblematic function, as a member of a class or era, is foregrounded. See Raymond Williams, *Marxism and Literature* (Oxford: Oxford University Press, 1977), 101. The specifically Eisensteinian notion of typage includes these ideas, but also draws on a variety of other dramatic traditions, such as the *commedia dell'arte*, and emphasizes the rapidity of classification that a system of social types enables. For further comment, see the analysis of *Strike* in Chapter 6.

32. The 'positive hero' refers to the revolutionary hero totally committed to the social struggle, characteristic of socialist realist narratives. In fact, the type has its modern origin in Chernyshevsky's didactic novel, *What Is To Be Done?* (1862). See Rufus Mathewson, *The Positive Hero in Russian Literature* (New York: Columbia University Press, 1958).

33. Heath, 'Film and System: Terms of Analysis', Part II, 104. I differ from Heath here, in that a stick figure may be perceived as an agent without being sufficiently individuated to be re-identified; thus, I do not agree that 'individuation is given in the very identification of agents as such'. Recognized characters—those which are individuated and continuous—are the norm for classical filmmaking, but as discussed at the beginning of this chapter, the medium allows several stages of 'proto-recognition', before an agent is individuated. At the most, one might

argue that there is a tendency towards such individuation in the medium of film which does present a problem for overtly anti-individualistic political doctrines. The value of Heath's remark is the way it makes explicit beliefs which were implicit in the doctrines and practice of certain Soviet filmmakers in the 1920s.

34. And, more generally, Eisenstein's interest in the use of masks in Asian theatre. Eisenstein discusses Lavater's physiognomy in 'Film Form: New Problems', in Sergei Eisenstein, *Film Form and the Film Sense*, trans. Jay Leyda (New York: Meridian Books, 1957). Kuleshov's remarks on the face and its relation to psychological acting can be found in 'The Art of the Cinema', in Lev Kuleshov, *Kuleshov on Film*, trans. Ron Levaco (Berkeley: University of California Press, 1974), 93. See Chapter 6 for a consideration of this issue with respect to allegiance.

Screens and Filters: Alignment

[As] Mildred waits in the Los Angeles 'Hall of Justice' for interrogation, it is with her that the audience is forced to identify. Her nerve-racked state is conveyed by increasingly amplified sounds: a ticking clock, ominously echoing voices, off-key whistling, a rustled newspaper, and finally an intercom buzzer exploding like a gunshot . . .

John Davis[1]

In the last chapter, I discussed the fact that our recognition and construction of certain characters, like Louis Bernard and the Draytons, is peculiarly tentative. The overturning of the first substantive characterization of the Draytons (as an affable English couple) would be more shocking if we did not receive the initial information about them in such a clearly marked, highly mediated fashion, which leads us to make only a provisional construction. What is the nature of this mediation? I refer here to the way in which the narration of a film may 'guide our perception by linking it to the perceptions of certain of the characters'.[2] The narration, I will argue, may place the spectator in an alignment with a certain character or characters. Structures of alignment are produced by two, interlocking character functions, cognate with narrational range and depth: *spatio-temporal attachment* and *subjective access*. By attachment, I refer to the way a narration may follow the spatio-temporal path of a particular character throughout the narrative, or divide its attention among many characters each tracing distinct spatio-temporal paths. In this way, attachment may be more or less exclusive. By subjective access, I refer to the way the narration may vary the degree to which the spectator is given access to the subjectivities—the dispositions and occurrent states—of characters. Within a given narrative, this may vary from character to character, ranging, in each case, from subjective transparency to opacity. One way of grasping the distinction between the two functions is to relate them to the notions of agent and subject respectively. Attachment is that function of narration which renders characters as agents, entities that act and behave; subjective access is the function that represents characters as entities that desire, believe, feel, think, and so forth.

No particular degree of subjective access is entailed by attachment to a character.[3] There is a historical association, in the classical film, between attachment and subjective transparency: if we follow the actions of a character, we normally know a good deal about what she is up to, in terms of her desires, motives, and feelings. But this is a contingent association. Alfred Hitchcock's *Stage Fright* (1950), the same director's *Psycho* (1960), and Michael Anderson's *Chase a Crooked Shadow* (1958) all attach us to subjectively opaque characters, as a result of which we are led to misjudge the characters played by Richard Todd, Anthony Perkins, and Anne Baxter, either within a substantial but limited proportion of the film, or across its entirety. Alignment, as a level of engagement, refers to the entire range of possible articulations of spatio-temporal attachment and subjective access.

Let us look more closely at the examples from *The Man Who Knew Too Much*. The McKennas meet Louis Bernard on the bus to Marrakesh. Jo asks him a number of questions, but he is curiously reticent and unforthcoming about his background and occupation. On the way to the hotel, Jo reveals her suspicions about Louis to Ben, and he is unable to counter them with anything other then dismissals. No alternative explanation for Louis Bernard's guarded behaviour is offered. (And at this point, we have no reason to think that Jo may be prone to paranoid judgements.) The McKennas first encounter the Draytons as they arrive at the hotel. Jo believes that the Draytons are behaving in an impolite, if not hostile manner by staring rather obviously at them. The narration supports Jo's opinion by ending the scene with a medium close-up of the Draytons, grim-faced, looking off-screen towards the Mckennas. In both cases, we are inclined to accept Jo's judgements of the new characters. The narration exclusively attaches us to the McKennas, so that there is no possibility of countervailing evidence, of narrative information about Louis or the Draytons conveyed to the spectator without the mediation of the McKennas. Ben McKenna offers no alternative explanation for the behaviour of Louis and the Draytons, and so within the 'alignment unit' formed by the McKennas, Jo's opinion dominates. The narration also differentiates the degree of subjective access we have to the characters: the McKennas, as we have seen, are far more expressive about their backgrounds and dispositions than Louis Bernard, and our lack of access to the Draytons is overtly marked by the rapid fade on the shot in which they stare at the McKennas. We do not even have access to what they might have whispered to each other ('isn't that Jo—, the singing star?').

Another process is at work here, which also contributes to the tentativeness with which we construct Louis Bernard and the Draytons. The McKennas are likeable, by the norms of bourgeois Western society, and the spectator may share many of their values. Our sympathy for the McKennas inclines us to accept their judgements. If we knew about Jo's depression and paranoia— character traits which become apparent later in the narrative—we might be more inclined to doubt her perceptions and judgements. But we should not confuse this mode of engagement, *allegiance*, with alignment. As I argued in Chapter 3, alignment and allegiance are quite distinct phenomena, though they do interact. For this reason, they have almost universally been conflated under single terms like 'identification' or 'point of view'. But we get more purchase on the nature of this interaction by distinguishing the two modes of engagement. In this chapter, then, we will restrict our attention to alignment, occasionally assuming the effects of allegiance, and turn more squarely to allegiance in the next chapter.

Recognition is a prerequisite for alignment. Our narrative experience cannot be said to have been filtered through a particular character's perspective until we have at least individuated that character. Once a character has been recognized, and we have been placed in some form of alignment with that character, however—in the above example, the McKennas—the recognition of any new character may be subject to the effect of mediation produced by the alignment. Thus, alignment may affect subsequent recognitions. In the case of *The Man Who Knew Too Much*, the effect is to force a suspension of the primacy effect: we do not assume that the first information we receive about Louis Bernard or the Draytons is accurate or reliable.[4]

It is crucial that we grasp here both the distinctness of attachment and subjective access as functions—it clouds matters to reduce them to a singular 'narrative point of view' or 'focalization'—and the fact that they interlock to produce a pattern or structure of alignment. Our suspicions concerning Louis Bernard and the Draytons arise not simply because we have access to the McKennas' thoughts about them (that is, because the McKennas are subjectively transparent), but also because the narration attaches us to the McKennas alone: we do not follow the Draytons or Louis Bernard outside of their interactions with the McKennas. Subjective access alone cannot account for the filtering effect: it must be combined with a complementary limitation with respect to other characters.[5]

We must also be careful not to confuse this 'filtering' effect, produced by a particular orchestration of attachment and subjective access, with the phenomenon of alignment more generally: the broad range of alignment structures generated by the various articulations of attachment and subjective access. In its purest form, the alignment pattern which produces this filtering involves a continuous and exclusive attachment to a character combined with subjective transparency: complete access to what that character knows, thinks, feels, and perceives. (The pragmatic measure of 'complete' subjective access is that we are given access to all significant thoughts or perceptions as the character experiences them; no perception which has significance is revealed retroactively.) Examples of such a 'pure' adherence to this pattern are in fact rare. The detective film might seem to fit the bill, but it is conventional that at certain points in the course of the narrative we know either a little less or a little more than the detective. This is the case even with Robert Montgomery's notorious *Lady in the Lake* (1946), in which virtually the entire film is represented from the detective's POV. If there is a generic type of film narrative that conforms to the pattern, it is rather the 'female gothic', in which we are aligned with a female protagonist who suspects that her husband intends to kill or harm her in some way.[6] Hitchcock's *Suspicion* (1941) and Roman Polanski's *Rosemary's Baby* (1968), for example, both develop exclusive and intimate structures of alignment.[7] In both cases, it is crucial that the spectator is aligned with the protagonist in this fashion, so that we can be as suspicious of the husband as she is: is Johnnie Aysgarth (Cary Grant) a well-meaning if irresponsible and shallow husband— or is he a con man, who sadistically uses these charms to break down his wife and drive her to suicide? The hesitation between these interpretations is crucial to the effect of the film, and played out in miniature in many scenes. In one such scene, Johnnie reveals to Lina (Joan Fontaine)—after he has allowed her (playfully? sadistically?) to believe otherwise—that he has bought back the family chairs which she had believed he had casually sold in order to finance his gambling. The fact that there may be some doubt at the end of the film as to Johnnie's character—in spite of the apparent resolution—is also a consequence of the alignment structure: since the film attaches us to Lina to the very end, the crucial information regarding Johnnie and the poison, and his whereabouts during Beaky's death in Paris, is only reported to Lina by him. On previous occasions, his verbal accounts of himself have been shown to be unreliable.

For all its interest, and the way in which it tends to foreground alignment as a particular level of engagement, the 'filtering' pattern remains but one pattern of alignment, and an unusual one at that. In what follows, therefore, I shall be concerned with how variations in the articulation of attachment and subjective access within scenes and over the course of entire films result in various alignment patterns. However, as in the case of character recognition, my concern is not to produce an exhaustive taxonomy, but to examine the schematic prototypes underlying this level of character engagement.

Alignment is closely related to the concepts of 'point of view' and 'focalization' in literary theory.[8] First propounded and elaborated by Gérard Genette, the term 'focalization' designates one of the two forms of 'that regulation of narrative information' which, for Genette, constitutes the 'mood' of narrative:

The narrative can . . . choose to regulate the information it delivers, not with a sort of even screening, but according to the capacities of knowledge of one or another participant in the story (a character or group of characters), with the narrative adopting or seeming to adopt what we ordinarily call the participant's 'vision' or 'point of view'.[9]

Although I will make occasional reference to this body of thought within literary theory, the model of narration described in Chapter 3 enables the analysis of alignment without recourse to more specifically literary models of narrative analysis.[10] Over the next three sections, I consider the roles of both attachment and subjective access, and the ways in which filmmakers use cinematic technique in order to produce structures of alignment. As in the last chapter, I will analyse both classical prototypes and alternative practices. I also consider some perennial problems, pertinent to alignment, raised by prior theories of 'identification', such as the nature of character 'interiority' in various types of narrative, and the role of particular techniques, such as performance style and optical point of view (POV), in our apprehension of character psychology. Too often, such devices become essentialized, associated with a fixed meaning or effect, regardless of context. Although I too discuss these stylistic techniques at length, I want to stress the variety of functions they may perform within structures of alignment.

Spatio-Temporal Attachment

A film like *Suspicion* exclusively attaches us to its protagonist; we follow her actions throughout the film, and witness the actions of other characters only when they are within proximity to her. By contrast, Douglas Sirk's *Written on the Wind* (1956) and—to take a more extreme example—Miklós Jansco's *The Red and the White* (1967) involve multiple attachments, in that in each case the narration successively traces the distinct spatio-temporal paths of many different characters. (Sirk's melodrama attaches us to three characters, while Jansco's film—which depicts a group of Hungarian volunteers fighting against the White Guard in 1919—attaches us to dozens of characters over its course, both as individual agents and as members of groups.) The two types of films represent the extremes within which all narrative films must move with respect to attachment; and most of them will carve out a pattern of attachment somewhere in between the two extremes.[11]

A narration establishing a pattern of multiple attachment will typically represent the distinct lines of action successively, by cutting from one spatio-temporal location, represented visually and aurally with synchronous sound, to another, represented in the same fashion. Certain techniques have been favoured historically for certain patterns of attachment: cross-cutting for a temporally concentrated sequence involving attachment to several spatially separate characters, for example. But other variations are possible, both in the use of technique, and in the nature of the attachment produced. One line of action, attaching us to a character in the normal iconic fashion, might alternate with another line in which a different character's actions are represented by a non-character voice-over narration, or by a series of expository intertitles. Different techniques may be used to produce innovative as well as conventional patterns of attachment. By virtue of certain technical possibilities, a film can generate not only a multiple and successive pattern of attachment, as a literary narrative might, but in addition a structure of multiple and simultaneous attachment. This can be accomplished by attaching us to one character on the sound-track, and one on the image track, as Godard does at certain moments in *Sauve qui peut (la vie)* (1980). A split-screen device can be used to the same end. At the beginning of Stephen Frears's *The Grifters* (1990), for example, a split screen attaches us to the three major characters simultaneously. Similarly, Frears's *Sammy and Rosie Get Laid* (1987) simultaneously attaches us to three lines of action at its climactic moment, again by using a split screen. Zbigniew Rybczyński's *New Book* (1975) takes the technique further, by splitting the screen into nine distinct spaces, each representing the action in a different part of a city at the same moment, through which several characters and objects move and reappear (frame 36).[12]

The purest form of exclusive attachment is produced by a narration which intercuts only two kinds of shot: shots of a character, and eyeline match shots representing the objects of that character's attention. Now a narration which never strayed from a character and the objects of her attention would be rare indeed. Nevertheless, with the complications noted in Chapter 3, the first movement of *The Man Who Knew Too Much* does, by and large, articulate such a pattern of attachment. In the second movement, not only does the narration splinter the previously exclusive attachment to the McKennas on a scene by scene basis; it also disperses the attachment within certain scenes involving the McKennas, that is, on a shot-by-shot basis. The organization of attachment at this fine-grained or shot-by-shot level affects what I labelled the 'texture' of narration in Chapter 3.

One of the clearest cases exemplifying a shift in the texture of the narration in *The Man Who Knew Too Much* involves Ben McKenna's visit to Ambrose Chappell, the taxidermist. Louis Bernard utters the words 'Ambrose Chappell' as he dies, and Ben interprets this as a proper name, not the name of a House of God, as it turns out to be. In many ways, the sequence inverts the murder sequence from the first movement. Rather than attaching us to Ben McKenna ever more narrowly, the narration begins by attaching us to McKenna exclusively, but progressively intersperses the sequence with shots which neither represent him nor the objects of his attention. The exclusive alignment with Ben, marked by POV shots and subjectively distorted sound as he approaches

Frame 36 New Book: multiple, simultaneous alignment

the taxidermist's shop, carries with it all the associations of the first movement of the film (frames 37, 38). Aligned and allied with Ben outside the shop, Ambrose Chappell Jnr. (Richard Wordsworth) seems very suspicious as he walks past Ben. The portentous atmosphere is further charged by Chappell Jnr.'s lugubrious expression, foreboding music, and a canted framing (frame 39). On entering the shop, however, the shots are composed in such a way that comically grotesque stuffed animals interpose themselves between the spectator and the characters (frames 40, 41, 42). The scene culminates in an utterly farcical struggle, involving Ambrose Chappell Snr. embracing a giant stuffed swordfish while another employee shimmies back and forth with a semi-stuffed leopard (frame 43). The displacement of McKenna in the shot-by-shot pattern of attachment occurs in these shots by virtue of compositions which foreground the stuffed objects which are not the objects of his attention. The displacement is sealed by the final shot in the sequence, of a stuffed, roaring lion's head mounted on a wall, which cannot be motivated through character attention (frame 44). The narration clearly works to undermine the intensity of our sympathetic engagement with Ben McKenna here; not by asking us to re-evaluate him, but by dividing our attention through a splintered pattern of attachment on both the global (scene-by-scene) and local (shot-by-shot) levels.

37 38

39 40

41 42

43 44

Frames 37–44 The Man Who Knew Too Much: Ben McKenna encounters Ambrose Chappell, taxidermist

Subjective Access

Once a narration attaches us to a character, it may stipulate the degree of access we have to the subjectivity of the character. But can we assume that all characters in all films have an inner life to the same degree and in the same sense? The structuralist tradition is right to insist that we cannot, although positing subjective access as a variable function in narrative should help us to move beyond this denial, towards a discrimination of the possible types of character subjectivity. Clearly, most films develop the inner lives of the major characters more fully than those of incidental characters; indeed, a complex, developed psychology is an important criterion by which we judge which characters will count as major ones in classical films.[13] Significantly, though, we may assume that minor characters, and even the unindividuated figures who populate the background, have the same potential for an inner life as the major characters; the narration is simply more interested in Hamlet than in Rosenkrantz and Guildenstern—in *Hamlet*. From a broader perspective, Mauss's anthropology of personhood, discussed in Chapter 1, warns us against assuming the universality of our contemporary notion of individuality, central to which is the notion of a private and unique psychological existence, at the same time that it suggests there is a more limited cross-cultural concept of 'the person'. But it is difficult to find major characters who do not have subjectivity in some sense. Such subjectivity may be more or less complex, transparent, and more or less foregrounded in the film, but it is rarely altogether absent.

The narration of a film will typically vary the degree of subjective access we have with respect to the character across time: there is no general requirement that a uniform degree of access be maintained throughout the text. The nature of these variations will depend upon generic conventions as well as the compositional needs of the particular text. As with attachment, the narration may represent the subjectivities of different characters both successively and (less commonly) simultaneously. Moreover, a kind of multiple or intersubjective access is possible, where a sequence in a film seems to represent not the subjectivity of an individual character, but a shared mental state or commingling of the states of different characters. Portions of the voice-over in Jean-Luc Godard's *Pierrot le fou* (1965), for example, mix the speech of Anna Karina and Jean-Paul Belmondo, suggesting an intersubjective state shared by the two characters they represent. Sam Peckinpah's *The Wild Bunch* (1969) suggests that a particular memory is shared by two characters, as the movement into the flashback is motivated through one character, while the movement out of the flashback is motivated through a different character. This second example involves not only the creation of 'intersubjective access', but also effects a shift in attachment from within a subjective sequence. This unusual narrational trope is also used in Friedrich Ermler's *Fragment of an Empire* (1929), in a flashback sequence in which the motivation shifts from Fillimonov, the protagonist, to the young soldier who rescues him, the shift beginning within the flashback itself (rather than in the framing action).

Of all the techniques which contribute to character subjectivity, performance style has had the least attention paid to it. This is a curious omission, given the centrality of performance to the construction of character in most narrative filmmaking, but an understandable one, in so far as few historical studies of performance have been undertaken, which theoretical studies like the present one could draw upon.[14] Acting style underwent a major shift during the first decade of the century, as facial expression displaced bodily gesture and attitude as the principal means by which emotions and other mental states were communicated, contemporaneous with the development of closer framings and shifts in narrative form.[15] However, aspects of the highly codified system of gestures persisted well into the 1920s, and contemporary Hollywood acting may be seen as a composite of such systems and the more 'naturalistic' styles developed since the turn of the century. While a stylistic history of performance is needed, it seems clear that the function of performance has remained constant in classical cinema: the revelation of the interior states of characters. As Noël Carroll has commented, 'The movie world is emotionally perspicuous through and through.'[16] This does not entail the impossibility of either false or opaque subjectivity within the classical cinema—indeed, it is integral to the mystery film and many suspense films (consider Phyllis in Billy Wilder's *Double Indemnity* (1944) or Lydecker in Otto Preminger's *Laura* (1944) (false subjectivity), and Louis Bernard in *The Man Who Knew Too Much* (opaque subjectivity)). In the case of false subjectivity, performance invites a construction of a character's psyche which is inaccurate; in the case of opaque subjectivity, performance does not allow us to form any clear picture of the character's motives and intentions. In neither case, however, is subjectivity itself put into question so much as the reliability of external and behavioural cues in constructing a character's psychology (both for other characters and for the spectator). Above all, in classical cinema, the narrative destination is always subjective revelation: false and opaque subjectivities are corrected by or exposed in the act of narrative closure. We will examine in greater detail a complex example of such a trajectory in Preminger's *Daisy Kenyon* (1947). In the work of Bresson, as we will see below, a radically different performance style both signals and produces a function different from the revelatory function of performance in classical filmmaking.

Music too is particularly important in conveying information about the inner states of characters, but as with performance this function of the film score has received little systematic attention. Claudia Gorbman has analysed the use of extradiegetic music to reveal and underline information about a character's mental state in the classical film:

The classical film may deploy music to create or emphasize a particular character's subjectivity. Several devices cue the spectator: the association of the music with the sight of the character in a shot, a thematic association repeated and solidified during the course of the narrative, orchestration of music that was previously sung by or to the character, and the marked addition of reverberation for suggesting strongly subjective experiences.[17]

Gorbman analyses an example from John Cromwell's *Of Human Bondage* (1934). A waltz motif, orginally played diegetically in a restaurant where the hero and heroine are dining, is later 'picked up' by the score and comes to signify the hero's romantic thoughts about the heroine (the motif does not accompany scenes in which the heroine is actually present). Film scores may interlock with the dramatic structure and the states of characters in other ways. For example, when a dramatic shock (say, the shocking revelation of a new piece of information to a character) is musically emphasized by a 'stinger'—an abrupt change in the volume or rhythm of the score—the musical and characterological structures are closely linked. In addition, Romantic orchestration—of the type made so familiar by Max Steiner in films like Michael Curtiz's *Mildred Pierce* (1945), Irving Rapper's *Now, Voyager* (1942), and Jean Negulesco's *Humoresque* (1946)— sets the affect-laden mood of the classical Hollywood woman's picture. Once again, though, the score is imbricated with specified, emotional states experienced by characters.

Godard's *Contempt* (1963) provides a striking contrast to these conventional relations between the score and character subjectivity. The film's score is Romantic in character, but the music is cut loose from any secure mooring in the character structure of the narrative. As with many of Godard's early movies, the story itself is fairly conventional material. On one level, *Contempt* is the story of a love triangle between a screenwriter (Michel Piccoli), his wife (Brigitte Bardot), and a producer (Jack Palance). However, the underdetermination of the characters' motivations and intentions results in a disjunction between the score and the narrative. Instead of hooking up with the narrative and characters through the association of musical motifs with characters and their subjective states, through stingers and 'mickey-mousing', the minor key music washes over the narrative in an almost aleatory fashion. The music, like the fragmented voice-overs, relates to the elliptical and self-conscious structure of characterization in the film which makes character subjectivity obscure and diffuse.

Structures of Alignment

By marking out a pattern of attachment and by controlling the degree of subjective access we have to the characters, cinematic narration produces a distribution of knowledge among characters and the spectator, which results in a certain structure or pattern of alignment. Needless to say, the possible articulations of the two functions are potentially infinite. There are, nevertheless, certain paradigmatic structures of alignment which are linked with familiar genres. Individual films which utilize these structures invariably put some idiosyncratic spin on them; but the general patterns are nevertheless recurrent.

The first of these relates to what David Bordwell has labelled 'detective narration'.[18] Bordwell derives this name from the classical detective film, in which the range of the narration is tightly restricted to the knowledge of the investigating character, although the pattern is not by any means limited to detective dramas. In our terms, the spectator is aligned with the protagonist in terms of the knowledge to which she has access: we are exclusively attached to the protagonist, and we have access to most of what she is thinking and feeling. In *Rosemary's Baby*, for example, the narration is carefully organized so that we know as much, but only as much, as Rosemary does about the real activities surrounding her traumatic pregnancy. (Although Polanski's film makes considerable use of POV shots, detective narration does not entail optical alignment, as we will see below.) This results in the 'filtering' alignment structure discussed at the beginning of the chapter: the spectator is aligned exclusively and completely with the protagonist. But most films manifesting 'detective narration' will break from this alignment pattern, briefly and intermittently, in two ways. First, the pattern of attachment will shift our attention away from the protagonist, thus giving us more information than the protagonist is party to. Secondly, the narration will modulate the degree of subjective access we have to the protagonist, so that we will not always know exactly what she is thinking. The spectator is thus placed either one step ahead or one step behind the protagonist.[19] As we noted before, the 'filtering' alignment structure, in the pure form exemplified by *Rosemary's Baby* and *Suspicion*, is comparatively rare.

'Melodramatic narration', by contrast, is characterized by multiple attachment and a high degree of subjective transparency across the various characters. In a melodramatic alignment structure, the spectator knows more than any individual character does.[20] Thus we watch for character reaction as much as for narrative progression. Bordwell points out that melodramatic narration is aptly designed for the production of irony and pathos, emotions perhaps equally present in the cross-cut sequence in *Written on the Wind* in which the death of Jasper Hadley is juxtaposed with the oblivious, salacious dancing of his daughter Marylee. The full pathos and irony of the juxtaposition is only apparent to the spectator, as only the spectator is aware of both events. Such narration is related to a broader dramatic and cultural tradition related to stage melodrama, and this obviously motivates Bordwell's choice of name. For reasons discussed below, however, I prefer to call this the 'expressive tradition'.

Although we may view these two structures of alignment in their 'pure' forms as the limits within which classical films operate, few films will adhere strictly to either the detective or melodramatic alignment structure. Most instead will tend towards one or the other form, while interweaving segments which are organized according to the other structure: 'In general, narrative films are constantly modulating the range and depth of the narration's knowledge.'[21] We have already suggested how the detective film usually injects moments of subjective opacity, or breaks the pattern of exclusive attachment. Irving Rapper's *Deception* (1946) illustrates parallel modulations in a film based upon the 'melodramatic' or expressive alignment structure. The film is concerned with a love triangle between a cellist (Karel), his wife (Christine), and a composer (Hollenius) who employs Karel to perform a new piece and who has in the past employed Christine as his mistress. Across the film as a whole, the narration attaches us to Christine, in that (with one exception) we are spatially attached to her throughout the film; but within scenes, the narration sometimes attaches us to other characters, so that we are party to information that Christine is not. Character subjectivity is generally transparent; the characters wear their hearts on their sleeves. But while the alignment structure is basically melodramatic, for certain stretches and within a subordinate line of action the narration reverts to a detective structure of alignment. For example, the beginning of the film—discussed in Chapter 3—does not conform to the melodramatic convention of a rapid and concentrated exposition, in which character subjectivity is established by character expressivity. In the context of the melodramatic structure of alignment, those few minutes constitute a striking delay: the sequence tells us virtually nothing about the characters. We will examine another 'intrusion' of the detective alignment structure into the film below.

Now, we have established that Christine is present in every segment bar one, and in this sense the narration attaches us to her. The structure of alignment thus places the spectator at the top of a 'hierarchy of knowledge', along with Christine:[22]

Christine   spectator
Hollenius
Karel

Within individual scenes, however, the narration does not attach us to Christine, but moves freely among characters within the general space defined by her movements, but not always within her perceptual purview. As in the encounter at the Ambrose Chappell workshop in *The Man Who Knew Too Much*, a shift in narrational texture occurs. In both cases, while the narration sustains an established pattern of attachment around a particular character from scene to scene, on a shot by shot level the narration is far less exclusive. As a consequence, the hierarchy of knowledge is shuffled. In *The Man Who Knew Too Much*, we realize before Ben McKenna does that he has made a mistake, because the narration undermines the initially menacing quality of the work-shop by drawing our attention, in an ironic fashion, to the stuffed animals which are peripheral to his attention. The reordering of the hierarchy of know-ledge in *Deception* also produces an ironic, though less comic, effect. In the scene in which Christine and Karel are married, the hierarchy among the characters is inverted, while the spectator remains more knowledgeable than any of them. Out of Christine's earshot, Hollenius tells Karel that in spite of his encourage-ment, Christine has never taught. This directly contradicts what Christine has told Karel: she is financially comfortable because she has taught rich students. After the party has broken up the narration has established, at the local or textural level, a detective alignment structure, in which we are aligned with Karel rather than Christine. The hierarchy *within the sequence* inverts the norm the film has established:

$$\text{Karel} \qquad \text{spectator}$$
$$\text{Hollenius}$$
$$\text{Christine}$$

In the aftermath of the party, we speculate about the way in which Karel will tell Christine about his conversation with Hollenius, and the way Christine will react to and handle this revelation (by virtue of our alignment with Christine on a scene by scene basis, we know that she is financially comfortable as a result of Hollenius's patronage). Hence, although the alignment pattern under-goes modification and the hierarchy of knowledge among the characters is inverted, the spectator remains at the top, and the distinctive form of and spectatorial attitude invited by the melodramatic alignment structure is sustained. But the film is typically classical in the way that this dominant structure of alignment is established and then varied within more local sequences.

If such variation in the pattern of alignment occurs only once, the narration generates what Genette calls an 'alteration', or temporary violation of the align-ment structure (in his terms, 'focalization code') that the text has established: 'a momentary infraction of the code which governs that context without thereby calling into question the existence of the code'.[23] For example, throughout most of Hitchcock's *Vertigo* (1958), we are not made party to the actions of Madeline/Judy outside of Scottie's presence, and we only have access to her inner states via external cues. Both norms are violated on a single occasion: the moment when, attached to Judy outside of Scottie's presence, we are given access to Judy's thoughts (in the form of a visualized flashback with voice-over), and discover the truth about Madeline, her double. Genette calls this a *paralepsis*: we are given more information than the code allows. The opposite situation, in which we are given less information than the code requires, Genette terms a *paralipsis*.

The importance of the notion of alteration is that it cautions the critic from too hastily celebrating a film as subversive. Alterations themselves are subject to normative patterns. As we have seen, where a film adopts a particular pattern of alignment as an underlying norm, be it that associated with the detective film or the melodrama, it will usually modify that pattern at the local level at some point, or subject it to some gradual evolution. Wim Wenders' *The Wings of Desire* (1987), for example, shifts from a pattern of multiple attachment to one of exclusive attachment, as the protagonist surrenders his angelic capacities. We will examine further examples of evolving alignment patterns in *Daisy Kenyon* and Bresson's *L'Argent* (1983). Such evolutions or temporary infractions are indeed the norm; the film which adheres without wavering to a particular structure of alignment established at its beginning is the true exception.[24]

The Place of POV

A further issue pertaining to alignment which deserves special attention concerns the status and function of point-of-view (POV) shots. Optical POV shots have always held a privileged place in discussions of 'identification' in film, perhaps because they are among the most obviously mediated of shots in cinema. To see (or hear) as a character does is to be in the place of that character, so the argument goes, and that is as close to identification as one may come. Close perceptual alignment makes us an 'accomplice' and not merely a 'witness' of a character's actions.[25] 'The audience must identify with Sarah,' claims an essay on *The Accused*, 'because the angle from which we see Dan's face is the one from which she must be seeing it.'[26] POV shots are thought to represent, synechdochically, the entire mind of the character—an assumption that I am tempted to call the 'fallacy of POV'. There is, moreover, a congruence and mutual reinforcement between the ideas that (1) in watching a film we lose consciousness of the fact that it is a film (the 'illusion' account of cinematic representation, examined in Part I), and that (2) a POV shot 'wires' us directly into the mind of a character. If we are brought to believe that we are 'in' the world of the fiction in general, then, logically, when the screen represents the field of vision of a character, we become absorbed specifically within the subjectivity of that character. Whether taken in conjunction with the broader assumption, or considered in its own right, however, this second assumption is as fundamentally misguided as the first.[27]

The fallacy is based on a simplistic, atomistic view of the function of optical POV shots. POV shots are considered to have a special effect in drawing us into the subjectivity of a character, regardless of context. We should not, however, think in terms of POV shots so much as POV structures, comprised of a point/glance function (the positing of a perceiver) combined with a point/

object function (the image of the perceived).[28] Moreover, these POV structures must be considered in the context of the larger narrational structures of the film as a whole. Obviously enough, POV structures can give us information about a character's thoughts, specifically about what the character is paying attention to: for example, the shots of isolated parts of Rosanna Arquette's anatomy designate very specifically the objects of Lionel Dobie's (Nick Nolte) attention in *Life Lessons* (Martin Scorsese's contribution to *New York Stories* (1989)). And this designation may in turn 'focus' the precise nature of the emotional state of the character who looks—in Dobie's case, lust.[29] But the mind is not always consumed by what the eyes see, and what the eyes see does not itself tell us what the mind thinks. Some brief counter-examples should serve to highlight the problems of a general account of POV based on the conflation of sight and subjectivity.[30]

At the beginning of Curtis Bernhardt's *Possessed* (1947), we are perceptually aligned with Louise Howell via a series of POV shots, but we cannot be said to 'identify' with her, as the suppressive narration delays the exposition of the narrative, withholding from the spectator any knowledge concerning the cause of her catatonic state, her background, and so forth. The opening shot of Dario Argento's *Profondo Rosso* (*Deep Red—Hatchet Murders*) (1975) represents the POV of a child as he witnesses a violent murder. But the status of the shot as a POV shot is withheld until the last moment of film, when the shot is repeated. On its first appearance, the shot can hardly be said to allow us to enter the subjectivity of the boy, as we do not know that the shot is from his point of view—indeed, we have not even individuated the character at this point. In the first case, we simply see as the character does: nothing more, nothing less. In the second case, we are not even aware that we are witnessing an event from the POV of a character. In Humberto Solás's *Lucía* (1968), there is a shot representing the 'POV' of a blindfolded character (that is, what the character would see if they were not blindfolded); Godfrey Reggio's *Koyaanisqatsi* (1983) includes a POV shot belonging to a twinkie on a production line in a cake factory. POV may even function to withhold the identity of the character whose vision is represented, as it often does in the horror film.[31] The identity of Arbogast's killer in *Psycho*, for example, is hidden by the fact that we see the murder from the killer's POV. In none of these cases can the POV shot be said to give us access to a character's subjectivity. In the light of such cases, we need to re-assess the claims made for the centrality of POV in the larger processes of alignment and character engagement.

On the face of it, external, behavioural information about a given character can obtain only in inverse proportion to optical alignment with that character. While we see from a character's optical viewpoint, we cannot, by definition, have access to her external features (except in the special case of a shot created to give the impression of a character's optical POV as she observes herself in a reflecting surface, like a mirror). This leads to an exactly opposed argument to the one we have just examined, most famously articulated by François Truffaut: '[A] subjective camera is the negation of subjective cinema. When it replaces a character, one cannot identify oneself with him. The cinema becomes subjective when the actor's gaze meets that of the audience.'[32] Performance rather than POV is the central device of 'identification' for Truffaut.

Theoretically, Truffaut's argument that the POV shot 'negates' subjective access by supplanting shots of the looking character holds little water. First, techniques like voice-over, expressive sound or music may be juxtaposed with POV shots and thereby provide the information, typically gleaned from facial expression and bodily gesture, lacking in an ordinary POV shot. In addition, the POV shot may be manipulated or contextualized in such a way that it does reveal information about the character's mental state beyond the merely perceptual. Such manipulations range from what Branigan calls 'perception' shots— the blurred vision of a drunkard, for example—in which we gain access to a character's state of mind through distortion of the POV shot, to character reflection and projection, in which the *mise-en-scène* itself, the objects seen in the POV shot, become 'charged with character semes',[33] and thus may provide information about the character's state of mind. *Vincent* (1986, directed by Paul Cox) constructs the eponymous character using only voice-over, expressive sound, POV and distorted 'perception' shots: the body of the character is never rendered visually. Again, POV shots must be analysed in the context of the structures in which they are placed. Both Truffaut's argument, and the obverse argument which holds that the POV shot wires the spectator directly into the mind of the character, fail to recognize that POV is a structure, not an autonomous device which produces an identical effect in all circumstances. Character subjectivity is an emergent quality of the narration as a whole, not the product of any single technique.

Truffaut's comment essentially asks us to recognize the importance of the expressive reaction shot—the shot in which a character reacts to the words or actions of another character, or to some discovery—in the creation of character subjectivity. A very common structure in classical cinema is one in which a scene or sequence is 'keyed' to the emotional state of a particular character through repeated reaction shots of the character. Truffaut again: '[I]f the audience feels the need to identify . . . it automatically does so with the face whose gaze it meets most frequently during the film, with the actor who is most often shot full on and in close-up.'[34] Consider the inquest scene in *Vertigo*, in which Scottie squirms as the coroner quietly assassinates his character in front of an impassive and inscrutable jury. As always, context is crucial: we are primed to focus our attention on Scottie because we have been attached to him thus far, and because he has been represented as an essentially sympathetic character. Hitchcock sets up a simple pattern of alternation in the scene, between reaction shots of Scottie, and shots of the judge and various other characters in the courtroom. The pattern puts the scene in Scottie's emotional 'key' by insistently returning to his expressions: roughly one-quarter of the shots in the scene are reaction shots of Scottie, occupying almost a third of the scene's screen duration.[35]

In stressing the importance of the reaction shot within the POV structure, I am not arguing that such shots have fixed meanings irrespective of context— that we know what Scottie feels through his facial expression alone. It is true that the 'Kuleshov-effect' greatly underestimates the power of facial expression, by suggesting that the meaning of facial expression is wholly determined by the surrounding shots, but of course the context of an expression will affect our interpretation of it.[36] (Consider the expression of 'George Kaplan' when Roger Thornhill confronts him in *North by Northwest* (Hitchcock, 1959): at first his expression appears to register his astonishment at the photograph Thornhill shows him, then it is revealed that it registers the shock and pain that inevitably follow on being stabbed in the back (frames 45, 46).) The point, rather, is that facial expression itself brings certain meanings into play, which work within narrative structures; and that specifically with respect to the POV structure, the importance of this has consistently been overlooked.

Neither does my argument overlook the fact that conventions of facial expressivity vary somewhat both within and between cultures. In Hollywood films, at least within certain genres, male characters are generally less expressive than female characters—indeed, this is a point I develop in the analysis of *Daisy Kenyon*. 'As a general rule', writes James Naremore, 'Hollywood has required that supporting players, ethnic minorities, and women be more animated or broadly expressive than white male leads.'[37] And there may well be a difference between conventions of facial expressivity in Western films and Japanese films, corresponding to the different 'display rules' in each culture

Frames 45 – 46 North by Northwest: emotional expression and context

45   46

regarding the aptness of the expression of emotions, according to the status of the agent, the context of expression, and the particular emotion in question.[38] Arguing for the importance of facial expression, and thus against 'strong' versions of the Kuleshov thesis, does not depend on viewing facial expressions as unvarying, universal phenomena.

The importance of the reaction shot and facial expression highlights a paradox in the use of the POV shot: the more a film attempts to render in a literal fashion the subjectivity of a character through the adoption of optical POV, the more it surrenders the power to evoke the full range of a character's mental states, through the powerful mechanism of facial expression. Branigan reaches a similar conclusion when, in discussing *Lady in the Lake*, he argues that 'if the purpose of Montgomery's film is to create an identity between spectator and character, the primary reliance on a single device of internal focalization—the point-of-view shot—actually *limits* what the spectator can easily know about the character.'[39] When Marlowe first encounters the killer, feigning the identity of the landlady of the house in which Marlowe is about to discover another victim, it is not clear whether he suspects her (as we do). Since the action is represented through a POV shot, we can only gauge Marlowe's reactions through his voice, and the reactions of the killer, a sparse array of clues relative to those available in a more conventional alternation of shot and reverse-shot.

From the standpoint of an empirical historical poetics, then, Truffaut's assertion concerning the importance of reaction shots becomes more powerful. Classical filmmaking has always depended overwhelmingly on facial expression and bodily gesture as the devices for conveying information about a character's inner states. In the hierarchy of all the devices which can perform this function, the face and the body have been consistently dominant: it is one of the most enduring, but automatized and therefore 'transparent', principles of classical filmmaking. Indeed, it is hardly apparent as a convention at all, until we look at a film like *Vincent*. When films attempt to subvert this hierarchy, by replacing (and not merely combining) facial expression and bodily gesture with other devices such as the voice-over, the results are striking but often troubling. The most familiar cases are those Hollywood films which attempt to construct a 'first-person' narration through continuous POV, such as *Lady in the Lake* and parts of Delmer Daves's *Dark Passage* (1947). In these cases, however, the disturbance caused by the reduced 'direct' visual representation of the protagonist is held in check by the use of mirror shots. Moreover, the POV shot itself carries the echo of human presence in the features that mark it as a POV shot: lack of stability, and a constriction of the mobility and ubiquity characteristic of normal Hollywood découpage. And the faces and bodies of other characters are still represented. Other films, such as *Vincent*, Chantal Akerman's *News from Home* (1976) and, as we will see, the films of Bresson, attempt a much more extreme subversion of the hierarchy of devices used for the representation of character psychology.

Truffaut's observation, then, has a certain amount of validity in the context of the historically developed systems of narration in which filmmakers and spectators work, though logically there are no reasons why we should not be able to 'identify' just as much with characters constructed through devices other than those of performance. Neither the argument that POV is the essence of subjective access, nor its converse which finds the POV shot antithetical to 'subjective cinema', holds up. The POV shot is not nearly as central to 'identification' as critics often assume. Nevertheless, it does perform a number of other functions related to alignment, some of which I have already touched upon. I will stress two of them here: the *marking* of alignment and the extreme *restriction* of narration.

We established above that POV shots do not always give us access to a character's subjectivity, so we cannot wholly subsume POV under the rubric of subjective access. Not all POV shots produce subjective access, and not all subjective access is produced by POV shots. In other words, POV is not a necessary feature of alignment, in that films do not need to use the kind of POV shot whose function is to provide subjective access in order to forge an alignment between a character and the spectator. There are many films which give us access to the inner states of characters without recourse to POV shots.[40] *Laura*, for example, rarely uses POV shots, though we are clearly aligned with certain characters over the course of the film: first Waldo Lydecker, then Mark McPherson. The narration in *Laura* rarely employs literal POV, and indeed comparatively few over-the-shoulder shot-reverse-shot structures (one step away from the optical POV structure in Branigan's scheme).

There are a few POV shots, scattered through the film. In the opening scene, there are two close-up shots of a small, handheld baseball game. The shots represent the POV of McPherson. In the context of this film, POV shots are extremely striking, precisely because they are so infrequently used (an effect made more emphatic by the sudden shifts in shot-scale which accompany the POV shots). Rather than slotting unobtrusively into the flow of character action and reaction, as they do in many classical films, here POV shots stand out. Far from effecting an absorption of the spectator, by virtue of the overstated connection between sight and subjectivity, the shots in fact 'endistance' the viewer. The POV shot functions as a 'marker', rather than as a foundation or necessary component, of alignment with a character. In many classical films, POV is used, as it is here, as a way of underlining a shift in the structure of alignment, or merely to recall and emphasize a continuing alignment with a particular character.

This practice is also used in *The Man Who Knew Too Much*. As Ben McKenna approaches the Ambrose Chappell workshop, POV shots mark the increasingly exclusive attachment to him (frames 37, 38, p. 149). But there are more complex instances, in which optical POV functions as a marker of shifts in alignment, at significant moments of change and complication in the alignment structure of the film. One scene in which such a shift occurs takes place in the restaurant where the McKennas first meet the Draytons. Up to this point in the film, the narration has aligned us with the McKennas, by spatially attaching us to them alone and by making them subjectively transparent. We have seen how the narration encourages the spectator to look upon the Draytons with suspicion through this pattern of alignment. Our perception of the Draytons has been 'filtered' through that of the McKennas, and especially Jo McKenna. However, these suspicions are rapidly overcome in the restaurant scene. The Draytons' rude staring in their earlier encounter with the McKennas is explained by their recognition of Jo as a famous performer (a fact of which we were not aware in the earlier scene). On the level of allegiance, the scene invites us to connect the two couples: the Draytons are British, and less ignorant of local customs, but like the Mckennas they are Westerners and outsiders to the Arab culture.

Several minutes into the scene, Ben and Jo begin to argue about Louis Bernard. It is at this point that a shift occurs in the pattern of alignment constructed in the film so far. As with the rest of the scene, the argument is visually structured through a series of two-shot reverse-shots between the Draytons and the McKennas. The pattern is interrupted by the unexpected arrival of Louis Bernard, whose appearance is represented in a POV shot showing Bernard from the McKennas' position. In this respect, the sequence simply marks our alignment with the McKennas in a manner similar to that in the sequence from *Laura*. What makes this sequence a more complex example is that a shift in the structure of alignment occurs during the argument, and this too is marked by the use of POV. Once the argument begins, the McKennas look at each other (frame 47), while the Draytons continue staring at the McKennas, with occasional glances of discomfort at each other (frame 48). The framing of the two-shots of both the Draytons and the McKennas becomes tighter at this point, so that the shots of the McKennas now function as the POV of the Draytons. This is a significant moment because it represents the first point in the film where we are aligned with the Draytons (or any other character, for that matter) independently of the McKennas. Within the scene, our engagement with the Draytons is no longer mediated by the McKennas.

The shift in the POV structure, then, signals a shift in the structure of alignment at the local level. It is, however, neither a necessary nor sufficient condition for the shift in the structure of alignment. The embarrassed and uneasy glances exchanged by the Draytons are more significant, as these are the actions which determine that we perceive the argument as much from the (metaphorical) viewpoint of the bystanders (the Draytons) as from the participants' perspective (the McKennas). All of the action occurring at the table could have been shot from the side on which none of the characters are sitting, in which case POV would not have been involved at any point in the scene. But the shift in the pattern of alignment would still have occurred, as our attention would still have been drawn to the actions and thoughts of the Draytons independent of the attention of the characters with whom we have been aligned so far (the McKennas). Up to this point, our attention to and construction of the Draytons has been entirely determined by the attention (both in degree and kind) paid to them by the McKennas.

POV shots, then, frequently function as a kind of emphasis, a rhetorical underlining of the narration's delegation of the storytelling function to a character (and the concomitant development of patterns of alignment). But this does not yet exhaust the functions performed by POV shots. Another function becomes apparent if we consider POV shots not under the rubric of subjective access, as they usually are, but under the rubric of attachment. In terms of subjective access, POV shots simply represent the field of vision of a character in the story world at a particular moment in the story. We are not 'put in the position' of a character by virtue of a new and deeper access to the character's subjectivity, but by knowing (or rather seeing) no more than the character does. It is an alignment characterized by an identical limitation of knowledge, by what is withheld rather than what is given. What effects does such a restriction to the visual field of a character produce?

In *Deception*, a film generally characterized by a rather unsuspenseful narration, a subordinate line of action involves a great deal of restriction, and the POV shot serves as a device in this restrictive sub-structure. The subordinate line of action concerns Gribble, a cellist whom Christine witnesses visiting Hollenius. Hollenius is, in fact, employing him as an understudy, but this information is withheld from us as the narration restricts our knowledge strictly

Frames 47–48 The Man Who Knew Too Much: POV and the marking of alignment

47   48

to that of Christine, who is not in the room in which the discussion between Hollenius and Gribble takes place. That is, for this stretch of the film, the narration aligns us with Christine by attaching us exclusively to her and by making her subjectively transparent. A POV shot gives us a brief glimpse of the action in the room in which Hollenius and Gribble talk; on the soundtrack, the sound of conversation fades as the door to the room closes. The perceptual (optical and aural) alignment does not give us any new or greater access to Christine's thoughts, but like her we are intrigued by the business between Gribble and Hollenius and frustrated that we cannot know more. It is an alignment of the spectator with the character based on an equal lack of knowledge. We are not made into an 'accomplice' by this POV shot; rather, we occupy a more limited position as an onlooker, in which we are given a tantalizing and partial view of an important incident (hence the usefulness of POV shots in generating enigmas and suspense). Here, then, we can grant that the POV shot serves to forge a close link between character and spectator, but only as part of a larger structure of alignment, and by virtue of restricting us to what the character sees, rather than by providing any new information in the shot itself concerning the character's state of mind.

The identical limitation of knowledge produced (in part) by the POV shot in *Deception* thus gives rise to a parallel frustration in character and spectator. Similarly, in the horror film, the POV shot often gives rise to parallel states of fear and shock in character and spectator. Restricted to the visual field of a character, we are as ignorant of the presence or location of the monster outside the frame as the character. Thus, the shock experienced by the character as the monster bursts into the character's field of vision is paralleled by that of the spectator. But it is important to see that the shock is not 'communicated' by the shot alone, but rather by the perceptual situation that the film has created for the spectator, of which the POV shot is but one element.

I now turn to more extended and detailed analyses in order to develop some of the claims and concepts that I have introduced. As in the last chapter, the examples have been chosen for the way in which they demonstrate the distinctness of a particular concept or structure. So far I have concentrated on typical patterns of alignment found in classical films. *Daisy Kenyon* serves to exemplify further the classical imperative of revealed subjectivity in an especially telling way, since the film features that play with the spectator's sense of character motivation so characteristic of Preminger's films, and yet, in the end, leaves us in no doubt as to what has driven the characters. We will see that this play with character motivation exploits two, somewhat conflicting social schemata pertinent to the period in which the film was made and the genre of which it is a member. These procedural schemata organize our understanding of the relationship between character expressivity and subjectivity, and may affect our assessment of the narration's reliability. Thus the film reveals how our construction of character psychology is in part determined by culturally and historically specific schemata. Bresson's films, even more than those of Preminger, are renowned for their opaque characters. *L'Argent*, however, inverts the classical movement towards subjective revelation (as enacted in *Psycho, Double Indemnity,* and *Daisy Kenyon*) by tracing a path to subjective opacity. The film departs from the powerful classical norm of a fully revealed psychology, and articulates very different relations between expressivity and subjectivity from those found in *Daisy Kenyon*.

Red Herrings and Purple Prose: Daisy Kenyon

'if you say so, doctor, though I don't see how you know . . .'

'The visible body is our only evidence for the invisible mind.'[41] Leo Braudy's statement hardly stands up as a generalization about the cinema: aside from performance, dialogue, voice-over, music, setting, cinematography, and editing may all contribute to our sense of a character's subjectivity. It serves very well, however, as a capsule explanation of the difficulties in determining the internal states and motivations of characters in *Daisy Kenyon* (and indeed in many of Preminger's films), since we are given access to the inner states of the characters solely through external behaviour.[42] In addition, Preminger exploits certain schemata regarding the relationship between external cues (facial expression, bodily gesture, speech) and character subjectivity with conflicting implications.

These schemata come into play in the context of a generic love triangle. Daisy (Joan Crawford) is a successful magazine artist living in New York. She is having an affair with Dan O'Mara (Dana Andrews), a wealthy lawyer, who is married with two children. Daisy is dissatisfied with the relationship because 'there isn't enough' (love, presumably). Dan will not divorce his wife because he fears traumatizing his children. Enter Peter Lapham (Henry Fonda), a disturbed war veteran, who also happens to be a widower looking for a new wife. After an initial period of hesitation, Daisy accepts Peter's proposal. At first, the marriage is haunted by their memories of former partners, but eventually these ghosts are exorcized.

However, Dan is still in love with Daisy, and one day attempts to force himself on her. Daisy resists. Dan's wife overhears him apologizing to Daisy over the phone and decides to sue him for divorce. When Peter perceives that the lives of Daisy and Dan are likely to cross in the course of the divorce, he decides to opt out of the marriage until the divorce is settled. Half-way through the trial Dan decides to marry Daisy (his affair with her has resumed in some way after Peter's walkout). He calls Peter to arrange a divorce between Peter and Daisy, and the two of them pursue the distraught Daisy to Peter's house on Cape Cod. There she apparently rejects both of them, but in a startling peripeteia Peter returns and reclaims her, and now Daisy gladly submits. A central node of my discussion is the surprise or disturbance that this last-minute *volte face* may engender in the spectator.

In what follows I shall only be considering some of the possible norms and expectations which might bear on a viewing of *Daisy Kenyon*. I do not, therefore, hold up my analysis as a complete reading or interpretation of the film; indeed, it is not a reading in that sense at all. As I argued in Chapter 2, 'the spectator' is a flexible construction which can be built up with a greater or lesser number of sets of expectations, depending on the aim of the analysis. In this case, the goal is to reveal how a number of schemata, pertaining to the way we grasp the motivations of characters, are both historically specific and highly automatized. The schemata in question are triggered, in part, by generic cues.

By genre I do not mean to indicate simply a set of properties shared by a number of texts, but rather clusters 'of norms and expectations which help the reader to assign functions to various elements in the work'.[43] The pertinent genre in the case of *Daisy Kenyon* would seem to be the 'melodrama' or 'woman's picture'. As a 'production genre'—one recognized by the film industry—the 'woman's picture' is a fairly delimited term, referring essentially to domestic dramas, centred on a female protagonist, thematically concerned with the family and maternity.[44] 'Melodrama', however, is a notoriously flexible word, that has undergone significant shifts in reference over its two-hundred-year existence as a term describing a certain kind of drama; it can refer to milieu, narrational qualities (as in Bordwell's distinction between detective and melo-dramatic narration), and moral structure. In the next chapter, we will have reason to question the coherence of our contemporary use of the term. Rather than becoming snared in a logomachical dispute, then, I will limit the use of the term 'melodrama' in this context, without denying that it has historical relevance. What is important here is to delineate the 'expressive tradition', a set of interrelated social assumptions and aesthetic forms, which have sometimes gone by the name 'melodrama'. Principal among these is the notion of expressivity—the assumption that characters have direct access to their desires and emotions and may express them forthrightly in speech or action: 'Melo-drama handles its feelings and ideas virtually as plastic entities, visual and tac-tile models held out for all to see and handle. Emotions are given a full acting-out, a full representation before our eyes.'[45] According to the Russian critic Sergei Balukhatyi, what is fundamental to the expressive tradition—or melodrama, in this use of the term—is its 'Emotional Teleology . . . the calling forth of "pure", "vivid" emotions'.[46] Balukhatyi goes on to suggest that the 'impassioned speech' of melodramatic characters is 'not only the direct expression of strong emo-tion, but . . . also contain[s] "analysis" of the emotion being experienced . . . the *character's self-appraisal* of the strength of his own feelings'.[47] Performative expressivity endows the narration with great depth, which, in combination with a pattern of multiple attachment, produces the distinctive alignment pattern that we have termed the melodramatic structure of alignment. In contrast to the detective structure, in which the spectator is often aligned with the protagonist in being ignorant of key events, in the melodramatic structure the spectator typically knows more than individual characters. The spectator of the melodrama hypothesizes as to how characters will react when they find out what she already knows.

The origins of the expressive tradition in the theatre are intimately tied to highly expressive theories of acting. Acting techniques underwent changes in the late eighteenth- and early nineteenth-centuries—broadly speaking, from an emphasis on facial expression to a greater use of gesture and attitude (a trend which cinema reversed).[48] Underlying these changes, however, was a functional continuity—maximized emotional expression to create an 'effect' in the spectator. Inarticulateness, according to Martin Meisel, was neither a cultural norm nor a theatrical convention in the nineteenth century: 'Only recently in the Western tradition have we accepted the convention that true feeling is always inarticulate and ultimately inexpressible.'[49] These are the assumptions of the expressive tradition, and they are manifested in many Hollywood genres, including the 'woman's picture', of which *Daisy Kenyon* is a member. The key link, then, is between *Daisy Kenyon*—as a 'woman's picture'—and the principle of expressivity, understood as a relation of directness between intentional states and their physical expression. We will see that the popularization of Freudianism challenges the assumptions of the expressive tradition, affecting the narrational character of many Hollywood genres, again including the woman's picture. For the moment, though, what is significant is that *Daisy Kenyon* emerges from the expressive tradition (albeit at a moment when the tradition is challenged) and that it is in this sense a 'melodrama'; that it is also a 'melodrama' in the modern sense (a drama of the domestic sphere, focusing on problems of family and maternity) is incidental to my argument.[50]

The opening of *Daisy Kenyon* immediately invokes the norm of expressivity. The drawn image of a middle-class house dissolves to a photographic analogue; a taxi draws up and Dan climbs out. There is then a short verbal exchange, as the cabbie explains in elaborate detail why he cannot wait for Dan. Though it is a small incident, it immediately establishes the norm of character expressivity. This is soon confirmed inside Daisy's flat. After some preliminary conversation in the first scene, which serves to establish the characters, Daisy's friend Angeles leaves, and Dan immediately kisses Daisy: a more obviously significant direct expression of emotion. They start to argue, and the 'self-appraisal' noted by Balukhatyi is apparent: 'I have to fight to stay happy, fight for everything' says Daisy. 'You're most of my life, Daisy, the only thing that matters,' replies Dan. And the expressivity of this somewhat purple prose is reinforced by physical performance. We are given no indication that we should doubt the veracity of what the characters say. In other words, the norm of expressivity in the text invites an attitude of trust on the part of the spectator towards the characters and the narration. The norm is tied into, and generated by, wider, cultural beliefs about expressivity, truth, and trust associated historically with the expressive tradition:

> Cultural assumptions . . . concerned with . . . 'transparency', 'sincerity', 'authenticity' and hence the 'true person' . . . seem in our culture to cluster around notions of the private and the uncontrolled. That is, when people are not in public . . . in circumstances defined as intimate (the family, bed), they are held to be more 'real' than otherwise; and when people 'let themselves go,' pour forth their thoughts and feelings in an untrammelled flow, then they are being their 'true selves.'[51]

We can refer to this belief as the Expressive Truth Schema. At one point, the film refers to the schema directly. When Peter abruptly proposes marriage to Daisy for the first time, she tells him that he is being 'melodramatic'. A moment later, she says, 'All right, have your melodrama, have your tragedy.' As she does this, she stands with her head tilted back, inviting and challenging him to kiss her. Thus, the film explicitly articulates the schema which defines melodrama as the forthright expression of emotions, such expressions being the most reliable indices of the desires and emotions of the character.

Other woman's pictures of the period are organized around a very different notion of the individual's access to her own 'truth', a difference which coincides to a large degree with the use of the detective, instead of the melodramatic, structure of alignment. Consider Dyer's comment in relation to two other woman's pictures starring Joan Crawford from the same period, *Mildred Pierce* (1945), and *Possessed* (1947). *Possessed* begins with a series of long shots following Crawford as she wanders through the streets of Los Angeles in a state of shock. She approaches various men addressing them as 'David', but we are given no specific clues as to the origins of her strange behaviour. The character is minimally expressive and the narration very uncommunicative. She falls into a catatonic stupor and has to be pumped with truth-serum to make her expressive. The sense of doubt and distrust these early moments create is not restricted to the framing narrative. The flashback narrative is invaded by the same features. Louise (the character played by Crawford) experiences a hallucination which is not cued as such to the spectator until after it is over. *Mildred Pierce* opens with a similarly repressive narration and inexpressive character. In this film, the narrative is constructed to suggest that Mildred is responsible for a murder which she has not in fact committed. But the very nature of the opening activates a different set of schemata in the spectator from those triggered by the opening of *Daisy Kenyon*. We are prompted to be suspicious of the most obvious hypotheses. We expect a red herring or two. Just as the corollary of narrational communicativeness and character expressivity is spectatorial trust, of both characters and the narration as a whole, so the suppressiveness and inexpressiveness in these films invites distrust, or at least caution, on the part of the spectator. The unreliability of characters and the potential duplicity of narration in American films of the 1940s is most fully realized in *Laura*, Robert Siodmak's *The Strange Affair of Uncle Harry* (1945), and Hitchcock's *Stage Fright* (1950), each of which mislead the spectator with respect to the epistemic status (reality, dream, lie) of substantial parts of the story.[52]

Associated with such detective narration is a notion of the individual's access to self-knowledge which is very different from that which relates to the expressive tradition. In this alternative schema, which I shall term the Repressive Truth Schema, the 'truth' of the self is buried beneath consciousness, and often can only be discovered by an external figure, be it doctor or policeman. Most woman's pictures of the period invoke one schema or the other, but rarely both. *Daisy Kenyon* is exceptional in this respect, in that although the film opens in an emphatically 'melodramatic' manner, immediately invoking the Expressive Truth Schema, later events throw this into question by explicitly invoking the Repressive Truth Schema. The disturbance at the end of the film arises, I will argue, as a result of the (mis-)reading of Peter Lapham's behaviour according to the inappropriate schema.[53]

This conflicting truth schema is invoked specifically in relation to Peter. What distinguishes him from the other characters is his initial lack of expressivity. An alignment structure is created in which we never see him for more than a few moments outside of his interaction with either Daisy or Dan. In the first scene in which we see him, he arrives at Daisy's flat, has a brief exchange with Daisy, who then disappears into another room to change. As he pours himself a drink, there is a dissolve which brings us to the moment when Daisy emerges. This would be insignificant were it not echoed in the larger structures of the narration. In his proposal to Daisy, he mentions a brother, a sister, and an aunt, but we never see or hear of these characters again. Once he has left Daisy, we do not see him again until Dan calls him to arrange the divorce.

Peter's lack of expressivity, however, is motivated very specifically by his war experiences and the death of his wife. The key scene in this respect is the nightmare scene, where Daisy interprets Peter's nightmare as a symptom of the continuing trauma of the loss of his wife. He resists any definite interpretation, simply responding to Daisy, 'if you say so doctor, though I don't see how you know'. Marriage, however, apparently 'normalizes' Peter; in the world of the woman's picture, love cures all. After the nightmare scene, Daisy declares her love for him, and his morbid fixation with the death of his wife and the war fall away. The text, then, raises the alternative, Repressive Truth Schema in relation to Peter, only to deny it. From this point on, we judge Lapham's behaviour according to the Expressive Truth Schema. This leads up to the scene in which Dan brings Daisy, Peter, and himself together to discuss the divorce proceedings his wife has taken out against him. Peter's reaction is as follows:

I pushed my way into your life Daisy because I needed you. Well, I'm fine now, better then either of you. . . . The only reason I was able to break in was that he [Dan] didn't love you enough then . . . you can work this out without the technical drawback of a husband—that's a formality we can dispose of any time you signal.

Now admittedly Peter also says that he is 'all in favour' of Daisy deciding her fate for herself, but the overwhelming sense of the speech is Peter's determined self-sufficiency—his observable behaviour gives every indication that he is willing to annul the marriage. Daisy's comment to Dan after Peter has left is absolutely crucial: 'There's nothing like a crisis to show what's really inside people.' Another textual invocation of the Expressive Truth Schema, the statement reinforces the sense that what Peter has just said is the plain and simple truth, rather than a ruse, which is what the end of the film suggests it is. It does this by invoking the cultural belief that permeates the expressive tradition—that when people 'let go', express themselves strongly, they express the truth. We have been led to judge Peter by the Expressive Truth Schema, and thus to believe that we understand his motives. If the film does effect this, then the ending—in which Peter calmly and inexplicably returns to Daisy, after his apparently sanguine departure—will be a surprise.

Surprising endings are, of course, perfectly congruent with the norms of the expressive tradition, but the 'unexpected event' here is peculiar. It is not achieved through the usual 'melodramatic' device of chance or coincidence—the fateful slip on the cliff's edge, for example, in Sirk's *All That Heaven Allows* (1955)—but rather through an inexpressive character and an uncommunicative strand of narration (that concerning Peter) embedded within an otherwise highly communicative narration and a highly expressive set of characters. Through these textual strategies, the spectator is encouraged to read the behaviour of all of the characters according to what I have designated the Expressive Truth Schema. The spectator is led to believe that her knowledge is superior to that of any character, and directs her energies not so much towards determining the mysteries of a character's motives, but rather towards predicting how characters will react to information she already has. Since Peter's stolidity in the final scene can be comprehended as a continuation of the self-sufficiency he declares in the earlier scene, the spectator is unlikely to suspect that he has a concealed strategy.

Once again, I do not want to argue that the analysis of the film that I have delineated has any absolute critical or social priority. A spectator's experience of the film will depend on the balance in that viewer of expectations built up by this particular film and—crucially—expectations which result from intertextual and social norms. I have tried to represent some of these other, sometimes competing norms, in Figure 5.1, which shows how expectations are initiated at various levels of specificity, and how they interrelate. The diagram represents a field of expectations which would be realized in a particular balance in a particular individual.[54] A narrative text can attempt to regiment the viewer's experience, it can encourage the activation of certain schemata over others, but it cannot 'position' the spectator. Like any film, it is constructed in the knowledge of what schemata spectators are likely to bring to it. The film-maker hypothesizes a shared background of knowledge and seeks to create certain effects against this beckground. But empirical spectators will differ, in both social and purely personal terms, in the knowledge that they in fact bring to the text. The construal or 'appropriation' of a text by a particular spectator thus may or may not match the interpretation of the film anticipated by the filmmaker.[55]

The Expressive Truth Schema and the Repressive Truth Schema are associated, then, with the melodramatic and detective structures of alignment respectively. In addition, there is an affinity between the detective structure, the Repressive Schema associated with it, and the implications of popularized psychoanalysis.[56] *Daisy Kenyon* makes the connection explicitly, by evoking psychoanalysis in relation to the one strand of detective narration in the film, that is, the line of action concerning Peter Lapham ('if you say so doctor'). The principle of expressivity and the genres which depend upon it encounter a challenge as psychoanalytic character types and imagery enter the rhetoric of Hollywood filmmaking. This is surely one of the major cultural factors behind the burgeoning of duplicitous or unreliable narration in American films of the 1940s, discussed formally by Kristin Thompson and, from a more overtly social perspective, Diane Waldman and Dana Polan.[57] Self-appraisal and expression are exactly those human abilities which are problematized by the psychoanalytic framework (and *Possessed* is explicitly based upon the psychoanalytic framework, as are a considerable number of films from the 1940s). 'Truth' is repressed and emerges symptomatically, rather than directly expressed. Psychoanalysis is raised in association with Peter's problem in expression, but, as I have argued, that problematic does not come to dominate the entire film. It is the mixing of the two truth schemata that has interesting repercussions for the way we make sense of character motivation in the film.[58]

More generally, since psychoanalysis entails a very different yardstick for what is read as the 'truth', it may be that the permeation of Freud's theories (in popularized form) into the woman's picture had a profound effect on the nature of the genre, in the norms and expectations which it inculcated in spectators. If we examine such films solely on a textual level, we will doubtless reach the conclusion that they are fundamentally classical, and that Hollywood

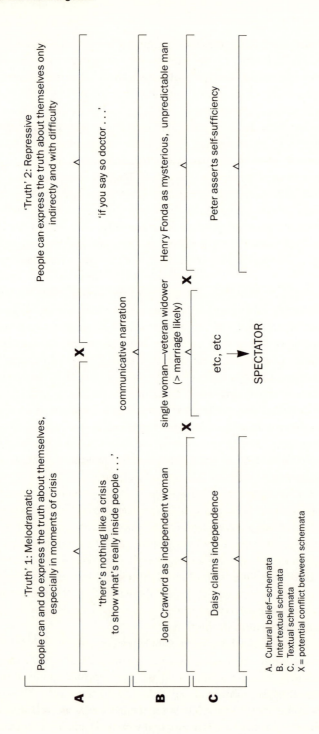

Figure 5.1 Schemata in *Daisy Kenyon*

A. Cultural belief–schemata
B. Intertextual schemata
C. Textual schemata
X = potential conflict between schemata

incorporated Freudianism without changing its own forms, just as, on a stylistic level, it had absorbed elements of Soviet montage and German expressionism.[59] But a history attentive to the cultural context(s) in which these films were viewed might suggest that the period of 'integration' was more turbulent—in terms of audience experience of these films. This is a mere speculation, but it serves to show how a cognitive approach to character engagement, which conceives of the spectator as a being who comprehends films through norms (embodied in mental schemata), allows for the entrance of historical specificity. We can talk about how formal expectations interact with wider cultural beliefs in particular groups at particular historical moments.

In the post-classical period, the assumptions and expectations associated with the expressive tradition are much less stable and less automatized. In Alan Rudolf's *Choose Me* (1984), for example—a film which alludes to many woman's pictures of the classical era—the relations between character expressivity, subjective transparency, and narrational reliability no longer hold. The affective outpourings of the characters no longer guarantee the persistence or reliability of the traits and occurrent states that such expressions appear to establish. This is especially true of the protagonist, Mickey (Keith Carradine). His expressions are subject to rapid revision if not immediate erasure, as his opening self-description as a compulsive liar indicates. Classical films often represent moderately complex characters, but the bounds of such characterization are definitely exceeded by the appearance of Mickey's photo-album, which verifies every one of the radically incompatible claims made by Mickey about his past life. The major factors in this erosion of the expressive tradition in Hollywood cinema, I would suggest, are the incorporation of the vulgarized psychoanalysis that we have been examining, and the influence of post-war European cinema.[60]

In spite of the narrational intricacies of *Daisy Kenyon*, which arise as a consequence of the challenges to the cultural and dramatic assumptions of the expressive tradition by the dissemination of psychoanalysis, the film ultimately conforms to the dramatic curve of the classical movie, with its movement towards subjective revelation. *L'Argent* reverses this movement, and flouts the classical association of attachment with subjective transparency: the more the narration restricts itself to the protagonist, the more inscrutable he becomes. The direct link between expression (action and appearance) and psychology (trait and occurrent state), central to the expressive tradition, qualified in *Daisy Kenyon*, is undercut entirely in Bresson's film.

Outside Yvon Targe: L'Argent

In the final scene of *L'Argent*, Yvon Targe (Christian Patey), the protagonist of the film, gives himself up to the police. Framed in a medium shot, he confesses in a concise, affectless monotone to several murders that he has committed. I would guess that many spectators interpret the flat delivery to be a sign of the desensitized nature of the character: his humanity worn away by victimization, the death of his daughter, and loss of his wife. He has, after all, just brutally murdered a woman who had taken him in and protected him, knowing that he had murdered previously. A viewer more familiar with Bresson's characteristic style might explain the lack of expressivity by reference to a stylistic pattern, and find no readily discernable semantic import in the flat delivery. I shall argue that neither response is wholly wrong, but that taken individually, neither response does justice to the complexity of the text.

Though I have called Yvon the protagonist of the film, there are many other important characters. The film begins by tracing the path of some counterfeit bank notes, as they pass from two schoolboys, Norbert (Marc Ernest Fourneau) and Martial (Bruno Lapeyre), to the owners of a photographic store, and finally to Yvon, as payment for the fuel he has just pumped into the store's tank. The narrative circles through these characters, moving from Yvon to the store owners and their employee Lucien (Vincent Risterucci), and back to Norbert and his parents. As the film progresses, though, the film focuses its attention more closely on Yvon's story. The pattern of looping away from Yvon continues, but on a smaller scale: when Yvon arrives at the farmhouse where he will commit the climactic massacre, the narration breaks away from him briefly, following the woman around the house as she checks on the members of her family. As the narration attaches us to Yvon ever more exclusively, however, his motivations become much more difficult to fathom. The film develops a paradoxical pattern of alignment, in which the more it restricts itself to Yvon, the less access we have to his psyche, and the greater the difficulty in describing with confidence the relationship between his actions and his psychology. Thus while *Psycho* suppresses our access to the internal states of the killer but ultimately reveals his psychology—enabling us to get 'inside Norman Bates', as Raymond Durgnat puts it[61]—*L'Argent* moves in the opposite direction. The difference is, perhaps, the measure of *Psycho's* ultimate adherence to classical principles, and, conversely, *L'Argent's* understated but devastating dismantling of the emotional rhetoric of the traditional movie.

Bresson is famous for constructing opaque characters, a consequence of a purportedly 'flat' or unmodulated acting style. Most narrative filmmaking—especially that within the expressive tradition—relies heavily on facial expression, bodily gesture, and dialogue to communicate information about characters. Cinematography co-operates with staging and performance, by rendering action predominantly within a certain range of anthropomorphic shot-scales, which enable us to discern the specificity of facial expressions. Antonioni sometimes stages scenes with the performers turned away from camera, and even some Hollywood films of the 1940s (like *Now, Voyager*) play with the norm of frontal

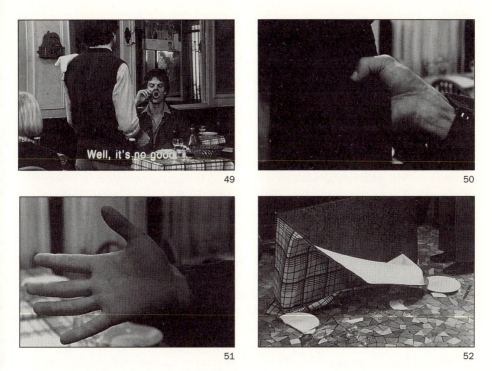

Frames 49–52 L'Argent: Yvon's argument with the waiter

staging; but Bresson subverts these conventions more systematically and persistently. In *L'Argent*, the rise and fall of dramatic tension is planed down to a level surface by a number of interlocking techniques: the acting style, an absence of anything closer than a medium-shot of the human face, and a complementary tendency to cut to parts of the body other than the face at moments of dramatic intensity. For example, Yvon's angry exchange with the cafe waiter who recognizes the notes as counterfeit is represented by three shots. In the first, Yvon and the waiter are framed in medium-shot, with the waiter's back to the camera (frame 49). They argue. Yvon stands up in response to the insult. Cut to a close-up of Yvon's hand grasping the shirt of the waiter (frame 50); he grips it tighty and then explosively shoves the waiter backwards. The shot lingers on the hand, opened out like a fan (frame 51). The third shot shows us an overturned table, with the waiter's legs just visible at the edge of the frame (frame 52). Similar constructions include the car chase, the episode with the skimmer in the prison mess-hall, and the coffee bowl held by the woman as she is slapped by her father. In each case, the classical technique of communicating the emotions of characters at moments of great intensity by recourse to facial close-ups is replaced by an attention to the limbs of the characters and the

props involved. These examples differ from the elliptical narrative constructions Bresson is fond of, like the decision to sustain the shot of the credit-card
machine while a character is assailed off-screen. In this case, the film generates
a degree of ambiguity about what has happened, a quality which is not present
in the previous examples. What makes these cases interesting from our perspective is that in them the narrative event is clear, but the rendering of character subjectivity is attenuated.

The inexpressivity of Bresson's characters has been somewhat overstated, I
think, at least with respect to *L'Argent*. Rather than characterizing the performance as 'flat', as a total absence of inflection on the part of the actors, it is better
described as operating within a compressed amplitude. A narrower repertoire
of gestures and attitudes is used to represent the same spectrum of inner states
that we find in classical films, both in terms of the type and intensity of inner
states. In other words there is a subtle modulation of acting, most noticeable
in *L'Argent* in vocal delivery. Certain characters are consistently more expressive in their vocal delivery than others.[62] The shop owner (Didier Baussy) and
the blind father (Michel Briguet) stand out in this respect. Indeed, we are introduced to the owner via the vituperative articulation of the words 'Imbecile!
Idiot!' But other characters too are infected by this sporadic emotionality:
Norbert's voice is very excited as he speaks to Martial on the phone in the first
scene; a fellow prisoner shouts in Yvon's defence in the mess-hall scene. Yvon's
'philosopher cell-mate' seems to take pleasure in the lilting rise and fall of his
sermon on the absurdity of the world and the centrality of money. In all but
the last of these cases, however, the performer either has his back to the camera, or the head of the performer is off-screen altogether, so we are still far
from a classical construction.

Yvon's vocal style is not uniformly inexpressive either. When Lucien and the
owner of the photo-shop both deny recognizing him, a note of bemusement is
present in his response to the detective, expressed in the rising pitch of the line:
'Ils sont fous.' When his wife Elise (Caroline Lang) visits him in prison, he
raises his voice in desperation as she leaves. This example is particularly useful because the vocal modulation here is juxtaposed with lack of modulation
in facial expression. Bresson establishes a kind of flat ground with respect to
facial expression and bodily gesture, over which subtle modulations of voice
play.

In addition, there are some moments when Bresson, in a sideways glance to
early cinema, places his actors in strikingly expressive bodily 'attitudes'. The
most memorable example is the shop owner's histrionic removal of a tear, shed
in response to Lucien's 'noble' gesture of returning the stolen money, accomplished with a broad sweep of the arm (frame 53). On returning to his apartment after having been accused of wilfully trying to pass counterfeit money,
Yvon sits, body stooped, with his head in his hands (frame 54). In prison, he lies

53   54

Frames 53–54 L'Argent: bodily attitudes and gestures

face down on his cot, having received news of his daughter's evidently painful death, and later he beats his head against a door in frustration as Lucien attempts to escape. These are very broad strokes, especially in the context of the generally compressed amplitude of performance. They provide a basic sense of a character's inner state, and they certainly do not conform to the stereotype of the unperforming, utterly opaque Bressonian performer. Having acknowledged these qualifications—the occasional modulations of vocal delivery and sporadic use of highly expressive gestures—I should reaffirm that they occur in the context of a generally inexpressive performance style. These deviations do have an important effect, however, which I pursue below.

For roughly the first third of the film, we have little difficulty in determining the subjective states of characters. In spite of the somewhat elliptical narration and the generally inexpressive style of performance, the basic motivations and reactions of characters are made clear by the vocal modulations, occasional bodily attitudes struck by the performers, and by cues provided by narrative context, dialogue, and genre. We have no difficulty in understanding the tie between action and character traits in the opening scenes: Norbert is a spoilt child of the *haute bourgeoisie* who wants more money than his parents are willing to give him. As a result, he is willing to pass a counterfeit banknote. His pamperedness is later confirmed when he runs to his mother after being questioned about the counterfeit money. Yvon is poor but dignified (or perhaps stubborn), traits established by his angry reaction to the waiter's accusations, and confirmed by his refusal to 'grovel like a dog' for his job. As in this example, dialogue is often crucial in establishing the narrative situation and the state of mind of a character. Thus, early in the plot *L'Argent* exhibits that economical, mutually sustaining motivation of action and character disposition that is a feature of classical cinema.[63] Furthermore, many of the situations in the first half of the film are generically familiar from the 'wrong man' thriller (Fritz Lang's *You Only Live Once* (1937), Hitchcock's *The Wrong Man* (1956)); our intertextual knowledge clarifies to some degree the psychological states of characters where the film itself is unforthcoming. Once again, generic schemata allow us to go beyond what it is literally given. But as we noted in Chapter 3, the 'inexpressive' performance style of the film, together with the placement of shots of objects and inert limbs at dramatic moments, undercut the process of affective mimicry, which provides the viewer with an empathic gauge of the emotional states of characters. While the first third of the film is quite comprehensible, it lacks the 'emotional intimacy' generated in classical films by mimicry.

Moreover, as the narration becomes more elliptical, so the narrative veers away from any obvious generic destination, and we strive to accommodate our genre schemata to less familiar narrative developments. If there is a single point at which a shift can be located, it is Yvon's release from prison. Nothing, not even the agony Yvon experiences over the death of his daughter and the knowledge of his wife's decision to leave him, prepares us for the nonchalant manner in which he murders the hotel owners. The increasing subjective opacity generated by the narration is underlined in the scenes where he first sees and follows the woman (Sylvie van den Elsen) into the countryside. The film teases the spectator with the idea that the two may know each other somehow—they first exchange glances in an oddly meaningful manner, and when Yvon enters the farmhouse that night, he casually walks in as if he were returning from a hard day's work into his own home. It is not clear that they are unrelated until they engage in conversation, which is deferred until the woman has checked on all the other members of the household.[64]

However, we have been prepared for the lack of depth in the last scenes by a gradual increase in the opacity of the characters. Compare the scene in which Yvon sits morosely with his family following the 'failure' of Lucien to recognize him, with the scene in which he is sentenced to three years in prison. By contrast with the earlier scene, Yvon does not fall into a conventionalized pose to express anger or defeat, for example. Can we say that he takes the decision stoically? Or is that a misreading of the expressionless visage of the performer, a projection of our own to fill this emotional void? The problem posed by the final scene has already begun to present itself.

The scene during which prison officials question Yvon about 'brandishing the skimmer' is key in this progression towards impenetrability. Dialogue establishes, in this instance, Yvon's occurrent emotional state: 'Is he agitated?' one governor asks; 'No. Calm', replies a second. Asked about his motives, Yvon is first evasive, and then facilely compliant:

GOVERNOR. You took the skimmer and what did you do?
YVON. Nothing. [*Pause.*] You think I wanted to kill him?
GOVERNOR. We think so. What do you think?
YVON. I think that's what happened.

Such, at least, is one interpretation of his actions. The exact dynamic of his thoughts is quite obscure. Henceforth, motivations will not be available for scrutiny. Although he verbalizes certain motivations for his actions with the woman in the farmhouse, his statements are not wholly convincing. He says he killed the hotel owners because he enjoyed doing it, although their bodies disgusted him. He takes money from the hotel, searches the farmhouse presumably for money, and asks 'Where is the money?' before murdering the woman. But the traits predicated upon him by these actions—the monomania of an obsessed and brutalized thief—clash with those suggested by his relationship with the woman. In his brief stay at the farmhouse, he shows himself to be sensitive to her mistreatment by the others. In the scene immediately preceding that in which he murders the family, he picks berries, offers them to the woman, and helps her hang out some washing. These seemingly incompatible traits are not resolved by an inner struggle or some higher-order personality model (schizophrenia, for example) which would explain the relationship between his apparent compassion and palpable violence. Clearly, the direct link between action and character motivation—exemplified early in the film by Norbert's desire for some extra pocket money—has been broken. To some degree, this is a feature that L'Argent shares with many 'art' films, which frequently deal with characters who have divergent and incompatible traits. The protagonist of Polanski's The Tenant (1976), for example, is both 'a sensible young man' and a paranoid cross-dresser. But typically a degree of resolution, or at least mediation, is offered by the high degree of access we have to the character's subjectivity. Such films may not go so far as to provide a pseudo-scientific explanation of apparently contradictory behaviour, as many Hollywood films from the 1940s and 1950s do (e.g. Anatole Litvak's The Snake Pit (1948), John Brahm's The Locket (1946), Psycho, Possessed), but neither do they block all access to the character's subjectivity, as Bresson does in L'Argent.

If the development of Yvon's character becomes opaque and unpredictable, then the revelations regarding Lucien are even more astounding. Characterized at first as thoroughly egotistic and venal by his willingness to perjure himself, only for the sake of a new suit and of protecting himself from the consequences of his own thievery in the shop, it is suddenly revealed that Lucien has an altruistic streak, and has been donating his ill-gotten gains to charity (albeit eccentric ones). The narration has concealed this from us simply by presenting his acts of theft in isolation, concentrating on the mechanics of the jobs (the repricing of the camera, the metal strip technique with the cash-point machine) rather than revealing his motivations in performing them. Character development in both Yvon's and Lucien's cases contrasts starkly with the adumbration of character development in the Hollywood film, where the possible trajectories of development are severely constrained by the established star persona, and hence tend to be highly predictable.

The puzzle of Lucien returns us to the problem posed at the beginning of this analysis: whether and to what degree the film licenses our habitual practice of inferring interior states from external expressions and gestures, given the peculiar nature of performance in the film. When Lucien makes some extra money by overpricing the camera, the narration refuses to cut to his face at any point to give us access to Lucien's occurrent emotional state (fear, exhilaration). Instead, the film concentrates on the physiognomy and rhythm of the trick, as it does with all exchanges involving money or goods in the film (passing the counterfeit bills, Norbert's mother paying off the woman in the photo shop, the exchanges of goods between prisoners, even the letters in the prison mail room). But we may be tempted to take the construction of the scene as a way of commenting on Lucien: it shows his absolute self-possession, reinforcing our sense (at this point in the film) of his corruption. I am less inclined to call this a misreading than to see it as an inevitable part of the viewing process; the most powerful schemata for all of us continue to be those associated with classical form, in which the ascription of traits on the basis of actions and expressive performance is constantly in play. The text itself keeps drawing us back to this process of inference by the deviations from inexpressivity examined above. The 'flattening' of expressive performance is neither complete nor consistent, as it would have to be in order to 'train' the spectator to relinquish this habit altogether.

By the end of the film, however, the structure of increasing opacity puts this habit in question, and we are left in doubt as to whether to assign a trait to Yvon on the basis of his cold confession, or to suspend this impulse and see it merely as part of a style of performance which does not allow the inference of character subjectivity from gestures and expressions (vocal and facial). Is the mode of performance to be taken as part of the story world, or is it a narrational intervention? Performance, like the other technical parameters in Bresson's films, is not as subordinate to the narrative as it is in the classical film; but as the principal bearer of character, performance is perhaps more resistant to being perceived as part of a pattern of purely stylistic variation. Indeed, the history of Bresson criticism suggests that even cinephiles have been more apt to fill the vacuum created by the tamped down acting style with a transcendental presence than to find the opaque actions meaningless or 'nonsignifying', a worktop enabling the exploration of cinematic style.[65] We should acknowledge that this hesitation between rigorous formal patterning and an intense (if suppressed) emotionality is integral to the experience of Bresson's films, not a lamentable distraction from such formal patterning.

The nature and structure of alignment in L'Argent suggests one way in which cinematic narration may depart from the typical features of classical alignment, especially the requirement of a revealed psychology. While both of the films we have examined in detail explore the relationship between exterior, physical expression, and interior states, L'Argent replaces the pattern of convergence between expression and psychology that characterizes Hollywood cinema with one of divergence. Based on an understanding of the way film narration, using various techniques, both attaches us to characters and provides varying degrees of access to their subjectivities, the concept of alignment enables us to talk about such non-classical strategies with more precision than the dichotomy 'identification–distanciation' allows.

One general conclusion may be derived from the foregoing examination of alignment in the context of various types of film. There is, on occasion, a legitimacy to the notion of a spectator and a character sharing an identical emotional or cognitive state. Noël Carroll has argued, as we saw in Chapter 3, that 'identification' is a fundamentally wrong-headed notion, a concept ill-suited for the purposes of building a theory of spectatorial response. Instead he prof-fers the concept of 'assimilation', in which the spectator comprehends the mental states of a character and then reacts with a suitable but typically different emotion: the grief of the tragic hero provokes pity in the spectator, not more grief.[66] While I share Carroll's suspicions at the global level, we have seen examples where a close alignment between spectator and character at the local level amounts to the two entities sharing an identical mental state: curiosity about the transaction between Hollenius and Gribble in *Deception*, for example. In saying this, I do not mean to translate 'alignment' back into 'identification': such an action would violate the impetus behind my own project. Eager as Carroll is to throw out the murky bathwater, however, I believe he throws out a baby which should be preserved, albeit thoroughly hosed down.

I have discussed how the spectator goes about recognizing characters, that is, individuating and re-identifying them; and how she is (or is not) given access to and limited to the actions and psychologies of characters in different ways, that is, is aligned with characters. I have tried to set in relief the conventions of classical filmmaking—among the most automatized of schemata—by juxta-posing them with films which operate according to fundamentally different principles. But I have yet to examine in detail the question of how films elicit and organize our emotional responses to character, and it is to this subject— the level of engagement I term *allegiance*—that I turn in the next chapter.

1. John Davis, 'The Tragedy of Mildred Pierce', *The Velvet Light Trap*, 6 (Autumn 1972), 27.
2. Kristin Thompson, *Breaking the Glass Armor; Neoformalist Film Analysis* (Princeton, NJ: Princeton University Press, 1988), 168.
3. Moreover, subjective access can exist without attachment, although this might seem counter-intuitive. That is, it is possible to render the subjective state of a character without ever establishing attachment to that character, that is, placing and following the character in a determined spatio-temporal context. The 'trance' films of the early American avant-garde— Maya Deren's *Meshes of the Afternoon* (1943), many Stan Brakhage films—often represent the subjective states of a character without anchoring these states in an objectively depicted character or world. We come to recognize the character, and the fictional world, only through

a subjective narration. The independence of subjective access from attachment is more evident in literary narrative, in which the spatial position of a character is often indeterminate (see Boris Uspensky, *A Poetics of Composition: The Structure of the Artistic Text and Typology of a Compositional Form*, trans. Valentina Zavarin and Susan Wittig (Berkeley: University of California Press, 1973), 76–80).

4. *Stage Fright* might at first appear to be a powerful counter-example, in so far as we mistakenly trust information which is clearly marked as mediated by character. Although the explanation of the murder we receive at the beginning of the movie is clearly 'filtered' through Johnnie's subjectivity, as it is narrated in the form of a flashback told by him, we do not question the validity of the information. A powerful norm of classical narration assures us that in spite of the mediation the images we see are accurate: images in flashbacks (indeed images in general) do not 'lie', and if some form of subjective distortion is present, this will be promptly signalled. This convention cues us to rely on the information rather than view it sceptically, as in the case of *The Man Who Knew Too Much*. *Stage Fright* appeals to a 'meta-convention': the convention that the image does not lie overrides the convention that information obviously filtered through a character lacks the authority of impersonally narrated information.

5. Here I depart from Chatman, who treats filtration not as an effect produced by attachment and subjective access working in concert, but as a consequence of subjective transparency (in his scheme, 'filter') alone. See Seymour Chatman, 'A New Point of View on "Point of View"', in *Coming to Terms: The Rhetoric of Narrative in Fiction and Film* (Ithaca, NY: Cornell University Press, 1990).

6. See Diane Waldman, 'At Last I Can Tell It to Someone! Feminine Point of View and Subjectivity in the Gothic Romance Film of the 1940s', *Cinema Journal*, 23: 2 (Winter 1984), 29–40; and my 'Film Noir, the Female Gothic and *Deception*', *Wide Angle*, 10: 1 (1988), 62–75.

7. Even in these two films, the narration breaks the pattern of exclusive and complete alignment occasionally, although the information we receive at these moments does not give us any greater insight into the guilt or innocence of the suspected parties (Aysgarth in *Suspicion*, the Castevets in *Rosemary's Baby*).

8. The material on narrative 'point of view' in literary narrative is prolific, having been addressed, in somewhat different ways, by Anglo-American authors (James, Lubbock, Forster, Booth, Chatman), Continental authors (Genette, Bal), and Soviet authors (Bakhtin, Voloshinov, Uspensky).

9. Gérard Genette, *Narrative Discourse: An Essay in Method*, trans. Jane E. Lewin (Ithaca, NY: Cornell University Press, 1980), 162.

10. Such literary models stress problems which have only marginal relevance to the poetics of film narration. The distinction between 'who tells?' and 'who sees?' (or, more correctly, 'who perceives?'), for example, while crucial to literary narratology, is not a fundamental issue for film theory because only very loose analogies can be drawn between verbal and cinematic narration.

11. We are attached to a character if the character's actions are directly represented (that is, enacted) by the narration. If a character's actions are recounted by another character within the diegesis—whether verbally, or visually in the form of a flashback—then the narration may be said to establish an embedded attachment. Direct representation depends on the absence of a mediating level of narration—in the form, for example, of character dialogue or voice-over—not on which channel of the medium is used to perform the function. On the distinction between enacting and recounting, see Seymour Chatman, *Story and Discourse: Narrative Structure in Fiction and Film* (Ithaca, NY: Cornell University Press, 1978), 32; and David Bordwell, *Narration in the Fiction Film* (Madison: University of Wisconsin Press, 1985), 77–8.

12. For a discussion of similar issues with respect to literary narrative, see Uspensky, *Poetics of Composition*, 57–65.

13. This is not the case, however, in Soviet montage films, whose protagonists are salient because of a more committed rather than a more complex mindset.

14. The most comprehensive scholarly work is James Naremore, *Acting in the Cinema* (Berkeley: University of California Press, 1988).

15. Janet Staiger, ' "The Eyes are Really the Focus": Photoplay Acting and Film Form and Style', *Wide Angle*, 6: 4 (1985), 14–23; see also Roberta E. Pearson, *Eloquent Gestures: The Transformation of Performance Style in the Griffith Biograph Films* (Berkeley: University of California Press, 1992).

16. Noël Carroll, *Mystifying Movies: Fads and Fallacies in Contemporary Film Theory* (New York: Columbia University Press, 1988), 224.

17. Claudia Gorbman, *Unheard Melodies: Narrative Film Music* (London: BFI, 1987), 83.

18. Bordwell, *Narration in the Fiction Film*, 64–70.

19. Ibid. 67.

20. Ibid. 70–3; see also Steve Neale, 'Melodrama and Tears', *Screen*, 26: 6 (1986), 6–22.

21. Bordwell, *Narration in the Fiction Film*, 58.

22. The concept of a 'hierarchy of knowledge' is the cognate concept within Bordwell and Thompson's system to my own 'structure of alignment'. Bordwell and Thompson, however, discuss the concept under the rubric of the range of narration (attachment), before they have even defined the depth of the narration (subjective access) (David Bordwell and Kristin Thompson, *Film Art: An Introduction*, 3rd edn. (New York: McGraw-Hill, 1990), 65). But a hierarchy of knowledge, like a structure of alignment, is the product of both functions.

23. Genette, *Narrative Discourse*, 195.

24. For Genette, 'alterations' are contrasted with the truly subversive polymo(o)dality of Proustian narrative, in which there is an overlaying of focalization structures which are decreed exclusive by tradition (rather than logic).

25. The word 'accomplice' is used by V. F. Perkins, *Film as Film: Understanding and Judging Movies* (Harmondsworth: Penguin, 1972), 142. Two further examples of the fallacy: Walter Lasally's description of the heavily-POV shot-laden *Lady in the Lake*: 'The task of making the patron believe that he is actually getting into, and driving a car, or crawling along the road on his hands and knees and hiding behind some bushes while in reality comfortably seated in his chair is not an easy one—but both these effects have been secured with remarkable reality' ('Subjective Cinema: An Analysis of the MGM Film *Lady in the Lake*', *Film Industry*, Apr. 1947, 12); and Jonathan Demme's comment on *The Silence of the Lambs*: 'I thought it was essential that the movie really put the viewer in Clarice's shoes. That meant shooting a lot of subjective camera in every sequence she was in; you always had to see what Clarice was seeing. So as the scenes between her and Lecter intensify, inevitably we work our way into the subjective positions' ('Identity Check', interview with Gavin Smith, *Film Comment*, 27: 1 (Jan.–Feb. 1991), 33).

26. Larry W. Riggs and Paula Willoquet, 'Up Against the Looking Glass! Heterosexual Rape as Homosexual Epiphany in *The Accused*', *Film/Literature Quarterly*, 17: 4 (1989), 221.

27. The fallacy underpins the notion of 'suture', in so far as the latter assumes an 'identification' between the spectator and the character whose vision motivates the space seen (which may or may not be in the form of POV shot, strictly defined). See Jean-Pierre Oudart, 'Cinema and Suture', *Screen*, 18: 4 (Winter 1977–8), 35–47; for an overview of the development of the concept by Stephen Heath and others, see Kaja Silverman, *The Subject of Semiotics* (New York: Oxford University Press, 1983), 213–14.

28. Edward Branigan, *Point of View in the Cinema: A Theory of Narration and Subjectivity in Classical Film* (New York: Mouton, 1984), ch. 5.

29. Noël Carroll, 'Toward a Theory of Point-of-View Editing: Communication, Emotion, and the Movies', *Poetics Today*, 14: 1 (Spring 1993), 134. Carroll summarizes his argument in the following way: 'the point/glance shot *sets the range* of the relevant emotions and *guides the reception* of the point/object shot'—via our capacity to recognize basic affective states through facial expression, as discussed in Chapter 3—'while the point/object shot *focuses* or *specifies* the particular emotion represented' (p. 136).

30. François Jost has made a distinction between *focalization* (information) and *ocularization*

(perception), which shares with my argument here a concern to show that seeing is not simply equivalent to knowing: 'Narration(s): En deçà et au delà', *Communications*, 38 (1984), 192–212.

31. See Branigan, *Point of View*, 58. Elena Dagrada, 'The Diegetic Look. Pragmatics of the Point-of-View Shot', trans. James Hay, *Iris*, 7 (1986), 120, examines at length an example from *The Nutty Professor* which exploits this form of POV in order to trick the spectator into making some mistaken inferences, for comic effect.

32. Quoted in Peter Graham, *The New Wave: Critical Landmarks* (New York: Viking, 1968), 93. There is some question as to what Truffaut means by the gazes 'meeting'. I do not interpret him literally, but understand him to mean the representation of the character's face rather than the object of her glance.

33. Branigan, *Point of View*, 122.

34. Quoted in Graham, *The New Wave*, 93.

35. There are some POV shots from Scottie's position in the scene, but their role is insignificant compared with the role of the reaction shots in the 'keying' of the scene to Scottie's subject-ivity. Shots of the coroner and the jury are necessary to focus (in Carroll's terms: see note 29) Scottie's emotional state, but they need not be POV shots to perform this function.

36. For an instance of the assumption that facial expressions in film are intrinsically meaningless, and given meaning only by context, see Ben Brewster, 'Film', in Dan Cohn-Sherbok and Michael Irwin (eds.), *Exploring Reality* (London: Allen and Unwin, 1987), 157; for a critique of the Kuleshovian assumptions embodied in Brewster's remarks, see Stephen Prince and Wayne Hensley, 'The Kuleshov Effect: Recreating the Classic Experiment', *Cinema Journal*, 31: 2 (Winter 1992), 59–75.

37. Naremore, *Acting in the Cinema*, 43.

38. Paul Ekman (ed.), *Emotion in the Human Face*, 2nd edn. (Cambridge: Cambridge University Press, 1982), 18–19, 149–52. My thanks to Thomas Elsaesser for bringing the example from *North by Northwest* to my attention, and for grilling me about the status of both the Kuleshov-effect, and the cultural dimension of facial expression, within my argument.

39. Edward Branigan, *Narrative Comprehension and Film* (London: Routledge, 1992), 157.

40. Cf. Ben Brewster's remarks on the contingent relationship between optical POV and 'nar-rative point of view' (in my terms, alignment), and in particular his remarks on Griffith's Biograph films of the period 1909–12, in 'A Scene at the "Movies"', *Screen*, 23: 2 (July–Aug. 1982), 9.

41. Leo Braudy, *The World in a Frame: What We See in Films* (Garden City, New York: Anchor, 1976), 184.

42. In *Daisy Kenyon*, the ambiguities about character motivation and intention which result from Preminger's style of narration are finally clarified. In some Preminger films, the ambiguities are sustained and left as ambiguities at the end of the film—as in the later *Anatomy of a Murder* (1959), for example.

43. Jonathan Culler, 'Stanley Fish and the Righting of the Reader', *Diacritics*, 5: 1 (Spring 1975), 28.

44. Steve Neale states that an awareness of films addressed specifically or especially to a female audience became prevalent in American trade papers in the late 1910s and 1920s; the earliest use of the term 'woman's picture' he finds is in 1911: 'Melo Talk: On the Meaning and Use of the term "Melodrama" in the American Trade Press', *The Velvet Light Trap*, 32 (Fall 1993), 80 n. 55.

45. Peter Brooks, *The Melodramatic Imagination: Balzac, Henry James, Melodrama, and the Mode of Excess* (New York: Columbia University Press, 1984), 41; see also 44.

46. Sergei Balukhatyi, 'Russian Formalist Theories of Melodrama: Balukhatyi and the *Poetics of Melodrama*', *Journal of American Culture*, 1: 1 (Spring 1978), 154.

47. Ibid. 156; see also Richard Dyer, *Stars* (London: BFI, 1979), 156.

48. See Staiger, '"The Eyes are Really the Focus"'.

49. Martin Meisel, *Realizations: Narrative, Pictorial and Theatrical Arts in Nineteenth-Century England* (Princeton, NJ: Princeton University Press, 1983), 7. I should point out here that the presence of mute figures in nineteenth-century melodrama is not a sign of inexpressivity, but rather an indication of the impetus towards non-verbal expression in this era. There is a debate over how this relates to the psychoanalytic revolution—Peter Brooks sees it as a prefiguration of Freudian theory, Louis James sees it as 'exploded' by the same. I sympathize with the latter view. See Brooks, *Melodramatic Imagination*, 35–6, 201–2; and James, 'Was Jerrold's Black Ey'd Susan more popular than Wordsworth's Lucy?' in David Bradby, Louis James, and Bernard Sharratt (eds.), *Performance and Politics in Popular Drama: Aspects of Popular Entertainment in Theatre, Film, and Television, 1800–1976* (Cambridge: Cambridge University Press, 1980), 7.

50. With somewhat different emphases, both Ben Singer and Steve Neale argue that in the nineteenth and early twentieth century, 'melodrama' was associated with 'masculine' adventure dramas, rather than domestic dramas or romances: Ben Singer, 'Female Power in the Serial-Queen Melodrama: The Etiology of an Anomaly', *Camera Obscura*, 22 (Jan. 1990), 91–129; Neale, 'Melo Talk', 69. Drawing on Frank Rahill, however, Neale points towards an encompassing notion of expressivity in a comment on the 'modified melodrama', a late nineteenth-century form in which 'firearms and the representation of the convulsions of nature yielded the centre of the stage to high voltage emotionalism [and the] examination of soul states' (Frank Rahill, *The World of Melodrama* (London: Pennsylvania State University Press, 1967), p. xv; quoted by Neale, 'Melo Talk', 76). It is this sort of broad connectedness that I have tried to capture with the phrase 'expressive tradition'.

51. Dyer, *Stars*, 138.

52. See Kristin Thompson's analyses of the latter two films, *Breaking the Glass Armor*, 135–94.

53. I am, of course, treating these popularized psychoanalytic beliefs in a most un-Freudian manner, by treating them as schemata which structure our comprehension of behaviour. But there is no contradiction here: our belief-schemata do not have to match that which is really the case. Religious beliefs could also be modelled on the schema theory of mental representation. Schema theory describes the nature of mental activity, and does not prescribe particular thought-contents.

54. The 'field' I have represented is by no means complete. A total field for a particular historical moment would be much larger, but given a principle of cultural salience, would not be limitless.

55. The schemata a spectator brings to a text are largely determined by her socio-cultural status. In the case of post-war melodrama, the gender of the spectator might be crucial in determining the saliency of a particular schema. Indeed, the two conceptions of 'truth', and the different expressive conventions of the melodramatic and detective structures of alignment, may have a special relationship to 'femininity' and 'masculinity' respectively, as these aspects of identity were then (and to a large degree still are) understood: femininity characterized by a propensity for emotion and openness with others, masculinity defined by a kind of macho truculence, in which speech misleads more than it reveals.

56. Carlo Ginzburg, in 'Morelli, Freud and Scientific Method', *History Workshop*, 9 (Spring 1980), 5–36, argues for a link between psychoanalysis and the detective novel in terms of what he calls the 'conjectural method'—that is, methods of analysis which go beyond what is materially available and verifiable. This is akin, in terms of interpersonal understanding, to what I am calling the Repressive Truth Schema, which also assumes that the truth is not always directly available through expressive manifestations.

57. Dana Polan, *Power and Paranoia: History, Narrative, and American Cinema, 1940–50* (New York: Columbia University Press, 1986). Waldman discusses the popularization of psychoanalysis in connection with the 'female gothic' cycle (*Gaslight, Rebecca, The Secret Beyond the Door*) of the 1940s, in 'Horror and Domesticity: The Modern Gothic Romance Film of the 1940s', Ph.D. thesis (University of Wisconsin–Madison, 1981), 230–8.

58. This 'mixing' should not be confused with the intermingling of the detective and melodramatic narrational modes discussed in relation to *Deception* earlier in the chapter. The withholding of significant information at certain moments in *Deception* is explicitly signalled. By contrast, in *Daisy Kenyon*, Peter's actual opacity is hidden—ironically—under the appearance of transparency; the withholding of significant information is entirely unsignalled.

59. See the first section of David Bordwell, Janet Staiger, and Kristin Thompson, *The Classical Hollywood Cinema: Film Style and Mode of Production to 1960* (New York: Columbia University Press, 1985). As I noted earlier, Thompson, *Breaking the Glass Armor*, argues that particular films from this period, such as *Laura* and *Stage Fright*, did adopt duplicitous narrations which dramatically challenge classical conventions. My hypothesis is that the viewing of certain genres during this period may have been marked by a kind of uncertainty as a result of the new force and pervasiveness of the Repressive Truth Schema, as a consequence of the spread of psychoanalysis beyond the detective movie with which it has a certain 'natural' affinity.

60. I do not mean to suggest that Hollywood no longer produces straightforward melodramas, based on the aesthetics of the expressive tradition. But such films, I submit, no longer constitute the highly automatized background against which we view all dramas exhibiting the melodramatic structure of alignment.

    That said, *Choose Me* adheres to classical conventions in other respects. Although Mickey's sexual desire seems undirected, it is still channelled towards the two female stars of the film; and Mickey ends up with Eve, the female character with whom he first makes love. The symmetry of classical narrative form, and the regulating power of the star system have, as it were, the last laugh in the film, in spite of its play with the classical conventions of character expressivity.

61. Raymond Durgant, 'Inside Norman Bates', *Films and Feelings* (Cambridge, Mass.: MIT Press, 1971).

62. Cf. Thompson's comments on Bresson's *Lancelot du Lac* (1974), *Breaking the Glass Armor*, 297.

63. Ibid. 169; Boris Tomashevsky, 'Thematics' (1925), in Lee T. Lemon and Marion J. Reis (trans. and eds.), *Russian Formalist Criticism: Four Essays* (Lincoln: University of Nebraska, 1965), 90.

64. The lack of a developed backstory (another feature of Bresson's technique of characterization) is also important here.

65. Bordwell, *Narration in the Fiction Film*, 306. Critics who pursue the 'spiritual' or 'transcendental' interpretation of Bresson include Susan Sontag, 'Spiritual Style in the Films of Robert Bresson', in *Against Interpretation and Other Essays* (New York: Delta, 1966), 181–98; and, specifically with respect to *L'Argent*, Dave Kehr, 'The Shock of the Immediate', *Chicago Magazine*, June 1984, 124–6.

66. Noël Carroll, *The Philosophy of Horror; or, Paradoxes of the Heart* (New York: Routledge, 1990), 95–6.

Soot and Whitewash: Allegiance

6

Most poetry is built on sympathy and aversion, on the evaluation of the material as it is presented. In literary works the conventional virtuous hero and the villain directly express this positive or negative evaluation. Because the feelings and emotions of the reader must be oriented, the theme of a work is usually emotionally colored; it evokes and develops feelings of hostility or sympathy according to a system of values.

Boris Tomashevsky[1]

I am not a dictator. I just have a grumpy face.

General Pinochet[2]

The phenomenon of allegiance is distinct from those of recognition and alignment in that it is an emotional as well as a cognitive response. It is particularly important that we grasp the distinction between alignment and allegiance here, since a great deal of narrative theory and criticism either conflates the two, or regards allegiance as simply a feature of alignment. Wayne Booth, Mieke Bal, and Seymour Chatman have all argued or implied that alignment with a character necessarily creates a basic sympathy for that character. Discussing Kafka's *Metamorphosis*, for example, Booth argues that 'because we are absolutely bound to [Gregor Samsa's] experience, our sympathy is entirely with him'.[3] Let us recall the example of *Maniac* in order to reveal the error of this argument, and to underline the distinction between alignment and allegiance. In this film, the spectator is aligned with a brutal rapist and murderer; we are spatially attached to this character and have access to his thoughts. But such alignment is distinct from our evaluation of the character. *Maniac* could be remade in such a way that the same events are narrated according to an entirely different pattern of alignment, in which the narration alternately attaches us to the murderer and a detective. Such a restructuring on the level of alignment would not in itself, however, affect our moral evaluation of the rapist—and it is to this evaluative level of structure and response that the concept of allegiance refers. The most we can say is that the conventional association of alignment and allegiance—most narratives in practice do elicit sympathy for those characters with whom they align us—primes us to be sympathetic to characters with whom we are aligned. If this relationship were necessary, however, it would be impossible to conceive of anti-heroes—protagonists around which the alignment structure of the film is built, but who remain unsympathetic.

To become allied with a character, the spectator must evaluate the character as representing a morally desirable (or at least preferable) set of traits, in relation to other characters within the fiction. On the basis of this evaluation, the spectator adopts an attitude of sympathy (or, in the case of a negative evaluation, antipathy) towards the character, and responds emotionally in an apposite way to situations in which this character is placed. I have chosen the term allegiance in part because it captures this combination of evaluation and arousal. As Tomashevsky recognizes, narratives engage us not simply through the cognitive interest generated by plot construction and the play of style, but through the 'emotional colouration' of thematic material. This 'colouration' is articulated through narrative agents.

In spite of the prominence accorded to these observations by Tomashevsky—they constitute the introduction to his essay—neither he nor other theorists within the Formalist and structuralist traditions have developed the notion of a 'system of values' or 'moral structure' in narrative works.[4] This is surely because of the suspicion of 'realist' conceptions of character within this tradition, a suspicion expressed by Tomashevsky himself later in the essay (on these matters, see also Chapter 1). In focusing on the way narratives elicit emotional responses towards characters, it is held that we analyse them according to a spurious criterion of realism, instead of assessing them 'according to laws proper to' works of art. Tomashevsky, for example, criticizes certain Russian critics of the 1860s for evaluating the character Vasilikov, in Ostrovsky's *The Bankrupt*, according to their 'everyday personal or political feelings', instead of examining how an emotional attitude towards the character is elicited by the structure of the novel.[5] Over time, the study of emotional response to character has come to be regarded as the area in which the hapless critic is most likely to wander astray into the slough of simplistic mimeticism.

The phenomenon of 'emotional colouration' has been forced to lead a subterranean existence within the Formalist and structuralist traditions because of these early interdictions on the study of character. While the causal, rhetorical, temporal, and spatial structures of narrative have been extensively and minutely examined, very little systematic attention has been directed towards moral structure (although critics and theorists of all stripes frequently rely upon an unreflective, pre-theoretical notion of moral structure). Nick Browne, for example, has written of the 'moral commentary' and 'moral order' of film texts,[6] in an attempt to examine the relationship between characters and values, but his analysis of this system is rudimentary in comparison with his examination of the relationship between characters and space. Of course, one response to this lack of systematic attention is to suggest that it simply reflects the actual insignificance of moral structure. It is obvious, the argument goes, that narrative films articulate, more or less explicitly, ideologies, doctrines, religious ethics, and so forth; and it is equally obvious that our reactions to these clusters of beliefs and values will depend entirely upon our own moral, political, and religious beliefs. Fashionable as this argument is, it leaves a very striking aspect of fictional experience unexplained. How is it that our emotions can be aroused by fictions which represent characters engaged in actions in which we have either no interest, or find simply deplorable? We may, for example, find ourselves caught up in a film like John McNaughton's *Henry: Portrait of a Serial Killer* (1990), responding with sympathy at certain moments to Henry, though in reality the phenomenon of serial killing *tout court* is repugnant to us. Do we all have a little Henry deep inside of us—or is there some other explanation for such a response?

I will have more to say on this question later in this chapter and in the concluding chapter, but as a starting-point we should note here Tomashevsky's imperative: 'To read, one must be innocent, must catch the signs the author gives.'[7] We may find the idea of an 'innocent' reader or spectator, taken literally, implausible. But something like a suspension of values must occur, if we are to explain the spectator aroused by the gangster film, against her 'better' (i.e. everyday) judgement. As Victor Perkins has suggested, 'Within limits the film-maker can recast our normal priorities of response';[8] and it is here that the importance of the internal 'system of values'—or moral structure—of a text becomes apparent. The task of this chapter will be to consider, first, how such 'systems of value' are constructed; secondly, the range of possible types of moral structure; and thirdly, the different ways in which a narration may unfurl these moral structures through time, a process I shall refer to as 'moral orientation'. Allegiance, as with the other levels of response considered thus far, is conceived of as a dynamic phenomenon which develops across the text.

Before examining these matters in more detail, a brief comment on my use of the term 'moral' is in order. I choose the word 'moral' rather than 'ideological' because, with respect to characters, ideological judgements are expressed as moral evaluations. Within contemporary film and cultural theory, however, the Marxist rejection of morality, as an inherently bourgeois notion, has been highly influential. There can be no doubt that the application of moral principles derived from scenarios of interpersonal behaviour (i.e. direct, local exchanges between human agents) to the behaviour of supraindividual forces (institutions) is often spurious. But it is not clear that radical programmes, like Marxism, really do escape notions of morality. Most basically, capitalism is an unjust form of social organization because it systematically exploits most members of society. Certain Marxists recognize this, and do not see Marxism as a system which transcends moral concepts or language. Moreover, nothing in my use of the term 'moral' denies the three fundamental insights that, it has been argued, Marxist literary theorists have contributed to the debate over the relationship between morality, politics, and ideology: first, that moral systems may be expressions of group solidarity; secondly, that they may vary historically and culturally; and thirdly, that different moral schemes may be more or less 'progressive' with respect to particular political goals.[9] 'Morality', then, might be added to agency, imagination, and mimesis, as another term which contemporary theory has been overhasty in rejecting.

As Noël Carroll suggests, 'Character . . . is the most integral factor in establishing the spectator's moral perspective on the action.'[10] It will be helpful here to re-examine the various techniques which contribute to the construction of character, focusing on the specifically moral dimensions of these stylistic devices. As in the case of alignment, these techniques must be understood in terms of how they function within certain structures—in this case, moral structures and patterns of moral orientation. These structures and patterns are the central concern of this chapter.

Obviously enough, one of the crucial mechanisms of moral orientation is that of character action. (We have already seen, in Chapter 5, that within the classical Hollywood cinema 'character' is virtually synonymous with 'character action'.) Carroll picks out the behaviour of major characters towards minor characters as an important device of moral orientation: Hannay's kindness towards Mrs Jordan in Hitchcock's *The 39 Steps* (1935), for example, contributes to our positive evaluation of him. More generally, thoughtful, generous, solicitous behaviour on the part of characters towards physically and socially weaker characters (children, the old, the sick, the oppressed) elicits a positive evaluation. Along similar lines, we might consider the behaviour of characters towards domestic pets. Near the beginning of *Daisy Kenyon*, for example, Peter Lapham pets Daisy's dog Tubby. His behaviour towards the dog is in marked contrast to the self-involved behaviour of his rival suitor, Dan O'Mara, who ignores the dog altogether. We hardly notice Lapham's gesture, because it constitutes the default value of our 'behaviour towards pets' schema: it is what people usually do with pets. Imagine, though, the effect on Fonda's characterization, and our

55

Frame 55 The Man Who Knew Too Much: Rien (Reggie Nalder), the ugly assassin

moral stance towards him, if he were to kick the dog instead of petting it (with no apology or explanation by phobia). This aggressive action towards the dog would be much more noticeable, occupying a lower place in the default hierarchy and being thus less automatized. But the automatized quality of our perception of the action of petting the dog makes it no less significant as part of our induction into the moral system of the film. Trivial as the gesture may seem, it is an important cue in the on-going process of moral orientation, especially given that it is among the first actions we witness Lapham perform (see the comments on the primacy effect, Chapter 4).

Similarly, iconography may have a pervasive but only peripherally perceptible influence on the development of a film's moral structure. Eisenstein drew on a particular tradition of 'physiognomic' iconography in *Strike*, and later commented directly on its value:

[Lavater's physiognomy] in its day was regarded as an objective scientific system. . . . We do not attribute to physiognomy any objective scientific value whatsoever, but the moment we require, in [the] course of the all-sided representation of character denoting some type, the external characterization of a countenance, we immediately start using faces in exactly the same way as Lavater did.[11]

The role of iconography in the process of allegiance has hardly been touched on, however (except in the self-pitying remarks of dictators, like General

Pinochet). I know of no work which runs a thread from the establishment of character via physical attributes (facial and bodily features, dress style, props), through the construction in the text of a moral structure, to the process of allegiance and emotional response. The work of iconography in this respect, however, is omnipresent, and rapid: consider the way in which the conventional ugliness of the assassin in *The Man Who Knew Too Much* immediately fixes him as a suspicious character (frame 55). The effects of iconography range from very general assumptions embedded within cultures regarding, for example, racial types, through to implications specific to particular genres, cycles, even individual texts. For example, as Eisenstein suggests, we still use terms and iconography which have their origins in discredited sciences like physiognomy. The terms 'highbrow' and 'lowbrow' derive from phrenology, in which certain races were deemed to be less intelligent because of a characteristic shape of skull.[12] The concomitant stereotypical iconography of race, used to represent blacks, Native Americans, and other minorities, persisted in Hollywood films until at least the 1960s. (An unusually explicit manifestation of such racist iconography appeared in the pages of *Time* during World War II, in the form of a guide claiming to enable readers to discriminate friendly Chinese from hostile Japanese, on the basis of physiology alone.)[13] Within a much smaller group of films, Richard Dyer has suggested that the physical attributes of Jane Fonda were invested with very particular connotations from the beginning of her career ('Americanness', liberalism), by virtue of the obvious resemblance between Jane and her father Henry.[14] These examples capture the range of possible phenomena: widespread cultural assumptions, concerning the relationship between appearance and inner 'moral character', used by a great many films, and very specific associations generated by a small number of texts. Whether we consciously assent to the moral associations of iconography or not, they are part of the 'automatized' level of filmic comprehension.[15]

There are good reasons for the lack of detailed attention to the relationship between the physical attributes and moral status of characters. The risk that such research would result in an untenably precise typology of physical types is high in a medium based on indexical representation. On the other hand, there is the possibility that the critic would come up with nothing more impressive than the stark oppositions noted by Panofsky: the Vamp (cigarette, vanity mirror) and the Straight Girl (apron, hair tied in homely bun), the Family Man (clean-shaven, stocky build, upright posture) and the Villain (black moustache, walking stick). And yet the use of physical traits with conventionalized meaning in the construction of types persists as an important part of contemporary filmmaking: consider the similarities in facial and bodily type, and costuming, in the representation of FBI agents in Martin Scorsese's *The King of Comedy* (1983), John McTiernan's *Die Hard* (1988), and Roger Donaldson's *No Way Out* (1987), for example. The fact that physiognomy and phrenology are dead as sciences does little to affect the generation of popular galleries of types based on physical features. The practice extends back to Chaucer's lascivious Wife of Bath, marked as such by the gap between her front teeth, and still further to Aristotle's *Physiognomonica*.

A third salient factor in the process of moral orientation is music. Claudia Gorbman notes that the 'girl next door is [often] graced with a sentimental tune in a major key; the seductress is often accompanied by a cocktail-lounge jazz clarinet or saxophone'.[16] In addition to character action, iconography, and music, the moral structure of a film may draw upon the arsenal of linguistic techniques developed in literature: sociolects, epithets with a moral dimension, and symbolically charged proper names. In D. W. Griffith's *Broken Blossoms* (1919), an intertitle describes Battling Burroughs as an 'abysmal brute'. In Soviet montage films, to be tagged 'bourgeois' is to occupy the pole of absolute 'evil' in the moral structure. In certain Hollywood films, 'Commie', 'pinko', or 'red' function as an equally succinct moral shorthand. (The epithets do not have to be specifically political or ideological; indeed, I shall argue below that it is a characteristic of the Hollywood film that it takes originally political and ideological terms and drains them of their specificity, retaining only the broad outline and general cultural evaluation of the term, to ensure that films will not appeal only to the very limited politicized segment of the audience.) Naming a character 'Eve' (as Alan Rudolf does in *Choose Me*) inevitably invokes widely understood (if not shared) cultural associations, which initiates and informs the process of evaluation, as do all of the following names in some degree: Sam Spade and Caspar Gutman (*The Maltese Falcon* (John Huston, 1941)), Jim Wormold (*Our Man in Havana* (Carol Reed, 1960)), Barney Millsap (*Kiss Me, Stupid* (Billy Wilder, 1964)), and Rupert Pupkin (*The King of Comedy*). Even the most naturalistic names—those designed, according to Barthes, to establish the absolute uniqueness of the character—carry some representative implications, which feed into our evaluation of characters.[17]

A thread running through my comments on character action, iconography, and naming is the star system. In Chapter 4, I indicated the importance of the star system in the process of recognition. It is equally significant with respect to allegiance; whatever else stars may be, they are, as Richard Dyer has shown, embodied clusters of (often conflicting) traits. We cannot tackle the complexities of the star system here, mired as we are in the overlapping, but distinct, question of our emotional responses to characters. Nevertheless, we should acknowledge that the process by which we evaluate characters and respond to them emotionally is often framed or informed by our evaluation of the star personae of the stars who perform these characters. Star 'charisma'—the elusive appeal that stars possess, often deriving from their embodiment of central social concerns in a particularly intense or compelling way—can obviously be used to direct our sympathies. Indeed, this is another technique by which the spectator can be brought to entertain sympathetically actions, characters, and domains of experience that they might otherwise reject.[18]

Text and Co-text

You have not seen yourself, you say. These people are all violent and suicidal. You are none of these.

The End (Christopher Maclaine, 1953)

Carroll, like Tomashevsky, regards moral-orientation-through-character as an internal feature of the text.[19] We can best understand the force of this claim if we return to those narratives which elicit from us responses of sympathy towards actions and characters with which we would have either no interest in or an active aversion towards in reality. For example, towards the end of Claude Chabrol's *The Story of Women* (1988), we sympathize with the heroine, a woman who has eked out a relatively privileged life for herself in occupied France, by performing abortions and by taking a Nazi informer as a lover. At first, the character seems entirely self-centred and attracts little sympathy; but once she is arrested, her crimes seem puny compared with the sanctimonious and hypocritical actions of the collaborationist authorities who decide to execute her for her 'moral weakness'. Our sympathies are determined here not simply by external factors—that is, by our real-world attitudes towards collaborators, informers, and the like—but by the internal 'system of values' of the text, in which such real-world attitudes are organized by the on-going placement of characters into positions of relative desirability. On the basis of this process, we form preferential and hierarchized sympathies and antipathies towards the various characters. Thus Henry, in *Henry: Portrait of a Serial Killer*, is quite repulsive by any external standard of morality; but, within the text's moral system, he is perhaps preferable over Otis. The difference hinges on their respective attitudes and behaviour towards Becky, Otis's sister; though Henry finally kills her, he protects her from Otis's sexual abuse and forms some kind of affectionate bond with her.

Nevertheless, such claims about our emotional responses to characters do rest upon the assumption that actions have fairly determinate moral 'valences'. The character actions Carroll discusses, the icons, names, and musical motifs which contribute to the construction of characters, only have a determinate moral valence within the terms of the text's 'co-text'. The co-text is the set of values, beliefs, and so forth which form the backdrop to the events of the narrative—the context within the text, as it were.[20] Individual works will establish this moral co-text more or less explicitly: some rely on overt, propositional statements to fix the moral nature of actions (through intertitles, for example), while others simply assume that the social context, shared by the contemporary spectator, will perform this function. Thus, the charitable actions Carroll discusses only have their positive moral valence in a world which endorses power structures and class differentiation, but which also values highly agents who do not abuse their power by (habitually) mistreating those in subordinate positions.[21] With contemporary works, the 'co-text' is often 'invisible' in so far as it conforms to the values of the social world in which we actually live. In the terms of the cognitive model of the spectator advanced in Chapter 2, the co-text may match the belief-schemata of the spectator, producing that 'automaticity' of perception (in this case, evaluation) that Edwin Hutchins terms 'referential transparency'.[22]

Similarly, many practices and values are stable enough such that their moral valence alters little over time. Dogs are still a common type of domestic pet. Consequently, Peter Lapham's affection towards the dog is still entirely recognizable as a 'humane' gesture, functioning to characterize him as warm and sensitive, and so to elicit our favour. But if dogs had been discovered to carry a harmful tick in 1950, had ceased to be kept as domestic pets, and had come to be regarded as no more than an oversized form of vermin, a contemporary spectator's reaction to Lapham's gesture would not carry the same 'automatic' sympathetic charge. (The correct moral valence of the action would still be determinable within the co-text, but this may not always be a simple matter because of the largely implicit nature of the co-text.) Indeed, such a spectator might misread the kick, in the revised version of the film, as merely the defensive action of a threatened person, with no negative moral charge. Thus, in stressing the importance of the internal 'system of values' of a text, we are not reverting to the anti-mimeticism of structuralism. The mimetic hypothesis has as much pertinence to moral evaluation as to other kinds of response; and as with these other responses, our mimetic assumptions, in this case concerning the moral valences of actions and agents, are subject to revision. Fictional narratives may 'recast' these external moral assumptions and beliefs, as both *The Story of Women* and *Henry: Portrait of a Serial Killer* strikingly illustrate.

We do not need to rely on fictional conjectures about the impact of killer ticks on our relations with domestic pets, however, in order to demonstrate the importance of the co-text in evaluating character behaviour. One need only look at D. W. Griffith's *The Birth of a Nation* (1915) in order to find a co-text of values which clashes with our own (or at least with the ostensibly accepted political-moral system of contemporary American society). Austin Stoneman's kindness towards Silas Lynch and other black characters is assumed to carry a negative moral charge, just as the paternalistic behaviour of the Cameron family to their black servants is approved within the co-text of the film. At best, Stoneman is morally weak—this much is directly stated by an intertitle; at worst, he is morally corrupt, the 'evil' within the text's moral system.

It is in this context that I would situate much of the work on cinema influenced by psychoanalysis, such as that concerning the relationship between gender and POV in Hollywood cinema, initiated by Laura Mulvey. In the political and cultural co-text of patriarchy, of which Hollywood films are a part, POV shots may take on an intrinsic moral or political meaning, being symptomatic of both a masculine voyeuristic urge to control the object of 'the look', and a narcissistic impulse to identify (in the Freudian sense) with the object of the look.[23] The male spectator, and 'masculinized' female spectator, find such shots pleasurable, and may therefore be sympathetic to the character whose look is represented. By contrast, Michael Powell's *Peeping Tom* (1960) links POV shots with psychotic, murderous acts, thus creating a co-text in which the POV shot possesses an unmistakably negative valence. But can we read a shot of a factory owner, representing the POV of an angry peasant in Pudovkin's *The End of St. Petersburg*, as equally symptomatic of patriarchal male desire or male psychosis? The varieties of 'male subjectivity' in the first two scenarios, and the 'proletarian subjectivity' in the last, and the degree of authority or sympathy which attaches to these particular 'subjectivities', are 'emergent qualities' of the narration which neither depend solely on nor can be reduced to the device of POV alone. Pudovkin's film creates a co-text very different from those in the other films, and any knowledge we have of the social context of *The End of St. Petersburg* will only serve to reinforce this alternative moral background set; and it is against this co-textual backdrop that the POV shots in the film must be seen. In accepting the insights of research based on psychoanalysis in this fashion, I am not contradicting my earlier caveats about the doctrine. Nothing here commits us to believing that the processes posited by psychoanalysis really do occur, just as nothing committed us to the truth of either of the two truth schemata invoked by *Daisy Kenyon*. This is no different, in essence, to arguing that it is legitimate and sometimes necessary to recognize the social power of Christianity, its influence on behaviour and the way we understand and above all evaluate behaviour, without endorsing it metaphysically. We are treating these doctrines as beliefs about human functioning which have informed both filmmakers and spectators at certain points, and which may therefore be crucial to an understanding of the moral co-texts of certain films.[24]

Ultimately, the problem of assigning a moral valence to a character's action, appearance, or any other constitutive factor, is part of the larger problem of interpretation. While in theory one can come up with conjectures about any number of audiences who might interpret a text in a radically 'inappropriate' way—as in the hypothetical example of *Daisy Kenyon* and the killer ticks—these only become interesting in concrete cases. As the Soviet critics Scheglov and Zholkovskii have remarked, 'if there really are different audience perceptions, they are several orders fewer than the number of cinema-goers'[25]—precisely because spectators share schemata. It is no surprise that an endless variety of interpretations can be produced within an institution largely devoted to it, as a number of metacritical analyses have pointed out.[26] I do not wish to argue that a reconstruction of the probable comprehension and interpretation (in this case, of specifically moral signs) of a contemporary audience is privileged in any absolute sense. But it has at least pragmatic value, for any striking 'mis-' or 're-'reading of a text can only be recognized as such by comparison with a normative contemporary reading, which sets up an implicit, descriptive standard for other interpretations.

The Manichaean Moral Structure: Strike

The objects the imitator represents are actions, with agents who are necessarily good men or bad—the diversities of human character being nearly always derivative from this primary distinction, since the line between virtue and vice is one dividing the whole of mankind.

Aristotle[27]

The kind of moral structure which articulates an unqualified opposition of good and evil values—the 'old "soot-and-whitewash" polarity', as Raymond Durgnat calls it[28]—is often identified with the melodrama, understood as a tradition of narrative representation originating in the late eighteenth century and extending through to the present day, evident in many Hollywood films among other cultural products (TV, pulp novels of various sorts, wrestling, and so forth). We noted in the last chapter that 'melodrama' has also been defined as a kind of narration. In the context of allegiance, yet another designation of the term will come to the fore: the domestic or family drama. The complex and shifting reference of the term demands caution in our use of it. In particular, the claim that 'melodrama' designates a persisting genre defined principally by a Manichaean moral structure, if it is to be maintained at all, requires considerable revision. To begin with, then, I will examine a type of film which I think exemplifies less problematically what I will term the Manichaean moral structure: the agitational film. The agitational film I define as one which is overtly designed to promulgate a particular doctrine, be it ideological or religious, and hence either to change the spectator's beliefs in accordance with the doctrine, or to reinforce these same ideas if they are already held by the spectator. Thus, the Manichaean moral structure and the agitational film are not synonymous, or even commensurate, terms. The agitational film is a type of film defined by several other factors which work in conjunction with the Manichaean moral structure: a doctrinal intertext explicitly evoked within the text (the scriptures, or the works of Marx and Lenin), and an exemplary narrative which concludes with a 'rule of action' ('turn the other cheek'; 'be vigilant for traces of bourgeois values in your own behaviour'). It is a mode of narration, of which the Manichaean moral structure is only one prototypical feature.[29] By the same token, the Manichaean structure appears in other types of film, defined by different narrational patterns and performing different functions. I shall draw my examples of agitational cinema from the cycle of Soviet montage films, examining Eisenstein's *Strike* (1925) in some detail.

In the agitational film, a particular doctrine is dramatized according to a dualistic value system, or Manichaean moral structure. The poles of the value system are occupied and embodied by characters or groups of characters. The dramatic structure is a genuinely antagonistic one, where that term suggests a powerful moral dimension: not only do the opposing dramatic agents have conflicting goals, but the goals themselves are situated at opposite ends of a moral spectrum. The striking workers in *Strike* seek to improve the conditions of the proletariat; the factory bosses and the military seek to suppress the uprising and continue exploiting the workers. The dramatic structure is thus not 'agonistic', as in the epic (or a film like *North by Northwest*), in which the struggle between opposing forces is conceived as a sort of game, where what is at stake is ingenuity, but rather as a moral struggle waged in the name of transcendental, absolute values (God, History, Manifest Destiny).[30] The ending of the socialist realist film *Battle for Siberia* (1940, directed by the Vasiliev 'brothers') furnishes an interesting demonstration of the difference between the two forms. The film is clearly agitational, and the action of the body of the film is marked by the kind of absolute moral opposition discussed here, between the embattled Soviets and their deceitful Japanese enemy, along with the presence of Bolshevik doctrine both within the text and invoked as an intertext. The film ends, however, with more than a hint of comradely bonding between the victorious Bolshevik commander and the heretofore 'evil' Japanese commander. The film seems to accept that the Japanese commander was only doing what was expected of him as a soldier, rather than characterizing him unequivocally as a class enemy. The ending, in other words, is more characteristic of the agonistic than the antagonistic, Manichaean narrative structure, and a striking departure from the norms of socialist realist narrative.

The Manichaean moral structure is generated in *Strike* principally through character types. Typage, for Eisenstein, was a technique by which abstract, social processes could be concretized in a character through external, physical traits associated with particular classes. This was accomplished in *Strike* by drawing on an iconographic repertoire established in cartoon satire, puppet theatre, and poster art.[31] Both the social position and the moral valence of the various characters are made immediately apparent through exaggerated physical traits. The second shot of the film (discounting intertitles) is a close-up of the director of the factory, his grotesquely fat, laughing face framed by a silk top hat at the top of the image and a frock coat and tie at the bottom (frame 56). The principal physical traits—obesity, expensive clothing, excessive

56

57

58

59

60

61

62

63

Frames 56 – 63 Strike: iconography and morality

laughter—lead directly to certain social and moral judgements: material self-indulgence and a sadistic insensitivity to the plight of others. The type of the wealthy capitalist, and the connections between its physical and moral attributes, would have been immediately recognized by a contemporary Soviet audience, as the figure had been an icon of anti-capitalist visual satire since at least the 1905 revolution. The moral evaluation invited by the type was secured by this enduring background set of visual icons (which were drawn upon again during World War II).

In addition to iconography, the film also employs certain linguistic devices in order to elicit rapid and absolute moral judgement from the spectator. Characters on both sides of the conflict are identified by their occupation and social role, rather than by a unique proper name: foreman, manager, worker, and so forth.[32] The linguistic and the iconographic techniques converge in the typing of the government spies, several of whom are known by animal names: the Owl, the Monkey, the Fox, the Bulldog, and the Bear. The names and images (an image of each animal is superimposed over the characters when they are first introduced) function to predicate a single, overriding, negative trait upon the character: cunning in the case of the Fox, for example (frame 57).

In order for a Manichaean moral structure to be sustained, however, the dualistic system of values has to be redundantly established. This is accomplished in *Strike* in a number of ways. First, on either side of the conflict, a great number of characters participate in the action and make pronouncements on the nature of the conflict. This is particularly clear in the case of the workers. Even more so than in *Arsenal*, the important actions within the revolutionary situation are distributed across many different characters: here no single leader emerges, along the lines of Timosh in *Arsenal*. There is a systematic difference in the relationship between individual characters and the mass of secondary figures, within the proletarian group and the bourgeois group respectively. While the bourgeois figures are individuated and re-identified early on in the film (the owner, the manager, the foreman, the stockholders), and only later are seen to be backed by large social groups (the hoodlums, the police, and the military), few proletarian figures are re-identified at any point in the film (on the concepts of distribution, individuation, and re-identification, see Chapter 4). Emblematic of the difference in the strategy of characterization here is the juxtaposition, in the first few minutes of the film, of the caricatured but individuated director and foreman, with the various groups of workers, all of whom are seen either in long shot, in silhouette, obscured by machinery, or positioned with their backs to the camera (frames 58, 59). The workers are composed, in other words, in such a way as to stress their typical features and downplay their individuality, thus retarding recognition (cf. the analysis of these and other techniques in *Arsenal* in Chapter 4).[33] The individualism of bourgeois society, as it is understood within Bolshevik doctrine, is represented by this difference in the degree and type of individuation within the two antagonistic groups.

Secondly, moral redundancy is accomplished by linking the various members of the opposing dramatic forces in the film through recurrent and overlapping iconographic motifs. Thus, several capitalists and military men are obese. Those capitalists who are not obese are identified with their peers through their formal and expensive dress style (frame 60). Both the young manager of the factory and the head foreman wear striped shirts (associated with the figure of the Kulak) (frame 61). The tramps enlisted by the government as provocateurs are depicted as deluded imitators of the bourgeoisie, decked out in the discarded remnants of their employers (worn hats, oversized overcoats, striped shirts, and so forth) (frame 62). On the other hand, among the striking workers, the men wear plain jackets and cloth caps, the women long work dresses and scarves (frame 63). In this way, the principal associations of the two sets of icons—self-indulgence and decadence, on the one hand, hard work, frugality, and selflessness, on the other—are continually reinforced. This was precisely the function of iconography grasped by Panofsky: '[A] method of explanation . . . a fixed iconography . . . from the outset informed the spectator about the basic facts and characters, much as [in a medieval scroll] the two ladies behind the emperor, when carrying a sword and a cross respectively, were uniquely determined as Fortitude and Faith.'[34]

Redundancy is also achieved through the mutual reinforcement between the overt narration of the film and the actions and speeches of characters. While the narration in the film as a whole is highly self-conscious, it is most overt in its use of tendentious (as opposed to expository or dialogue) intertitles. The film opens with a quotation from Lenin, stressing the need for organization and unity among the proletariat. These sentiments are echoed by characters at several points in the film—for example, on the 'labour rostrum' after the strike breaks out. Susan Suleiman suggests that in the *roman-à-thèse*—the novelistic equivalent to the agitational film—'actions and events are continually doubled by interpretive commentary',[35] which reinforces the moral structure of the text. In film, of course, the 'commentary' cannot be equated with the linguistic device of the intertitle; the 'commentary' pervades the iconographic structure of the film, as discussed above. Nevertheless, the intertitles further reinforce the dualistic value system by attaching moral epithets to events and characters: the underclass characters are 'hoodlums'; the bargain struck between 'the King' of the underclass and the government spy is a 'dirty deal'; and the killing of children by the military in the sixth section of the film ('Liquidation') is dubbed 'savagery'.

Certain critics have argued that far from producing a univocal meaning through the strategies of redundancy outlined here, Eisenstein's films are in fact 'writerly' texts which reveal the process of meaning production, and hence

64   65

Frames 64–65 Strike: iconography and morality

generate a certain instability of meaning.[36] Judith Mayne, for example, argues that women in *Strike* destabilize the opposition between the bourgeoisie and the proletariat. In support of this claim, she cites the scenes of domestic discord, in which one wife lambasts her husband for the lack of food during the strike, while another resists her striking husband's decision to pawn some domestic goods for the purchase of food.[37] The subordinate position of women under patriarchy undermines the binary opposition between bourgeoisie and proletariat that the film explicitly sets up. Mayne does not comment on the resolution of this conflict within the proletarian couples, however. The second wife comes to accept not only the need to pawn the goods her husband has collected (including part of their young child's clothing), but volunteers a piece of jewellery in addition. This gesture marks her off from the lavish, bejewelled bourgeois women in the film (frame 64). The conflict between man and woman is contained within the dominant opposition between bourgeoisie and proletariat. A controlled contradiction is rhetorically useful to an agitational film: 'A crisis overcome . . . becomes . . . a sign of coherence'.[38]

Arguments of this sort derive in part from too homogeneous a view of 'modernism', understood as a phase of aesthetic practice. Modernism, it is assumed, involves an attack on univocal meaning. If we are to understand what makes Eisenstein's films modernist, we must probe the apparent clarity of the films' political messages, and discover ambiguity and 'undecidability' (a Derridean term used by Mayne) within them. The modernity of *Strike*—as of a great deal of European art from the 1920s—resides not in thematic ambiguity or semantic equivocation, however, but in the formal dynamism put in the service of the straightforward political message. An instance of this formal inventiveness may be found in the use of playful intertitles. The third intertitle of the film reads: 'All is quiet in the factory' (На заводе всё спокойно). A new intertitle frames in close-up the last two letters of the preceding intertitle ('но'), meaning in Russian 'but'. The letters are animated so that the 'н' lays itself sideways in the centre of the frame, and the 'o' moves on top of it; the 'н' then fades out. A dissolve to a fan follows, graphically similar to the form of the 'o', in front of which two workers, in silhouette, discuss strategy. The film then cuts to a further intertitle. The redundancy on the iconographic level —established in the film and in advance of it by the artistic intertext—enables the use of such laconic, ironic, and playful intertitles. The codes of iconography and character action, far from being unique to the film, are derived from a familiar intertext. This secures a stability of meaning, which in turn enables an inventiveness of technique and play with the codes of editing, performance, intertitling, and so forth, with little risk of ambiguity disrupting the underlying political thesis. The redundancy evident in the moral structure of the film permits a stylistic play with the spatial, temporal, and causal structures of the film without any weakening of its agitational function.

A further technique of redundancy is identified by Suleiman as the 'amalgam', in which 'a character is constructed in such a way that his or her culturally negative qualities are redundant with qualities whose pertinence is specifically ideological'. Her example concerns the character Rébecca Simonovitch from the novel *Gilles* by Pierre Drieu La Rochelle, an anti-Communist *roman-à-thèse* from the late 1930s. Rébecca is ugly, envious, and 'promiscuous to the point of lubricity' (culturally negative qualities) and Jewish and Communist (specific ideological qualities).[39] Suleiman further postulates a causal relationship between the two sets of qualities: it is as if the character is Communist as a result of being ugly, and vice versa. In *Strike*, the culturally negative qualities of greed, decadence, and brutality towards children (represented by the excessive consumption of food, drink, and tobacco among the bourgeois characters, and the murder of children in the raid on the factory) (frame 65) are 'amalgamated' with the ideology of capitalism. And the amalgam works just as surely at the opposing, positive ideological pole: kindness to children, witnessed in several scenes depicting the proletariat, is connected with a sense of communal welfare (frame 63) which is in turn amalgamated with specifically Bolshevik ideology (recall the emphasis placed on organization and unity in the quotation from Lenin which opens the film).

It is characteristic of the Manichaean moral structure that the antagonistic principles are externalized and embodied by physically discrete agents. The 'positive hero' of socialist realist narratives is wholly committed to the aims and ideals of the revolution; his White Guard or bourgeois factory owner antagonist is equally committed to the absolute destruction of these goals. The 'positive hero' is not at all 'typical', then, in the Lukácsian sense, where the typicality involves a literal em*bodi*ment of the contradictions of a given historical moment: the contradictory impulses adhere to a single person. Fillimonov in Friedrich Ermler's *Fragment of an Empire* (1929) is a typical hero in this sense, struggling internally with the contradictions between capitalist and socialist value systems. Similarly Lucía, in the first part of Humberto Solás's *Lucía* (1968), is typical in the Lukácsian manner, embodying the conflict between bourgeois values (her obsession with romantic love) and the nationalistic passion for independence. By contrast, in the Manichaean moral structure, a single principle, represented by a character or group of characters, is placed in contradiction with an opposing principle, represented by a separate character or group of characters. Lukács criticized such narrative forms for producing a 'merely external picture of mutual destruction incapable of arousing the human sympathies and enthusiasms of the reader'.[40]

Why should the Manichaean structure, and the agitational film, favour the externalized conflict over the interior struggle? From an agitational point of view, it is more persuasive—or merely, perhaps, rhetorically simpler—to represent the enemy as a physically separate 'Other' rather than as a part of the fabric of the self. The violence of extermination is not then directed against the self. It is this absence of externalization, so central to the Manichaean moral structure, that distinguishes *Fragment of an Empire* from *Strike*. By the same token, *Fragment of an Empire* reminds us that the agitational film should not be equated with the Manichaean moral structure, for though it lacks this kind of moral structure the film is clearly agitational. The Manichaean structure is not the peculiar possession of the agitational film; equally, the agitational film can 'survive' a less absolute division of characters according to utterly opposed values.

The breakdown of the Manichaean structure occurs in *Fragment of an Empire* when Fillimonov visits his pre-revolutionary employer. Still surrounded by the trappings of his bourgeois lifestyle, and angry at his relative poverty ('I've been robbed!—ruined!'), the employer resists Fillimonov's attempts to show obeisance to him: 'You musn't do that. We are all equal now—no master and workman any more.' Fillimonov leaves his former boss, still confused and unable to grasp mentally the new values and practices of socialist life. No 'resolution' occurs, of the type discussed in relation to the proletarian wives in *Strike*, whereby the 'liminal' figure of the boss would be placed as either an enemy or an active proponent of the new society. In moral terms, the boss occupies a grey zone in between, a zone obliterated by the Manichaean structure. Like Fillimonov, he is truly a 'fragment of empire', adrift from both his previous life and the new world.

In spite of this, *Fragment of an Empire* remains an agitational work. The film evokes the doctrinal intertext of Bolshevism, and, like *Strike*, ends with an explicit address to the spectator, who is exhorted to continue working for change, as 'there is still much to do'. The narrative functions as an exemplum, inviting an interpretation which in turn furnishes a 'lesson' and an implicit rule of action: 'Be vigilant for the traces of the old, bourgeois ways, in others, but especially in yourself.'

The Hollywood Manichaean

If *Fragment of an Empire* provides us with an instance of an agitational film which forgoes the Manichaean structure, what film or class of films utilize the Manichaean structure outside of an agitational imperative? Here I return to the aesthetic form that many readers would have expected me to begin with: the classical stage melodrama and its purported successor in cinema, the Hollywood melodrama. Neither Hollywood cinema in general, however, nor Hollywood melodrama in particular, is wedded to the Manichaean moral structure. I shall argue that the Manichaean structure constitutes an option, and, as an element of classical stage melodrama, a historically important antecedent, but it is not a necessary component of either the classical Hollywood cinema in general or the Hollywood melodrama in particular. Discussion is complicated here by shifts in the sense and reference of the term 'melodrama'—an issue already touched on in Chapter 5. I will argue that an older sense of the term 'melodrama', evoking the Manichaean moral structure, has been transferred—inappropriately—to the primary reference of the term in academic film criticism, that is, Hollywood 'woman's pictures' and 'family melodramas' produced between 1930 and 1960.

The integral relationship between classical stage melodrama and the Manichaean moral structure has been most influentially theorized by Peter Brooks in *The Melodramatic Imagination*. For Brooks, melodrama emerges as a form in the wake of the French Revolution and the more general process of Enlightenment desacralization. In the absence of a transcendental system guaranteeing morality, Brooks speculates that one of the functions of melodrama is the reconstitution of a legible moral landscape in purely 'personal' (that is, human, rather than divine) terms. Brooks argues that classical French melodrama hinges on the revelation of a 'moral occult': a Manichaean moral structure which is initially hidden ('occulted'), but which the action of the drama reveals with absolute clarity. The outcome of the melodramatic text 'turns less on the triumph of virtue than on making the world morally legible, spelling out its ethical forces and imperatives in large and bold characters'.[41]

Much of the work on Hollywood melodrama ('woman's picture', 'family melodrama') of the 1930s, 1940s, and 1950s either implicitly or explicitly assumes that the Manichaean moral structure is a core feature of the genre.[42] We do occasionally find examples of the 'soot-and-whitewash' structure in such films, as, for example, in *Johnny Belinda* (1948, directed by Jean Negulesco). Belinda, a mute woman, is raped in the small village community in which she lives. She gives birth to a child, but the local community decides that she is incapable of looking after her child, and the rapist (with new wife) is dispatched to appropriate it. In the ensuing struggle, Belinda shoots the rapist in self-defence. She is then tried for murder, but is vindicated at the last moment. The narrative thus conforms quite closely to Brooks's moral occult, in which the true moral nature of the principal characters, known to the audience all along, is inverted in the world of the characters, until a final dramatic turn forcefully reveals the true moral world.

Among 'woman's pictures' and 'family melodramas', however, such cases are the exception rather than the rule. If the Manichaean structure is evident anywhere within Hollywood cinema, then it is within genres other than those we now recognize as 'melodramatic': the gangster film, the Western, the horror movie, the thriller, the adventure film, and the war picture. Steve Neale has shown that such films were regularly termed 'melodramas' and 'mellers' by the trade press, continuing the nineteenth-century association of melodrama with action and sensation ('blood and thunder'), rather than with domesticity and the feminine.[43] The problem here is that what academic film criticism has identified as 'melodrama' derives from what was, at most, a sub-tradition within classical stage melodrama, born of a fusion of the latter (as analysed by Brooks) with the 'romantic' or 'sentimental' novel of the nineteenth century.[44] The Hollywood descendant of this 'modified melodrama' may indeed be the 'woman's picture', but the latter did not inherit the Manichaean structure of the central, 'blood and thunder' tradition of classical stage melodrama. The Manichaean structure was bequeathed not to the domestic and family drama, but to the 'masculine' genres Neale discusses.

Given, though, that certain Hollywood films do exhibit Manichaean structures, how are we to distinguish between the Manichaean agitational film (*Strike*), on the one hand, and the Manichaean Hollywood film on the other (*Johnny Belinda*)? Again, the distinction hinges on the differing function of the same moral structure within distinct narrational modes with different imperatives. Both are characterized by the Manichaean structure, and yet they perform quite different social functions, and offer very different aesthetic experiences. Unlike the agitational film, the 'Manichaean Hollywood' film does not typically map its dualistic value system on to a particular doctrine, either elaborated within the film or present as an immediate and unavoidable intertext. The narrative therefore does not function as an exemplum, furnishing a rule of action.[45]

A detailed historical account of Hollywood cinema would reveal some complications here. While I believe that the broad distinction between the 'Manichaean agitational' film and the 'Manichaean Hollywood' film holds, the Production Code certainly lent to many Hollywood films of the 1930s and 1940s a didactic aura (even if the 'message' was somewhat less explicit than in the Soviet films we have been examining). 'Immoral' subject-matter was sometimes defended by an appeal to the negative exemplary function of the narrative, as in the Biblical epigraph attached to the beginning of Mervyn LeRoy's *Little Caesar* (1930) ('for all they that take the sword will perish with the sword'), or in the prologue which opens King Vidor's *Beyond the Forest* (1949): 'This is a story of evil. Evil is headstrong—is puffed up. For our soul's sake, it is salutary for us to view in all its naked ugliness once in a while. Thus we may know how those who deliver themselves over to it, end up like the Scorpion, in a mad fury stinging themselves to eternal death.' In addition, there have been several cycles of filmmaking in Hollywood which can only be characterized by their agitational imperative: anti-Fascist films during World War II, and anti-Communist films in the 1950s, for example. Nevertheless, even in these cases, the form of such films is significantly different from that of the truly agitational film, exemplified here by *Strike*. But in order to see how this is so, we need to examine a type of moral system distinct from the Manichaean structure: what I will term the graduated moral structure.

The Graduated Moral Structure

The graduated moral structure is characterized by a spectrum of moral gradations rather than a binary opposition of values. Characters are not sorted into two camps, the good and the evil, but rather occupy a range of positions between the two poles. André Bazin's high regard for Italian Neo-Realist films was in part based upon their articulation of this kind of moral structure, in contrast to what he saw as the Manichaeanism of propaganda films. The graduated structure is seen as another strategy by which films like Vittorio De Sica's *Bicycle Thieves* (1948) capture the 'ambiguity' of phenomenological reality: 'Although on the basis of the workman's misfortune we have no alternative but to condemn a certain kind of relation between a man and his work, the film never makes the events or the people part of an economic or political Manicheism. It takes care not to cheat on reality.'[46] It would be a mistake, however, to regard the graduated structure as one of the characteristics of art cinema which marks it off from Hollywood cinema. As we have already noted, the Manichaean structure constitutes only an option within the classical mode as a whole: many Hollywood films are organized around graduated structures. Indeed, ironically, it is the graduated rather than the Manichaean structure that typifies Hollywood melodrama from the 1930s to the 1950s—the very obverse of the moral structure characteristic of classical stage melodrama, again revealing the difficulties of the term 'melodrama', or at least of its use in academic criticism. *Daisy Kenyon*, Edmund Goulding's *The Old Maid* (1939), Sam Wood's *Kings Row* (1942), Douglas Sirk's *All That Heaven Allows* (1955)—to take a casual sample of films that we would categorize as melodramas, in the contemporary academic sense—all feature a range of more or less good and more or less bad characters, detailing compromise and reconciliation between them, rather than imposing a clear dichotomy between the irreproachably virtuous and the irredeemably evil. Consider, as a further example, Orson Welles's *The Magnificent Ambersons* (1942). The story provides ample opportunity for a Manichaean struggle, pitting gentle, selfless Eugene Morgan against the selfishness and arrogance of George Minnifer. 'Virtue', embodied in Isabel and Eugene, suffers long and hard; and yet the film avoids characterizing George as a purely 'evil' force which is purged, a requirement of classical melodramatic form as described by Brooks: 'The [classical French melodramatic] play ends with public recognition of where virtue and evil reside, and the eradication of one as the reward of the other.'[47] Thus, empirically, the graduated structure provides a better general model of the moral structure of the 'mature' Hollywood melodrama than does the Manichaean (though as we have seen in *Johnny Belinda*, there are instances in which the latter is present). A major flaw in much of the work on the Hollywood 'woman's picture' and 'family melodrama'—in addition to the terminological problems of referring to such works as 'melodramas'—has been a lack of attention to the history of the form. Instead, a hypostasized, timeless model of 'the melodramatic' is constructed, which then becomes the yardstick by which the formal inventiveness and ideological subversiveness of individual films are measured. On this basis, individual texts which seem to undermine an absolute, dualistic moral structure are valorized as subverting the melodramatic system of representation, and in this way are seen as symptomatic of ideological problems of the era.[48] Often, however, the formal background against which the 'subversive' text is measured is a false one, in so far as it ignores the historical developments outlined here, in which the Manichaeism of classical stage melodrama is, in general, replaced by the graduated moral structure.

Of course, Hollywood did produce domestic dramas very clearly drawing on classical stage melodrama, both in terms of specific sources and more general conventions. Many of Griffith's films, like *Orphans of the Storm* (1922), are good examples. Historically, the fault line between such films, often manifesting Manichaean structures, and the domestic dramas characterized by graduated structures, is a complex and, at this stage, empirically unsettled matter. Alan Williams has argued that this shift occurred, and was in some measure caused by, the coming of sound.[49] But there is evidence that the shift may have occurred much earlier. On the stage, the 1860s witnessed a shift in subject-matter and narrative structure, which was in some sense 'repeated' in American film around the end of the first decade of this century. 'Modern-life dramas' and 'everyday dramas' were recognized, within films themselves and in criticism, as distinct from their nineteenth-century forebears by virtue of, first, their attention to contemporary subject-matter, and secondly, their relatively complex narrative structures (less reliant on simple character types) and subtle (in my terms, graduated) moral structures. These formal changes were linked to struggles over class, the newer form being part of an appeal to 'refined' middle-class audiences, as contrasted to the unwashed rabble perceived to be the audience for the older form. The rhetoric of differentiation existed not just in criticism but in films themselves: *Hoodoo Ann* (1916, directed by Lloyd Ingraham) embeds within itself a parodically crude Western, *Mustang Charley's Revenge*, in order to highlight its own contemporaneity, complexity, and sublety.[50] There may, then, have been a transitional period in which domestic dramas manifesting Manichaean structures continued to be produced, while those articulating more graduated structures became more pervasive. By the time of Hollywood's 'Golden Age', most domestic dramas, I would suggest, were characterized by graduated structures.

If the Manichaean structure finds its way into film from the classical stage melodrama, the graduated structure derives in large part from the nineteenth-century realist novel. A particular strategy of characterization stands out by way of contrast with the amalgam. In the context of the agitational film, the amalgam produces a redundancy by overlaying culturally negative qualities with the specifically ideological values which are under attack. More generally— the amalgam is not peculiar to the agitational film—the Manichaean structure is founded upon characters defined by either wholly negative or wholly positive attributes, eliciting an uncomplicated sympathy or unqualified aversion.[51]

The graduated structure, by contrast, tends to generate characters through the combination of culturally negative with culturally positive traits, producing what we might call an 'alloy', in the sense that morally 'base' and 'precious' qualities are combined in the name of a 'stronger' representation, where strength is measured in terms of verisimilitude.[52] In Hitchcock's *Saboteur* (1942), for example, Tobin (Otto Kruger) is a (neo-)Fascist who heads an organization committed to undermining, via sabotage, the efforts of the USA in World War II. He is not, however, a wholly despicable character, in terms of his actions within the film. In particular, in the first scene in which we see him, he displays great affection and solicitude towards his grand-daughter. He is not, as it were, an interpersonal fascist. By contrast with the capitalists in *Strike*, Tobin is not a grotesque amalgam of obesity, ugliness, and self-interest, but rather, an alloy of kindness, civility, condescension, and a commitment to an 'un-American' social doctrine. As in the case of Henry in *Henry: Portrait of a Serial Killer*, a cluster of undesirable traits are linked with more desirable ones, and this has the effect of ameliorating the severity of our judgement of the character. The alloy, as a key element of the graduated moral structure, denies the spectator the absolute, 'primal' responses associated with the Manichaean form.

Interestingly, though, whatever specifically Fascist activities one imagines Tobin engaging in (Jew baiting, for example), these are not represented within the plot, any more than the hero of the film, Barry Kane, is involved in specifically democratic activities. Their ideological positions are determined simply by their functions in the story of the film: Kane works in an aircraft factory, building planes for the Allies, while Tobin works to sabotage such efforts.

We are now in a position to pinpoint more accurately the differences between the authentically agitational film and its Hollywood cousin. First, in the
Hollywood agitational film, the specific contents of the antagonistic doctrines
(Fascism and liberal democracy in the case of *Saboteur*) are drained of much of
their substance. Barry Kane is an attractive person, by the vaguely Graeco-
Roman and Christian standards that govern the moral codes of Hollywood
cinema (a point to which I will return), but hardly a spokesman for a doctrine—
a set of propositions—of liberal democracy: contrast his one overtly 'political'
speech in the film with the quotations from Lenin, and the political speeches
of various characters, in *Strike*. (For similar reasons, Don Siegel's *Invasion of the
Body Snatchers* (1956) has been interpreted as an attack on both Communism
and McCarthyism.) This evacuation of political substance is nicely summed up
in a speech made by Huntley Haverstock, the hero of Hitchcock's earlier espi-
onage drama, *Foreign Correspondent* (1940): 'I don't know the ins and outs of
your crackpot peace movement, and I don't know what's wrong with Europe,
but I do know a story when I see one, and I'll keep after it until I get it or it
gets me.' For the Hollywood agitational, a dynamic story organized around a
character who is (by the standards of Western society) transparently 'good'
does not require the explicit articulation of the ideological values being fought
for—they are supposed to be embodied in the very being of the protagonist.
Secondly, the prototypical Soviet agitational film employs a Manichaean moral
structure. This is much less clear in the case of the Hollywood agitational film.
Here I can only propose that the Manichaean structure may not be typical of
the Hollywood agitational film: *Saboteur* certainly demonstrates that it is not
mandatory.[53] Of course, the characters in the film are divisible into two opposed groups—those in sympathy with the Allies, and those working to sabotage Allied efforts—but the presence of the alloy alerts us to complications
in this apparently dualistic scheme. Similarly, the ending of the film directs
some sympathy towards the heretofore detestable Fry, the 'on-the-ground'
saboteur. As he dangles helplessly from the Statue of Liberty, the expression of
terror on his face evokes, as I argued in Chapter 3, an empathic response,
which in turn complicates the moral structure of the film, underlining its graduated form.

Given that both the Manichaean and the graduated structures are options for
both the agitational and classical narrational modes—the permutations possible
among the two narrational modes and the two types of moral structure are set
out in Figure 6.1—we might ask if there are particular social and historical
circumstances which favour each of these moral structures. For Peter Brooks,
the Manichaean structure of the classical stage melodrama, its 'moral occult',
is a response to the collapse of the traditional guarantors of moral meaning:
the melodrama 'comes into being in a world where the traditional imperatives
of truth and ethics have been violently thrown into question, yet where the

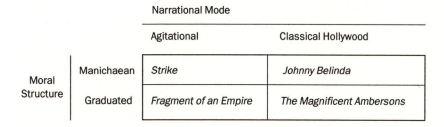

	Narrational Mode	
	Agitational	Classical Hollywood
Moral Structure — Manichaean	*Strike*	*Johnny Belinda*
Moral Structure — Graduated	*Fragment of an Empire*	*The Magnificent Ambersons*

Figure 6.1 Permutations of narrational mode and moral structure

promulgation of truth and ethics, their instauration as a way of life, is of immediate, daily, political concern'.[54] It is not difficult to see how a revolutionary period produces social and ideological polarization, and severe political schisms, which in turn often emerge in narrative art in the form of Manichaean structures. In this sense, there are direct parallels between French stage melodramas made in the wake of the French Revolution of 1789, and the Soviet agitational films inspired by the October Revolution of 1917.

What of the status—and co-existence—of the Manichaean and graduated moral structures in the Hollywood melodrama of the classical era? It is possible that there is a relationship between these different kinds of moral structure and two social forces, one with a specific, institutional base, the other more dispersed: the Production Code, and the popularization of Freudian psychoanalysis. My comments here are offered as a hypothesis rather than as a fully documented argument. The Production Code was formulated in 1928 and then revised in 1934, and exercised considerable influence over Hollywood filmmaking for the following fifteen years, after which its influence gradually subsided. Psychoanalysis was popularized in the USA in two waves: in the 1910s, and then again in the late 1930s and 1940s.[55] During this second period the influence of this popularized version of psychoanalysis became visible in Hollywood filmmaking, with the production of films incorporating Freudian figures, language, narrative structures, and imagery (*Kings Row*, Edmund Goulding's *Nightmare Alley* (1947), Jacques Tourneur's *Cat People* (1942), Alfred Hitchcock's *Spellbound* (1945), Curtis Bernhardt's *Possessed* (1947), Otto Preminger's *Whirlpool* (1949), Anatole Litvak's *The Snake Pit* (1948), and so on).

I have argued that it is a mistake to see a simple continuity on the level of moral structure between classical stage melodrama and Hollywood melodrama, as the latter, quite possibly from its earliest years, had been influenced by the graduated moral structure of the realist novel as much as the Manichaean structure of stage melodrama. What is fascinating about the period of the 1930s and 1940s is that the two more immediate social forces in question here—the

Production Code and psychoanalysis—push the moral structure of the Hollywood melodrama in opposite directions. On the one hand, the Code demands a return to the harsh moral landscape of the Manichaean structure: 'No picture shall be produced which will lower the moral standards of those who see it. Hence the sympathy of the audience shall never be thrown to the side of crime, wrong-doing, evil or sin' (General Principle No. 1). This accounts for the prevalence of retributive endings, often tacked on with insufficient motivation, in which characters guilty of some moral transgression pay with their lives (as, for example, in William Wyler's *The Letter* (1940)). Recall here the convention of classical stage melodrama that evil be eradicated (see above, p. 208). On the other hand, psychoanalysis on the whole tends towards an attenuation of the severity of the Manichaean universe.[56] The language of 'good' and 'evil' is replaced by that of 'health' and 'maladjustment'; responsibility for immoral actions is often removed from the individual, who may now be regarded as subject to unconscious motivations; and the boundaries between the moral and the immoral, the normal and the abnormal, are blurred. 'Thus a healthy person, too,' in Freud's words, 'is virtually a neurotic.'[57] The tensions between the two forces are evident in films like *Possessed*. The film initially sets up a Manichaean opposition between Louise Howell (Joan Crawford) and her one-time lover David Sutton (Van Heflin), with Louise occupying the 'just' moral pole. However, as the film progresses, this simple opposition is complicated. Louise becomes a paranoid psychotic, finally shooting Sutton. But this trajectory does not exemplify the emergence of a moral occult, with Louise and Sutton simply trading places in the original, dualistic moral scheme. Rather, Louise's psychoanalyst Dr Willard states that she was 'neither mentally nor morally responsible for any of her actions', and is hopeful that she can be rehabilitated with love and attention from her husband Dean Graham (Raymond Massey). Thus, the 'sinful' actions of the heroine—to use the language of the Code—do not result in a punitive resolution. My thesis, then, is that the popularization of psychoanalysis is one of the factors which accounts for this attenuation of the stern, Manichaean morality of the Production Code.

In saying this, I do not wish to argue that psychoanalysis was the only determinant, or even a primary causal factor, in the attenuation of the Code strictures. A full account would obviously have to examine the Production Code as an institution, and examine the material factors which led to its loss of power (for example, the rise of independent production). Nevertheless, I think we can say, at the very least, that psychoanalysis provided a powerful new language in which the relative moral tolerance of secular American society could be expressed, against the wrathful Christian sentiment given a platform by the institution of the Code. The attenuation of a Manichaean moral attitude fits far more happily with the ethos of entertainment which underpins Hollywood as an institution than does the didacticism of the Code.

Moral Structures and the Classical Hollywood Film

The notion of the classical Hollywood cinema that I have assumed throughout this study defines it as a particular organization of causality, space, and time, and of relations among these systems. Does the classical Hollywood film possess a normative moral structure, in the same way that it has, in this sense, a characteristic narrative form? Certainly not in the sense that it uniformly promulgates a particular moral doctrine. Raymond Durgnat has revealed the problems besetting any attempt to find in Hitchcock's work a narrowly defined moral code and religious doctrine, the critical strategy associated with Chabrol and Rohmer.[58] The difficulties would only be exacerbated by widening the field to the whole of classical American cinema.

It is true that Hollywood films reflect, in general, the mixture of Graeco-Roman and Christian values which govern interpersonal behaviour in modern Western societies. It is only against such a background—or co-text—that the combination in characters of fortitude with solicitude for the less fortunate, discussed earlier in the chapter, elicits moral allegiance. These values are tacitly accepted norms, usually characterized by the 'referential transparency' of default values, not a highly visible set of propositions for which our assent is explicitly sought (although the Production Code made Old Testament retribution more visible within Hollywood cinema in the 1930s and 1940s). Just as Hollywood cinema transforms social and ideological conflicts into personal dramas, so it reshapes alien doctrines to the contours of this 'default' morality. But the system, at this level, is fairly flexible, accommodating both the egoism of King Vidor's *The Fountainhead* (1949) and the populist communitarianism of *It's a Wonderful Life* (1946) and other Capra films. As Noël Carroll argues, sympathetic characters need not be 'moral in respect of extant ethical codes or sets of categorical imperatives'.[59] It is this transformation which accounts for the dilution of doctrines in Hollywood cinema, functioning to make the text palatable to audiences with no interest in—or even an aversion towards—the particular doctrines in question. This is, of course, a function of the mass nature of Hollywood art—the maximization of audiences—though it has also been taken, by Wayne Booth, to be one of the features of 'great' art.[60]

Rather than seeking the norms of the moral structure of Hollywood cinema at the level of particular doctrines, then, we need to consider norms at a more abstract level. Classical Hollywood films require, I propose, moral 'resolution' and a moral centre. Moral resolution entails that the text makes the moral status of characters clear (if not in the course of the narrative, then at its end, as in the mystery film).[61] A moral centre entails a locus of positive moral value. This is perhaps even more fundamental than the 'happy ending' of the classical Hollywood film, since the latter is dependent on a moral centre. That is, for a happy ending to be recognized as such, we must have previously identified a morally desirable character and outcome. We have seen how Hitchcock, in *The Man Who Knew Too Much*, toys with the moral centre of the narrative without eliminating it. It should be apparent that both the Manichaean and the graduated moral structures may accommodate moral centring and moral resolution (indeed, the Manichaean cannot do without them). We may say, then, that the Manichaean and the graduated structures, in combination with moral resolution and moral centring, constitute the formal boundaries within which the typical Hollywood film produces its 'system of values'. We may term this the 'classical moral system'.

Beyond the Classical Moral System

We began the chapter by arguing for the importance of the concepts of moral structure and moral orientation. I have made one broad distinction, between the Manichaean and the graduated moral structures; and argued that these structures function differently within different narrational modes (the agitational and the classical). In the last few pages I have been concerned principally with the different ways in which the norms of moral structure in the classical Hollywood film in general, and the melodrama in particular, might be defined. I have argued that the norms of moral resolution and moral centring persist under the historical pressures examined in the case of melodrama.

For the remainder of this chapter, I want to consider some other modes of filmmaking which undermine, in different ways, these requirements of the classical moral system. First, we might consider those films which refuse moral resolution, across the entire narrative. In the last chapter, I argued that 're-vealed interiority' was a feature of the classical film. The psychic traits of characters are unambiguously revealed to the spectator, even if this occurs towards the end of the plot. When a character's attributes are 'underdetermined'—that is, when they are not redundantly established—the moral valence of the character also becomes unclear. We encounter here an inverse relationship between complex, ambiguous interiority and lucid exterior typing, decried by an early French observer of the cinema: 'Action, only action, which is rapid and brutal. From this comes the almost total suppression of any psychology.'[62] The more complex a character's interiority, the less she can function as a person-alized emblem of a clear moral state. *The Suspended Vocation* constitutes an extreme example of this lack of moral resolution, as it is well-nigh impossible to determine either the moral valence of individual characters, or any stable allegiances among characters, even though an amorphous sense of moral urgency pervades their actions.

Ellipticality in the representation of narrative events may also result in a moral haziness. In Jean-Luc Godard's *A bout de souffle* (1959), one of the central actions of the story—Michel's killing of the policeman—is represented in such a discontinuous, elliptical fashion that it is impossible to make a confident moral assessment of the action, and therefore, to some degree, of the character. Does Michel simply reach for the gun as the cop approaches him, and casually fill him with lead? Or is the shooting an impulsive act of desperation? Like Eisenstein, to borrow a phrase from Bazin, Godard does not so much represent the action as 'allude to' it.[63] But unlike Eisenstein's abstract 'hieroglyphs', Godard's discombobulated montage sequences obscure rather than clarify the moral valence of the action or character in question. In less drastic style, many European art films of the 1960s deny the viewer moral resolution.

Similarly, moral centring may be attenuated. Oshima Nagisa's *Cruel Story of Youth* (1960), *The Story of Women*, the films of Jean-Pierre Melville, and several of those directed by R. W. Fassbinder (*The Bitter Tears of Petra Von Kant* (1973), *Chinese Roulette* (1976), *The Third Generation* (1979)), effectively flatten all moral dynamism, such that even the subtle moral hierarchies of the graduated structure look exaggerated by comparison. Consider the differences in moral structure between *Cruel Story of Youth* and Nicholas Ray's *Rebel Without a Cause* (1955) (to which there are several allusions in the Japanese film). The nominal hero and heroine of *Cruel Story of Youth*, Mako and Fujji, spend half the film exploiting and beating up others, and the other half being exploited and beaten up, either by each other or by a gang of thugs. In the end, they die simultaneously but separately. Mako throws herself from a moving vehicle, while Fujji is beaten and strangled by the gang. This is just about as gloomy an ending as one can imagine. But the survival of the characters at the end of the film could not alone transform it into a happy ending. Mako and Fujji are barely any more attractive than the various thugs and sanctimonious hypocrites that we encounter in the course of the film, and it is in this sense that the film lacks a moral centre. The film does not lack moral resolution; it is just that all the characters are crammed into a small part of the moral spectrum at the 'immoral' pole. In so far as there is moral hierarchization among the characters, it is absolutely minimal. There is, as it were, no outcome which is desirable or preferable. (It is for this reason, I think, that many viewers complain that the film leaves them feeling 'indifferent'.) A genuinely happy ending would require the kind of moral centring present in *Rebel Without a Cause*, where the 'authenticity' of Jim Stark (James Dean) furnishes a clearly preferable value (within the co-text of the film), when compared with the pettiness of his family and the spinelessness of his father in particular.

I must emphasize that I am not arguing that the Japanese film is agonistic, that is, that it does not engage us morally or emotionally. Rather, my suggestion is that it fails to produce even that moral hierarchy based on preference (as opposed to genuine desirability) that Carroll finds in *The Wages of Fear*

(Henri-Georges Clouzot, 1953): 'The four drivers are not moral men in terms of normal Western standards of morality. Mario and Jo, at least, are hooligans. Yet, within the film's moral system, they are initially more moral than the other morally relevant forces in the town.'[64]

Moral (Dis-)Orientation: Le Doulos

Another aspect of the moral system of a text pertains to the manner in which the moral structure (whether Manichaean or graduated) is revealed. Moral orientation is the narrational complement to the notion of moral structure. In a moment, I want to demonstrate the way in which Jean-Pierre Melville employs a pattern of orientation which subtlety raises questions about the reliability of the narration as a whole, and in doing so abrogates the conventional limits of the classical moral system. Yet Melville achieves this not by positing a wholly different set of norms, but by stretching the classical conventions to or even beyond breaking-point. In order to see how this is so, then, we need to consider the range of patterns of moral orientation typically found in classical films.

Manichaean structures are often the basis of both mystery and suspense films ('thrillers'). That is, in terms of moral structure, mystery films often employ the same kind of moral dualism present in *Johnny Belinda* and *Strike*. But there is a key difference in the pattern of moral orientation. In the classical stage melodrama, as defined by Brooks, the true moral valence of the characters is obvious to the spectator throughout: the moral categories of the world are inverted only within the diegesis, and it is in this sense that morality is 'occulted'. The pattern of moral orientation in this case is stable. In the mystery film, a suppressive narration conceals the identity of the criminal—and hence the locus of 'evil' in the moral structure—not only from the view of characters within the diegesis, but from the spectator as well. 'False' alignment, in which we mistakenly believe that we have access to the mental states of a character, is created with at least one character (the criminal). Consequently, mystery films, such as Siodmak's *The Spiral Staircase* (1945), often undermine at the last minute the moral structure as it has been constructed by the viewer. The responsible, charming, and handsome Professor (George Brent) emerges as the murderer, rather than his unstable and dissolute younger brother Stephen (Gordon Oliver). The pattern of moral orientation in such cases is, by contrast with that in the classical stage melodrama, dynamic. From the viewpoint of moral structure, then, the mystery film is akin to the classical stage melodrama; but the process of orientation to the Manichaean structure in the former is dynamic, by contrast with the stable orientation of the latter. And while the agitational film and the mystery film often manifest the same kind of

| McKennas vs. Draytons | > | McKennas/Draytons vs. Bernard/assassin | > | McKennas vs. Draytons/assassin | > | McKennas/Mrs Drayton vs. Mr Drayton/assassin |

Figure 6.2 Moral allegiances in *The Man Who Knew Too Much*

moral structure, in the mystery film the visible signs of moral character—physiognomy, dress style, and so on—cannot always be trusted.

Similarly, many suspense films depend upon the Manichaean moral structure, while presenting the structure through a dynamic pattern of moral orientation. One of the striking features of Hitchcock's films is the intricacy of this dynamic moral orientation. *The Man Who Knew Too Much*, for example, depends, at any given point in the text, on a generally stark division between benign and malign agents. But we are forced to revise, several times, the way in which we sort the characters into these categories. The Draytons are initially perceived as malignant. This perception is overturned when the McKennas meet them in the restaurant, in the scene discussed in the last chapter, in which they are presented as a kindly retired couple. The Draytons are then revealed to be the agents of the kidnapping, and we must revise our judgement of them again. Later in the film, the pattern of moral orientation is further complicated by a division within the villainous group of characters, between Mrs Drayton, on the one hand, and her husband, the assassin, and another woman accomplice on the other hand. Mrs Drayton is now presented as guilt-ridden and solicitous towards Hank; ultimately, she switches her allegiance to the McKennas. The dynamism of the moral orientation in the film is represented in Figure 6.2. This process of splitting and inversion within or over a basically dualistic opposition of values perhaps explains the peculiar combination in Hitchcock of the crass and the complex.

Moreover, it is surely one factor contributing to the oft-noted 'sympathy for the devil' elicited by Hitchcock's films; our evaluation of characters is continually revised, but the 'drag' of emotions (see Chapter 2) results in a lingering sentiment for unattractive characters with whom we were once (at least somewhat) sympathetic. We can see this process at work in our responses not only to the Draytons, but also to Bruno in *Strangers on a Train* (1951), Eve in *North by Northwest* (1959), and Norman in *Psycho* (1960). This works in concert with a number of other strategies dealt with previously. First, the rhetoric of the internal moral structure, whereby a character with whom we would have little sympathy in reality attracts our sympathy by virtue of their relative desirability. A variant of this is the creation of a local situation in which an otherwise undesirable character is herself victimized, or is placed in a dreadful situation. An episode of *NYPD Blue* pursues this Hitchcockian tactic. A murderer is made to confess by a ruthless psychological strategy, including threats of physical force—in the police cell, the police have all the power, the murderer none. The immediate situation at least temporarily obscures the larger context, in which the character is more or less repellent. This, of course, is true of Fry in *Saboteur*, though in his case I have argued that it is a second technique, the use of affective mimicry, which is most significant in forcing a suspension of the firmly established antipathy towards him. To these two strategies we should add the third, namely, the combination of sympathetic and antipathetic traits, or at least actions, in a given character, which may may attenuate unalloyed condemnation—a factor in our response to Mrs Drayton, the German captain in *Lifeboat* (1944), and Tobin in *Saboteur*. Along with the inertia of emotional response, these three factors not only explain the particular case of Hitchcock, but also provide a framework for the way in which fiction in general is capable of 'recasting' our everyday responses to unsympathetic characters. Such a framework makes any appeal to repressed, aggressive urges, shared by spectator and character, quite otiose.

Where Hitchcock in *The Man Who Knew Too Much* effects a series of moral reversals, Melville's *Le Doulos* (1962) stuns us with a single, monumental inversion. As in *The Spiral Staircase*, the moral structure of the film, constructed at the beginning of the film and the basis on which we interpret new narrative information, is inverted at the eleventh hour, but in *Le Doulos* this occurs in such a dramatic fashion that we are left questioning the reliability of the narration itself. (See the Appendix for a detailed breakdown of the plot.) The first third of the film is structured so that we make an incorrect series of inferences, which in turn invite us to 'misread' subsequent narrative information. Having murdered fellow criminal Gilbert Varnove (René Lefèvre), Maurice Faugel (Serge Reggiani) is hiding out at his girlfriend Thérèse's (Monique Hennessy) apartment. His friend Silien (Jean-Paul Belmondo) arrives with safe-cracking equipment, for a robbery that Maurice is planning in the vicinity of Neuilly. Therese returns from a 'reconnaisance' mission at the site of the robbery. In the following scene, Silien makes a telephone call from a public telephone, asking for an Inspector Salignari (Daniel Crohem). We infer that Silien, while behaving like an accomplice of Maurice, is in fact the eponymous *doulos*, 'fingerman' or informer. (Gilbert, prior to being murdered, raises questions about Silien's loyalty in segment 2, the first scene following the credits.) We see Maurice and Rémy (Philippe Nahon), his partner in the robbery, on the Metro. Silien returns to Thérèse's apartment in the next scene, where at first he acts seductively, and then brutally beats her. He slaps and punches her until she is unconscious, ties and gags her very securely, finally pouring a bottle of whisky on her head to wake her. He wants to know the exact address of the robbery, and, having slapped her a few more times, extracts the information. Silien leaves the apartment, promising to return.

At Neuilly, Maurice and Rémy are interrupted by the police as they attempt to crack the safe. Rémy is shot and killed as they flee; their final conversation indicates that they believe that Silien has informed the police of the Neuilly plan. Maurice is shot in the shoulder, but escapes the police, and in doing so kills Salignari. As he collapses, a car pulls up alongside him. We do not see the occupant, but before Maurice passes out, he whispers: 'Thérèse . . .' In the subsequent scene, Maurice is treated for his wound at the home of Jean (Aimé de March), another gangster acquaintance. Maurice leaves in a hurry to find Silien, planning to avenge Rémy. Thus, there are multiple cues which lead us to infer that Silien has acted treacherously. Above all, our lack of access to Silien's inner states—his subjective opacity—precludes any alternative explanation, a point I will expand on below.

Our (mis-)construction of events may be explained, up to a point, in cognitive terms. The plot is organized in such a way that we lack crucial information, which would lead us to interpret events differently. For example, we do not know at this point that Silien recognizes Thérèse as Salignari's girlfriend. Silien's suspicion and brutality towards her seem explicable only in terms of a general misogyny, and of his need, as the informer, for more information about the robbery. When we discover, much later in the plot, that Thérèse is a (the?) professional informer, Silien's actions take on a very different moral valence. Moreover, these initially cognitive factors lead to certain moral assessments and emotional reactions which reinforce the train of mistaken inferences, a fact which undermines the viability of Bordwell's assumption 'that a spectator's comprehension of [a film's] narrative is theoretically separable from his or her emotional responses'.[65] Silien's attack on Thérèse seems to confirm the suspicions raised about him by Gilbert; the brutality of the attack, following as it does his apparently seductive behaviour, seems sadistic in the extreme and fixes our negative evaluation of him. The emotion we experience, a deep aversion towards Silien, functions as a 'pattern of salience' which deflects us from filling in the narrative gaps in a way that would be favourable to Silien's character; as Ronald de Sousa writes, the 'emotion limits the range of information that the organism [i.e. in this context, the spectator] will take into account'.[66]

For example, there is a significant gap between segments 8 and 9. Maurice is rescued, and taken to Jean's, but at no point does the spectator, or any character, see his saviour. Maurice mutters 'Thérèse' as he is discovered, but, logically, we have no reason to suppose that she has managed to escape from the bondage Silien places her in in segment 7 (and, to reiterate, the professionalism of the job is dwelt upon). The police, as they interview Silien, reveal that they do not believe that Thérèse was driving the pick-up car, and suspect that

Silien was the driver. The narration places before us what turns out to be a more accurate version of events, but we do not regard this, at this point, as a plausible reconstruction. I suggest that these logical inconsistencies are overridden by our emotional reaction to Silien. Having negatively evaluated Silien, our mind is deflected from the possibility that Silien may have rescued Maurice. In addition, the primacy effect adds to the force of the negative evaluation. From the very beginning, doubt is cast on Silien's reliability; and his initial actions apparently support the qualms voiced by Gilbert.

The fact that *Le Doulos* is not a mystery film—even though it shares with the mystery film a certain pattern of moral orientation—is also significant in this respect. In the mystery film, we are invited to speculate about a number of different explanations for the crime; and the final explanation is typically not the one that seems to fit the facts at first. *Le Doulos* does not seem to encourage this kind of scepticism; the film invites us to assume that Silien is the 'fingerman', and our interest subsequently focuses on whether he will be able to continue double-crossing the various parties he works for. Indeed, another intertextual plot schema—'the hero with two masters', exemplified by the Dashiel Hammett novel *Red Harvest* (1929), and such films as Akira Kurosawa's *Yojimbo* (1961), Sergio Leone's *A Fistful of Dollars* (1964), and the Coen brothers' *Miller's Crossing* (1990)—may predispose or 'prime' the spectator to perceive Silien in this way.

Moreover, the pattern of alignment established in the film serves to reinforce the negative evaluation of Silien. An important norm of the film is its uncommunicative narration, and in particular the subjective opacity of the characters. For almost the entire film, our only access to the thoughts and motivations of the characters is limited to the terse and elliptical dialogue, and to the mostly understated facial expressions of the characters. These norms are established at the beginning of the film. Maurice, recently let out of prison, is talking with Gilbert, about the Parisien gang world in general and about the planned Neuilly robbery. Gilbert is solicitous towards Maurice, inviting him to eat a stew that he has cooked, and advising him on how to alleviate his depression. (In particular, as we have seen, he warns Maurice about Silien; but Maurice defends Silien's character.) Maurice seems to be grateful. He asks Gilbert for his revolver, which he says he will need for the robbery, since he is physically weak after his term in prison. Reluctantly, Gilbert agrees to lend it to him, and tells him where to find it. Maurice takes the gun and cartridges out of a drawer, sits down, and weighs the gun in his hands. In a POV shot from Maurice's vantage point, we see Gilbert examining jewels at a table, talking to Maurice as he does so. The film cuts back to Maurice, framed in medium-shot, placidly listening, and then again back to the POV shot of Gilbert. Gilbert looks up from his work towards Maurice. He stands up, horror-stricken. A gun shot, from off-screen, levels Gilbert.

Maurice has shot Gilbert, but nothing has prepared us for this action; indeed, the preceding conversation had led us to infer that the two characters were allied. Nowhere is the reticence of the narration, with regard to the internal states of characters, better exemplified. Maurice's intention, in this case to kill Gilbert, is made available to us only as it registers in the world of objects and actions—that is, when it is no longer merely an interior, mental phenomenon.[67] Another emblem of the opacity of the characters are two shots which virtually frame the film. As Maurice enters Gilbert's hideout in segment 2, he stops to check his appearance in a mirror. Nothing in particular is accomplished by this; Maurice is not vain, and he is not checking a disguise. Similarly, in the final moments of the film, Silien, on the brink of death, staggers to a mirror, re-arranges his hat, looks at himself, and collapses. What matters in this world is not motivation, but appearance—which itself reveals very little.

Once again, we should note that the POV shot representing Maurice's view of Gilbert does not establish, for the spectator, a simple 'identification' with Maurice. We discover his intention as Gilbert—the object rather than the sub-ject of the look—does. The extreme lack of narrational depth here may be highlighted by comparison with Hollywood films of the same genre, such as Billy Wilder's *Double Indemnity* (1944), which provide us with far more informa-tion about at least the focal character's interiority (in this case, through the voice-over narration of the protagonist, Walter Neff). In *Le Doulos*, the lack of depth is sustained as a norm until the penultimate segment (22) of the film, in which a startling narrational transgression effects a reversal of the film's moral polarity. Up to this point, Silien's inexpressivity and the lack of any other access to his psyche lead us to doubt his stated motivations, and thus to regard him as a mendacious, vicious thug. (The process is the exact reverse of that which we saw at work in *Daisy Kenyon*. In Preminger's film, expressivity leads to apparent subjective transparency, and an attitude of trust towards the expres-sions of the characters; in *Le Doulos*, lack of expressivity fosters an attitude of distrust in the spectator.) After all, the epigraph of the film reads: 'It is neces-sary to choose. Die . . . or lie?' Silien appears to be the ultimate survivor. In this way, the structure of alignment works to maintain our aversion towards Silien.

Segment 22, however, overturns many of the assumptions and evaluations we have relied upon, forcing a rereading of events and reinterpretation of certain gaps in the narrative. This is accomplished narrationally by what Genette terms an 'alteration': a singular violation of a narrational norm. Maurice has just been released, unexpectedly and without explanation, from prison. Along with Jean, he meets Silien in a bar (complete with black jazz pianist). Silien explains his actions via a series of flashbacks: thus we gain a far greater degree of access to Silien's thoughts than we have enjoyed up to this point (with respect to Silien or any other character). Silien explains that he had recognized Thérèse as Salignari's girlfriend, and as an informer. His phone call to Salignari in segment 5, in which we had assumed that he informs Salignari of the robbery, had been made simply to invite Salignari to dinner (!). Salignari declines the invitation, telling Silien that he has to deal with a tip-off concerning a robbery in Neuilly. Silien realizes that Thérèse has given the information to Salignari. He beats Thérèse, therefore, in order to obtain the address of the robbery, so that he can warn or rescue Maurice. After the aborted robbery, Maurice passes out before seeing that it is Silien—as the police suspected—who has rescued him. Following Silien's interview with the police, he agrees to telephone various bars asking for Maurice only because he believes that Maurice is safely hidden at Jean's, where he had left him. Prior to the police interview, Silien had spent all day trying to acquire a false passport for Maurice. Finally, Silien is responsible for Maurice's release. Maurice had been imprisoned for the murder of Gilbert; but Silien has successfully framed the rival gangsters Nuttheccio (Michel Piccoli) and Armand (Jacques de Leon) for the murder (segment 20).[68]

The narration asks us, then, to reverse our evaluation of Silien. He has, at the very least, been utterly loyal to Maurice, a major virtue in the gangster world, that is, within the moral co-text of this film. On a purely cognitive level, his story 'fits the facts' as we have seen them; indeed, his version of events makes better sense than the incorrect version we had been encouraged to infer by the plot construction and the emotional responses elicited by the film's pattern of moral orientation. But the duration and intensity of our aversion towards Silien precludes a simple cognitive revision of our understanding of events and of our moral allegiances. The 'drag' of emotions may make us resist the revision, prompting us to question the reliability of the narration. As one contemporary reviewer commented: 'Jean-Paul Belmondo . . . may or may not be a finger man (stool pigeon, informer, *doulos*) and may or may not run the Paris narcotics trade.'[69] The classical moral system—defined by moral resolution and moral centring—is suspended in this context of extreme equivocation. *Le Doulos* undermines these norms as surely as *The Suspended Vocation* thwarts the process of character recognition.

I hope to have demonstrated several points in the course of this analysis of *Le Doulos*, which I will conclude by reviewing in order of their increasing generality. First, that in order to capture the experiential, and specifically emotional, qualities of a film, we must consider not only its moral structure, but its pattern of moral orientation. Secondly, that patterns of alignment and allegiance are mutually influential: moral judgements about a character's actions may determine what we take to be the content of a character's interiority, and more obviously, what we take to be the content of a character's mind influences how we evaluate her. (Note, though, that this is a far cry from conflating the two levels of engagement under the concept of 'identification'.) The example also clearly demonstrates that alignment alone does not result in allegiance. In the cases cited by Booth (*Metamorphosis*, Jane Austen's *Emma*, and Henry James's 'The Beast in the Jungle'), it is not the mere fact of being aligned with a character that makes sympathetic to them, so much as what is revealed to us through that alignment. Sustained alignment can give us a developed picture of the motivations as well as the actions of a character, the detail of which may serve to exonerate actions which, viewed in isolation from this larger picture, might be easier to condemn. But such alignment does not necessarily have this effect. In the many scenes in which we are aligned with Silien (attached to him, and given what we take to be a limited, but reliable degree of access to his subjectivity) we feel little sympathy for him. The ending asks us to reverse our judgement of him, by revealing that the context and motivation of his actions were not what we took them to be: again, what counts is what is revealed by the alignment, not the mere fact of it.

This brings us to the third implication of the analysis of *Le Doulos*, that allegiance is a distinct level of engagement. I began this chapter by noting how the question of moral structure and emotional response had been ignored or marginalized by most narrative theorists. This attitude is reiterated by Chatman when he stipulates that questions of objectivity in narration (how do we assess the reliability of a narration?) are 'more narratologically relevant' than questions of moral judgement in narration (does the narration present a character in a sympathetic light?).[70] The analysis of *Le Doulos* demonstrates that moral structures themselves have important effects on the putatively more basic, informational structures of narrative and narration. My aim has been to show that the mistaken inferences that a playful—or duplicitous—narration like that of *Le Doulos* encourages us to make, often involve emotional as well as cognitive factors (bearing in mind, of course, that emotions themselves have a cognitive component, and are not irrational forces opposed to cognition). Perception, cognition, and emotion are thus interdependent; the theory of emotions underpinning this analysis 'thickens' cognitive accounts of spectatorial response, which are often thought to be incapable of handling emotional responses.

1. Boris Tomashevsky, 'Thematics', in Lee T. Lemon and Marion J. Reis (trans. and eds.), *Russian Formalist Criticism: Four Essays* (Lincoln: University of Nebraska Press, 1965), 65.
2. General Pinochet, quoted in Jonathan Glover, *I: The Philosophy and Psychology of Personal Identity* (London: Allen Lane, 1988), 71.
3. Wayne C. Booth, *The Rhetoric of Fiction*, 2nd edn. (Harmondsworth: Penguin, 1991), 280–1; Mieke Bal, *Narratology: Introduction to the Theory of Narrative* (Toronto: University of Toronto Press, 1985), 104–5; Seymour Chatman, *Coming to Terms: The Rhetoric of Narrative in Fiction and Film* (Ithaca, NY: Cornell University Press, 1990), 158–9.
4. Greimas and Hamon comment briefly on the problem under the rubric of 'axiological investment', but both view it as an issue of very minor importance: A. J. Greimas, *On Meaning: Selected Writings in Semiotic Theory*, trans. and ed. Paul J. Perron and Frank H. Collins

(Minneapolis: University of Minnesota Press, 1987), 105; Philippe Hamon, 'Pour un statut semiologique du personnage', in Roland Barthes, *et al.* (eds.), *Poetique du récit* (Paris: Seuil, 1977), 151–2. Seymour Chatman is openly dismissive of 'the study of mechanisms of judgement': *Story and Discourse: Narrative Structure in Fiction and Film* (Ithaca, NY: Cornell University Press, 1978), 125–6. In his later work, Chatman posits a notion of 'interest-focus', but devotes precious little attention to it; moreover, Chatman equivocates in his use of the term between the notion of a text concentrating our attention on the interests of a particular character, and eliciting our sympathy for those interests—the very distinction which I argue must be made clearly. See Chatman, *Coming to Terms*, 177.

5. Tomashevsky, 'Thematics', in Lemon and Reis (trans. and eds.), *Russian Formalist Criticism*, 90.

6. Nick Browne, *The Rhetoric of Film Narration* (Ann Arbor, Mich.: UMI Research Press, 1982), 11–14.

7. Tomashevsky, 'Thematics', in Lemon and Reis (trans. and eds.), *Russian Formalist Criticism*, 90.

8. V. F. Perkins, *Film as Film: Understanding and Judging Movies* (Harmondsworth: Penguin, 1972), 138.

9. See Christopher Butler, *Interpretation, Deconstruction, and Ideology* (Oxford: Clarendon Press, 1984), 133. See also Norman Geras, *Discourses of Extremity* (London: Verso, 1990); and Steven Lukes, *Marxism and Morality* (Oxford: Clarendon Press, 1985).

10. Noël Carroll, 'Toward a Theory of Film Suspense', *Persistence of Vision*, 1 (Summer 1984), 76.

11. Sergei Eisenstein, *Film Form and the Film Sense*, trans. Jay Leyda (New York: Meridian Books, 1957), 127.

12. Lawrence W. Levine, *Highbrow/Lowbrow: The Emergence of Cultural Hierarchy in America* (Cambridge, Mass.: Harvard University Press, 1988), 221–2.

13. Sheila K. Johnson, *American Attitudes toward Japan, 1941–1975* (Washington, D.C.: AEI-Hoover Institute, 1975), 9. James Naremore notes that until the late 1930s, Humphrey Bogart was typed as a villain because executives at Warner Brothers thought that his large (by implication, 'black') lips disqualified him from playing sympathetic leading men: *Acting in the Cinema* (Berkeley: University of California Press, 1988), 106. For an overview of the iconography of racial stereotypes in the USA in the nineteenth century, and the 'racial theories' which formed their original context, see Michael H. Hunt, *Ideology and U.S. Foreign Policy* (New Haven, Conn.: Yale University Press, 1987). I take this tradition to be the most powerful cultural influence on the iconography of racial stereotyping in Hollywood cinema.

14. Richard Dyer, *Stars* (London: BFI, 1979), 72–98.

15. For a brief consideration of some of these issues from a philosophical perspective, see Glover, *I: Philosophy and Psychology of Personal Identity*, 115.

　　Later in this chapter, I draw on iconographic research by Roberta Reeder, in which she examines the traditions of visual representation (portraiture, caricature, and so forth) which fed into *Strike*. For an attempt to deal with a much broader tradition of iconography in relation to the novel, see Graeme Tytler, *Physiognomy in the European Novel: Faces and Fortunes* (Princeton, NJ: Princeton University Press, 1982); and on teeth as emblems of potency and beauty, Theodore Ziolkowski, 'The Telltale Teeth: Psychodontia to Sociodontia', *PMLA* 91 (1976), 9–22.

16. Claudia Gorbman, *Unheard Melodies: Narrative Film Music* (London: BFI, 1987), 83.

17. Cf. Booth's comment on the contempt elicited by the name 'Gerald Scales' in a novel by Arnold Bennett, and Boris Uspensky's discussion of naming in relation to 'phraseological' and 'ideological point of view': Booth, *Rhetoric of Fiction*, 145; Boris Uspensky, *A Poetics of Composition: The Structure of the Artistic Text and Typology of a Compositional Form*, trans. Valentina Zavarin and Susan Wittig (Berkeley: University of California Press, 1973), 20–32. Ian Watt comments on the balancing of the 'appropriate and suggestive' with the 'realistic' in the naming of novelistic characters in *The Rise of the Novel* (Berkeley: University of California

Press, 1957), 19; and Dyer remarks on the 'residue of the emblematic' in the names of certain stars, *Stars*, 110.

18. On star 'charisma', see Dyer, *Stars*, 34–6.

19. Carroll, 'Toward a Theory of Film Suspense', 75; Tomashevsky, 'Thematics', in Lemon and Reis (trans. and eds.), *Russian Formalist Criticism*, 65.

20. Butler, *Interpretation, Deconstruction, and Ideology*, 4; see also Booth, *Rhetoric of Fiction*, 137–47.

21. I do not wish to suggest that such values represent a particular ideology or doctrine, but rather a very general and enduring set of tacit beliefs and practices which are derived from both classical (Graeco-Roman) and Christian moral doctrines.

22. Edwin Hutchins, *Culture and Inference: A Trobriand Case Study* (Cambridge, Mass.: Harvard University Press, 1980), 12.

23. Laura Mulvey, 'Visual Pleasure and Narrative Cinema', *Screen*, 16: 3 (Autumn 1975), 6–18. I am not concerned here with the detail of Mulvey's argument, or the many pieces which have followed it. Rather, I am concerned to establish the way in which psychoanalytic research relates to the model of character engagement.

24. On one reading, Mulvey would accept this point, since it amounts to saying that the functions of POV in Hollywood cinema are historically determined by the needs of patriarchy, a system she vehemently opposes. However, the essay also contains passages which strongly imply that looking (and its counterpart in film, the POV shot) is part of an extremely basic, ahistorical, and—even though this contradicts the expressed intention of the piece—natural process by which humans mature. See, for example, the hesitation between language in general and 'the language of patriarchy' specifically: Mulvey, 'Visual Pleasure', 7.

25. Yu. K. Scheglov and A. K. Zholkovskii, 'Towards a "Theme—(Expression Devices)—Text" Model of Literary Structure', trans. L. M. O'Toole, *Russian Poetics in Translation*, 1 (1975), 20.

26. e.g. David Bordwell, *Making Meaning: Inference and Rhetoric in the Interpretation of Cinema* (Cambridge, Mass.: Harvard University Press, 1989).

27. Aristotle, *The Rhetoric and Poetics of Aristotle*, trans. W. Rhys Roberts and Ingram Bywater (New York: The Modern Library, 1984), 224.

28. Raymond Durgnat, *Films and Feelings* (Cambridge, Mass.: MIT Press, 1971), 186.

29. See Susan Rubin Suleiman, *Authoritarian Fictions: The Ideological Novel as a Literary Genre* (New York: Columbia University Press, 1983), 56. See also David Bordwell, *Narration in the Fiction Film* (Madison: University of Wisconsin Press, 1985), ch. 11, on 'historical-materialist narration'.

   Many of the concepts in this section on the Manichaean structure as it is manifested in the agitational film are drawn from Susan Suleiman's work on the *roman-à-thèse*, a close novelistic relative of the agitational film. Where Suleiman is interested in the 'dualistic value structure' of the *roman-à-thèse* as one of a number of defining features of that genre, however, I am interested in that structure as it is manifested in different genres and modes of narrative cinema.

30. Suleiman, *Authoritarian Fictions*, 101.

31. Roberta Reeder, 'Agit-prop Art: Posters, Puppets, Propaganda, and Eisenstein's *Strike*', *Russian Literature Triquarterly*, 22 (1989), 255–78.

32. A few characters have proper names—the worker who hangs himself, some of the government spies, for example—but the names are revealed in a cursory, almost incidental fashion. In accordance with the principle of typage, characters are linguistically designated by names which identify their occupation, social class, or role within the conflict ('the leader', 'the organizer', and so forth).

33. It is worth noting, however, that the strategies of typification in *Arsenal* and *Strike* do not preclude emotional responses to the characters in the way that I argued the strategies of instability and contradiction, exemplified by *The Suspended Vocation*, do. *Strike* clearly does elicit sympathy and outrage on behalf of the proletarian characters, even though it limits the individuation of them.

34. Erwin Panofsky, 'Style and Medium in the Motion Pictures', in Gerald Mast and Marshall

Cohen (eds.), *Film Theory and Criticism: Introductory Readings* (New York: Oxford University Press, 1974), 162.

35. Suleiman, *Authoritarian Fictions*, 185.

36. The most notable example of this approach to Eisenstein is Marie-Claire Ropars, 'The Overture of *October*', trans. Larry Crawford and Kimball Lockhart, *Enclitic*, 2: 2 (Fall 1978), 50–72, and 3: 1 (Spring 1979), 35–47. Judith Mayne's chapter on *Strike* in *Kino and the Woman Question: Feminism and Soviet Silent Film* (Columbus: Ohio State University Press, 1989) seems, in a general way, to be influenced by Ropars's study.

37. Mayne, *Kino and the Woman Question*, 77.

38. Suleiman, *Authoritarian Fictions*, 172.

39. Ibid. 190–2.

40. Georg Lukács, *The Historical Novel*, trans. by Hannah and Stanley Mitchell (Lincoln: University of Nebraska Press, 1984), 36.

41. Peter Brooks, *The Melodramatic Imagination: Balzac, Henry James, Melodrama, and the Mode of Excess* (New York: Columbia University Press, 1984), 42.

42. D. N. Rodowick, 'Madness, Authority, and Ideology in the Domestic Melodrama of the 1950s', *The Velvet Light Trap*, 19 (1982), 44; Tania Modleski, *Loving with a Vengeance: Mass-Produced Fantasies for Women* (New York: Methuen, 1984), 90.

43. Steve Neale, 'Melo Talk: On the Meaning and Use of the Term "Melodrama" in the American Trade Press', *The Velvet Light Trap*, 32 (Fall 1993), 69, 76. Such adventure and action genres were, in the nineteenth and early twentieth centuries, regarded as melodramas. Within trade discourse, Neale argues that the term 'drama' was used as a broad term for films focusing on domestic life: on these matters, see the references in Chapter 5, n. 50.

44. Neale, 'Melo Talk', 76; Frank Rahill, *The World of Melodrama* (London: Pennsylvania State University Press, 1967), p. xv; see also Maria LaPlace, 'Producing and Consuming the Woman's Film: Discursive Struggle in *Now, Voyager*', in Christine Gledhill (ed.), *Home is Where the Heart is: Studies in Melodrama and the Woman's Film* (London: BFI, 1987), 151–5.

45. I am not claiming that only overtly didactic texts may have some impact on the ideas and behaviour of the audience, but simply that the Hollywood film does not, in general, rhetorically position itself as an exemplary narrative, in which its social worth is to be found in the positive or negative fate of the major characters.

46. André Bazin, *What is Cinema?* ii, trans. and ed. Hugh Gray (Berkeley: University of California Press, 1971), 51.

47. Brooks, *Melodramatic Imagination*, 32.

48. See e.g. Rodowick, 'Madness, Authority, and Ideology'.

49. Alan Williams, 'Historical and Theoretical Issues in the Coming of Recorded Sound to the Cinema', in Rick Altman (ed.), *Sound Theory/Sound Practice* (New York: Routledge, 1992), 133–5.

50. On stage melodrama, see Brooks, *Melodramatic Imagination*, p. xii; and Rahill, *World of Melodrama*, p. xv; and more generally Martin Meisel, *Realizations: Narrative, Pictorial and Theatrical Arts in Nineteenth-Century England* (Princeton, NJ: Princeton University Press, 1983). On early cinema, see Singer, 'Female Power'; Janet Staiger, ' "The Eyes are Really the Focus": Photoplay Acting and Film Form and Style', *Wide Angle*, 6: 4 (1985), 14–23; and Tom Gunning, *D. W. Griffith and the Origins of American Narrative Film: The Early Years at Biograph* (Urbana: University of Illinois Press, 1991), esp. 106–7.

51. Cf. Brooks, *Melodramatic Imagination*, 35.

52. The mark of that verisimilitude being, for us, precisely a lack of moral purity. An early screenwriting guide recommends that the heroine should have certain flaws, in order 'to make her human, having a thoughtless and a tender side': George Rockhill Craw, 'The Writing of a Scenario', *Moving Picture World*, 8: 17 (29 Apr. 1911), 940. Verisimilitude—itself a shifting quality, as we saw in Chapter 2—constitutes only one possible criterion of rhetorical power, the directness and exaggeration of caricature and allegory furnishing alternative criteria.

Suleiman comments on the potential conflict between these two rhetorical strategies in the *roman-à-thèse*, *Authoritarian Fictions*, 189.

53. The question of the typicality of the Manichaean structure within agitational Hollywood films is, of course, an empirical question, and, given the much greater size of the corpus of Hollywood films as compared with Soviet agitational films of the 1920s and early 1930s, one that would require a much more specific and detailed study than the present one.

54. Brooks, *Melodramatic Imagination*, 15.

55. Nathan G. Hale, Jr., *Freud and the Americans: The Beginnings of Psychoanalysis in the U. S., 1876–1917* (New York: Oxford University Press, 1971); and Diane Waldman, 'Horror and Domesticity: The Modern Gothic Romance Film of the 1940s', Ph. D. thesis (University of Wisconsin–Madison, 1981), 230–8.

56. The issue here is not the political nature of psychoanalysis—whether it is reactionary or progressive. Rather, the question is the affinity between certain doctrines and the two basic kinds of moral structure outlined in this chapter. I argue that when represented in narrative, psychoanalysis tends to generate the graduated structure.

57. Sigmund Freud, *Introductory Lectures on Psycho-Analysis*, trans. and ed. James Strachey (New York: W. W. Norton and Co., 1966), 568.

58. Raymond Durgnat, *The Strange Case of Alfred Hitchcock; or, the Plain Man's Hitchcock* (London: Faber, 1974), ch. 2.

59. Carroll, 'Toward a Theory of Film Suspense', 75.

60. Booth, *Rhetoric of Fiction*, 141.

61. This should not be confused with the Manichaean structure *per se*. A graduated structure possesses moral resolution if the traits and moral valences of the characters within it are clearly established. Resolution is not synonymous with dualism.

62. Louis Haugmard, 'The "Aesthetic" of the Cinematograph', trans. Richard Abel, in Richard Abel (ed.), *French Film Theory and Criticism: 1907–39*, i (Princeton, NJ: Princeton University Press, 1988), 83; cf. Singer, 'Female Power', 96.

63. André Bazin, *What is Cinema?* i, trans. and ed. Hugh Gray (Berkeley: University of California Press, 1967), 25.

64. Carroll, 'Toward a Theory of Film Suspense', 74–5.

65. Bordwell, *Narration in the Fiction Film*, 30.

66. Ronald de Sousa, *The Rationality of Emotion* (Cambridge, Mass.: MIT Press, 1988), 195.

67. The technique is redolent of Bresson's in *L'Argent*, examined in the last chapter.

68. In the case of this last narrative event, we see it prior to the flashback sequence. Furthermore, Silien states that one of his intentions in framing Nuttheccio and Armand is to help Maurice (segment 19). However, by this point in the film, we do not trust Silien's stated motivations. Here, our antipathy towards him results in a perceived lack of access to Silien's true mental states. Just as the structure of alignment—in particular, the subjective opacity—of the narration supports our aversion towards Silien, so, in parallel fashion, the moral structure of the film affects the structure of alignment. Allegiance affects, but is not reducible to, alignment.

69. Joan Didion, review of *Le Doulos*, *Vogue*, 1 Apr. 1964, 42.

70. Chatman, *Coming to Terms*, 150–1.

Conclusion

Cultural symbolism creates a community of
interest but not of opinions, which—be it said
in passing—has always troubled churchmen
and politicians, manufacturers of ideology,
obstinate misappropriators of symbolism.

                                    Dan Sperber[1]

The influence of aesthetic value is not that it
swallows up and represses all remaining values,
but that it releases every one of them from
direct contact with a corresponding life-value.

                              Jan Mukařovský[2]

Whatever the faults of the model of character engagement set forth here, I hope to have demonstrated that it is possible to discuss with rigour what I take to be undeniable and central aspects of our experience of narrative films. The examination of characters as analogues of persons does not have to result in the impressionistic quality and 'imbecilities of rhapsodic gush'[3] associated with most writing on the subject. The purpose of this study has been to set out a detailed description and functional explanation of character engagement, or what is casually referred to as 'identification'. Given that we do respond in a variety of ways to fictional characters, I have sought to describe the different elements comprising this phenomenon, and to explain how these elements (the person schema, the three levels of engagement, mimicry, simulation, and so forth) function within the process of character engagement. The main purpose of this concluding chapter will be to sketch an explanation of character engagement as a whole. Prior to this, however, a few remarks need to be made regarding other questions raised by this study.

Many issues related to character engagement which deserve exploration have been left untouched. There is, obviously, much more to be said about the functions of music in relation to emotional response, both as it works directly upon us and in concert with an overtly representational medium like the cinema. The role of facial expression, and especially the significance of Ekman's 'display rules', is a potentially rich area of investigation. This study springs in part from a contradiction in the evaluation of certain kinds of emotional response between various groups—the entertainment industries on the one hand, and various artistic movements and philosophies on the other (Brecht, formalism of the type associated with the philosopher Ortega y Gasset)—and much more needs to be said concerning the relationship between types of emotional response and the social ranking of different types of fiction. Some kinds of fiction elicit univocal, or mixed but complementary, emotional responses, while others invite conflicting and ambiguous emotional responses, and this division corresponds in general to the ranking of what our society deems 'serious fiction' (or 'art') over 'mere fantasy' or 'entertainment'. And all too often this dichotomy is assumed to be isomorphic with a divide between 'Hollywood movies' and 'art films'. But this is surely a contingent relationship—one with a history which one might begin tracing in the development of the novel. Some fictions which elicit strong emotional responses are lauded for their sincerity and profundity, others—usually when they effect an imaginative recasting of the spectator's beliefs and values in a direction that they do not like—are rejected as 'manipulative'. Some theorists of postmodernity, talking of the 'death of affect', might be seen as making the (dubious) argument that any kind of emotional response to fictional representations is impossible in a culture of pervasive irony. All of these questions, it strikes me, have to do with the way our society predisposes us to evaluate emotions themselves—the relative worth of different emotions, but also emotions as such. I offer these remarks only as indications of what another, rather different but complementary work on emotion and fiction might examine.

The most influential paradigms for the explanation of character engagement or 'identification' are Brechtianism and psychoanalysis. Although I have been concerned to emphasize the differences between my approach to engagement and that of many contemporary theorists working within the psychoanalytic tradition, we share some goals. In reaction to the sweeping generality of the accounts of Baudry and Metz, many theorists have stressed the ways in which cultural and social difference affect our experience of the cinema. I believe that my model is wholly in line with this impetus, although it combines this concern for cultural and historical specificity with a parallel concern for breadth and generality. One of the advantages of the character engagement model is that it posits a variety of levels, ranging from the universal to the local and specific. It enables us to acknowledge cultural and social difference, and to specify at what level these factors become salient.

We cannot do without some general assumptions about the nature of a phenomenon in considering specific instances of it. Whether we are studying contemporary responses to Tim Burton's *Batman* (1989) or the original reception of Erich Von Stroheim's *Foolish Wives* (1922), we will approach the problem equipped with a notion of how spectators in general relate to films and the characters within them.[4] In a study of the American war film, Dana Polan suggests that we can understand its workings as 'a particular inflection of psychoanalytic principles like the death-drive'.[5] In other words, these psychoanalytic principles form a bridgehead between the historian and the specific period and film in question. Psychoanalysis is presumed to have some kind of universal explanatory capacity. Though I disagree about what the general model should be, I share with Polan an approach which rests on a variety of levels of generality. (Oddly, though, elsewhere in the same article Polan criticizes Sartre for adopting a 'universal hermeneutic' in the form of the notion of 'empathy'.) An explanation requires such a variety of levels: we need to acknowledge the dialectic between abstract theorizing and detailed historical study. We cannot simply 'get stuck into' empirical, historical work any more than we can blithely construct ideal notions of the spectator with no acknowledgement of social and historical particularity. In my view, historical reception studies are not well served by the general assumptions supplied to us by the folk model of identification, or any of the alternatives examined in passing in this study. The model of character engagement is an attempt to improve our model of spectatorship, but it is not a simple return to the 'ahistoricism' of much theoretical work from the 1970s. It is intended as a complement to historical study.

In Chapter 3, I made reference to some discussions of 'identification' which have suggested that we should think in terms of 'multiple identification', that is, the way in which, over the course of a film, the 'subject position' we occupy shifts. In my terms, we may experience a variety of different kinds of emotional response to characters, our sympathy moving among several characters rather than being directed only at a singular 'identification figure'.[6] (Freud's 'A Child is Being Beaten' essay is often cited here, as a scenario in which the subject phantasizes occupying, or identifying with, several different roles within it.) I am wholly in sympathy with the general aim of this shift, although I would argue that my model of character engagement offers a much more sensitive instrument for registering the diverse range of emotional responses that the spectator may experience than any theory which begins with a particular narrative (or set of narratives)—like the Oedipal scenario—with a predetermined range of roles.[7] The person schema combined with various cultural models constitutes an extremely flexible and productive generative system, which in principle may produce an infinite range of engagement patterns. One of the aims of this study has been to supplant the notions of role and identification with those of representation and response. Engagement is not a process in which we vicariously experience the emotions of characters in any simple sense, nor one in which we are 'possessed' wholly by a single character. It is, rather, a complex, heterogeneous set of interacting responses—autonomic, cognitive, affective—to what we know to be fictional entities.

For all its influence, the Brechtian explanation of the function of character engagement is extremely limited. In many ways, the Brechtian account mirrors the folk model, assuming that the traditional fictional film induces a loss of consciousness on the part of the spectator, and a complete identification with a particular character. This 'empathic' form of response is then counterposed to an 'alienated' type of response, elicited by films with highly self-conscious narrations. Critics of Peter Greenaway's *The Baby of Mâcon* (1993), for example, regularly appealed to this Brechtian dichotomy.[8] Conceived as an elaboration of 'defamiliarization', the notion of 'alienation' (*Verfremdung*) is compelling, as I suggested in Chapter 2. The problem lies in defining the term as simply the opposite of 'identification' or 'empathy'. The dualism of 'empathy' and 'alienation' needs to be recast in terms of the various levels of engagement and different degrees of intensity of engagement at each level. An 'empathic' response—in the Brechtian sense of the term—is elicited by a text which allows recognition to proceed swiftly and 'automatically', attaches us to a character for a substantial proportion of the text, gives us access to her subjectivity, and makes her a predominantly sympathetic character. This is the form of textual organization we saw in the first half of *The Man Who Knew Too Much*. From the very beginning of this study, however, I have stressed that alignment and allegiance need not converge at all, thus creating the possibility of perceptual and cognitive 'empathy' being combined with emotional 'alienation'. Moreover, a text like *The Suspended Vocation* reveals that the process of recognition may engage us just as intensely, in its own way, as alignment or allegiance. As Wayne Booth has suggested, 'Every literary work of any power . . . is in fact an elaborate system of controls over the reader's involvement and detachment along *various* lines of interest,' and much the same can be said for fiction films.[9]

The real difference between the Brechtian and everyday model lies in the evaluation of the 'empathic' response. What the everyday model regards as 'harmless entertainment' is, for Brecht, a damaging escapism leading to quiescence and conformism. Neither of these positions is satisfactory; it is doubtful that character engagement has a univocal ideological effect. It may reinforce oppressive norms, but it may lead us to question them.[10] The Brechtian challenge to the value of empathy is vitally interconnected with an attack on the very notion of the aesthetic, as a domain in some way disengaged from everyday interests, activities, and beliefs. Brecht's position can be set in relief by juxtaposing his statement regarding the attitudes of spectators within the theatre with Tomashevsky's call for an 'innocent' perceiver of art, willing to engage a fiction by surrendering his or her everyday prejudices:

Rushing out of subway stations, eager to be turned into putty at the hands of magicians—grown men, tried and tested in the struggle for existence, scurry to the box-office. There they check their hats, and along with those, their customary habits, their normal attitudes of everyday life.[11]

[The ideology of a work of fiction] may create a completely insurmountable wall between the reader and the work if the reader begins to evaluate the emotions generated within the work in terms of his everyday personal or political feelings. To read, one must be innocent, must catch the signs the author gives.[12]

The Brechtian adherence to the 'normal attitudes of everyday life' confronts the Enlightenment assumption that the aesthetic stands apart from practical, everyday concerns. For Brecht, theatre should have political use value, that is, direct practical value in the advancement of socialism. If, however, a spectator carries over all her everyday prejudices into the theatre, why should she be any more likely to reflect critically upon them in the theatre than outside it? Why should she suspend her everyday values and beliefs? Unless, that is, the spectator does regard the theatre as a qualitatively different sphere of activity, a forum precisely for the suspension and reconsideration of everyday values. This, of course, contradicts the very point that Brecht is urging, creating a paradox. The spectator is encouraged to bring into the theatre her everyday attitudes, but at the same time to subject these attitudes to a kind of analysis from which they are ordinarily protected. In reality, then, the spectator is asked to bring into the theatre all her everyday attitudes *bar one*—the 'pragmatic' or 'instrumental' attitude which allows us to act on the basis of beliefs without reconsidering the rationality or morality of these beliefs on each occasion. This is, as it were, a 'meta-' attitude, one which underpins all others enabling us to pursue ends without continually diverting ourselves by questioning the worth of the ends—an attitude eminently suited to, though hardly unique to, the capitalism that Brecht abhorred. It is precisely the surrender of this one key attitude which gives rise, in combination with an aesthetic 'prompt' (such as a fictional text), to an aesthetic situation. The solution to the Brechtian paradox is clear. While Brecht overtly attacks the notion of the aesthetic, he covertly assumes it, or assumes a revised version of it.

What, then, is the nature of the aesthetic principle that Brecht does depend upon, albeit covertly? A lot of confusion in this debate turns on the vague definition of the phrase 'practical interest' and its antonym 'disinterested'. If aesthetic interest is defined as 'disinterested' in the sense of a complete separation from the beliefs, values, and themes drawn from social life, one can have little quarrel with Brecht's rejection of aesthetics. But this is surely an unduly narrow definition of 'aesthetic interest'. A more precise definition of 'disinterested' would be 'divorced from our direct, specific practical interests'. That is to say, we can make a distinction between my attending to something in a way that reflects its direct and specific relevance to me, and attending to something in a way that reflects its indirect and general relevance to me. A fictional representation of a rape, like *The Accused*, which implies and evokes claims concerning the causes of rape and the (in-)just treatment of rape victims by the legal system, commands my interest in two senses: it captures my attention, and, as a member of the society the film refers to, it represents phenomena in which I have a stake. But now imagine that someone has been raped in my neighbourhood, and that a security camera has recorded the incident, and that I am asked to watch the film to see if I recognize the assailant. My relationship to this film—my interest in it—I want to say, is direct and specific, in contrast to the indirect and general relevance of the fictional film. The distinction, however, is not between mundane, practical interest (I need to identify the suspect) and abstract 'disinterest' (the narrative of *The Accused* achieves an exquisite balance though rigorous closure). Both forms of attention are socially embedded. Indeed, I might well become distressed or angry in response to the fictional film of the rape, either because I believed the film reveals horrific injustices in the world or because I believed it failed to represent an important phenomenon in an accurate way, but I could only react this way if I understood the film as a representation of—no matter how mediated—real, social phenomena. On this account, my attention to the film can be at once disinterested and profoundly engaged with the social experiences depicted and addressed by the film. 'Disinterest' can be defined so as to make a distinction not between a social and an asocial practice, but between different kinds of social practice.

'Aesthetic' in the sense that I am using the term thus assumes that art stands apart from the everyday, not in the sense of emerging from a separate realm of 'the spirit', but rather in that it provides a forum for reflection on the nature and structure of automatized beliefs and practices. This definition is akin not only to the Russian Formalist notion of 'defamiliarization', but also to Dan Sperber's definition of symbolism as the placing of our 'encyclopaedia' of knowledge about the world 'in quotes'. For Sperber, a representation becomes symbolic as it resists or ceases to function in an instrumental or communicative way. Resisting literal comprehension or use, the symbolic representation becomes a prompt for 'evocations' whose meanings cannot be completely determined; in Sperber's words, a 'representation is symbolic precisely to the extent that it is not entirely explicable'.[13] Thus, 'symbolicity' is not a property of an object but a function that any object can come to play if it is treated in a symbolic fashion—a definition closely mirroring Jan Mukařovský's definition of the aesthetic.[14] Overtly aesthetic representations—objects or acts in which the defamiliarizing or evocative function is signalled and emphasized—mark the existence of institutionalized practices in which these functions are recognized and facilitated.

I should perhaps stress here, in view of the Formalist lineage of this argument, that it does not exclude social and ideological phenomena as objects of reflection and defamiliarization. That is, placing a representation 'in quotes' does not amount to abstracting it, evacuating it of all referential meaning, as the insult 'merely formalist' usually implies. It is true that Shklovsky focused on how art makes the 'stone *stony*', that is, on those levels of experience that the term 'aesthetic' originally designated: sensuous and perceptual experience.[15] Shklovsky, however, represents only one voice in this tradition, and there can be no doubt that defamiliarization works as much on cognitive, propositional knowledge, such as beliefs and values, as it does on non-propositional, perceptual experience. The 'revaluation of value' is central for Mukařovský, for example, and as I have suggested, Brecht's notion of 'alienation' is in effect a reworking of 'defamiliarization' which emphasizes conceptual knowledge and the social shaping of conceptual knowledge, rather than the sensuous experience dwelt upon by Shklovsky.

As an abstract definition of the aesthetic, perhaps it will be felt that the account presented here ascribes far more self-consciousness to the average spectator than is plausible. But I would remind the reader of the tempered definition of 'consciousness' given in Chapter 2, and draw her attention back to some of the examples given over the course of this study. If I begin to form the impression that a character is not to be trusted, I am more likely to ask myself what it is about the character that leads me to form this impression than I would in a real situation with a comparable person, precisely because in the experience of fiction my immediate interests are not at stake: such feelings are 'more coolly tested without the overload of consequence that life provides'.[16] To take a more elaborate example, the ending of *Le Doulos* may make us reflect on the automatized beliefs—the schemata—which lead us to rush to judgement of Silien. How did the film manipulate us—what assumptions and expectations did it elicit? Similarly, after watching *Daisy Kenyon* or *L'Argent*, we may reflect on our assumptions about the social conventions of expressivity and their relation to the ways in which we apprehend the inner states of others. This, I would suggest, is one function of the institutions of fiction and aesthetics. Along similar lines, the anthropologist Victor Turner argues that art is a 'liminal' phenomenon—a process which is both within a social system and yet at the threshold of the system, in the sense that it may provide a member of the society with a reflexive view of the system which her normal functioning within it precludes.[17] The argument here is only that one of the functions of the institution of fiction is to provide such opportunities, not that it guarantees that an individual spectator will reflect in this way, nor that fiction may not perform other non-aesthetic functions.

Along with a number of other shared attitudes, this conception of the aesthetic links this study with the work of other film scholars sometimes gathered under the rubrics of 'neoformalism' or 'historical poetics', who draw their principal inspiration from Russian Formalist literary theory and cognitive psychology. What distinguishes this study from other work in this tradition is that it is centrally concerned with questions which are often thought to be effectively answered only by 'mimetic' theories—theories which emphasize thematic material, and the embodiment of that material in the form of characters, rather than the formal structures of texts. Throughout, though, I have been concerned to argue that mimetic concepts, like character, do not depend on naïve confusions and assumptions about their status as artifices. Consequently, the antipathy held to exist between questions of character and emotional response and the 'neoformalist' approach does not really exist.[18] But there is no doubt that its presumed existence has led to a paucity of attention to the nature and functions of character within theory—including 'neoformalist theory'—a meagreness that this study has attempted to enrich.

One last argument is worth making in this regard, an argument which ascribes to fiction (especially the novel and classical filmmaking, which share the norm of narratives based largely on the actions of individuals) a very different function from the one ascribed to theatrical fiction by Brecht. Iris Murdoch argues that literature is essentially 'anti-egoistic'—that it offers the reader an opportunity to experience imaginatively situations, value-systems, and persons radically different from those with which we are familiar.[19] Thus, while both the novel and Hollywood films are 'individualistic' forms, it would be simplistic in the extreme to argue that they merely reflect the individualism of modern Western society and, equally univocally, perpetuate this individualism. Fiction—or at least, fiction when it functions aesthetically—involves not so much the suspension of 'disbelief' as of the values which ordinarily guide us. The 'anti-egoism' argument stresses the fact that character engagement encourages the reader to confront unfamiliar experiences, fostering our 'imaginative mobility'. A viewer may learn about the contradictions of the social situation of the 'mulatta' in Douglas Sirk's *Imitation of Life* (1959); about the conditions of existence for Jews under the Nazis in *Schindler's List*, as well as the attitudes of some of those who participated in the genocide; about the experiences of rural Germans which led them either to support or to accept Fascism in Edgar Reitz's *Heimat* (1984); about the horror of being raped, as well as the array of subsequent social and legal oppressions awaiting rape victims in *The Accused*. Of course, like all fictions, these films shape our imaginative experience of social 'otherness'; in the language of semiotics, they 'signify' rather than simply reflect reality. And the way that particular films shape our perception of aspects of social reality can be contested in terms of their validity, relevance, and value—as it has been in the case of all of the films mentioned here. The fact that we can argue over the merits of particular fictions in these terms should not, however, obscure the fact that this is a function that fictions in general perform.

Once again, this 'quasi-experiential' form of interest is not the only one that fiction films possess, but it is an important one. Certain philosophers have suggested that such experience actually amounts to a distinct kind of knowledge, to be placed alongside the more widely acknowledged forms (knowing how to do something, and knowing that something is the case): knowing what it is like to be someone or something other than oneself, what it is like to be in a situation of a type one has never experienced, and so forth.[20] On my account, though, this is not achieved through a wholesale 'identification' of spectator with character, but through a process whereby centrally imagining 'other' perspectives is imbricated with imagining situations as if we (rather than the character) occupied a position within them, and where both are held within a structure of acentral imagining. Character engagement need not, according to this view, accommodate us to timeless human predicaments or anaesthetize our will to act on social problems, as Brecht argues; rather, it may enable us to apprehend experiences other than our own, and—possibly—use this new knowledge to act in the world in a more informed way.

The argument for the 'anti-egoistic' function of fiction depends on a conception of knowledge wholly opposed to that embedded in the version of psychoanalysis which has been so influential in studies of cinematic 'identification'. For Jacques Lacan, social experience irrevocably 'alienates' us from our 'true' being; as we learn language we become permanently enmeshed in a social system ('the Symbolic') which alienates us from 'the Real'. On the view advanced here, we are largely social entities; we are biologically endowed with certain potentials and capacities which are shaped and constrained by different societies and cultures in different ways. Since human experience is social experience, knowledge may be said to be acquired as we become aware of how our experiences are socially produced, and how they differ from the experiences of others, constrained and shaped by different factors. We may have knowledge in and of 'the Other'; it is not an intrinsically self-deluding and self-alienating experience.

I have posited a theory of character engagement which assumes the interdependency of social structure and personhood, and which attempts to tackle the questions of agency and consciousness from a fresh vantage point (fresh within film studies, at least). It is a theory which attempts to account for both the very general processes which must take place for engagement to occur at all, and the particular instantiations of these processes in Western cultures. It is a 'humanistic' approach, in that it rests upon the assumption that humans share certain capacities, and that cultures share certain features. It is not a humanism, however, which assumes that History unfolds to reveal an ideal human essence, nor a humanism which seeks to overlook the social differences between humans. It is a humanism which argues that while individual agents are far from the masters of their own lives, neither are they hopelessly subjected to structural determination. Such a perspective can only lead to a paralysing and destructive pessimism, a far cry from the 'complex seeing' advocated by Brecht.

1. Dan Sperber, *Rethinking Symbolism*, trans. Alice L. Morton (Cambridge: Cambridge University Press, 1975), 137.
2. Jan Mukařovský, *Aesthetic Function, Norm and Value as Social Facts* (1936), trans. Mark E. Suino (Ann Arbor: Michigan Slavic Contributions, 1979), 89.
3. The phrase is W. J. Harvey's (*Character and the Novel* (Ithaca, NY: Cornell University Press, 1965), 206).
4. On *Batman*, Henry Jenkins and Lynn Spigel, 'Same Bat Channel, Different Bat Times: Mass Culture and Popular Memory', in Roberta E. Pearson and William Uricchio (eds.), *The Many Lives of the Batman: Critical Approaches to a Superhero and his Media* (New York: Routledge, 1991), 117–48; on *Foolish Wives*, Janet Staiger, *Interpreting Films: Studies in the Historical Reception of American Cinema* (Princeton, NJ: Princeton University Press, 1992), ch. 6.
5. Dana Polan, 'Film as Language, Film as Power', *East–West Film Journal*, 2: 2 (June 1988), 108.
6. See the essays cited in Ch. 3, n. 15; see also Robert Lapsley and Michael Westlake, *Film Theory: An Introduction* (Manchester: Manchester University Press, 1988), 92; and Carol Clover, *Men, Women, and Chainsaws: Gender in the Modern Horror Film* (London: BFI, 1992).
7. Beyond this broad kinship, however, there are considerable difficulties in integrating the two approaches. See the conclusion to 'Altered States: Character and Emotional Response in the Cinema', *Cinema Journal*, 33: 4 (Summer 1994), 34–56.
8. e.g. Kate Bassett, 'Distance Lends Enchantment', *The Times*, 14 Sept. 1993, 39; and Adam Mars-Jones, 'Baby, It's True', *Independent*, 17 Sept. 1993, 20.
9. Wayne C. Booth, *The Rhetoric of Fiction*, 2nd edn. (Harmondsworth: Penguin, 1991), 123.
10. For a similar argument made in direct response to Brechtian criticisms of the American television series *Holocaust* (1978), see Andreas Huyssen, 'The Politics of Identification: "Holocaust" and Wert German Drama', *New German Critique*, 19 (Winter 1980), 117–36.
11. Bertolt Brecht, quoted in Frederic Ewen, *Bertolt Brecht: His Life, His Art and His Times* (New York: Citadel Press, 1967), 201.
12. Boris Tomashevsky, 'Thematics' (1925), in Lee T. Lemon and Marion J. Reis (trans. and eds.), *Russian Formalist Criticism: Four Essays* (Lincoln: University of Nebraska Press, 1965), 90.
13. Sperber, *Rethinking Symbolism*, 113.
14. Mukařovský, *Aesthetic Function*, 3.
15. Viktor Shklovsky, 'Art as Device', in *Theory of Prose*, trans. Benjamin Sher (Elmwood Park, Ill.: Dalkey Archive Press, 1990), 6; cf. Victor Erlich, *Russian Formalism: History—Doctrine*, 3rd edn. (New Haven, Conn.: Yale University Press, 1981), 209.
16. Martin Price, *Forms of Life: Character and Moral Imagination in the Novel* (New Haven, Conn.: Yale University Press, 1983), 23.
17. Victor Turner, *Dramas, Fields and Metaphors: Symbolic Action in Human Society* (Ithaca, NY: Cornell University Press, 1974).
18. Cf. Mukařovský, *Aesthetic Function*, 88–9.
19. Iris Murdoch, *The Sovereignty of Good* (London: Routledge, 1991), esp. pp. 34, 59, 65–6, 86–7; Murdoch is also cited by Price, *Forms of Life*, 12.
20. On 'knowing what': Dorothy Walsh, *Literature and Knowledge* (Middleton, Conn.: Wesleyan University Press, 1969); and Catherine Wilson, 'Literature and Knowledge', *Philosophy*, 58 (1983), 489–96. The phrase 'quasi-experience' is used by Paul Taylor in 'Imagination and Information', *Philosophy and Phenomenological Research*, 42 (1981), 205–23. Both Taylor's argument and the argument put forward by Paul Ricoeur in 'The Function of Fiction in Shaping Reality', trans. David Pellauer, in Mario J. Valdés (ed.), *A Ricoeur Reader: Reflection and Imagination* (London: Harvester-Wheatsheaf, 1991), 117–35, discussed in Chs. 1 and 2, relate to the concept of 'knowing what'.

The Suspended Vocation (Ruiz, 1977)

0. Preface(s).

1. (B/W) Jérôme discusses with the Spiritual Director (both unnamed at this point) the doctrine of 'excessive virilism'.

2. (C) Jérôme meets two members of La Dévotion, and discusses with them the planned crossing of another character to 'the other zone'. Jérôme and one of the two leave the apartment in which they have been meeting.

3. (B/W) Jérôme repeats the admonition—'Regarde!'—and warns his companion about the ubiquity of the Black Party.

4. (C) As we glimpse Jérôme standing behind a window overlooking a courtyard, a voice-over is heard in which he talks of a rival whom he follows. The rival has 'raped' the woman he loves.

5. (B/W) Jérôme's voice-over continues, though now 'in' the voice of the other performer. The 'rape', it appears, was more of a *ménage à trois* involving Jérôme, his wife, and a friend, and the images suggest that this was set-up by Jérôme at a dinner party. The incident partially explains Jérôme's entrance into the clergy: 'This temptation to do evil . . .'

6. (C) Jérôme's voice-over finishes with a description of how administering the sacraments deflects him from evil.

7. (B/W) Jérôme is informed that 'his friend' has made it to the other zone, but that he is in danger because of an incriminating letter.

8. (C) In direct contradiction of 7, Jérôme is informed that his friend was intercepted, but that the letter is safe.

9. (B/W) Jérôme tears up the letter, and scatters the remains; after he leaves, a stream of Brothers rush into the room and retrieve the pieces.

10. (C) Jérôme is interviewed by a Father, and addressed as Jérôme for the first time. He is questioned about the letter, his allegiance to La Dévotion, and the doctrine of 'excessive virilism'.

11. (B/W) The interview continues. Jérôme is chastised. Outside, he accuses another Brother of spying. A different Brother tells him that La Dévotion will be grateful, and that he must leave for a church (?) in another zone.

12. (B/W) Jérôme arrives at his new clerical institute. He is told about a certain peculiar division of labour that is maintained within the establishment, involving the rotation of physical tasks.

13. (C) Jérôme inquires about the labour system. The Prior—in leather jacket, jeans, smoking—assures Jérôme that he trusts him.

14. (C) Jérôme witnesses a Brother being slapped over a disagreement concerning a scriptural fresco.

15. (C) Jérôme meets up with his companion from segment 2, also in this establishment. He tells Jérôme that he (Jérôme) is suspected of being a double agent.

16. (B/W) A Father gives a talk to a table of other priests about the requirement to leave the institution. An off-screen voice twice disrupts the speech with the cry 'Inversion!'

17. (C) In discussion with Jérôme, the Prior advocates a pluralist, disunified style for the painting of the fresco. The Prior leaves, and the Painter Brother—who had been slapped in 14—advocates a traditional approach to the painting of the fresco, which should be unified and conducted by a master painter.

18. (B/W) A Brother comes to Jérôme's room, and leads him through a bizarre catechism. The Brother addresses this performer as 'Jérôme' for the first time. Jérôme finds a double-ended cross under his pillow.

19. (C) In discussion with the Painter Brother, Jérôme offers some compositional advice, at which point the Painter Brother physically ejects him.

20. (B/W) As Jérôme stumbles away, he finds a note secreted in (another?) double-ended cross on a wall. We have seen another Brother leave the note and steal away.

21. (C) The Prior, the priest from 10, and a Bishop perform the 'fresco test' on Jérôme, by asking him to express and justify his opinions on how the fresco should be painted. He fails. The Bishop says he must come to his diocese.

22. (C) As the Bishop and Jérôme leave, the Bishop is mobbed by 'priest-fans'. A nun picks the two of them up in a van, and the mobbing continues as they drive away.

23. (B/W and C) In the abbey (?) to which he has been transferred, Jérôme is contacted by two nuns who show him pictures by the artist Malagrida, including fresco images (in C). Jérôme identifies Malagrida as an old acquaintance, 'a trickster' from his 'years of subversion'. He complains about his perceived allegiance with the Black Party. One of the nuns replies that this is hardly suprising in view of the letter showing his agreement to write a secret report for La Montagne.

24. (C) A new set of characters, centred around La Montagne. The latter's boy servant falls into a fit, muttering the names of figures in the fresco.

25. (B/W) The boy servant has ordered some statuettes. His room is found to be full of statues of the Virgin Mary. He falls into (another?) fit.

26. (C) The camera pans over a room in La Montagne's house, full of statues. A voice-over describes La Montagne's conversion and Malagrida's relationship to it.

27. (B/W) Jérôme is again beckoned by the nuns.

28. (C) Jérôme meets Malagrida in the courtyard, who asks Jérôme to help him in the pursuit of Sister Vincent, the cousin of La Montagne. He reveals that the photo of the exhumed nun, shown to Jérôme in 23, is a fake.

29. (B/W and C) A conversation between a Father (in C), later identified as Euthanasien Persienne, and Jérôme (generally in B/W), who advocates that the Church be seen merely as an invention of the human psyche.

30. (B/W and C) Jérôme returns to his room, and finds a note. He proceeds to a room where he witnesses two nuns dressing in evening gowns.

31. (C) Jérôme goes to Malagrida's room, where he finds the two nuns. While Malagrida dances with one of the nuns, he talks with the other one, who urges him to 'play along'. She seems to have her own ends, but these are not made clear.

32. (B/W) At La Montagne's, the latter chides Jérôme for acting as a go-between between Malagrida and his niece (not cousin).

33. (B/W) Jérôme talks to his present Father Superior about the motivations of Mother Angelique in denouncing him (Jérôme) to La Montagne. It seems this was a simply a diversion from her initiation of the seduction plot with Malagrida. Part of the motivation for the plot is to experiment with Sister Theophile's emotions. Theophile was the model in the fake photo of the exhumed nun, and a former lover of Malagrida.

34. (C) Jérôme attempts to talk to one of the nuns. She resists, and finally tears off the cover of a painting which she is carrying. The painting is a portrait of La Montagne (by Malagrida) as a Bishop (?). She instructs him to go to his room, where Mother Angelique awaits him.

35. (B/W) Mother Angelique denies that she denounced Jérôme. She suggests that they publish their ideas together in a broadsheet, and expresses her opinion of 'the necessity for marriage within the priesthood'. Jérôme's Father Superior enters in the background.

36. (C) The Father Superior talks to Jérôme about Euthanasien Persienne—the 'atheist' priest from 29, justifying his presence within the Church.

37. (B/W) Jérôme is approached by another Brother, who encourages him to produce a broadsheet and his report, in the interests of debate and clarification. He introduces Jérôme to a group from the Black Party, from whom Jérôme distances himself. Finally, he is informed by one of the nuns that 'the Community' has been secularized.

38. (C and B/W) Jérôme watches a service performed by Malagrida, along with many other transfixed priests and nuns. Shocked, he tells Malagrida that he is leaving the Church. Malagrida predicts that he will return.

39. (B/W) Jérôme walks out on to the steps of the church, as the bells ring.

40. End credits, including cast list which identifies which characters were played by more than one performer.

Arsenal (Dovzhenko, 1929)

1. Prologue: the Great War, and its impact on those left at home.

2. {T} The Ukrainian 'deserters' return, by train, to their homeland.

3. 'Who/Qui/Wer?' They find their spouses with illegitimate children.

4. {T} Timosh's immediate fortunes (refused re-employment).

5. (T) Religious ceremony, celebrating Ukrainian independence.

6. (T) Petlyura addresses the soldiers, enjoining them to the nationalist cause. Timosh intervenes.

7. (T) Meeting of Ukrainian landowners.

8. (T) Bolshevik revolution across the country: the outbreak of the strike at the arsenal.

9. (T) Build-up to the Civil War.

10. (T) The Civil War, the struggle for the arsenal, the defeat of the Ukrainian proletariat, and Timosh's last stand.

{T} = sequence structured around Timosh.

(T) = Timosh appears but is framed by other figures.

No T = complete and utter absence of Timosh.

Le Doulos (Melville, 1962)

1. Credits: Maurice Faugel walks through an industrial district.

2. Maurice enters a house in which fellow gangster Gilbert Varnove is examining the jewels from the famous Mozart robbery. Maurice persuades Gilbert to lend him his gun; he claims that he cannot handle an upcoming robbery unarmed because he is physically weak from serving time in prison. Maurice shoots Gilbert with the gun, steals the jewels and some money, and leaves just before Nuttheccio and Armand, joint heads of a powerful gang, enter the house. Nuttheccio's girlfriend, Fabienne, sits outside in their car.

3. Maurice buries the money, jewels, and gun next to a lamp-post in an abandoned lot.

4. Maurice is hiding out at his girlfriend Thérèse's apartment. Silien, a close friend of Maurice's, arrives with safe-cracking equipment for Maurice, who is planning a robbery in the Neuilly district. Another friend, Jean, arrives. Thérèse returns from a scouting trip to the site of the upcoming robbery.

5. Silien calls Inspector Salignari from a public phone.

6. Maurice and his accomplice, Rémy, board a train to Neuilly.

7. Silien returns to Thérèse's apartment. He beats her, ties her up, and forces her to reveal the address of the robbery. He leaves.

8. Maurice and Rémy are discovered as they attempt to crack the safe. They assume that Silien has informed on them. As they flee, Rémy is shot and killed. Maurice kills Salignari and is wounded himself. He staggers away, and is rescued by an unseen saviour. As he passes out, he utters the word: 'Thérèse . . .'

9. At Jean's, Maurice is treated for the gunshot wound. No one knows who brought Maurice to Jean's. Immediately after the doctor leaves, Maurice rips the dressing off, draws a map for Jean with the location of the money and jewels, and leaves. He is in a hurry to take revenge on Silien.

10. Three policemen cruise the streets looking for Silien. They find him.

11. At the police station, Silien is interviewed. He denies tipping off Salignari about the Neuilly robbery. The police reveal that Thérèse has been found dead, crushed in a flattened car in a quarry. Silien is also suspected of having driven the getaway car in which the murderer of Salignari escaped. Silien denies all knowledge, insisting that as a friend of Salignari's, he would like to kill the murderer.

The police then interrogate him about the Gilbert Varnove murder. They suspect Maurice. Silien denies that he is a friend of Maurice. The police coerce Silien into helping them find Maurice, by threatening to help the Vice Squad, who, they claim, are investigating him for drugs trafficking.

12. Silien is taken by the police to a phone booth.

13. He calls several bars, until he discovers one which Maurice has just left.

14. Maurice is arrested in an adjacent bar as he reads a newspaper report about Thérèse's crushed body.

15. Maurice is interrogated. The police are convinced that he shot Gilbert, but they have no idea that he shot Salignari; in fact, they offer to drop the charge that he murdered Gilbert, if he will 'finger' Rémy's accomplice—that is, himself! Maurice claims to have been Gilbert's friend. He refuses to say anything further.

16. Silien digs up the money and jewels, and takes the gun as well.

17. In prison, Maurice contracts Kern, a fellow prisoner soon to be released, to kill Silien.

18. Silien arrives at Nuttheccio's club, 'The Cotton Club'. He sits with Nuttheccio's girlfriend, Fabienne, apparently a former lover. Nuttheccio avoids a confrontation with Silien. Silien arranges a clandestine meeting with Fabienne.

19. Silien reveals to Fabienne that he wants to set up Nuttheccio and Armand for the murder of Gilbert. For her, this offers a way out of her relationship with Nuttheccio. Silien persuades her to 'remember' hearing a gun shot from inside Gilbert's house, as she waited outside for Nuttheccio and Armand (1).

20. With Fabienne's aid, Silien breaks into Nuttheccio's bar and safe room. Nuttheccio enters. Silien calls Fabienne, who in turn calls Armand, telling him that Nuttheccio needs to meet him at the club. At gunpoint, Silien forces Nuttheccio to handle the Mozart jewels—originally stolen from Gilbert's. Then Silien shoots him. Armand arrives and is shot by Silien. Silien arranges the scene so that it appears that the two gang leaders have shot each other in a struggle over the jewels.

21. Maurice talks with Jean, having been unexpectedly pardoned and released from jail. He does not know who was responsible for his release.

22. Maurice and Jean meet with Silien at a bar. Silien explains the nature of his involvement in the various plots. He had recognized Thérèse as Salignari's girlfriend, a professional informer. Silien's phonecall to Salignari (5) had been an attempt to distract him, as he knew that Thérèse would have tipped Salignari off about robbery in Neuilly. Later, Maurice passed out before he saw that it was Silien who had come to his rescue (8). Silien and Jean together killed Thérèse. Silien had only agreed to phone around the various bars searching for Maurice, on behalf of the police (13), because he believed that Maurice was in safe hiding at Jean's, where he had left him. When Maurice was imprisoned, Silien had formulated the plan to implicate Nuttheccio and Armand in the Mozart robbery and the murder of Gilbert.

Silien declares that he is going to retire, before he is 'filled with lead'. He leaves.

Maurice receives a phone call informing him that Kern is about to fulfil his contract—that is, murder Silien. He leaves to find Silien.

The police arrive and arrest Jean. A shred of the raincoat he is wearing was found in the car in which Thérèse was found.

23. Maurice drives quickly to Silien's country house. Unwittingly, he passes Silien filling his car with gas. Maurice arrives at the house first; mistaking him for Silien, Kern shoots him. Silien returns and finds the expiring Maurice. Maurice warns Silien about Kern; Silien shoots him. Silien turns away, believing that Kern is dead; however, Kern manages to shoot Silien in the back with his last bullet. Silien struggles to the telephone, calls Fabienne, and tells her that their plans for the evening are cancelled. He rearranges his hat in a mirror, and collapses.

Bibliography

ABEL, RICHARD (ed.), *French Film Theory and Criticism: 1907–39*, 2 vols. (Princeton, NJ: Princeton University Press, 1988).

ALLEN, RICHARD, *Projecting Illusion: Film Spectatorship and the Impression of Reality* (New York: Cambridge University Press, 1995).

ALLOWAY, LAWRENCE, 'The Iconography of the Movies', *Movie*, 7 (Feb. 1963), 4–6.

ALTHUSSER, LOUIS, *For Marx*, trans. Ben Brewster (London: Allen Lane, 1969).

—— *Lenin and Philosophy and Other Essays*, trans. Ben Brewster (London: New Left Books, 1971).

ANDERSON, PERRY, *In the Tracks of Historical Materialism* (London: Verso, 1983).

ARBIB, MICHAEL, and HESSE, MARY, *The Construction of Reality* (Cambridge: Cambridge University Press, 1986).

ARCHARD, DAVID, *Consciousness and the Unconscious* (La Salle, Ill.: Open Court Publishing Co., 1984).

ARISTOTLE, *The Rhetoric and Poetics of Aristotle*, trans. W. Rhys Roberts and Ingram Bywater (New York: The Modern Library, 1984).

ARMSTRONG, PAUL B., *Conflicting Readings: Variety and Validity in Interpretation* (Chapel Hill: University of North Carolina Press, 1990).

ARNHEIM, RUDOLF, *Art and Visual Perception: A Psychology of the Creative Eye* (The New Version) (Berkeley: University of California Press, 1974).

ASCHENBRENNER, KARL, and ISENBERG, ARNOLD (eds.), *Aesthetic Theories: Studies in the Philosophy of Art* (Englewood Cliffs, NJ: Prentice-Hall, 1965).

BAL, MIEKE, *Narratology: Introduction to the Theory of Narrative* (Toronto: University of Toronto Press, 1985).

BALUKHATYI, SERGEI, 'Russian Formalist Theories of Melodrama: Balukhatyi and the *Poetics of Melodrama*', trans. and paraphrased by Daniel Gerould, *Journal of American Culture*, 1: 1 (Spring 1978), 154–63.

BARTHES, ROLAND, *Mythologies* (1957), trans. Annette Lavers (New York: Noonday Press, 1990).

—— 'Introduction to the Structural Analysis of Narratives' (1966), in *A Barthes Reader*, ed. Susan Sontag (New York: Hill and Wang, 1982), 251–95.

—— *S/Z*, trans. Richard Miller (New York: Hill and Wang, 1974).

—— *Roland Barthes by Roland Barthes*, trans. Richard Howard (London: Macmillan Press, 1977).

—— KAYSER, W., BOOTH, W., and HAMON, P. (eds.), *Poétique du récit* (Paris: Seuil, 1977).

BARTLETT, FREDERIC, *Remembering: A Study in Experimental and Social Psychology* (Cambridge: Cambridge University Press, 1932).

BASSETT, KATE, 'Distance Lends Enchantment', *The Times*, 14 Sept. 1993, 39.

BAUDRY, JEAN-LOUIS, 'Ideological Effects of the Basic Cinematographic Apparatus' (1970), trans. Alan Williams, *Film Quarterly*, 28: 2 (Winter 1974–5), 39–47.

BAZIN, ANDRÉ, *What is Cinema?* i (1967) and ii (1971), trans. and ed. Hugh Gray (Berkeley: University of California Press).

BERGSTROM, JANET, 'Enunciation and Sexual Difference', *Camera Obscura*, 3/4 (Summer 1979), 33–69.

BOOTH, WAYNE C., *The Rhetoric of Fiction*, 2nd edn. (Harmondsworth: Penguin, 1991).

BORDWELL, DAVID, *Narration in the Fiction Film* (Madison: University of Wisconsin Press, 1985).

—— 'A Case for Cognitivism', *Iris*, 9 (May 1989), 11–40.

—— *Making Meaning: Inference and Rhetoric in the Interpretation of Cinema* (Cambridge, Mass.; Harvard University Press, 1989).

—— and THOMPSON, KRISTIN, *Film Art: An Introduction*, 3rd edn. (New York: McGraw-Hill, 1990).

—— STAIGER, JANET, and THOMPSON, KRISTIN, *The Classical Hollywood Cinema: Film Style and Mode of Production to 1960* (New York: Columbia University Press, 1985).

BRADBY, DAVID, JAMES, LOUIS, and SHARRATT, BERNARD (eds.), *Performance and Politics in Popular Drama: Aspects of Popular Entertainment in Theatre, Film, and Television, 1800–1976* (Cambridge: Cambridge University Press, 1980).

BRANIGAN, EDWARD, *Point of View in the Cinema: A Theory of Narration and Subjectivity in Classical Film* (New York: Mouton, 1984).

—— 'Diegesis and Authorship in Film', *Iris*, 7 (Oct. 1986), 37–54.

—— *Narrative Comprehension and Film* (London: Routledge, 1992).

BRAUDY, LEO, *The World in a Frame: What We See in Films* (Garden City, New York: Anchor Press, 1976).

BRECHT, BERTOLT, *Brecht on Theatre: The Development of an Aesthetic*, trans. and ed. John Willett (London: Methuen, 1964).

BREWSTER, BEN, 'Introduction to "Documents from *Novy Lef*"', *Screen*, 12: 4 (Winter 1971–2), 59–66.

—— 'From Shklovsky to Brecht: A Reply', *Screen*, 15: 2 (Summer 1974), 82–102.

—— 'A Scene at the "Movies"', *Screen*, 23: 2 (July–Aug. 1982), 4–15.

—— 'Film', in Dan Cohn-Sherbok and Michael Irwin (eds.), *Exploring Reality* (London: Allen and Unwin, 1987), 145–67.

BRITTON, ANDREW, 'The Ideology of *Screen*', *Movie*, 26 (Winter 1978–9), 2–28.

—— 'The Philosophy of the Pigeonhole: Wisconsin Formalism and "The Classical Style"', *CineAction!*, 15 (Winter 1988–9), 47–63.

BROOKS, PETER, *The Melodramatic Imagination: Balzac, Henry James, Melodrama, and the Mode of Excess* (New York: Columbia University Press, 1984).

BROWN, E. J., *The Proletarian Episode in Russian Literature* (New York: Columbia University Press, 1953).

BROWN, S. C. (ed.), *Philosophical Disputes in the Social Sciences* (Brighton: Harvester Press, 1979).

BROWNE, NICK, *The Rhetoric of Film Narration* (Ann Arbor, Mich.: UMI Research Press, 1982).

BUDD, MIKE, and STEINMAN, CLAY, 'Television, Cultural Studies, and the "Blind Spot" Debate in Critical Communications Research', in Gary Burns and Robert J. Thompson (eds.), *Television Studies: Textual Analysis* (New York: Praeger, 1989), 9–20.

BURCH, NOËL, *Theory of Film Practice*, trans. Helen R. Lane (Princeton, NJ: Princeton University Press, 1981).

BUTLER, CHRISTOPHER, *Interpretation, Deconstruction, and Ideology: An Introduction to Some Current Issues in Literary Theory* (Oxford: Clarendon Press, 1984).

CAMERON, IAN, 'The Mechanics of Suspense', *Movie*, 3 (Oct. 1962), 4–7.

—— 'Suspense and Meaning', *Movie*, 6 (Jan. 1963), 8–12.

CARPENTER, TERESA, 'Slouching Toward Cyberspace', *Village Voice*, 12 Mar. 1991, 34–42.

CARR, DAVID, 'Discussion: Ricoeur on Narrative', in David Wood (ed.), *On Paul Ricoeur: Narrative and Interpretation* (London: Routledge, 1991), 160–74.

CARRITHERS, MICHAEL, COLLINS, STEVEN, and LUKES, STEVEN (eds.), *The Category of the Person: Anthropology, History, Philosophy* (Cambridge: Cambridge University Press, 1985).

CARROLL, NOËL, 'Toward a Theory of Film Suspense', *Persistence of Vision*, 1 (Summer 1984), 65–89.

—— 'Belsey on Language and Realism', *Philosophy and Literature*, 11: 1 (Apr. 1987), 124–35.

—— *Mystifying Movies: Fads and Fallacies in Contemporary Film Theory* (New York: Columbia University Press, 1988).

—— *The Philosophy of Horror; or, Paradoxes of the Heart* (New York: Routledge, 1990).

—— 'Toward a Theory of Point-of-View Editing: Communication, Emotion, and the Movies', *Poetics Today*, 14: 1 (Spring 1993), 123–41.

CHATMAN, SEYMOUR, *Story and Discourse: Narrative Structure in Fiction and Film* (Ithaca, NY: Cornell University Press, 1978).

—— 'Characters and Narrators: Filter, Center, Slant, and Interest-Focus', *Poetics Today*, 7: 2 (1986), 189–204.

—— *Coming to Terms: The Rhetoric of Narrative in Fiction and Film* (Ithaca, NY: Cornell University Press, 1990).

CHISMAR, DOUGLAS, 'Empathy and Sympathy: The Important Difference', *Journal of Value Inquiry*, 22 (1988), 257–66.

CHURCHILL, CARYL, *Churchill Plays: One* (London: Methuen, 1985).

CLOVER, CAROL, *Men, Women, and Chainsaws: Gender in the Modern Horror Film* (London: BFI, 1992).

COOK, MALLORIE, 'Criticism or Complicity? The Question of the Treatment of Rape and the Rape Victim in Jonathan Kaplan's *The Accused*', *CineAction*, 24/25 (1991), 80–5.

COWIE, ELIZABETH, 'Fantasia', *m/f*, 9 (1984), 70–105.

CRAW, GEORGE ROCKHILL, 'The Writing of a Scenario', *Moving Picture World*, 8: 17 (29 Apr. 1911), 938–40.

CRAWFORD, MARY, and CHAFFIN, ROGER, 'The Reader's Construction of Meaning: Cognitive Research on Gender and Comprehension', in Elizabeth A. Flynn and Patrocinio Schweickart (eds.), *Gender and Reading: Essays on Readers, Texts, and Contexts* (Baltimore: Johns Hopkins University Press, 1986), 3–30.

CULLER, JONATHAN, 'Stanley Fish and the Righting of the Reader', *Diacritics*, 5: 1 (Spring 1975), 26–31.

—— *Structuralist Poetics: Structuralism, Linguistics and the Study of Literature* (London: Routledge and Kegan Paul, 1975).

DAGRADA, ELENA, 'The Diegetic Iook. Pragmatics of the Point-of-View Shot', trans. James Hay, *Iris*, 7 (Oct. 1986), 111–24.

D'ANDRADE, ROY, 'A Folk Model of the Mind', in Holland and Quinn (eds.), 1987, 112–48.

DAVIS, JOHN, 'The Tragedy of Mildred Pierce', *The Velvet Light Trap*, 6 (Autumn 1972), 27–30.

DENNETT, DANIEL, *Brainstorms: Philosophical Essays on Mind and Psychology* (Cambridge, Mass.: MIT Press, 1978).

DE SOUSA, RONALD, *The Rationality of Emotion* (Cambridge, Mass.: MIT Press, 1988).

DIDION, JOAN, Review of *Le Doulos*, *Vogue*, 1 Apr. 1964, 42.

DOANE, MARY ANN, *The Desire to Desire: The Woman's Film of the 1940s* (Bloomington: Indiana University Press, 1987).

DOCHERTY, THOMAS, *Reading (Absent) Character* (Oxford: Clarendon Press, 1983).

DURGNAT, RAYMOND, *Films and Feelings* (Cambridge, Mass.: MIT Press, 1971).

—— *The Strange Case of Alfred Hitchcock; or, the Plain Man's Hitchcock* (London: Faber, 1974).

DURKHEIM, EMILE, 'The Dualism of Human Nature and its Social Conditions', in K. H. Wolff (ed.), *Emile Durkheim 1858–1917: A Collection of Essays with Translation and a Bibliography* (Columbus: Ohio State University Press, 1960).

DYER, RICHARD, *Stars* (London: BFI, 1979).

EISENSTEIN, SERGEI, *Film Form and the Film Sense*, trans. Jay Leyda (New York: Meridian Books, 1957).

—— and TRETYAKOV, SERGEI, 'Expressive Movement' (1923), trans. Alma H. Law, *Millenium Film Journal*, 3 (Winter/Spring 1979), 30–8.

EITZEN, DIRK, 'Negotiated Readings of *The Civil War*: A Cognitive Perspective', paper delivered at the 1992 Society for Cinema Studies Conference, University of Pittsburgh, USA.

—— 'The Reception of *The Civil War* and the Popular Conception of History', unpublished manuscript, 1992.

EKMAN, PAUL (ed.), *Emotion in the Human Face*, 2nd edn. (Cambridge: Cambridge University Press, 1982).

—— 'About Face: Information Signalled by Facial Expression', Hilldale Lecture Series, University of Wisconsin–Madison, Sept. 1990.

—— LEVENSON, ROBERT W., and FRIESEN, WALLACE, 'Autonomic Nervous System Distinguishes among Emotions', *Science*, 221 (Sept. 1983), 1208–10.

ELSAESSER, THOMAS, 'Tales of Sound and Fury', *Monogram*, 4 (1972), 2–15; reprinted in Gledhill (ed.), 1987.

ELSTER, JON, *Sour Grapes: Studies in the Subversion of Rationality* (Cambridge: Cambridge University Press, 1983).

ERLICH, VICTOR, *Russian Formalism: History—Doctrine*, 3rd edn. (New Haven, Conn.: Yale University Press, 1981).

EVANS-PRITCHARD, E. E., *Nuer Religion* (Oxford: Clarendon Press, 1956).

EWEN, FREDERIC, *Bertolt Brecht: His Life, His Art and His Times* (New York: Citadel Press, 1967).

FEAGIN, SUSAN, 'Getting Into It', unpublished manuscript, 1990.

FISH, STANLEY, *Is There a Text in this Class? The Authority of Interpretive Communities* (Cambridge, Mass.: Harvard University Press, 1980).

FISKE, JOHN, '*Cagney and Lacey*: Reading Character Structurally and Politically', *Communication*, 9 (1987), 399–426.

FLECK, PATRICE, 'The Silencing of Women in the Hollywood "Feminist" Film: *The Accused*', *Post Script*, 9: 3 (Summer 1990), 49–55.

FORSTER, E. M., *Aspects of the Novel* (London: Edward Arnold and Co., 1927).

FREUD, SIGMUND, *Introductory Lectures on Psycho-Analysis* (1917), trans. and ed. James Strachey (New York: W. W. Norton and Co., 1966).

FROW, JOHN, 'Spectacle Binding: On Character', *Poetics Today*, 7: 2 (1986), 227–50.

GALAN, F. W., *Historic Structures: The Prague School Project, 1928–46* (Austin: University of Texas Press, 1985).

GEERTZ, CLIFFORD, 'Person, Time and Conduct in Bali', in *The Interpretation of Cultures* (New York: Basic Books, 1973), 360–411.

GENETTE, GÉRARD, *Narrative Discourse: An Essay in Method*, trans. Jane E. Lewin (Ithaca, NY: Cornell University Press, 1980).

GERAS, NORMAN, *Discourses of Extremity* (London: Verso, 1990).

GINZBURG, CARLO, 'Morelli, Freud and Scientific Method', *History Workshop*, 9 (Spring 1980), 5–36.

GLEDHILL, CHRISTINE (ed.), *Home Is Where the Heart Is: Studies in Melodrama and the Woman's Film* (London: BFI, 1987).

GLOVER, JONATHAN, *I: The Philosophy and Psychology of Personal Identity* (London: Allen Lane, 1988).

GOMBRICH, E. H., *Art and Illusion: A Study in the Psychology of Pictorial Representation* (Princeton, NJ: Princeton University Press, 1969).

—— 'The Edge of Delusion', review of David Freedberg, *The Power of Images*, *New York Review of Books*, 15 Feb. 1990, 6–9.

GOODMAN, NELSON, *Languages of Art: An Approach to the Theory of Symbols* (Indianapolis: Hackett, 1976).

GORBMAN, CLAUDIA, *Unheard Melodies: Narrative Film Music* (London: BFI, 1987).

GORDON, ROBERT M., *The Structure of Emotions: Investigations in Cognitive Psychology* (Cambridge: Cambridge University Press, 1987).

GRAHAM, PETER, *The New Wave: Critical Landmarks* (New York: Viking, 1968).

GREENBLATT, STEPHEN J., 'Culture', in Frank Lentricchia and Thomas McLaughlin (eds.), *Critical Terms for Literary Study* (Chicago: University of Chicago Press, 1990).

GREENSPAN, PATRICIA, *Emotions and Reasons* (New York: Routledge, 1988).

GREIMAS, A. J., *On Meaning: Selected Writings in Semiotic Theory*, trans. and ed. Paul J. Perron and Frank H. Collins (Minneapolis: University of Minnesota Press, 1987).

GUNNING, TOM, *D. W. Griffith and the Origins of American Narrative Film: The Early Years at Biograph* (Urbana: University of Illinois Press, 1991).

HALE, NATHAN G., Jnr., *Freud and the Americans: The Beginnings of Psychoanalysis in the U.S., 1876–1917* (New York: Oxford University Press, 1971).

HAMON, PHILIPPE, 'Pour un statut semiologique du personnage', in Barthes *et al.* (eds.), 1977, 115–80.

HANDEL, LEO, *Hollywood Looks at its Audience: A Report of Film Audience Research* (Urbana: University of Illinois Press, 1950).

HARVEY, W. J., *Character and the Novel* (Ithaca, NY: Cornell University Press, 1965).

HATTERSLEY, ROY, 'Endpiece: What Would the Rake Make of our Progress?', *Guardian*, 18 Nov. 1991, 24.

HAUGMARD, LOUIS, 'The "Aesthetic" of the Cinematograph' (1913), trans. Richard Abel, in Abel (ed.), 1988, 77–85.

HEATH, STEPHEN, 'Lessons from Brecht', *Screen*, 15: 2 (Summer 1974), 103–28.

—— 'Film and System: Terms of Analysis', parts I and II, *Screen*, 16: 1 (Spring 1975), 7–77; and 16: 2 (Summer 1975), 91–113.

—— 'Notes on Suture', *Screen*, 18: 4 (Winter 1977–8), 48–76.

HOLLAND, DOROTHY, and QUINN, NAOMI (eds.), *Cultural Models in Language and Thought* (Cambridge: Cambridge University Press, 1987).

—— and SKINNER, DEBRA, 'Prestige and Intimacy: The Cultural Models behind Americans' Talk about Gender Types', in Holland and Quinn (eds.), 1987, 78–111.

HOLLIS, MARTIN, and LUKES, STEVEN (eds.), *Rationality and Relativism* (Oxford: Basil Blackwell, 1982).

HORTON, ROBIN, 'Material Object Language and Theoretical Language: Towards a Strawsonian Sociology of Thought', in S. C. Brown (ed.), 1979, 197–224.

—— 'Tradition and Modernity Revisited', in Hollis and Lukes (eds.), 1982, 201–60.

HUNT, MICHAEL H., *Ideology and U.S. Foreign Policy* (New Haven, Conn.: Yale University Press, 1987).

HUTCHINS, EDWIN, *Culture and Inference: A Trobriand Case Study* (Cambridge, Mass.: Harvard University Press, 1980).

HUYSSEN, ANDREAS, 'The Politics of Identification: "Holocaust" and West German Drama', *New German Critique*, 19 (Winter 1980), 117–36.

ISER, WOLFGANG, *The Implied Reader: Patterns in Communication in Prose Fiction from Bunyan to Beckett* (Baltimore: Johns Hopkins University Press, 1974).

JAMES, LOUIS, 'Was Jerrold's Black Ey'd Susan more popular than Wordsworth's Lucy?', in Bradby *et al.* (eds.), 1980, 3–16.

JAMESON, FREDRIC (ed.), *Aesthetics and Politics* (London: Verso, 1980), writings by Adorno, Benjamin, Bloch, Brecht, and Lukács.

JENKINS, HENRY and SPIGEL, LYNN, 'Same Bat Channel, Different Bat Times: Mass Culture and Popular Memory', in Pearson and Uricchio, 1991, 117–48.

JOHNSON, MARK, *The Body in the Mind: The Bodily Basis of Meaning, Imagination, and Reason* (Chicago: University of Chicago Press, 1987).

JOHNSON, SHEILA K., *American Attitudes Toward Japan, 1941–1975* (Washington, DC: AEI-Hoover Institute, 1975).

JOHNSON-LAIRD, PHILIP, *Mental Models: Towards a Cognitive Science of Language, Inference and Consciousness* (Cambridge: Cambridge University Press, 1983).

JOST, FRANÇOIS, 'Narration(s): En deçà et au delà', *Communications*, 38 (1984), 192–212.

KAHNEMAN, DANIEL, SLOVIC, PAUL, and TVERSKY, AMOS (eds.), *Judgment under Uncertainty: Heuristics and Biases* (Cambridge, Mass.: Harvard University Press, 1982).

KEHR, DAVE, 'Hitch's Riddle', *Film Comment*, 20: 5 (May–June 1984), 9–18.

—— 'The Shock of the Immediate', *Chicago Magazine*, June 1984, 124–6.

KENNY, ANTHONY, 'Are You a Person?', *New York Times Book Review*, 27 Aug. 1989, 21.

KERMODE, FRANK, *The Genesis of Secrecy: On the Interpretation of Narrative* (Cambridge: Harvard University Press, 1979).

KINTSCH, WALTER, and GREENE, EDITH, 'The Role of Culture-Specific Schemata in the Comprehension and Recall of Stories', *Discourse Processes*, 1 (1978), 1–13.

KOSSLYN, STEPHEN, *Image and Mind* (Cambridge, Mass.: Harvard University Press, 1980).

KULESHOV, LEV, *Kuleshov on Film*, trans. Ron Levaco (Berkeley: University of California Press, 1974).

LACAN, JACQUES, *Écrits: A Selection*, trans. Alan Sheridan (New York: W. W. Norton and Co., 1977).

LAKOFF, GEORGE, *Women, Fire, and Dangerous Things: What Categories Reveal about the Mind* (Chicago: University of Chicago Press, 1987).

—— and JOHNSON, MARK, *Metaphors We Live By* (Chicago: University of Chicago Press, 1980).

LAMARQUE, PETER, 'How Can We Fear and Pity Fictions?', *British Journal of Aesthetics*, 21: 4 (Autumn 1981), 291–304.

LAPLACE, MARIA, 'Producing and Consuming the Woman's Film: Discursive Struggle in *Now, Voyager*', in Gledhill (ed.), 1987, 138–66.

LAPSLEY, ROBERT, and WESTLAKE, MICHAEL, *Film Theory: An Introduction* (Manchester: Manchester University Press, 1988).

LASALLY, WALTER, 'Subjective Cinema: An Analysis of the MGM Film *Lady in the Lake*', *Film Industry*, Apr. 1947, 12–13, 20.

LAWRENCE, D. H., *The Letters of D. H. Lawrence*, ed. Aldous Huxley (London: Heinemann, 1932).

LEVINE, LAWRENCE W., *Highbrow/Lowbrow: The Emergence of Cultural Hierarchy in America* (Cambridge, Mass.: Harvard University Press, 1988).

LÉVI-STRAUSS, CLAUDE, *The Savage Mind*, trans. unknown (Chicago: University of Chicago Press, 1966).

—— *Anthropologie structurale II* (Paris: Plon, 1973).

LEWIS, DAVID, 'Survival and Identity', in Rorty (ed.), 1976, 17–40.

LIPPS, THEODOR, 'Empathy and Aesthetic Pleasure' (1905), in Aschenbrenner and Isenberg (eds.), 1965, 403–12.

LOTMAN, JURIJ, *Semiotics of Cinema*, trans. Mark E. Suino (Ann Arbor: Michigan Slavic Contributions, 1976).

LOVELL, TERRY, *Pictures of Reality: Aesthetics, Politics, and Pleasure* (London: BFI, 1983).

LUKÁCS, GEORG, *The Historical Novel* (1937), trans. Hannah and Stanley Mitchell (Lincoln: University of Nebraska Press, 1983).

LUKES, STEVEN, 'Conclusion', in Carrithers *et al.* (eds.), 1985, 282–301.

—— *Marxism and Morality* (Oxford: Clarendon Press, 1985).

McARTHUR, COLIN, *Underworld U.S.A.* (London: BFI, 1972).

MacCABE, COLIN, 'The Politics of Separation', *Screen*, 16: 4 (Winter 1975–6), 46–61.

MacCARTHY, THOMAS, 'Ironist Theory as a Vocation', *Critical Inquiry*, 16: 3 (Spring 1990), 644–55.

McCrone, John, *The Myth of Irrationality: The Science of the Mind from Plato to Star Trek* (London: Macmillan, 1993).

Margolin, Uri, 'Characterization in Narrative: Some Theoretical Prolegomena', *Neophilologus*, 67 (1983), 1–14.

—— 'The Doer and the Deed: Action as a Basis for Characterization in Narrative', *Poetics Today*, 7: 2 (1986), 205–25.

—— 'Introducing and Sustaining Characters in Literary Narrative: A Set of Conditions', *Style*, 21: 1 (Spring 1987), 107–24.

Mars-Jones, Adam, 'Baby, It's True', *Independent*, 17 Sept. 1993, 20.

Matejka, Ladislav, and Titunik, Irwin R. (eds.), *Semiotics of Art: Prague School Contributions* (Cambridge, Mass.: MIT Press, 1976).

Mathewson, Rufus, *The Positive Hero in Russian Literature* (New York: Columbia University Press, 1958).

Mauss, Marcel, 'A Category of the Human Mind: The Notion of the Person; the Notion of Self' (1938), trans. W. D. Halls, in Carrithers *et al.* (eds.), 1985.

Mayne, Judith, *Kino and the Woman Question: Feminism and Soviet Silent Film* (Columbus: Ohio State University Press, 1989).

Meisel, Martin, *Realizations: Narrative, Pictorial and Theatrical Arts in Nineteenth-Century England* (Princeton, NJ: Princeton University Press, 1983).

Merquior, J. G., *From Prague to Paris: A Critique of Structuralist and Post-Structuralist Thought* (London: Verso, 1986).

Metz, Christian, *Film Language*, trans. Michael Taylor (New York: Oxford University Press, 1974).

—— 'History/Discourse: Note on two Voyeurisms', *Edinburgh '76 Magazine*, 1 (1976), 21–5.

—— *Psychoanalysis and Cinema: The Imaginary Signifier*, trans. by Celia Britton, Annwyl Williams, Ben Brewster, and Alfred Guzzetti (London: Macmillan, 1982).

Mitchell, Stanley, 'From Shklovsky to Brecht: Some Preliminary Remarks Towards a History of the Politicisation of Russian Formalism', *Screen*, 15: 2 (Summer 1974), 74–81.

Mitchell, W. J. T. (ed.), *On Narrative* (Chicago: University of Chicago Press, 1981).

Modleski, Tania, *Loving with a Vengeance: Mass-Produced Fantasies for Women* (New York: Methuen, 1984).

Morin, Edgar, *The Stars* (New York: Grove Press, 1960).

Mukařovský, Jan, *Aesthetic Function, Norm and Value as Social Facts* (1936), trans. Mark E. Suino (Ann Arbor: Michigan Slavic Contributions, 1979).

Mulvey, Laura, 'Visual Pleasure and Narrative Cinema', *Screen*, 16: 3 (Autumn 1975), 6–18.

Murdoch, Iris, *The Sovereignty of Good* (1970) (London: Routledge, 1991).

Naremore, James, *Acting in the Cinema* (Berkeley: University of California Press, 1988).

Neale, Steve, 'Melodrama and Tears', *Screen*, 26: 6 (1986), 6–22.

—— 'Melo Talk: On the Meaning and Use of the Term "Melodrama" in the American Trade Press', *The Velvet Light Trap*, 32 (Fall 1993), 66–89.

Nisbett, Richard, and Ross, Lee, *Human Inference: Strategies and Shortcomings of Social Judgment* (Englewood Cliffs, NJ: Prentice-Hall, 1980).

NOVITZ, DAVID, *Knowledge, Fiction and Imagination* (Philadelphia: Temple University Press, 1987).

NUSSBAUM, MARTHA, *The Fragility of Goodness: Luck and Ethics in Greek Tragedy and Philosophy* (Cambridge: Cambridge University Press, 1986).

OUDART, JEAN-PIERRE, 'Cinema and Suture', *Screen*, 18: 4 (Winter 1977–8), 35–47.

PANOFSKY, ERWIN, 'Style and Medium in the Motion Pictures' (1934), in Gerald Mast and Marshall Cohen (eds.), *Film Theory and Criticism: Introductory Readings* (New York: Oxford University Press, 1974), 151–69.

PARFIT, DEREK, *Reasons and Persons* (Oxford: Clarendon Press, 1984).

PEARSON, ROBERTA E., *Eloquent Gestures: The Transformation of Performance Style in the Griffith Biograph Films* (Berkeley: University of California Press, 1992).

—— and URICCHIO, WILLIAM (eds.), *The Many Lives of the Batman: Critical Approaches to a Superhero and his Media* (New York: Routledge, 1991).

PERKINS, V. F., *Film as Film: Understanding and Judging Movies* (Harmondsworth: Penguin, 1972).

PETERSON, JAMES, *Dreams of Chaos, Visions of Order: Understanding the American Avant-garde Cinema* (Detroit: Wayne State University Press, 1994).

PHELAN, JAMES, *Reading People, Reading Plots* (Chicago: University of Chicago Press, 1989).

PILGER, JOHN, 'Vietnam, Another Hollywood Fairy Story', *Manchester Guardian Weekly*, 11 Mar. 1990, 22.

POE, EDGAR ALLAN, 'The Purloined Letter' (1845), in *The Fall of the House of Usher and Other Writings* (Harmondsworth: Penguin Classics, 1986), 330–49.

POLAN, DANA, *Power and Paranoia: History, Narrative, and the American Cinema, 1940–50* (New York: Columbia University Press, 1986).

—— 'Film as Language, Film as Power', *East–West Film Journal*, 2: 2 (June 1988), 87–114.

PRICE, MARTIN, *Forms of Life: Character and Moral Imagination in the Novel* (New Haven, Conn.: Yale University Press, 1983).

PRINCE, STEPHEN, and HENSLEY, WAYNE, 'The Kuleshov Effect: Recreating the Classic Experiment', *Cinema Journal*, 31: 2 (Winter 1992), 59–75.

PROPP, VLADIMIR, *Morphology of the Folktale* (1928), 2nd edn., trans. Laurence Scott and Louis A. Wagner (Austin: University of Texas Press, 1968).

QUINN, NAOMI, and HOLLAND, DOROTHY, 'Culture and Cognition', in Holland and Quinn (eds.), 1987, 3–40.

RADFORD, COLIN, 'Philosophers and their Monstrous Thoughts', *British Journal of Aesthetics*, 22 (1982), 261–3.

—— and WESTON, MICHAEL, 'How can We be Moved by the Fate of Anna Karenina?', *Proceedings of the Aristotelian Society*, Supplementary Volume 49 (1975), 67–93.

RAHILL, FRANK, *The World of Melodrama* (London: Pennsylvania State University Press, 1967).

REEDER, ROBERTA, 'Agit-prop Art: Posters, Puppets, Propaganda, and Eisenstein's *Strike*', *Russian Literature Triquarterly*, 22 (1989), 255–78.

REY, GEORGES, 'Survival', in Rorty (ed.), 1976, 41–66.

RICOEUR, PAUL, *Time and Narrative*, i, trans. Kathleen McLaughlin and David Pellauer (Chicago: University of Chicago Press, 1984).

—— 'The Function of Fiction in Shaping Reality', trans. David Pellauer, in Mario J. Valdés (ed.), *A Ricoeur Reader: Reflection and Imagination* (London: Harvester-Wheatsheaf, 1991), 117–35.

RIGGS, LARRY W., and WILLOQUET, PAULA, 'Up Against the Looking Glass! Heterosexual Rape as Homosexual Epiphany in *The Accused*', *Film/Literature Quarterly*, 17: 4 (1989), 214–23.

RIMMON-KENAN, SHLOMITH, *Narrative Fiction: Contemporary Poetics* (London: Methuen, 1983).

RODOWICK, D. N., 'Madness, Authority, and Ideology in the Domestic Melodrama of the 1950s', *The Velvet Light Trap*, 19 (1982), 40–5.

ROMAINS, JULES, 'The Crowd at the Cinematograph' (1911), trans. Richard Abel, in Abel (ed.), 1988, 53–4.

ROPARS, MARIE-CLAIRE, 'The Overture of *October*', trans. Larry Crawford and Kimball Lockhart, *Enclitic*, 2: 2 (Fall 1978), 50–72, and 3: 1 (Spring 1979), 35–47.

RORTY, AMÉLIE OKSENBERG (ed.), *The Identities of Persons* (Berkeley: University of California Press, 1976).

ROSE, JACQUELINE, 'Paranoia and the Film System', *Screen*, 17: 4 (Winter 1976–7), 85–104.

SARRAUTE, NATHALIE, *Tropisms and the Age of Suspicion*, trans. Maria Jolas (London: John Calder, 1963).

SARTRE, JEAN-PAUL, *The Psychology of the Imagination* (1940), trans. unknown (London: Methuen, 1972).

SCHAPER, EVA, 'Fiction and the Suspension of Disbelief', *British Journal of Aesthetics*, 18 (1978), 31–44.

SCHEGLOV, YU. K., and ZHOLKOVSKII, A. K., 'Towards a "Theme—(Expression Devices)—Text" Model of Literary Structure', trans. L. M. O'Toole, *Russian Poetics in Translation*, 1 (1975), 4–50.

SCHRADER, PAUL, *Transcendental Style in Film: Ozu, Bresson, Dreyer* (Berkeley: University of California Press, 1972).

SHKLOVSKY, VIKTOR, 'The Resurrection of the Word' (1914), in S. Bann and J. E. Bowlt (eds.), *Russian Formalism* (New York: Barnes and Noble, 1973), 41–7.

—— *Theory of Prose* (1929), trans. Benjamin Sher (Elmwood Park, Ill.: Dalkey Archive Press, 1990).

SHWEDER, RICHARD A., and LEVINE, ROBERT A. (eds.), *Culture Theory: Essays on Mind, Self and Emotion* (Cambridge: Cambridge University Press, 1984).

SHWEDER, RICHARD A. and BOURNE, EDMUND J., 'Does the Concept of the Person Vary Cross-Culturally?' in Shweder and LeVine, 1984, 158–99.

SILVERMAN, KAJA, *The Subject of Semiotics* (New York: Oxford University Press, 1983).

SINGER, BEN, 'Female Power in the Serial-Queen Melodrama: The Etiology of an Anomaly', *Camera Obscura*, 22 (Jan. 1990), 91–129.

SMITH, ADAM, *The Theory of Moral Sentiments* (1759) (Oxford: Clarendon Press, 1976).

SMITH, GAVIN, 'Identity Check', interview with Jonathan Demme, *Film Comment*, 27: 1 (Jan.–Feb. 1991), 28–30, 33–7.

SMITH, MURRAY, 'Film Noir, the Female Gothic and *Deception*', *Wide Angle*, 10: 1 (1988), 62–75.

—— 'Character Engagement: Fiction, Emotion and the Cinema', Ph.D. thesis (University of Wisconsin–Madison, 1991).

—— 'Altered States: Character and Emotional Response in the Cinema', *Cinema Journal*, 33: 4 (Summer 1994), 34–56.

—— 'The Logic and Legacy of Brechtianism', in David Bordwell and Noël Carroll (eds.), *Post-Theory: Reconstructing Film Studies* (Madison: University of Wisconsin Press, 1995).

SONTAG, SUSAN, 'Spiritual Style in the Films of Robert Bresson', in *Against Interpretation and Other Essays* (New York: Delta, 1966), 181–98.

SORLIN, PIERRE, *European Cinemas, European Societies 1939–90* (London: Routledge, 1991).

SPERBER, DAN, *Rethinking Symbolism*, trans. Alice L. Morton (Cambridge: Cambridge University Press, 1975).

STAIGER, JANET, ' "The Eyes are Really the Focus": Photoplay Acting and Film Form and Style', *Wide Angle*, 6: 4 (1985), 14–23.

—— *Interpreting Films: Studies in the Historical Reception of American Cinema* (Princeton, NJ: Princeton University Press, 1992).

STERNBERG, MEIR, *Expositional Modes and Temporal Ordering in Fiction* (Baltimore: Johns Hopkins University Press, 1978).

STRAWSON, PETER, *Individuals: An Essay in Descriptive Metaphysics* (London: Methuen, 1959).

SULEIMAN, SUSAN RUBIN, *Authoritarian Fictions: The Ideological Novel as a Literary Genre* (New York: Columbia University Press, 1983).

TANNEN, DEBORAH, 'What's in a Frame? Surface Evidence for Underlying Expectations', in Roy O. Freedle (ed.), *New Directions in Discourse Processing* (Norwood, NJ: Ablex, 1979), 137–44.

TAYLOR, PAUL, 'Imagination and Information', *Philosophy and Phenomenological Research*, 42 (1981), 205–23.

THOMPSON, KRISTIN, *Breaking the Glass Armor: Neoformalist Film Analysis* (Princeton, NJ: Princeton University Press, 1988).

TODOROV, TZVETAN, 'Introduction: Le Vraisemblable', *Communications*, 11 (1968), 1–4.

—— *The Poetics of Prose*, trans. Richard Howard (Ithaca, NY: Cornell University Press, 1977).

TOMASHEVSKY, BORIS, 'Thematics' (1925), in Lee T. Lemon and Marion J. Reis (trans. and eds.), *Russian Formalist Criticism: Four Essays* (Lincoln: University of Nebraska Press, 1965), 61–95.

TURNER, VICTOR, *Dramas, Fields and Metaphors: Symbolic Action in Human Society* (Ithaca, NY: Cornell University Press, 1974).

TYTLER, GRAEME, *Physiognomy in the European Novel: Faces and Fortunes* (Princeton, NJ: Princeton University Press, 1982).

USPENSKY, BORIS, *A Poetics of Composition: The Structure of the Artistic Text and Typology of a Compositional Form*, trans. Valentina Zavarin and Susan Wittig (Berkeley: University of California Press, 1973).

VAN LAAN, THOMAS L., *The Idiom of Drama* (Ithaca, NY: Cornell University Press, 1970).

VERNET, MARC, 'Le Personnage de film', *Iris*, 7 (Oct. 1986), 81–110.

WALDMAN, DIANE, 'Horror and Domesticity: The Modern Gothic Romance Film of the 1940s', Ph.D. thesis (University of Wisconsin–Madison, 1981).

—— 'At Last I Can Tell it to Someone! Feminine Point of View and Subjectivity in the Gothic Romance Film of the 1940s', *Cinema Journal*, 23: 2 (Winter 1984), 29–40.

WALSH, DOROTHY, *Literature and Knowledge* (Middleton, Conn.: Wesleyan University Press, 1969).

WALTON, KENDALL, 'Fearing Fictions', *Journal of Philosophy*, 75: 1 (Jan. 1978), 5–27.

WATT, IAN, *The Rise of the Novel* (Berkeley: University of California Press, 1957).

WHITE, HAYDEN, 'The Value of Narrativity in the Representation of Reality', in W. J. T. Mitchell (ed.), *On Narrative* (Chicago: University of Chicago Press, 1981).

WILKES, KATHLEEN V., *Real People: Personal Identity without Thought Experiments* (Oxford: Clarendon Press, 1988).

WILLIAMS, ALAN, 'Historical and Theoretical Issues in the Coming of Recorded Sound to the Cinema', in Rick Altman (ed.), *Sound Theory/Sound Practice* (New York: Routledge, 1992), 126–37.

WILLIAMS, BERNARD, *Problems of the Self: Philosophical Papers 1956–72* (Cambridge: Cambridge University Press, 1973).

WILLIAMS, LINDA, '"Something Else Beside a Mother": *Stella Dallas* and the Maternal Melodrama', *Cinema Journal*, 24: 1 (1984), 2–27.

WILLIAMS, RAYMOND, *Marxism and Literature* (Oxford: Oxford University Press, 1977).

WILSON, CATHERINE, 'Literature and Knowledge', *Philosophy*, 58 (1983), 489–96.

WILSON, GEORGE M., *Narration in Light: Studies in Cinematic Point of View* (Baltimore: Johns Hopkins University Press, 1986).

WOLLEN, PETER, *Signs and Meaning in the Cinema*, 3rd edn. (Bloomington: Indiana University Press, 1972).

WOLLHEIM, RICHARD, *On Art and the Mind* (Cambridge, Mass.; Harvard University Press, 1974).

—— *The Thread of Life* (Cambridge, Mass.; Harvard University Press, 1984).

WOOD, ROBIN, *Hitchcock's Films Revisited* (New York: Columbia University Press, 1989).

ZAJONC, R. B., 'Emotion and Facial Efference: A Theory Reclaimed', *Science*, 228 (Apr. 1985), 15–21.

ZIOLKOWSKI, THEODORE, 'The Telltale Teeth: Psychodontia to Sociodontia', *PMLA* 91 (1976), 9–22.

Index

Page numbers in italics denote illustrations.